Maren Freudenberg, Astrid Reuter (eds.)
Social Forms of Religion

Religious Studies | Volume 38

Maren Freudenberg, born in 1983, is a sociologist of religion at the Center for Religious Studies, Ruhr-Universität Bochum, Germany. She obtained her PhD in sociology at Freie Universität Berlin, where she was a member of the Graduate School of North American Studies. Her research focuses on contemporary religion in the United States, global Charismatic Christianity, the connections between religion and the economy, and theoretical approaches in the sociology of religion.
Astrid Reuter, born in 1968, is a professor for religious studies at Universität Münster and principal investigator at the Cluster of Excellence Religion & Politics. Her main research areas are the history and theory of religious studies, religion and law in Europe, Charismatic Catholicism and African religions in Latin America (with special focus on Brazil).

Maren Freudenberg, Astrid Reuter (eds.)
Social Forms of Religion
European and American Christianity in Past and Present

[transcript]

Funded by the Deutsche Forschungsgemeinschaft (DFG, German Research Foundation) under Germany's Excellence Strategy - EXC 2060 "Religion and Politics. Dynamics of Tradition and Innovation" - 390726036.

Bibliographic information published by the Deutsche Nationalbibliothek
The Deutsche Nationalbibliothek lists this publication in the Deutsche Nationalbibliografie; detailed bibliographic data are available in the Internet at https://dnb.dnb.de/

This work is licensed under the Creative Commons Attribution 4.0 (BY) license, which means that the text may be remixed, transformed and built upon and be copied and redistributed in any medium or format even commercially, provided credit is given to the author.

Creative Commons license terms for re-use do not apply to any content (such as graphs, figures, photos, excerpts, etc.) not original to the Open Access publication and further permission may be required from the rights holder. The obligation to research and clear permission lies solely with the party re-using the material.

First published in 2024 by transcript Verlag, Bielefeld
© Maren Freudenberg, Astrid Reuter (eds.)

Cover layout: Maria Arndt, Bielefeld
Printed by: Elanders Waiblingen GmbH, Waiblingen
https://doi.org/10.14361/9783839468265
Print-ISBN: 978-3-8376-6826-1
PDF-ISBN: 978-3-8394-6826-5
ISSN of series: 2703-142X
eISSN of series: 2703-1438

Contents

Introduction
Maren Freudenberg and Astrid Reuter 7

The Four Phases of the Catholic Charismatic Renewal (1967–2017)
Valérie Aubourg 25

'Catholic' and 'Charismatic'
Two Logics of Legitimization and the Negotiation of Belonging
in the German Catholic Charismatic Renewal
Hannah Grünenthal 49

"I am happy to be Catholic"
The Catholic Charismatic Renewal and the Dynamics of the Religious Field in Brazil
Astrid Reuter 79

Everyday Familialism in the Emmanuel Community
Samuel Dolbeau 107

The Capital of Closed Churches
Heritage Buildings as Social Entrepreneurship in Quebec
Hillary Kaell 131

God Is Not at Church
Digitalization as Authentic Religious Practice in an American Megachurch
Ariane Kovac 153

Shapeshifting the Christian Right
The Moral Majority as a Faith-Based Organization and the Immanent Turn
of Evangelicalism in the Late 20th Century
Sebastian Schüler 183

Social Forms in Neo-Pentecostal Prosperity Contexts
From Network to Market Exchange
Maren Freudenberg 207

Pentecostal Social Engagement in Contemporary Guatemala
Virginia Garrard 225

Social Forms in Orthodox Christian Convert Communities in North America
Sebastian Rimestad and Katherine Kelaidis 251

Forever Into Eternity
Social Forms of Religion in the Temple Wedding of The Church of Jesus Christ
of Latter-day Saints
Marie-Therese Mäder 273

Organizing "Private Religion"
Types of Governance in US Protestantism
Insa Pruisken 299

Authors 323

Introduction

Maren Freudenberg and Astrid Reuter

Abstract *This introduction briefly sketches the aims and scope of the present volume before providing an overview of existing typologies of social forms in the sociology of religion and beyond and presenting the volume's theoretical framework, which assumes (1) a congruence between social forms and religious semantics, (2) a shift from organizational to community structures in the religious field, and (3) a marked influence on the emergence of particular social forms as a result of competition, both within the religious field and on the border to other fields. The final section summarizes the main arguments of the volume's contributions against this theoretical backdrop.*

Keywords *Social forms of religion, religious semantics, organization, group, market exchange, network, movement, church, sect, mysticism, cult*

1. Aims and scope of the volume

The present volume sheds light on the various social forms Christianity in Europe and the Americas takes and has taken since the mid-20th century. It examines the religious, cultural, social, and historical context of diverse empirical cases, from Charismatic Catholicism to Evangelicalism and Pentecostalism, and asks how different social forms have contributed to the success or failure of the respective Christian communities. Social forms can be understood as the ways in which people come together to shape social interaction. Religious social forms are then the modes in which people congregate to structure aspects of their religious lives, such as religious practices or social practices that are religiously motivated. Religious social forms include not only religious interaction per se, as during a worship service or group prayer, but also the 'background coordination' that makes religious interaction possible, such as maintaining a congregation or organizing an event. Social forms in this sense must be seen as 'ideal types' as Max Weber defined them (Weber 2012 [1904]). Ideal types, in line with Weber, are concepts with an extremely high degree of abstraction. They do not exist in empirical reality in their 'pure' forms, nor do they serve as a scheme to simply classify social complexity. Rather, they are points of reference to which social phenomena are compared. They are heuristic tools: by observing correspondences and divergences between real phenomena and ideal types, we gain a better understanding of social and historical reality.

In this introduction, we begin by providing an overview of existing typologies of social forms in the sociology of religion and beyond (2.). Next, we present the volume's theoretical framework (3.), which assumes a congruence between social forms and religious semantics, a shift from organizational to community structures in the religious field, and a marked influence on the emergence of particular social forms as a result of competition, both within the religious field and on the border to other fields. The final section (4.) summarizes the main arguments of the volume's contributions against the theoretical backdrop.

2. Typologies of social forms in the sociology of religion and beyond

Various typologies of social forms exist in the sociology of religion (both its German-speaking and anglophone variants) and beyond. In this section, we provide a brief overview of central literature on the subject.

The older sociology of religion, in the form of Max Weber and, interacting with and building on Weber's work, Ernst Troeltsch, differentiates *church*, *sect*, and *mysticism* as three main social forms of religion. Broadly speaking, membership in a *church* (as an ideal type, with Weber) is usually not based on a personal decision or vocation, as people are born into the religious community; churches, as inclusive social forms, tend by and large to accommodate the values of majority society in order to retain adherents; expulsion is correspondingly rare; leadership positions require specialized training and are renumerated; church structures are hierarchical and bureaucratic, their practices traditional in the sense of being closely oriented towards liturgical rituals (Weber 2011 [1920; 1905]; Troeltsch 1931 [1912]). Membership in *sects*, on the other hand, is voluntary; people elect to join the group in an act of conversion and are eligible only through personal qualification, i.e., by adhering to strict behavioral rules; sects, as exclusive social forms, correspondingly reject many values of majority society and are swift to punish transgressions with expulsion; leadership requires no specialized training but a sense of calling and charisma, structures are more flexible and practices less ritualistic (Weber 2011 [1920]; Troeltsch 1931 [1912]).

While Troeltsch expanded Weber's types of church and sect, he added *mysticism* as a separate social form to refer to the "insistence upon a direct inward and present religious experience" which "takes for granted the objective forms of religious life in worship, ritual, myth, and dogma" (Troeltsch 1931 [1912]: 730). Although Troeltsch's acknowledgment of individual spirituality as (potentially) existing separately from organized, communal religion is highly important, we argue that mysticism does not present a genuine social form in its own right, as it designates an individual's personal, inner religious experience instead of a mode of social interaction. It is only the act of relaying this personal experience verbally to another individual or a group that gives it a social dimension. The conversion experience in Evangelicalism, Pentecostalism, or Charismatic Catholicism is a fitting case in point: The individual convert typically accepts Jesus "in her heart" as her personal savior before recounting the experience of being saved to fellow believers. But the act of sharing the conversion experience with the group is crucial to gain legitimacy as a 'true' believer, as without the confirmation of the group the experience is essentially worthless, at least in terms of socially integrating the individual believer in the larger collectivity of the "saved". Then again, it may also be the case that the group itself opens up the space for conversion experiences in the first place. Thus, in many Pentecostal or Charismatic groups, conversion experience – "baptism in the Spirit", as it is usually called – is prayed for together. The tension between religious individualism and communal integration deserves deeper exploration in its own right (cf. e.g. Hervieu-Léger 2007) and will not be elaborated on here for reasons of scope. We wish to point out that, in our view, Troeltsch's mysticism does not qualify as a social form as lacks the dimension of social interaction. This does not exclude, however, the possibility of mystic experiences shaping specific social forms of religion.

Weber's and Troeltsch's typology received appreciation and critique in equal amounts over the past century. It has been labeled as Eurocentric and too strongly molded on Christianity (cf. Dawson 2011 for an overview), and we add to this the observation that their typology comprises *generically religious* social forms instead of a range of social forms which may or may not be religious (such as the social form of organization, which may be religious or secular) (on this point, cf. also Petzke/Tyrell 2011). These observations notwithstanding, various scholars of religion have expanded the typology in different ways since its inception, the first being H. Richard Niebuhr, American historian and theologian (2005 [1929]). In the attempt to apply Troeltsch's typology, which was derived from the European context, to the American religious landscape, Niebuhr added *denomination* as an additional type to capture the internal diversity of Christian traditions in the United States. The American sociologist Howard Becker (1940), in turn, proposed an alternative that included the types *ecclesia, sect, denomination*, and *cult*, while another American sociologist, J. Milton Yinger, distinguished between *universal church, ecclesia, denomination, established sect, sect*, and *cult* (Dawson 2011: 528–29). In both cases, inclusiveness decreases the further one moves from church to cult, but for Becker, the denomination and cult are both sub-types of sects (with different degrees of formalization). British sociologist Bryan Wilson (1970) offered a sevenfold sub-typology of *sects* which includes the *conversionist, revolutionist, introversionist, manipulationist, thaumaturgical, reformist*, and *utopian* types; each has a different understanding of its role vis-à-vis majority religion and society. Along similar lines, British sociologist Roy Wallis (2019) developed a threefold sub-typology of cults that also denotes differing relationships to majority society: *world-affirming, world-rejecting*, and *world-accommodating cults*. American sociologists Rodney Stark and William S. Bainbridge (1985) distinguish between *churches* as established forms, *sects* as schismatic forms, and *cults* as independent forms. More recently, the term *new religious movement* (NRM) has increasingly become a substitute expression for the term *cult*, because the latter was deemed too pejorative for academic use due to its everyday connotations. However, NRM as a term and category is also disputed, raising questions of how new NRMs need to be to qualify as such and where the limits of what qualifies as religion should be drawn (Cowan 2016; Fox 2010; Dawson 2008). Importantly for the topic at hand, many of these (and other) expansions of Weber and Troeltsch's typologies look to degrees of organization, the dynamics of social or religious movements, and the role of communitizing forces, i.e. of deepening interpersonal relations.

The Austrian-American sociologist Thomas Luckmann displays a very different understanding of the social forms of religion, namely as dependent on the type of society in which a given religion develops. He argues that the social forms that religions take correspond to wider, non-religious social structures. In this regard, he distinguishes undifferentiated religion in "archaic" societies, religion in "early high cultures", religion in functionally differentiated societies, and privatized forms of religion in functionally specific, plural societies

(Luckmann 2003). This approach is located on a different scale, in terms of both geographical and temporal scope, than the preceding typologies. Canadian sociologist Peter Beyer follows a similarly global approach, yet his typology of the social forms of religion is more closely aligned with organizational sociology. He distinguishes between *organized religion, politicized religion, social movement religion,* and *communitarian/individualistic religion* (Beyer 2003). This brings us to newer approaches in the sociology of religion which partially draw from organizational sociology to distinguish between the social forms of *organization, group, market exchange, network, movement,* and *event*, among others. This framework is analytically situated on the meso-level of society, between micro-level social interactions and macro-level societal change or stasis, and functions to mediate between the micro and macro by way of coordinating and structuring social activity.

This newer perspective on social forms also draws from classical sociology. Social forms are subject to processes of *Vergemeinschaftung* (communitization, or communal relationships) and *Vergesellschaftung* (societalization, or associative relationships) and may, in turn, participate in shaping these processes. These terms were coined by Ferdinand Tönnies (1999 [1912]) and developed further by Max Weber (2013 [1922]), who emphasized their procedural nature, associating communitization with tradition, emotions, and personal relations, and societalization with rationality, reflexivity, and objectified relations. Particularly in his later works, Weber defined communitization as a social relationship based on a subjective sense of solidarity and shared identity, and societalization as a social relationship focusing on pursuing shared interests, emphasizing that all social relations contain elements of both (ibid.). The corresponding social forms in which the dynamics of communitization and societalization become manifest are (1) the *group*, defined by personal relationships between members, relative stability and durability, shared norms and values that forge a collective identity, and generalized reciprocity, and (2) the *organization*, defined by fixed membership criteria, the purpose of attaining specific goals, internal differentiation of tasks and responsibilities, formalized participation procedures, and a hierarchical structure (Krech 2018; Schlamelcher 2018; Lüddeckens/Walthert 2018). Group and organization represent two ends of a continuum of social forms, with others – network, market exchange, event, etc. – located between them.

German sociologists Volkhard Krech, Jens Schlamelcher, and Markus Hero differentiate between *group* (or *community*), *organization*, and *market exchange* as three main types of social forms as well as between *movement* and *event* as two sub-types (Krech et al. 2013). According to them, the *group* as the oldest existing social form is characterized by the personal inclusion of its members, the close emotional bond between them, their collective identity and general reciprocity to stabilize social relationships, its informal structures, and its resulting limitations regarding growth. The *organization*, in contrast, includes members based on their roles instead of their personalities, is characterized by formal structures, and is able to make decisions regarding its programmatic goals, structure, and staff via its personnel. As we elaborate in the next section, the fact that organizational roles are taken on by 'real people', individuals with their own personalities and preferences, presents a dilemma for organizations, as their formalized, rational structures are confronted with individual attitudes, opinions, and outlooks. While groups and organizations can exist for an unlimited amount of time, Krech et al. argue, the *market exchange* is a temporally limited social form that, like organizations and unlike groups, includes exchange partners based on their roles not personalities, because the exchange is a rational form of interaction. Social *movements* are constituted by both communal and organizational coordination mechanisms: The former serve to integrate members while the latter serve to propel the movement's aims and goals forward. *Events*, in turn, present a mix of market exchange and communitizing ritual (Krech et al. 2013: 54–58).

A similar typology is offered by German sociologists Patrick Heiser and Christian Ludwig (2014) in their volume on the transformation of social forms of religion. In the introduction, they distinguish five social forms of religion: *religious organizations*, which emerge from sects or charismatic movements and coalesce into formal organizations through institutionalization and denominalization; *religious networks* (including religious movements) with porous boundaries and the ability to integrate various actors, roles, and identities through communication via local and global channels; *religious communitization*, or alternatively, individualized forms of religious community (akin to the group discussed above); *marketization* as an exchange relationship between individuals and groups based on both a cost/benefit rationale and communal norms and values; and *eventization* as a spatially, temporally, and socially condensed form of communal religious experience which provides sensory stimulation that goes beyond everyday impressions (ibid.: 6–10). Regarding events, the authors draw from the extensive work of German sociologists Winfried Gebhard, Ronald Hitzler, and associates (Gebhard et al. 2000; e.g. Hitzler 2011; Hitzler et al. 2009; Gebhardt 2018).

Interestingly, Ludwig and Heiser categorize movements as a sub-type of networks instead of as a social form in its own right. In this sense, they somewhat parallel Krech et al.'s perspective on social movements as a type in between group and organization (on this, cf. also Roth/Rucht 2008). Social movement theory has of course long become a distinct field of research in the social sciences, and it is beyond the scope of this introduction to delve into it extensively. As it has been integrated in the sociology of religion as a social form, *religious social movements* (a more general category than new religious movements, briefly mentioned above) is defined as networks of groups and organizations that establish a collective identity, frame a common goal, and mobilize available resources in order to bring about societal and/or political change that is guided by transcendental aims (Kern/Pruisken 2018). Religion acts as a mobilizing force in seeking to give rise to societal transformation in that it typically provides the organizational structures necessary to coordinate action, the ideological framework to sustain participants over longer periods of time, and the resources to engage with the broader social environment it is situated within (Williams 2003). In these broad definitions of movement as a social form in the religious field, it becomes clear that social forms are first and foremost analytical categories that help understand and organize empirical reality from a sociological perspective. They do not exist in their 'pure' analytical form on the ground; as we elaborate in the next section, while a given social form may be dominant in a given religious context – such as the type organization is in the Roman Catholic Church – other social forms are evident in the same empirical case, such as group, movement, or event on different levels of the Catholic hierarchy. Against the background of these debates about social forms of religion, briefly sketched here, we will now outline the guiding questions and theoretical ideas that we address in this volume.

3. Framework of the volume: Theoretical considerations on social forms of religion

In this section, we propose three central arguments regarding social forms of religion: (1) As traditionally structured religions – by which we mean hierarchical and bureaucratic organizations – are declining both in terms of membership and of public relevance, these same organizations are trying to innovate and transform by strengthening community elements and downplaying hierarchy and bureaucracy. This attempt at more community, less organization may be called the societalization of communitization (*Vergesellschaftung von Vergemeinschaftung*). (2) This approach brings with it an approximation of the social form of community with the core idea of giving power to the people, i.e. empowering laypeople to voice their individual religious convictions and shape their own religious practices. In other words, congruence is sought between the social structure of religion and its semantics: religion develops social forms that correspond with its religious ideas, and these forms, in turn, structure religious interaction. (3) The aspect of competition thus has a crucial influence on the emergence and consolidation of social forms, as those religions that are most successful influence others in terms of dominant social forms and central semantics. In addition, competition plays a decisive role not only within the religious field, but also on the borders between religion and other social fields, such as between religion and economics, religion and health care, religion and (pop)culture, or religion and education.

Let us discuss these three arguments in more detail now. Our fundamental assumption (basically drawn from Troeltsch) is that religions try to develop social forms that correspond with their respective religious ideas (ideas of salvation, a God-pleasing life, etc.). In other words: they seek congruence of religious semantics and social structure. This correspondence between semantics and structure is not unique to social forms of religion, specifically. Social forms of religion, however, tend to be characterized in a particular way by the respective religious self-logic. This can be exemplified by the social form of *church*: In terms of the sociology of organization, the social form *church* can be described as *organization*. However, churches are atypical organizations (cf. Petzke/Tyrell 2011), and in several respects: One aspect is that churches are organizations that want to be *more* than organization. In terms of their religious ideas, they picture themselves as e.g. a community of sisters and brothers, God-chosen people, *corpus Christi mysticum*, etc.

Churches are thus hybrid social forms, characterized by a profound tension of community logics (motivated by religious ideals) and organizational logics (strictly functional), in other words – and that brings us to our second argument – by a tension between communitization and societalization. This tension strengthens a paradox that all organizations (religious or not) have in common: While the ideal type organization requires including members according to their function, i.e. not as the individuals they are, the thus formally excluded individual is nevertheless de facto present because roles and functions are necessarily taken on and carried out by people. Consequently, against their organizational logics, organizations 'host' people – with personalities, attitudes, preferences, and so on. This paradox is particularly pronounced in *religious* organizations, at least in Christian churches, for these claim to "call" every single "soul" to salvation by belonging to the church as the individual person they are.

Another aspect of the atypical character of churches as organizations is that while non-religious organizations usually reduce contingency by making decisions according to (ideal-typically) transparent formalized procedures, religious organizations, through sacralizing membership roles, leadership, and the decision-making process itself, make contingency invisible. The responsibility for decisions and decision-making procedures, for rituals, ethical principles, etc., is thus delegated to an authority beyond this world which is unavailable. It is precisely this mechanism that reduces the feeling of uncertainty and helps cope with contingency.

Despite the tension between community logics and organizational logics described above, organizations, including churches, may themselves be community-productive at the same time. As research on Mainline Protestantism in the United States has shown, denominations have responded to their massive membership decline by launching top-down, community-building initiatives on the congregational level in the attempt to get more people involved in local churches (Freudenberg 2018). Church organizations thus play a role in implementing the program 'more community, less organization'. Tensions between the religiously regulative idea of community and the requirement of the organization of this communality may also set religious change in motion. Thus, the longing for 'more community, less organization' as well as the longing for shared personal conversion experiences instead of rigid ritual practice seems to be an isomorphic tendency of our times in the Christian field in the Americas and, though less pronounced, in Europe. The Evangelical Lutheran Church in America, the country's second-largest Mainline denomination, for instance, has exhibited a strong orientation toward the congregational autonomy and pronounced community culture so prevalent in American Evangelicalism (ibid.). As community logics increasingly spread and are embedded on a societal scale, 'more community' seems to become a goal and ideal even for highly societalized forms of religion, e.g. religious organizations. We therefore suggest considering the societalization of communitization (*Vergesellschaftung von Vergemeinschaftung*) as a central framework in contemporary global Christianity.

If we now look at the dynamics of social forms of religion in a given religious field (Bourdieu 1985; 1987 [1971]; 1991 [1971]; Bourdieu/Saint Martin 1982), we must take into account that each religious field is composed of different religious 'sub-fields' (including e.g. the Catholic field, Protestant field, Christian field, Islamic field, Jewish field, etc.). Both levels of the field are entangled, and the dynamics of religious social forms within a sub-field (such as e.g. Catholicism) must be analyzed in the context of the dynamics (of social forms) in the broader religious field. This brings us back to our third argument regarding social forms of religion: The competition between religions or denominations or between religion and other social fields may lead either to the adoption of successful social forms from competing (religious or non-religious) actors or to their deliberate rejection with the aim of sharpening one's own profile. What is a given community's position in the respective religious sub-field, in the broader religious field, and in the structure of different social fields in relation to each other? And what role does its dominant social form play in the process of its positioning in the (sub-)field? If a given community fails, how might its demise be connected to the ways in which its adherents organize(d) to practice their faith? Religious or denominational competition is thus a decisive factor in the emergence and consolidation of social forms of religion.

Clearly, social forms are communally productive. When individuals come together to practice their faith, this creates and strengthens interpersonal relationships and community ties. At the same time, different social forms create different kinds of space for individual and collective religious experience and values to emerge. Social forms enable individual religious experience, which in Christianity requires communal grounding and validation to become legitimate and authentic. In this way, the tension between individual religion and religious community is negotiated by way of different social forms. This volume's case studies offer a range of empirical examples of the social forms to be found in Christianity and are briefly introduced in the next section.

4. Outline of the volume

The contributions bring together case studies that demonstrate the plurality and dynamics of Christianity in Europe and the Americas, with a focus on its (changing) social forms.

In *The Four Phases of the Catholic Charismatic Renewal (1967–2017)*, **Valérie Aubourg** focuses on the development of the Catholic Charismatic Renewal in light of its changing relationship to Pentecostalism. While the first phase (1967–1982) was characterized strongly by Pentecostal experience that entered

Catholicism through grassroots religious communities, the second phase (1982–1997) saw a routinization of charisma and a renewed emphasis on the Catholic Church as an organization. In the third phase (1997-early 2000s), the Charismatic Renewal sought renewed proximity to (neo-)Pentecostalism by adopting experiential practices; the fourth stage (since the early 2000s) is characterized by the continued adoption of typically Pentecostal elements over and above the Charismatic Renewal in the strict sense and the 'infiltration' of Charismatic-style elements into conventional Catholic practice. In terms of social forms, Aubourg traces a shift from organization to group and network, reflecting a larger process of adopting religious social forms to religious individualization within the Catholic Church.

In *'Catholic' and 'Charismatic': Two Logics of Legitimization and the Negotiation of Belonging in the German Catholic Charismatic Renewal*, **Hannah Grünenthal** analyzes this very tension between organization and network/group within the German Catholic Charismatic Renewal (GCCR). Tracing the GCCR's twofold logic of legitimization – the 'Catholic' and the 'Charismatic' logic – she shows which strategies are necessary for members to assert their position within two very different contexts: recognizing hierarchy, structure, tradition, and the doctrine of the Catholic Church, on the one hand, and emphasizing personal religious experiences and the experience of the Holy Spirit, on the other. Organizational logics are at times at odds with network or group logics, meaning that GCCR members require flexibility to adapt to a range of social forms to maintain adherence to both the Catholic and the Charismatic world.

In *"I am happy to be Catholic": The Catholic Charismatic Renewal and the Dynamics of the Religious Field in Brazil*, **Astrid Reuter** looks at ongoing changes within Latin American Catholicism, namely in Brazil. She takes as her point of departure the fact that Charismatic movements have experienced an unexpected boom in Brazilian Catholicism since the 1970s and increasingly since the 1990s and interprets this growth as resulting from both the dynamics of the religious field in Brazil as a whole and from the dynamics of the Catholic subfield. She argues that the rise of Pentecostalism since the 1950s and 1960s has set in motion a previously unknown dynamic of competition which coincides with converging religious beliefs and demands (beliefs in spiritual beings and aspirations for personal spiritual experiences). Competition and convergence are thus interconnected, which, Astrid Reuter argues, fosters a dynamic of 'mimicry' both in relation to the style of piety and to the religious social forms that support this style.

In *Everyday Familialism in the Emmanuel Community*, **Samuel Dolbeau** focuses on the family as the guiding model for social relations within Catholic Charismatic communities in Europe, as becomes evident in the Emmanuel Community. Here, familialism structures community life in various ways, including not only day-to-day activities but also religious, political, and social involvement in broader society. This serves to support recent Catholic initiatives on sexuality and gender issues. Members are involved in and committed to the community to different degrees, from sporadic to full-time engagement, which results in a range of social forms – from dyad and group to network and organization – and a distinct gender regime influencing not only family dynamics but also the perception of clerical roles. As the Emmanuel Community is the largest Catholic Charismatic community in Europe, the dynamics described by Samuel Dolbeau could point to future changes in the Catholic Church as a whole.

In *Capital of Closed Churches: Heritage Buildings as Social Entrepreneurship in Quebec*, **Hillary Kaell** highlights urban, historic churches that often also house community organizations and run the danger of closing as resulting in community hubs as a new social form within North American Christianity. She argues that such hubs derive value from their location on the border of historically religious forms (heritage churches), economic forms (corporate investment), and the public sphere, drawing from a case study in inner-city Montreal as an example. Showing that churches in decline are seizing the opportunity to leverage tax-free land as their primary asset, the chapter emphasizes social entrepreneurship as a key area where religion and market intersect: community hubs are framed as a smart real estate investment for private investors with social purpose goals, while Christian property, supported by private investment, becomes central to reinvigorating Christian influence in the public sphere.

In *God Is Not at Church: Digitalization as Authentic Religious Practice in an American Megachurch*, **Ariane Kovac** investigates how digitalization has fundamentally transformed the organizational structure of Churchome, an American Evangelical megachurch, and how the church justified this process and incorporated it into its theology. She argues that Churchome uses its digital approach to emphasize the ideal of communitization and to present itself as an authentic and exciting organization. The resulting changes in membership structure have led to a diversification of how members relate to the church and an eventization of church life. In this way, Churchome is able to counter internal and external criticism against megachurches per se and its move into the digital in particular. Kovac's case study reveals the manifold ways in which changing social forms influence religious semantics.

In *Shapeshifting the Christian Right: The Moral Majority as a Faith-Based Organization and the Immanent Turn of Evangelicalism in the Late 20th Century*, **Sebastian Schüler** looks at nonprofit organizations as a specific religious social form. The author starts from the premise that religious movements would hardly survive or gain social and political influence without organizations. He illustrates this assumption by using the Moral Majority as an example of how the Christian Right evolved from a loose network of church organizations into a politically successful movement by adopting new forms of organization. The Christian Right thus underwent an immanent turn, increasingly adapting its social forms and semantics to secular forms of organization and legal discourse. With his contribution, Schüler sheds light on a somewhat hidden aspect of social forms of religion by expanding the understanding of this concept to the social forms that allow religions to act efficiently in the political sphere. His case study is right-wing American Christianity, but his approach could also be applied to other religious settings.

In *Social Forms in Neo-Pentecostal Prosperity Contexts: From Network to Market Exchange*, **Maren Freudenberg** discusses the various social forms that play a role in prosperity theology. In these contexts, religious interaction and practice is coordinated by way of groups, events, organizations, networks, movements, and market exchanges, while the market exchange is a particularly salient social form due to its congruence with prosperity semantics. Freudenberg highlights that prosperity theologies teach that investment not only in one's personal faith and one's congregation, but also and importantly on the secular market, will be rewarded by God, and that these semantics are mirrored on a structural level by the market exchange as a form of transaction between two parties. She concludes that because financial risk-taking and success on the secular market are coded religiously as signs of depth of faith and divine grace, the market exchange complements these core tenets by translating semantics into structure.

In *Pentecostal Social Engagement in Contemporary Guatemala*, **Virginia Garrard** discusses emerging social forms in the context of Pentecostal social engagement in Central American Guatemala. Pentecostals in recent decades have shifted from a hermeneutics of separation from the world to a stance which embraces social and political participation, cohering into social forms that emphasize collective mobilization and participation. As Garrard shows, this development corresponds to a shifting emphasis on religious ideals and theologies that become self-reinforcing logics within the vertical and horizontal networks of the church. Pastors build strong vertical patriarchal relations with their congregants and purposefully encourage strong lateral networks within "small groups" that strengthen group cohesion and the church as an institution. As these social relationships evolve, Garrard argues, they transform the role of the church as an organization to one of increased, outward-facing social action.

In *Social Forms in Orthodox Christian Convert Communities in North America*, **Sebastian Rimestad** and **Katherine Kelaidis** examine conversion dynamics in the Orthodox Church in North America, which is a refuge from liberalism and perceived social relativism for many. Orthodox Christian convert communities use various social forms in order to create this image of the Orthodox Church as a divinely inspired counterculture, with the effect of challenging existing Orthodox Christian communities, who are often more concerned with ethnic and cultural affiliation and wish to integrate into Western culture. The authors argue that this kind of individualization of North American Orthodoxy indicates that hierarchical structures are becoming less important while community elements are gaining in prevalence, suggesting a dynamic of societalization of communitization.

In *Forever Into Eternity: Social Forms of Religion in the Temple Wedding of The Church of Jesus Christ of the Latter-day Saints*, **Marie-Therese Mäder** introduces us to the Mormon wedding ritual of the "sealing" ceremony at the temple to illustrate not only the profound significance of this event in the life of a Latter-day Saint but also to highlight the dyad of the martial couple as well as processes of religious communitization that occur during the ritual and its eventization as important social forms of religion in present-day Mormonism. Through interviews with long-married members of the Church of Jesus Christ of Latter-day Saints, the largest branch of Mormonism, Mäder retrospectively uncovers the impact of the collectively experienced temple ceremony.

Insa Pruisken's contribution *Organizing 'Private Religion': Types of Governance in American Protestantism* shifts the focus from empirical perspectives to systematic considerations. Pruisken adds a governance perspective to the social forms approach as we outline it in this introduction, discussing three elementary mechanisms of governance forms (mutual observation, influence, and negotiation) and relating these to types of actors in the American Protestant field, including individual believers, communities, congregations, denominations, and special purpose groups. Building on constellations of mutual negotiation, she then distinguishes six types of governance forms in American Protestantism –denominational regulation, democratic self-governance, hierarchical self-governance, stakeholder guidance, competition, and network governance – and discusses the role of organizations for what, following Thomas Luckmann, she calls the "private form" of religion.

Acknowledgements

This anthology is the result of a cooperation between the two editors as part of the Cluster of Excellence 'Religion and Politics' at the University of Münster. Funded by the Cluster, we were able to organize two international workshops: In June 2022, we discussed the history and present of 'Charismatic Catholicism in Europe and the Americas' at the University of Münster. 'Religious Social Forms in American Christianity Yesterday and Today' was the topic of the follow-up workshop held at the Center for Religious Studies at Ruhr University Bochum in March 2023. The Cluster not only provided funding for both workshops, but also made the publication of this volume possible through covering the printing costs. We are grateful for the generous support.

We also wish to thank all participants of the workshops for their presentations, their active engagement in the discussions, and their willingness to develop their presentations into contributions for this volume. We are very grateful for the fruitful cooperation with every contributing author!

A big thank you also goes to the administrative staff and student assistants who made the workshops possible. Finally, we would like to express our sincere thanks to Allegra Goldstraß, Paula König, and Emilia Bachmann for their invaluable support in the final editing of this volume.

Bibliography

Becker, Howard (1940): "Constructive Typology in the Social Sciences." In: American Sociological Review 5/1, pp. 40–55.

Beyer, Peter (2003): "Social Forms of Religion and Religions in Contemporary Society." In: Dillon, Michele (ed.), Handbook of the Sociology of Religion, Cambridge: Cambridge University Press, pp. 45–60.

Bourdieu, Pierre (1985): "Le champ religieux dans le champ de production symbolique." In: Centre de sociologie du Protestantisme Strasbourg (ed.): Les nouveaux clercs. Prêtres, pasteurs et spécialistes des relations humaines et de la santé, Genève: Labor et Fides, pp. 255–261.

Bourdieu, Pierre (1987 [1971]): "Legitimation and Structured Interests in Weber's Sociology of Religion." In: Whimster, Sam/Lash, Scott (eds.): Max Weber. Rationality and Modernity, London: Allen & Unwin, pp. 119–136.

Bourdieu, Pierre (1991 [1971]): "Genesis and Structure of the Religious Field". In: Comparative Social Research 13 (special issue: 'Religious institutions'), pp. 1–44.

Bourdieu, Pierre/Saint Martin, Monique de (1982): "La sainte famille. L'épiscopat français dans le champ du pouvoir." In: Actes RSS 44/45, pp. 2–53.

Cowan, Douglas E. (2016): "New Religious Movements." In: Linda Woodhead/Christopher H. Partridge/Hiroko Kawanami (eds.), Religions in the Modern World: Traditions and Transformations, London: Routledge, pp. 379–406.

Dawson, Lorne L. (2008): "New Religious Movements." In Robert A. Segal (ed.), The Blackwell Companion to the Study of Religion, Malden: Blackwell Publishing, pp. 369–384.

Dawson, Lorne L. (2011): "Church-sect-cult: Constructing Typologies of Religious Groups." In: Peter B. Clark (ed.), The Oxford Handbook of the Sociology of Religion, Oxford: Oxford University Press, pp. 525–544.

Dillon, Michele (ed.) (2003): Handbook of the Sociology of Religion, Cambridge: Cambridge University Press.

Fox, Judith (2010): "New Religious Movements." In John Hinnells (ed.), The Routledge Companion to the Study of Religion, London: Routledge, pp. 337–353.

Freudenberg, Maren (2018): The Mainline in Late Modernity: Tradition and Innovation in the Evangelical Lutheran Church in America, Lanham: Lexington Books.

Gebhardt, Winfried/Hitzler, Ronald/Pfadenhauer, Michaela (2000): Events: Soziologie des Außergewöhnlichen, Opladen: Leske & Budrich.

Gebhardt, Winfried (2018): "Religiöse Szenen und Events." In: Detlef Pollack/Volkhard Krech/Olaf Müller/Markus Hero (eds.), Handbuch Religionssoziologie, Wiesbaden: Springer, pp. 591–610.

Hervieu-Léger, Danièle (2007): "Individualism, the Validation of Faith, and the Social Nature of Religion in Modernity." In Richard K. Fenn (ed.), The Blackwell Companion to Sociology of Religion, Malden: Blackwell, pp. 161–175.

Hitzler, Ronald/Honer, Anne/Pfadenhauer, Michaela (2009): Posttraditionale Gemeinschaften, Wiesbaden: VS Verlag für Sozialwissenschaften.

Hitzler, Ronald (2011): Eventisierung: Drei Fallstudien zum marketingstrategischen Massenspaß, Wiesbaden: VS Verlag für Sozialwissenschaften.

Kern, Thomas/Pruisken, Insa (2018): "Religiöse Bewegungen – Das Beispiel des Evangelikalismus in den USA." In: Detlef Pollack/Volkhard Krech/Olaf Müller/Markus Hero (eds.), Handbuch Religionssoziologie, Wiesbaden: Springer, pp. 507–524.

Krech, Volkhard/Schlamelcher, Jens/Hero, Markus (2013): "Typen Religiöser Sozialformen und ihre Bedeutung für die Analyse religiösen Wandels in Deutschland." In: Kölner Zeitschrift für Soziologie und Sozialpsychologie 65/1, pp. 51–71.

Krech, Volkhard (2018): "Dimensionen des Religiösen." In: Detlef Pollack/Volkhard Krech/Olaf Müller/Markus Hero (eds.), Handbuch Religionssoziologie, Wiesbaden: Springer, pp. 51–94.

Luckmann, Thomas (2003): "Transformations of Religion and Morality in Modern Europe." In: Social Compass 50/3, pp. 275–285.

Lüddeckens, Dorothea/Walthert, Rafael (2018): "Religiöse Gemeinschaft." In: Detlef Pollack/Volkhard Krech/Olaf Müller/Markus Hero (eds.), Handbuch Religionssoziologie, Wiesbaden: Springer, pp. 467–488.

Ludwig, Christian/Heiser, Patrick (2014): "Zur Mesoebene Von Religion. Eine Einführung." In: Patrick Heiser/Christian Ludwig (eds.), Sozialformen der Religionen im Wandel, Wiesbaden: Springer, pp. 1–16.

Niebuhr, Helmut Richard (1929 [2005]): The Social Sources of Denominationalism, Whitefish: Kessinger Publishing.

Petzke, Martin/Tyrell, Hartmann (2011): "Religiöse Organisationen." In: Maja Apelt (ed.), Typen Der Organisation: Ein Handbuch, Wiesbaden: VS Verlag für Sozialwissenschaften, pp. 275–306.

Pollack, Detlef/Krech, Volkhard/Müller, Olaf/Hero, Markus (eds.) (2018): Handbuch Religionssoziologie, Wiesbaden: Springer.

Roth, Roland/Rucht, Dieter (2008): "Einleitung." In: Dieter Rucht/Roland Roth (eds.), Die sozialen Bewegungen in Deutschland seit 1945: Ein Handbuch, Frankfurt: Campus, pp. 9–35.

Schlamelcher, Jens. 2018. "Religiöse Organisation." In: Detlef Pollack/Volkhard Krech/Olaf Müller/Markus Hero (eds.), Handbuch Religionssoziologie, Wiesbaden: Springer, pp. 489–506.

Stark, Rodney/Bainbridge, William Sims (1985): The Future of Religion: Secularization, Revival, and Cult Formation, Berkeley, CA: University of California Press.

Tönnies, Ferdinand (1999 [1912]): Community and Society, London: Routledge.

Troeltsch, Ernst (1931 [1912]): The Social Teaching of the Christian Churches: Vol. I and II, New York: Harper.

Wallis, Roy (2019): The Elementary Forms of the New Religious Life, Ann Arbor: Routledge.

Weber, Max (2011 [1920; 1905]): The Protestant Ethic and the Spirit of Capitalism: The Revised 1920 Edition. Translated by Stephen Kalberg, New York: Oxford University Press.

Weber, Max (2013 [1922]): Economy and Society: An Outline of Interpretive Sociology, Berkeley: University of California Press.

Weber, Max (2012 [1904]): "The 'objectivity' of knowledge in social science and social policy." In: idem, Collected Methodological Writings, edited by Hans Henrik Bruun and Sam Whimster, London: Routledge, pp. 100–138.

Williams, Rhys H. (2003): "Religious Social Movements in the Public Sphere: Organization, Ideology, and Activism." In: Michele Dillon (ed.), Handbook of the Sociology of Religion, Cambridge: Cambridge University Press, pp. 315–330.

Wilson, Bryan R. (1970): Religious Sects: A Sociological Study, London: Weidenfeld & Nicolson

The Four Phases of the Catholic Charismatic Renewal (1967–2017)[1]

Valérie Aubourg

Abstract *This article focuses on the Catholic Charismatic Renewal by looking at its development from 1967 to the present day through the prism of its social forms in light of its relationship to Pentecostalism. I identify four phases: the first (1967–1982) during which the Pentecostal experience entered Catholicism and translated into the birth and development of the Catholic Charismatic Renewal; followed by a phase of retreat into its Catholic identity and 'routinisation' of charisma (1982–1997); then, in the third phase, the Charismatic Renewal sought to find new impetus by moving closer to neo-Pentecostal networks (since 1997); and, finally and simultaneously, a 'post-charismatic' stage (since the early 2000s) corresponding to the wide introduction of typically Pentecostal elements into Catholicism, over and above the Charismatic Renewal in the strict sense of the term.*

Keywords Catholicism, Charismatic Renewal, Church, Evangelicalism, Pentecostalism, Protestantism

1. Introduction

On June 3, 2017, the Charismatic Renewal celebrated its jubilee in Rome. Fifty thousand pilgrims from 120 countries were gathered for the vigil of Pentecost. The Circus Maximus was deliberately chosen over the Roman basilicas or Saint Peter's Square in order to accommodate the dozens of representatives of various Christian churches invited for the occasion. They were seated on the platform or in the front rows. Among them, Giovanni Traettino, pastor of the Evangelical Church of Reconciliation in Caserta, spoke for about 15 minutes. Not-

---

[1] This article is based on the book "Réveil Catholique. Emprunts évangéliques dans le catholicisme" (Aubourg 2020).

ing that 2017 was also the year of the 500th anniversary of the Reformation, he stressed that "Catholics and Evangelicals share a similar experience of the Holy Spirit". He went on to cite the various papal initiatives that had fostered "an unprecedented development" of relations with many pastors: "the visit to the Evangelical Church of Reconciliation in Caserta, asking Italian Pentecostals for forgiveness, the encouragement given to US pastors, and even this historic Pentecostal meeting ... Since the election of Cardinal Bergoglio as pope, another season has begun"[2]. When Pope Francis' turn at the microphone came, he stressed the importance of interfaith relations: "Today Christian unity is more urgent than ever [...] we desire to be a reconciled diversity"[3]. The Pope went on to preach conversion, a transformed life, and Baptism in the Holy Spirit.

This event provides an opportunity to look back at the history and development of the Charismatic Renewal through the prism of its links with Pentecostalism. As Pastor Traettino's words suggest, this is a long-standing relationship, since the Catholic Charismatic movement has its origins in Pentecostalism. Nevertheless, the Catholic Church was long suspicious of Catholic Charismatics, many of whom distanced themselves from Pentecostalism. The Roman event shows the extent to which the situation has changed.

In fifty years, the Charismatic Renewal has been through different phases, different 'seasons', to take up the Italian pastor's image, going from the opening up of springtime to the retreat into the Catholic identity of wintertime. The history of the Charismatic movement is generally divided into three major periods[4]: first, the blossoming years (1967–1982), during which the Pentecostal experience entered Catholicism in the form of an initial 'renewal', followed by a retreat into its Catholic identity (1982–1997). This second period led to its routinization. In a bid to reassure the ecclesiastical institution, certain Pentecostal practices were abandoned (demonic deliverance, resting in the spirit, etc.), emotional expressions became less and less exuberant, prayer meetings followed an increasingly repetitive format, turning into real paraliturgical assemblies. Finally, a period of rapprochement with the neo-Pentecostals followed with the aim of reviving the Renewal (since 1997). To this, I will add a

---

2   Pastor Traettino's statement, Rome, June 3, 2017, personal notes.
3   Pope's statement, Rome, June 3, 2017, personal notes.
4   In North America as in Europe, the number of years allocated to each period varies by country and by observer (in Quebec, for example, Côté and Zylberberg date the second period from 1974 to 1978, and the third from 1978 to 1982), but the substance of each phase is comparable.

fourth so-called 'post-charismatic' phase which corresponds to the introduction of typically Pentecostal elements into Catholicism outside of the Charismatic Renewal *sensu stricto*.

Since its birth, the Charismatic Renewal has taken the form of prayer groups and communities. We are dealing with believers who emphasize the Holy Spirit so that they, and through them, the world they live in, can be transformed. However, Jean-René Bertrand and Colette Muller note that the social forms of this current "are so different, it is difficult to provide a complete diagnosis and classify this whole variety of communities. Each one is active in its own way, spreads the evangelical message according to its ways of living and engaging, most often within the known ecclesiastical structures of the movements, the parish, the diocese, but also sometimes within the wider society in which members are involved, investing of their time and energy" (Bertrand/Muller 2004: 225). [5] As also underlined by Martine Cohen "at first the Charismatic Renewal was not a movement of social reconquest undertaken in the name of a Catholicism that saw itself as homogeneous. Rather, it was a kind of religious explosion whose social manifestations quickly became distinct" (Cohen 1986: 66). In France, when the Catholic Charismatic Renewal was born, the social form that dominated in the Catholic Church was that of activists invested in society, like "the salt in the dough" of the earth (Matthew 5:13-16). They were grouped around age or social classes: children, young farmers, workers, health professionals, pensioners, etc. In contrast, Charismatic activism brought together lay persons, ordained individuals, youths, families, workers, and senior executives around praying.

The first two phases have been widely documented in North America (Csordas 1995; Côté/Zylberberg 1990; Ciciliot 2019), in Italy (Pace 2020), and in France (Landron 2004, Pina 2001; Cohen/Champion 1993). We have benefitted from precise surveys in which several researchers have described one or several aspects of the Charismatic Renewal: healing (Charuty 1987), prayer assemblies (Parasie 2005), glossolalia (Aubourg 2014), prophecy (McGuire, 1977), the exercise of authority (Plet 1990), its meaning and significance (Vetö 2012), etc. We have also benefitted from quantitative studies which estimate there were 119 million charismatic Catholics in the world twenty years ago (Barrett/Johnson 2005). They show how the Renewal grew rapidly during its first twenty years, corresponding to the first stage of its development (the focus of the first part of this article) and the beginning of the second (the

---

5   All translations by the author unless indicated otherwise.

focus of the second part), before seeing a decline in the Western countries. In response, interdenominational initiatives were taken to revive religious enthusiasm. These will be presented in the third part of this article. Finally, I will conclude by showing how groups and parishes describing themselves as completely foreign to the Charismatic Renewal are now taking up Pentecostal practices (Aubourg 2020), demonstrating a certain "evangelicalization" of Christianity (Willaime 2011: 346). Throughout this paper, I will draw on data mainly from Europe (France and Italy) and North America.

2. Birth and development of the Charismatic Renewal

In January 1967, four lay teachers and students from Duquesne University in Pittsburgh, Pennsylvania, experienced "baptism in the Holy Spirit" among a group of Episcopal Pentecostals.

This experience quickly spread to student circles at the University of Notre-Dame du Lac in South Bend, Indiana, the University of Michigan in Ann Arbor, and the Franciscan University of Steubenville, Ohio. It then extended beyond the academic world through the creation of prayer groups in traditional parishes. In 1973, there were 855 prayer groups in the United States and 65 in Canada. 200.000 people had joined the movement in 1972, and 670.000 in 1976 (Barrett 1982). Edward Denis O'Connor's estimations arrive at a lower number. According to him, an American priest and theologian, by June 1974, 100.000 people had joined the movement in North America (O'Connor 1975: 19). The movement simultaneously traveled abroad, beginning with Anglo-Saxon countries. There were prayer groups in 13 countries in 1969, in 25 countries in 1970, and in 93 countries by 1975. In less than ten years, the movement had become established on all continents. In regions such as Africa, it was so successful that it led the Jesuit anthropologist Meinrad Hegba to speak of a "veritable tidal wave" (Hegba 1995: 67).

The Catholic Charismatic Renewal spread in a relatively spontaneous manner, thanks to laypersons, priests, or monks and nuns who discovered the movement whilst visiting the United States and then introduced it to their home countries. It also spread through American Charismatics who promoted it during their travels abroad. Finally, some groups that were initially formed outside the Catholic Charismatic Renewal subsequently joined it. The Charismatic Renewal included a very wide range of individuals all over the world who occasionally took part in various groups and activities: prayer assemblies, conferences, conventions, spiritual retreats, evangelization schools, publishing houses, new communities, etc.

The first phase of this Catholic Pentecostalism was characterized by "individual entrepreneurship and sacred effervescence" (Côté/Zylbergberg 1990: 84). It translated into a profusion of highly diverse prayer groups, several of which gave birth to so-called new communities: in the United States, The Word of God (1969); in France, L'Emmanuel (1972; cf. Dolbeau's chapter in this volume), Le Chemin Neuf (1973), La Théophanie (1972), Le Pain de Vie (1976), Le Puits de Jacob (1977) etc. Prayer groups and communities organized regular joint gatherings fostering relations between Catholics and Pentecostals. This social form was directly inherited from Pentecostalism and, more broadly, the Evangelical tradition of camp meetings (large revival conventions held in the 18th century).

Charismatic entities borrowed from Pentecostalism its emphasis on conversion (or reconversion), the proclamation of the Gospel, the experience of "baptism in the Holy Spirit", and the charismatic manifestations that are believed to flow from it (healing, glossolalia, prophecy).

Charismatic prayers were mainly prayers of praise, with an emphasis on religious emotions, real-life testimonies, and spontaneous expressions of faith. The body played a central part through rhythmic chants, dancing, and many gestures and postures such as clapping hands. This type of prayer attracted individuals in search of all kinds of divine favor, including healing, fertility, and marital success.

Apart from Pentecostal practices and beliefs, most of the communities emerging from the Charismatic Renewal adopted a strict orthopraxy characteristic of Evangelical circles: strong condemnation of behavior deemed immoral, such as adultery, prohibition of drinking and smoking, wariness of music (particularly rock music), a ban on gambling, as well as a condemnation of yoga, divinatory astrology, and spiritism. Proof of the condemnation of this type of practice in France can readily be found in the many books sold in Evangelical libraries. Authors bear witness to the way in which they categorically renounced astrology, New Age, esotericism, etc. (cf. Doerin/Von Der Wense 2009; Beekmann 1998; Foucart 2015).

Going beyond the strictly religious sphere, the changes linked to the experience of "baptism in the Holy Spirit" had to involve the whole life of a Catholic convert: from one's social relations through one's daily attitude to one's representation of society. This ethical dimension also affected gender relations: not only did women wear skirts and men grew beards, but male authority was ascribed to greater value. There was a strong distinction between male and female roles. The maternal function was highly valorized and charismatic women usually had more children than their fellow countrywomen and often chose to stay at home to raise them. They followed an ethic that placed mistrust of ostentatious attitudes over their bodies: hardly any make-up, tattoos, perfume, eccentric hairstyles, bare shoulders, visible knees, or tight-fitting clothes. However, the Charismatic Movement (like Pentecostalism) did its best to simultaneously endorse the symbolic advantages of male domination (in terms of both ethics and confessional practice) and promote the female virtues expounded by a theology that encouraged emotions (Malogne-Fer/Fer 2015: 13).

Nevertheless, while appropriating the major features of Pentecostalism, Charismatics retained their Catholic identity: they defended Catholic doctrine, attended parish services regularly, and respected the Church hierarchy. Distancing themselves from political issues and the progressivism of their Catholic coreligionists, Charismatics preferred to revive traditional practices abandoned in the post-conciliar years: recitation of the rosary, Marian pilgrimages, individual confession, prostration, adoration of the Blessed Sacrament, etc. From the point of view of their ecclesiastical integration, even if the new communities' way of life was similar to that of religious orders (vow of obedience, sharing of goods, daily life punctuated by the recitation of offices), Charismatic communities enjoyed the status of "associations of the faithful" (private or public) and were placed under the authority of the bishop of the diocese where they were set up. Some of them were subsequently recognized as international associations directly linked to the Dicastery for the Laity, Family, and Life, while others set up clerical associations of pontifical right. Since 1993, the Bishops' Conference of France has done an inventory of Charismatic communities and distinguished between several types of communities based on how they are organized and work and, secondarily, on their activities (Bertrand/Muller 2004).

The Charismatic Renewal was born in a church that was grappling with the effects of Vatican II. Indeed, the Council introduced reforms whose effects were perceptible in the birth of the Charismatic Renewal, such as opening up to other Christian denominations, the importance given to lay persons, and the renewal of the liturgy. In France, it was a continuation of the post-1968 countercultural protest movement. In this favorable context, the Renewal represented a form of social and religious protest. It challenged a Catholicism that was perceived to have become too prosaic, too aligned with the norms of global society, having eliminated all wonder and sensitive emotions from one's personal engagement and from the liturgy (Cohen/Champion 1993: 79). However, unlike in Pentecostalism, at that point, the protest occurred within the Church since the groups that belonged to this movement remained faithful to Rome.

The Catholic Church's view of the Renewal was largely skeptical, if not negative. The important role given to the laity in running the movement and their claim that they acted directly under the influence of the Holy Spirit made them uncontrollable in the eyes of some in the hierarchy. The Charismatic Renewal was viewed critically because of its tendency towards an emotional Christianity that seemed to devalue engagement in society, and because of the perceived arrogance of these new converts who presented themselves as the future of the Church.

Even though, unlike Pentecostal converts, Catholic Charismatics did not abandon the pews of the Church and did not break with their "lineage of believers" (Hervieu-Léger 1999), they nevertheless went through a process of individualization of their religious experience. This phenomenon manifested in the emergence of "elective fraternities" made up of Renewal prayer groups and the new communities. Indeed, their adherence to these groups represented a personal choice that emancipated them from the communities they belonged to, particularly their parishes. These voluntary affiliations further changed their relations with their family circles.

But over time, contrary to what the religious authorities feared, the Catholic Charismatics became integrated into the Church. The Jesuit theologian Sullivan even noted the opposite trend: "On the contrary, the evidence suggests that their Pentecostal experience turned Catholics into more faithful participants in the life of the Church" (Sullivan 1988: 87). This fidelity to the Catholic Church explains the fact that, after being called "Catholic Pentecostalism", "neo-Pentecostalism", or the "Pentecostal movement in the Church" (O'Connor 1975: 18), the movement was finally referred to as the "Charismatic Renewal" and, soon after, the "Renewal". It also explains the fact that several church leaders gradually began to look favorably upon the Charismatic movement and give it their support. On May 18 and 19, 1975, on the feast of Pentecost, 12.000 people from more than 60 countries took part in the third international Catholic Charismatic Renewal conference in Rome, where Pope Paul VI asked them this question: "How could this Renewal not be an opportunity for the Church and for the world? And how, in this case, could we not do everything possible to ensure that it remains so?" (La Documentation catholique 1975: 562). By calling the Renewal an "opportunity", the Pope not only offered the Charismatic Movement the legitimacy it hoped for, but he also encouraged the development of this "new spring for the Church". This event illustrates the opening up to Pentecostalism, but also the institutional assertion of control over the Charismatic Renewal. Pauline Côté and Jacques Zylberberg underline these two aspects: a "Protestant expansion and acculturation", on the one hand, and the beginning of an exogenous control closely interwoven with the endogenous structuring of the Charismatic Renewal, on the other (Côté/Zylberberg 1990: 83–84). The years that followed, and especially the 1980s, would be particularly marked by this second aspect: its integration into the Catholic matrix.

3. Retreat into Catholic identity

The 1980s represent a second stage in the development of the Renewal. After a difficult start between the Charismatic Movement and the Catholic Church, relations became easier. As Christine Pina points out, these pacified relations were "proof of a twofold movement whereby the Renewal mellowed and the Catholic Church adopted a more moderate stance as it wished to both make use of the vigor and mobilizing potential of this current and permanently anchor the Renewal in the universal Church by lessening its protest-oriented aspect" (Pina 2001: 29). It is true that some of the Renewal's innovations were "potentially destabilizing for the institutional system" (Cohen 1990: 144). Thus, in order to become less marginal and at the same time reassure the Church, the Charismatic Movement made a number of pledges to the Roman institution, namely that it would use emblematic figures (saints, mystics, popes), reappropriate the history of the ecclesiastical tradition and bring back devotions that had fallen out of favor. Pentecostal practices were either abandoned or transformed. Prophecies – particularly those related to the end times – became rare. There were fewer and less visible healings. Their conception changed to "conversion" or "inner healing". The ecclesiastical institution, which sought to regulate charismatic practices, issued warnings about them. In particular, the Church issued recommendations concerning certain practices such as exorcism, which it reserved for priests, or "resting in the Spirit", which it banned. According to Martine Cohen, this evolution led these Charismatic practices to become markedly less spectacular (Cohen 1986: 69). Delivery practices, for example, became more cautious. The Dominican Jean-Claude Sagne, an exorcist in the diocese of Lyon and a member of a charismatic Community, urged believers to be wary of "grand, noisy, and violent displays" and instead favor "detachment, silence, and adoration". He emphasized "discernment", which aimed to distinguish mental disorders from supernatural elements (Sagne 1994: 124). As for the idea of conversion associated with "baptism in the Holy Spirit", this was euphemized: groups such as the Emmanuel community replaced it with the term "outpouring of the Spirit" to clearly distinguish it from the Pentecostal experience. Prayer meetings became increasingly repetitive in format. In several French prayer groups, it was noted how, over time, these meetings turned into real paraliturgical assemblies. It was therefore clear that a process of "routinization of charisma" (Weber 1947) was at work.

The regulation of the Charismatic Renewal was attended by a restructuring of the movement. The Catholic charismatic landscape was organized around two main types of religious groupings: communities, on the one hand, and prayer groups, on the other. The communities themselves were subdivided into three categories: firstly, there were covenant communities, which brought together individuals that continued to be part of working life and civil society, including those who had taken vows. Then there were life communities, which brought all categories of people together in one place in order to engage in contemplative forms of prayer while observing rules of life similar to those of monasteries. Finally, a third category included mixed forms, that is, households that followed various rules and groups that met periodically to pray, for example (Bertrand/Muller 2004).

The communities were more visible, and their organization was more formal than that of the prayer groups. In most communities, irrespective of their specific social form, members made a solemn commitment, were subject to the obligations imposed by a code of conduct, and rendered mutual services. In these communities, the founder played a key role. The members of these communities were generally younger than those of the prayer groups and their involvement within the community was more restrictive than in a simple prayer group.

On the other hand, in prayer groups, the leader – called a "shepherd" – did not play a major part. This second type of assembly did not require intensive commitment from its members. However, even if their membership was more fluid and mobile, prayer groups made the effort to structure themselves by setting up national coordination bodies. In France they took the name Fraternité Pentecôte ('Pentecostal Fraternity').[6] Local Renewal delegates were appointed with the aim of "establishing dependence on the Bishop". An "ecclesiastical subsystem" was thus set up (Côté/Zylberberg 1990: 85).

This institutional evolution of the Charismatic Renewal was criticized by Protestants, who also noted that the movement had clearly distanced itself from ecumenism. "With a few exceptions, it was always the Protestants who took the initiative of organizing major interdenominational meetings. The Catholic authorities kept encouraging the charismatics of their denominations to organize themselves and invite their leaders to Rome", notes Olivier Landron (2004: 251). As Valentina Ciciliot has shown in her study on the relations between Catholic Charismatics and other US Christian groups in the late 1960s and 1970s, "the abundant interconnections between Catholic charismatic and Protestant leaders were put in the background, if not partially censored, for the sake of acknowledgement and acceptance" (Ciciliot 2021: 2).

In North America, the Charismatic Renewal predominantly involved middle and upper classes. In France, it also appealed to marginalized populations (homeless people, patients of psychiatric hospitals, backpackers, former drug addicts, conscientious objectors). It offered weekly meetings with a friendly atmosphere, helped by the norms of behavior implicitly prescribed in these assemblies: they called each other by their first names, used informal forms of address, kissed upon arriving and leaving, and did not make any mention of their professions... All these elements marked the fact that they belonged to a microsociety founded on a familial metaphor that erased the differences of generation and position within the social hierarchy. Furthermore, prayer groups and regional gatherings enabled followers to form relationships of friendship and mutual aid outside their families and professional circles (Charuty 1990: 75). This created a sense of psychological security and personal reassurance.

As for the new communities, they were characterized by the fact that they encouraged relations of solidarity rather than competition between members. They distanced themselves from modern societies' conception of social ties centered on individual will. This solidarity may be interpreted as an attempt to counteract the fragmentation experienced by societies in modernity. From

---

6 Founded in 1976, the group was initially made up of representatives of Charismatic communities and two representatives of prayer groups. Since 1988, it has brought together 23 individuals in charge of coordinating prayer groups not affiliated to communities. There are currently 1200 groups linked to this body, which is advised by a priest.

a sociographic perspective, the leaders of these Catholic communities were able to gather around them a number of followers who were sufficiently motivated and stable (they were in general better equipped culturally than prayer group members) to implement their innovations. That is why most founders belonged to the bourgeoisie or middle classes (Landron 2004: 85; Cohen 1990: 144).

In terms of the governance of the Renewal, Ralph Martin had set up a first International Communications Office (ICO) in Ann Arbor, USA, in 1972. Eager to strengthen the link between this entity and the Catholic authorities, in 1976, Cardinal Suenens transferred the ICO to the Bishopric of Mechelen-Brussels and, in 1978, changed it into the International Catholic Charismatic Renewal Office (ICCRO). The 1980s saw the institutionalization of this office and the consolidation of its links with the Roman authorities. It first moved to Rome in 1981, and finally to the Vatican in 1985. In 1993, the Pontifical Council for the Laity granted it pontifical recognition (i.e. approval of its statutes as an international service organization), and its name was changed to International Catholic Charismatic Renewal Services (ICCRS), thus emphasizing that it was a pastoral ministry service rather than merely an administrative office. The organization's aim was to promote relations between Catholic Charismatic entities and liaise with the Holy See.[7]

Throughout his pontificate (1978–2005), John Paul II gave his constant firm support to the Charismatic Renewal. The Polish Pope saw the movement's evangelizing potential and stressed its capacity to promote Christianity in societies "without God"[8] "infected by materialism"[9]. He interpreted the movement as "risposta provvidenziale" ('providential response') to secularization.[10] However, although he encouraged it, Pope John Paul II constantly reminded the Charismatic Renewal of "the importance of being rooted in that Catholic unity of faith and charity which finds its visible center in the See of Peter".[11]

---

[7] Cf. https://dev-iccrswp.day50communications.com/wp-content/uploads/ICCRS-STATUTES_EnOFFICIAL.pdf.
[8] https://www.vatican.va/content/john-paul-ii/en/speeches/1998/may/documents/hf_jp-ii_spe_19980530_riflessioni.html.
[9] https://www.vatican.va/content/john-paul-ii/it/speeches/1986/november/documents/hf_jp-ii_spe_19861115_rinnovamento-spirito.html.
[10] Cf. https://www.vatican.va/content/john-paul-ii/en/speeches/1998/may/documents/hf_jp-ii_spe_19980530_riflessioni.html.
[11] https://www.vatican.va/content/john-paul-ii/en/speeches/1981/may/documents/hf_jp-ii_spe_19810507_rinnovamento-carismatico.html.

He entrusted the leaders of the Charismatic Movement with "the primary task of safeguarding the Catholic identity of charismatic communities".[12]

The following two decades saw the continuation of the process of the Charismatic Movement's integration into Catholicism. New communities would increasingly take their place within the Church as they were entrusted with parishes, abbeys, and ecclesiastical responsibilities. Thus, several bishops came directly from within their ranks: Michel Santier (Créteil) founded "Réjouis-Toi" ('Rejoice'); Msgr. Dominique Rey (Toulon), Msgr. Guy de Kérimel (Grenoble), and Msgr. Yves Le Saux (Le Mans) were members of the Emmanuel Community. At the same time, however, another trend was emerging that sought to turn the tide.

4. The Charismatic Renewal's neo-Pentecostal reload

A third period began in the 1990s and continued into the 2000s. The Renewal's members were getting older, and the number of its prayer groups was beginning to decrease (Barrett/Johnson 2005).[13] However, there was a new impetus under the influence of the Pentecostal "third wave" which emphasized the power of a Holy Spirit that was supposed to manifest itself more strongly through "signs, wonders, healings, miracles"[14] and deliverances from demonic entities. New initiatives, taken from the fringes of the Catholic Renewal, reactivated Pentecostal-Charismatic emotions. They led to a transdenominational effervescence which the ecclesiastical institution struggled to control. In France, the Bishops' Conference devoted a seminar (in May 2009) and a book to this subject (CEF 2010). With the Toronto Blessing – a Canadian neo-Pentecostal movement which came to France in late 1997 – old Charismatic practices were updated, and new bodily phenomena promoted: resting in the Spirit, prolonged laughter, crying out, and even animal-like behavior (Poloma 2003). These phenomena occurred mainly during large group meetings organized by various Christian churches (Catholic, Protestant, Evangelical,

---

12 https://www.vatican.va/content/john-paul-ii/en/speeches/1998/october/documents/hf_jp-ii_spe_19981030_carismatici.html.

13 This slowing down, particularly noticeable in North America and Europe, did not prevent the Catholic Charismatic Movement from continuing to grow in Latin America and Africa.

14 http://www.laguerison.org/presentation/vision.

Pentecostal), such as the "Embrase nos cœurs" ('Fire up our hearts') conferences (since 1996) as well as gatherings at the Charlety Stadium in Paris (1998) and in Villefranche-sur-Saône (1998). Groups and entities bringing together Charismatics from different denominations were then set up.

Beginning in 1997, the Burning Bush initiative started by Kim Kollins spread throughout the Italian Renewal and then, in the course of 1999, in Europe, as it sought to achieve three goals: Christian unity, evangelization, and the renewal of the Church. The following year the interdenominational association 'Intercession France' was created, which encouraged fasting and praying for France. At the same time, the movement Dans la Gloire ('In the Glory') was introduced in France by Deborah Kendrick, a disciple of Ruth Ward Heflin. Beginning in 2002, there was a symbiosis between the intercessory networks, the Toronto Blessing, the annual Embrase nos cœurs-conventions, and the promotion of evangelization between Christians of different denominations (Chieux 2010: 65). The new way of conducting a prayer assembly, focusing on healing and praising, was gaining widespread acceptance, although there were still significant reservations. The healing practices prompted the Catholic Church to react by publishing, in 2000, *Instruction on Prayers to Obtain Healing from God*, a text written by Cardinal Ratzinger, Prefect of the 'Congregation for the Doctrine of the Faith'.[15]

All these new practices and initiatives brought together preachers working within interdenominational networks. The association called Paris tout est possible ('Paris, everything is possible'), established by Pastor Carlos Payan, is a good example. It set up training courses, prayer meetings, and evangelization days which focused on three areas: "Unity, Unction, Healing".[16] Another example is the healing methods introduced in Lyons, which brought together Catholic and Evangelical Charismatics in healing rooms and for monthly Miracles and Healing evenings. These initiatives were supported by the Consultation Charismatique Œcuménique Lyonnaise (CCOL) ('Lyon Ecumenical Charismatic Consultation'), whose activities were also part of the "third wave" movement. In 2004, this Lyons-based association began holding small intercession meetings for the city every month, as well as larger evening events every three months. The latter would begin with a long session of worship in

---

15   Cf. https://www.vatican.va/roman_curia/congregations/cfaith/documents/rc_con_cfa ith_doc_20001123_istruzione_fr.html.

16   *Unité Onction Guérison* ("Unity, unction, healing"), a pamphlet written by Pierre Cranga 2004. Flyer quoted by Chieux 2010: 71–72.

the neo-Pentecostal style and be followed by a dual Catholic and Evangelical sermon. Neo-Pentecostalism, also known as third-wave Pentecostalism or the neo-Charismatic Movement, is characterized by the promotion of extraordinary divine manifestations under the effect of "power evangelism". A greater variety of spiritual experiences was encouraged: uncontrollable laughter, intense sobbing, screaming and roaring, shaking, falling to the ground, showers of gold confetti, etc. Miracles, healings, and deliverances were already observed in "classical" Pentecostalism and the Catholic Charismatic Renewal, but the various movements that made up the "third wave" (Freston 1995) accentuated their importance. Their theology was accompanied by a particular emphasis on spiritual struggle, giving rise to new religious notions such as "spiritual warfare", "spiritual mapping", and prosperity theology (Coleman 2000).

Aside from the prayer groups and new communities whose members were partly active in these networks, this new Charismatic impulse went far beyond the Catholic Renewal: it involved the wider Evangelical Movement. In some contexts, the term Charismatic even went as far as to designate an interdenominational (and even transdenominational) movement that no longer referred to the 'borders of institutions' (Gonzalez 2014).

In terms of social forms, there was the novelty that those who participated in this movement did not seek to form interpersonal relationships that were likely to extend beyond the worship setting. Studies conducted among those who attended (Aubourg 2020) show that people came primarily in search of answers to personal or family needs (healing, well-being, resolving a difficulty, spiritual recharge). They would be re-energized by these collective meetings but then return to their homes as if nothing had happened. The prayer evening, prayer meeting, or Sunday's Eucharist service did not lead to the creation of new social ties. The attitude of these laypeople seemed in a sense more consumerist (ibid.). That said, these same individuals could belong to another Catholic group (Scouts, Itinéraires Ignatiens, family ministries, Équipes Notre Dame, etc.), where they developed close and sustained relationships. Their engagement with these groups sometimes reflected a high level of integration in the church institution. In other words, the difference from the Charismatic Renewal (in its initial and then routinized form) lay in the fact that the participants in the groups that were studied ("third wave") no longer combined spiritual regeneration with building community ties within the same entity.

Furthermore, there was a significant difference in the formation of each of these groups. Whilst in its early stages the Charismatic Renewal was characterized by a mix of social backgrounds, the Miracles and Healings events reached primarily individuals of modest means and believers from immigrant backgrounds (ibid.).

5. Towards a 'Post-Charismatic' period?

While the Charismatic Renewal corresponds to a church movement identified as such, many Evangelical and Pentecostal elements have spread within the Catholic Church beyond its Charismatic section. They have 'infiltrated', as it were, the parish as the basic social form of traditional Catholicism.

They take the form of prayer groups, healing assemblies, training courses, individualized arrangements, musical aids, books, body techniques, objects, etc. As noted by Henri Couraye, "a certain charismatic sensibility in the broadest sense has reached the Church by capillary action, without all the faithful always being aware of it" (Couraye 2011: 38). This includes, for example, the Mothers' Prayer Groups founded by the English Charismatic Veronica Williams (Williams 2004),[17] which brings women together for weekly prayer sessions (Aubourg 2016). Unlike Renewal prayer groups, there are no charisms and prayers are extremely formalistic. As certain gestures could look incongruous and surprising in a European cultural context (raised, clasped, or open hands), aspects that could threaten the respectability of the groups' members the most have been discarded. Nevertheless, Pentecostal features are still evident in several practices. Firstly, these meetings encourage spontaneous prayer and emphasize praise. When a biblical text is looked at, there are no theological discussions, but rather commentaries based on the participants' experiences and feelings. Secondly, as with Pentecostal-Charismatic circles, the rhetoric of salvation is favored and the proclamation "Jesus Christ is Lord and Savior" is at the heart of the message contained in prayers. Thirdly, the entity of the devil has been reintroduced. This phenomenon has been amply demonstrated in extra-European societies: in Africa, the Mascarene Islands (Boutter 2002), and South America (Boyer 1996). It is worth stressing the extent to which conceptions of Satan have accompanied religious revivals, including

---

17 Veronica Williams regularly attends charismatic conventions in Walsingham and her book mentions typically charismatic practices such as "perceiving inner images" or randomly opening one's Bible and attributing the text one's eyes land on to the Holy Spirit (Williams 2004: 15).

in groups of Anglo-Saxon origin. As noted by Birgit Meyer, the figure of the devil has proven to be "remarkably resistant to ideas which, ever since the Enlightenment, have criticized belief in its existence" (Meyer 2008: 4). Finally, it is worth noting the place given to lay people, who can address God directly, away from the presence of a priest and outside parish premises.

Parishes are also a good place to observe this 'Pentecostalisation' of Catholicism. From Baltimore (Mallon 2016) to Halifax (White/Corcoran 2015), Lyons, Hyères, Senlis, and Sophia-Antipolis, several Catholic parishes have adopted features that have made megachurches successful. Many of them have engaged in a process of "pastoral conversion" in order to produce "missionary disciples". Emphasis is laid on individual experience and personal appropriation of the Christian faith. The term "church" itself has replaced the term "parish". This semantic shift reflects a particular representation of the Church, conceived as a grouping of converts who evolve within networks made up of convinced Christians; this is the case of Amazing Parish,[18] an international network which brings together more than 200 parishes committed to renewing their pastoral project.

Since its beginnings in France in 1998, so-called "Alpha courses" have played a key role in disseminating Pentecostal practices and tools in Catholic circles, building an interdenominational and international network of leaders, and implementing a new model for organizing parishes. Alpha courses, which were started in an Anglican parish in London and take place over dinner, "are an evangelization tool characterized by the conviviality they seek to introduce and their well-honed logistical organization" (Rigou-Chemin 2011: 355). With Alpha, it is a whole vocabulary (related to conversion and evangelization), a set of practices (prayer of the brothers or even baptism in the Holy Spirit, Bible reading, small discussion groups, testimonies, welcome), and a way of running things (centered on the user, valuing lay people's input, presenting the faith with humor and in a relaxed way) which Catholic parishes have become familiar with over the last twenty years. Since 2012, Alpha has partnered with the Talenthéo Association of Christian Coaches to provide so-called Des pasteurs selon mon cœur ('Pastors according to my heart') courses. The aim of these training courses is to obtain the support of the church authorities and involve all parishioners in a new evangelizing dynamic. Currently in France, Des pasteurs selon mon cœur have already brought together 710 priests and vi-

---

18   Cf. https://amazingparish.org.

cars general, 29 bishops, and two cardinals committed to a process of "pastoral renewal".

Meanwhile, the diocesan prayer groups of the Charismatic Renewal – gathered within the Fraternité Pentecôte – have continued to lose ground: their members are aging, their numbers are dwindling, while social circles with a strong socio-cultural capital (who had previously provided the movement's leaders) are abandoning them. Charismatic prayer groups were initially seen as posing a threat to parish structures. Their members then emerged as major players thanks to their involvement in various parish services, while elements of Charismatic piety came to spread quietly through the parishes. In the end, the parish structure was not weakened by the Charismatic Renewal and its extensions (particularly the Alpha course) since it all happened within a sphere of Catholic membership that has steadfastly maintained its doctrinal and liturgical apparatus. The Catholic institution has tried not so much to exclude as to channel believers' energies, synthesizing doctrines, regulating practices, and bringing actors together under the banner of a unity it promoted with the watchword "visible communion". Thus, for centuries, parishes have been the "social core unit" of Catholicism. At first, the Charismatic Renewal was seen as a challenge and even a danger to parish structures. Today, Charismatic piety is a part of parishes and the latter even develop links with international and transdenominational networks. It is interesting to note here the union of two seemingly opposed rationales: the territorial organization of Catholic communities within the parish and their integration into a network.

For their part, the new communities have continued to develop on a global scale while showing real dynamism. As major places for priestly and religious vocations, they create an attractive pastoral offer for Catholic youth. The ecclesiastical institution has recognized this strength of theirs, going as far as appointing one of their priests in charge of youth ministry in France, after having constantly given an increasingly important role to charismatic communities during youth gatherings, especially World Youth Days.

However, Charismatic communities have not remained on the sidelines of the initiatives mentioned above. Indeed, they were the first to promote Alpha courses. The first course in a French Catholic environment was run by the Chemin Neuf community (1998) in the parish of Saint Denys de la Chapelle (Paris, 18th arrondissement). The following year, Marc and Florence de Leyritz, who were in charge of the program in France, trained Alpha course leaders at Paray-le-Monial in collaboration with the Emmanuel community. "It is a unifying project which draws together many charismatic communities", a member of the "Fondations du Monde Nouveau" ('New World Foundations') noted (De Galzain 1999). Furthermore, charismatic communities have engaged the parishes under their care in "pastoral conversion"-projects by drawing direct inspiration from the North American megachurch model,[19] or by participating in the training courses offered by Des pasteurs selon mon cœur. In the case of this latter association, it should be noted that several coaches are also members of one or another of the established Renewal communities. Thus, while retaining an important and well-defined place within Catholicism, Charismatic communities have taken part in this "process of developing a transdenominational Christianity centered on the individual and their personal conversion". They have joined the vast field of an "evangelizing ecumenism" (Willaime 2011: 349).

From an organizational point of view, Pope Francis has set up the International Catholic Charismatic *Renewal* Services (CHARIS) to replace the International Catholic Charismatic Renewal Service (ICCRS). The statutes of this new service begin by noting, in their preamble, the ecumenical dimension of the Charismatic Renewal. They go on to emphasize "the same fundamental experience of 'baptism in the Holy Spirit'" shared by all those belonging to this movement. Finally, they reflect a desire to restore flexibility to its organization and to encourage a plurality of charismatic expressions.[20]

6. Conclusion

The Catholic Charismatic Renewal is "a child of North American Pentecostalism" (Pina 2001: 26). Thus, in its initial form, it was characterized by its emphasis on religious emotions and closeness to Pentecostal circles. In the second phase, as it became institutionalized, the Renewal lost its momentum and left the margins of the Church. In reaction to this institutionalization of the Renewal, in the third phase, initiatives were taken with the aim of reconnecting with the Evangelical world and encouraging more intense emotional expressions. Currently, Pentecostal practices are being introduced into the

---

19 Some of them even went to the Saddleback Valley Community Church in California, founded by Rick Warren, and used the tools suggested by this pastor in *The Purpose Driven Church* (Warren 1998).

20 Cf. https://www.nsc-chariscenter.org/wp-content/uploads/2018/06/7_Charis-Statutes-Final-Text-Protocol-06.03.2018.pdf.

Catholic world again by groups who do not wish to be identified with the Catholic Charismatic Renewal. Could this fourth stage be a "post-charismatic" one?

In the end, we can ask ourselves what face of the Charismatic Renewal the above discussed developments reveal. Unlike rationalized faith, formalized religious practice, and abstract religious language, this type of Catholicism gave a chance to spontaneity, spiritual exigency, and the involvement of the believer's body. It favored the immediacy of faith's realities. Believers sought not so much future salvation as a pragmatic response to the desire to lead a successful life here and now. Echoing contemporary individual aspirations, the Charismatic Renewal rejoined the space of health and the desire for wellbeing by focusing its offer on healing and personal reassurance. This development of an enthusiastic type of Catholicism had obvious consequences in terms of political disengagement. Just as Veronica Williams renounced her work with the House of Lords to create mothers' groups, political activism was abandoned in favor of worshipping and praying. It was by transforming themselves that, alongside their coreligionists, these Catholics aspired to change society. The way in which their meetings were run left little room for debates. Conflicts and struggles were minimized, and tensions shifted to the psychological register.

Later, the Charismatic Renewal was increasingly marked by mobile forms of belonging. In its third (closer to neo-Pentecostalism) and fourth (post-Charismatic) phases, allegiances have become unstable and membership loose. Whether in relation to individuals searching for healing, women attending mothers' prayer, or laypersons and clerics following the US-American megachurch model, significant permeability is observed between these different groups, where commitment is reversible. Regardless of any pyramidal logic, individuals follow their own personal religious paths. Previously, the Catholic appropriation of the Pentecostal movement reflected a religious entity whose objectives, organization, orthodoxy, and orthopraxy corresponded to a very precise mission. The ICCRS statutes are ample proof of this (Pesare 2005: 141–142). Today, the Catholic Charismatic Renewal has become completely splintered. It has taken the form of international and interdenominational networks.

Many of its practices (testimony, prayer of the brothers, musical repertoire, etc.) have been adopted by parishes or Catholic movements not affiliated with the Renewal movement. Thus, the Charismatic Renewal's social forms partially evolved with time: at first, they gave rise to elective assemblies (life communities and prayer groups) which became institutionalized. Today, it rather takes the form of a network, attracting believers who do not place themselves exclusively under its banner, while its practices permeate very diverse Catholic realities. Networks, individual pragmatism, scattered forms of belonging, religious dissemination – all these features are echoes of "ultramodernity" (Giddens 1994; Willaime 1995).

Bibliography

Aubourg, Valérie (2014): Christianismes charismatiques à l'île le La Réunion, Paris: Karthala.
Aubourg, Valérie (2020): Réveil Catholique. Emprunts évangéliques dans le catholicisme, Genève: Labor et Fides.
Aubourg, Valérie (2014): "Chant céleste: la glossolalie en milieu pentecôtiste charismatique à l'île de La Réunion." In: Anthropologie et Sociétés, 38/1, pp. 245–264.
Aubourg, Valérie (2016): "L'Oraison des mamans: un nouvel entre soi religieux." In: Ethnologie Français, 162, pp. 323–333.
Barrett, David (1982): World Christian Encyclopedia: A comparative study of churches and Religions in the Modern Worlds, AD 1900–2000, Nairobi: Oxford University Press.
Barrett, David/Johnson Tood. M. (2005): "Le Renouveau charismatique catholique, 1959–2025." In: Oreste Pesare (ed.), "Et Pierre se leva...", pp. 163–178.
Beekmann, Sharon (1998): Séduite par la lumière. L'histoire terrifiante d'une femme séduite par le Nouvel Âge, Châteauneuf-du-Rhône: Vida.
Bertrand, Jean-René; Muller, Colette (2004), "De nouvelles figures de militants catholiques: les groupes du Renouveau charismatique dans l'Ouest de la France." In: Militants catholiques de l'Ouest: De l'action religieuse aux nouveaux militantismes, XIXe-XXe siècle, Rennes: Presses universitaires de Rennes, pp. 225–241.
Boutter, Bernard (2002): Le pentecôtisme à l'île de la Réunion. Refuge de la religiosité populaire ou vecteur de modernité?, Paris: L'Harmattan.
Boyer, Véronique (1996): "Possession et exorcisme dans une Église pentecôtiste au Brésil." In: Cahiers des Sciences Humaines 32/2, pp. 243–264.
CEF (2010): Les nouveaux courants charismatiques. Approches, discernement, perspectives. Paris: Bayard, Cerf, Fleurus-Mame.

Charuty, Giodana (1987): "Guérir la mémoire. L'invention rituelle du catholicisme pentecôtiste français et italien." In: Social Compass 34/4, pp. 437–463.

Charuty, Giodana (1990): "Les liturgies du malheur. Le souci thérapeutique des chrétiens charismatiques." In: Le Débat 59, pp. 68–89.

Chieux, Pierre (2010): "Bénédiction du Père, troisième vague, courant dans la gloire... De quoi parle-t-on? En quoi ces courants touchent-ils le Renouveau?" In: Les nouveaux courants charismatiques. Approches, discernement, perspectives, Conférence des Evêques de France, Paris: Bayard, Cerf, Fleurus-Mame, pp. 51–96.

Ciciliot, Valentina (2019): "The Origins of the Catholic Charismatic Renewal in the United States: Early Developments in Indiana and Michigan and the Reactions of the Ecclesiastical Authorities." In: Studies in World Christianity 25/3, pp. 250–273

Ciciliot, Valentina (2021): "'Pray Aggressively for a Higher Goal – The Unification of All Christianity': U.S. Catholic Charismatics and Their Ecumenical Relationships in the Late 1960s and 1970s." In: Religions 12/5: 353.

Cohen, Martine (1986): "Vers de nouveaux rapports avec l'institution ecclésiastique: l'exemple du Renouveau Charismatique en France." In: Archives de Sciences Sociales des Religions 62/1, pp. 61–79.

Cohen, Martine (1990): "Les Renouveau catholique et juif en France. L'individu et ses émotions." In: Françoise Champion/Danièle Hervieu-Léger (eds.), De l'émotion en religion: renouveau et tradition, Paris: le Centurion, pp. 121–167.

Cohen, Martine/Françoise, Champion (1993): "Recompositions, décomposition. Le renouveau charismatique et la nébuleuse mystique-érotique depuis les années soixante-dix." In: Débat 73, pp. 81–90.

Coleman, Simon (2000): The Globalisation of Charismatic Christianity: Spreading the Gospel of Prosperity, New York: Cambridge University Press.

Couraye, Henry (2011): "Le Renouveau charismatique – 40 ans." In: Il est vivant 284, http://fr.calameo.com/accounts/490358, pp. 32–45.

Côté, Pauline/Zylberberg, Jacques (1990): "Univers catholique romain, charisme et individualisme: les tribulations du renouveau charismatique canadien francophone." In: Sociologie et sociétés 22/2, pp. 81–94.

Csordas, Thomas (1995): "Oxymorons and Short-Circuits in the Re-Enchantment of the World. The case of the Catholic Charismatic Renewal." In: Etnoffoor 8/1, pp. 5–26.

Doerin, Martin/Von Der Wense, Sabine (2009): Le ciel décrypté. J'étais astrologue, Romanel-sur-Lausanne: Ourania.

De Galzain, Christophe (1999): "Les cours Alpha arrivent en France." In: La Croix November 15 (https://www.la-croix.com/Archives/1999-11-15/Les-cours-Alpha-arrivent-en-France-_NP_-1999-11-15-487169).

La Documentation Catholique (1975): "L'Église et le Renouveau charismatique catholique" 1678, pp. 562–568.

Foucart, Samuel (2015): L'occultisme dévoilé, Grézieu-la-Varenne: Viens et Vois.

Freston, Paul (1995): "Pentecostalism in Brazil: a brief history." In Religion 25/2, pp. 119–133.

Giddens, Anthony (1994): Les conséquences de la modernité, Paris: L'Harmattan.

Gonzalez, Philippe (2014): Que ton règne vienne – des évangéliques tentés par le pouvoir absolu, Geneva: Labor et Fides.

Hegba, Meinrad (1995): "Le mouvement charismatique en Afrique." In: Études 383/1, pp. 67–75.

Hervieu-Léger, Danièle (1999): Le pèlerin et le converti. La religion en mouvement, Paris: Flammarion/Champs.

Landron, Olivier (2004): Les communautés nouvelles: nouveaux visages du catholicisme français, Paris: Cerf.

Mallon, James (2016): Manuel de survie pour les paroisses. Pour une conversion pastorale, Paris: Artège.

Malogne-Fer, Gwendoline/Fer Yannick (2015): Femmes et pentecôtismes. Enjeux d'autorité et rapports de genre, Geneva: Labor et Fides.

McGuire, Meredith B. (1977): "The social Context of Prophecy: Word gifts of the Spirit among Catholic Pentecostals." In: Review of Religious Research 18, pp. 134–147.

Meyer, Brigit (2008): "Le Diable. Introduction." In: Terrain 50, pp. 4–13.

O'Connor, Edward Denis (1975): Le Renouveau Charismatique. Origines et perspectives, Paris: Beauchesne.

Pace, Enzo (2020): "The Catholic Charismatic Movement in Global Pentecostalism." In: Religions 11/7, unpaginated.

Parasie, Sylvain (2005): "Rendre présent l' 'Esprit-Saint'. Ethnographie d'une prière charismatique." Ethnologie française 35/2, pp. 347–354.

Pesare, Oreste (ed.) (2005): "Et Pierre se leva...". Documents des papes adressés au Renouveau Charismatique. Rassemblés par Oreste Pesare, Nouan-le-Fuzelier: Éd. des Béatitudes.

Pina, Christine (2001): Voyage au pays des charismatiques, Paris: Les Editions de l'Atelier.
Plet, Philippe (1990): L'autorité dans le mouvement charismatique contemporain, thèse de sociologie soutenue à l'université de Paris IV (unpublished manusript).
Poloma Margaret M. (2003): Main Street Mystics: The Toronto Blessing & Reviving Pentecostalism, Oxford: Alta Mira Press.
Rigou-Chemin, Bénédicte (2011): Les virtuoses religieux en paroisse. Une ethnographie du catholicisme en acte, Thèse de doctorat en anthropologie, Paris: EHESS.
Sagne, Jean-Claude (1994): "Le ministère d'exorciste." In: Jean-Baptiste Martin/ François
Laplantine/Massimo Introvigne (eds.), Le Défi magique, vol. 2, Satanisme et sorcellerie, Lyon: CREA, pp. 121–123.
Sullivan, Francis (1988): Charismes et Renouveau Charismatique. Une étude biblique et théologique, Nouan-Le Fuzelier: Éditions du Lion de Juda.
Vetö, Miklos (2012): "Le Renouveau charismatique dans l'Église Catholique." In: Les cahiers de psychologie politique 20. https://cpp.numerev.com/articles/revue-20/941-le-renouveau-charismatique-dans-l-eglise-catholique.
Warren, Rick (1998): The Purpose Driven Church, Grand Rapids, MI: Zondervan.
Weber, Max (1947): Wirtschaft und Gesellschaft, Tübingen: JCB Mohr.
White, Michael/Corcoran, Tom (2015): Rebuilt – histoire d'une paroisse reconstruite, Québec: Editions Néhémie.
Willaime, Jean-Paul (2011): "Protestantisme et nouvelle donne œcuménique." In: Sébastien Fath/Jean-Paul Willaime (eds.), La nouvelle France protestante. Essor et recomposition au XXIe siècle, Genève: Labor et Fides, pp. 328–351.
Williams, Veronica (2004): La joie de s'abandonner à Lui!, Caterham (GB): Transform Management Ltd.

Web References

Amazing Parish. "Amazing Parish." Accessed March 10, 2024. https://amazingparish.org.
Association Internationale des Ministères de Guérison. "Notre vision." Accessed September 16, 2016. http://www.laguerison.org/presentation/vision.

CHARIS. "Statutes." April 6, 2018. Accessed February 23, 2024. https://www.nsc-chariscenter.org/wp-content/uploads/2018/06/7_Charis-Statutes-Final-Text-Protocol-06.03.2018.pdf.

Congrégation pour la Doctrine de la Foi, instruction, « Sur les prières pour obtenir de Dieu la guérison », September 4, 2000

Congrégation pour la Doctrine de la Foi. "Instruction sur les prières pour obtenir de Dieu la guérison." September 4, 2000. Accessed March 10, 2024. https://www.vatican.va/roman_curia/congregations/cfaith/documents/rc_con_cfaith_doc_20001123_istruzione_fr.html.

International Catholic Charismatic Renewal Services. "Statutes." Accessed March 10, 2024. https://dev-iccrswp.day50communications.com/wp-content/uploads/ICCRS-STATUTES_EnOFFICIAL.pdf.

Pope John Paul II. "Address of the Holy Father to the Participants in the International Conference for Catholic Charismatic Leaders." Libreria Editrice Vaticana. October 30, 1998. Accessed March 10, 2024. https://www.vatican.va/content/john-paul-ii/en/speeches/1998/october/documents/hf_jp-ii_spe_19981030_carismatici.html.

Pope John Paul II. "Speech of the Holy Father Pope John Paul II. Meeting with Ecclesial Movements and New Communities." Libreria Editrice Vaticana. May 30, 1998. Accessed March 10, 2024. https://www.vatican.va/content/john-paul-ii/en/speeches/1998/may/documents/hf_jp-ii_spe_19980530_riflessioni.html.

Pope John Paul II. "Discorso di Giovanni Paolo II. Ai partecipanti al convegno nazionale del «Rinnovamento nello Spirito»." Libreria Editrice Vaticana. November 15, 1996. Accessed March 10, 2024. https://www.vatican.va/content/john-paul-ii/it/speeches/1986/november/documents/hf_jp-ii_spe_19861115_rinnovamento-spirito.html.

Pope John Paul II. "Address of John Paul II to the Participants in the Fourth International Leaders' Conference of the Catholic Charismatic Renewal." Libreria Editrice Vaticana. May 7, 1981. Accessed March 10, 2024. https://www.vatican.va/content/john-paul-ii/en/speeches/1981/may/documents/hf_jp-ii_spe_19810507_rinnovamento-carismatico.html.

'Catholic' and 'Charismatic'
Two Logics of Legitimization and the Negotiation of Belonging in the German Catholic Charismatic Renewal

Hannah Grünenthal

Abstract *This article explores how the German Catholic Charismatic Renewal (GCCR) navigates its positioning in the Catholic Church as well as in the Charismatic Movement. Focusing on the movement's two logics of legitimization – the 'Catholic' and the 'Charismatic' logic – this paper delves into the strategies employed by its members to assert their position within these two contexts. In order to be recognized within the Catholic Church, the GCCR needs to adopt a 'Catholic' logic of legitimization, which is based on the hierarchy, structure, tradition, and doctrine of the Catholic Church. With regard to the Charismatic Movement, the GCCR legitimizes its practices based on personal religious experiences and the experience of the Holy Spirit. The question of legitimization is tied back to the question of social forms in which German Catholic Charismatic practice takes place. The GCCR provides its members with a wide variety of social forms and opportunities for participation. By analyzing the two logics of legitimization connected to social forms, this article provides insights into the multifaceted strategies employed by the Catholic Charismatic Renewal Movement in Germany to navigate its intricate dual identity and foster a sense of belonging in both spheres, the Catholic Church and the Charismatic Movement.*

Keywords *Belonging, Catholic Church, Charismatic Catholicism, Charismatic Movement, German Catholic Charismatic Renewal, logic of legitimization*

1. Introduction

Scene 1: A Catholic Church, the smell of incense and the age of centuries lingers in the air. Approximately 300 people are gathered here, more than usual. They sit in the pews, looking at the altar where an elderly priest celebrates the Holy

Mass. A song is sung, then the sounds transition to a muttering and mumbling. No recognizable words are spoken, but people utter syllables and make noises; some stand up and open their arms widely, and many have their eyes closed. It grows louder, and their voices fill the high, gothic ceilings. After a few minutes, it grows silent again, and the priest continues his celebration.

Scene 2: Six people sit in a circle at the apsis of a small church around the altar. It is dark in the nave and only the apsis is illuminated. One after the other, sentence by sentence, they read out the gospel of the week. After the last one finishes, they remain silent. The Paschal candle flickers next to the icon of Mother Mary in the middle of the circle, next to the altar. Suddenly, one of the participants repeats a word from the gospel that has just been read. Someone else repeats a whole sentence, three times, with gravity. Then it is silent again. After a few minutes, one woman, the leader, begins to sing a song, and the others join her one by one.

Scene 3: A man in his early forties walks dynamically up and down the stage, wearing tight jeans, a casual jacket, and brand-new sneakers. He draws circles, lines, and arrows on a flipchart to illustrate his message: Men are men and women are women; they are created as such by God and must behave accordingly. In the audience, there are around 500 people of all ages, sitting on padded chairs, applauding, cheering, and nodding in agreement. After the presentation, a worship band begins to play. The stage is illuminated in bright green, yellow, and blue light. The people in the room stand up from their chairs, join the singing, clap their hands, and move to the rhythm.

All three of these scenes, though very different in mood, content, and character, were taken from meetings of the GCCR, the German Catholic Charismatic Renewal. German Catholic Charismatics go to the Holy Mass in their local parish, host Bible reading groups, and go to national and international faith events. They celebrate the sacraments and practice charisms. They are part of the Catholic Church as well as of the Charismatic Movement. In between those two, the GCCR has developed its own strategies of positioning itself within the Catholic Church on the one hand and the Charismatic Movement on the other. Those strategies include debates about legitimate and illegitimate practices and arguments as well as authority constructions, and the establishment of specific, yet fluid social forms according to the respective goals and needs.

Members of the GCCR are typically involved in several different religious social forms and contexts – some of them organized by members of the GCCR itself (like GCCR regional meetings), some situated in the Catholic Church (such as parish prayer groups with worship elements), some situated in the

Charismatic Movement (like weekend seminars on the charisms), and some situated somewhere in between (like Catholic Charismatic life-communities that are recognized by the Holy See). To grasp the GCCR's predominant social form is therefore not an easy task. In addition to the fluid social forms of GCCR activities, membership is also widely fluid.

In 2017, the Catholic Charismatic Renewal in Germany stated on its website that "currently about 12.000 Catholic Christians of all ages meet in about 500 prayer groups, house groups, and new spiritual communities",[1] and listed 32 Charismatic communities, initiatives, and ministries in addition to local prayer groups. Since the GCCR "does not accept 'members' in the manner of an association", there are neither membership statistics nor fixed criteria for who is part of the GCCR and who is not. It is merely the leaders and those who hold offices within the GCCR who are "tangible [...] – and these only as long as they participate in a 'binding' way" (Baumert 1998: 599). Elected communal, diocesan, and national spokespersons organize communication and networking on the regional and transregional level and form the 'Council of the GCCR' (Rat der CE), where matters of importance – structural as well as content-related – are discussed and decided. These structures are very much parallel to the Catholic diocesan structure. Furthermore, many members of the GCCR are actively involved in their local Catholic parishes and participate in Catholic activities. On the other hand, GCCR members are frequently involved in (non-Catholic) Charismatic group meetings, workshops, worship services, and other events. These social forms – or ways of coordinating interaction – are shaped by the different organizational structures in the Catholic Church and the Charismatic Movement: while the Catholic Church as an organization is hierarchically structured, the Charismatic Movement has the form of a network of individual churches, communities, and groups. The roles of hierarchy, authority, and members follow the respective organizational logics. As the GCCR positions itself in both contexts, this results in different points of contact with the two contexts. Apart from that, there are other, equally important social forms within the GCCR, such as prayer circles, religious life communities, open prayer meetings, blessings, praise services, seminars and lectures, and regional and national GCCR events.

As seen from these examples, the GCCR refuses to adopt one specific social form that can be understood as typical, permanent, or even exclusively Catholic

---

[1]   https://www.erneuerung.de/wer-wir-sind. All translations from German (written sources and empirical data) by the author unless indicated otherwise.

Charismatic. Is the GCCR a network, event community, group, organization within an institution, or movement? I argue that the GCCR can be understood as all of the above, and adapting different social forms in different contexts is one of the GCCR's core strengths. The GCCR, although bound together by a head association, is not a static construct. Rather, it is a crowd of individuals and groups meeting in different, changing contexts and social forms, shaping and maintaining their collective identity, ascribing religious authority in different contexts, and facing different challenges. They are, as I will argue in this article, bound together not only by a strict sense of belonging, but also by the simultaneous application of two parallel, yet exclusive, logics of legitimization: the 'Catholic' logic and the 'Charismatic' logic. The decision which logic is applied in which situation is a matter of constant negotiation, which at the same time embeds and demarcates the GCCR from both reference groups: the Catholic Church and the Charismatic Movement.

The data and reflections presented here were derived from a research project on positioning processes and the construction of religious authority in the case of the GCCR (Grünenthal 2021). The project covered a wide range of data: on the one hand, ethnographical data was collected and interpreted (extensive fieldwork in 2016–2017 with 43 protocols of participant observation and eight qualitative interviews). On the other hand, the media discourse of the GCCR between 2015 and 2018 was evaluated (the website[2], 16 issues of the quarterly journal "CE Info", an e-mail newsletter, and six publications by the theological committee). The total number of documents analyzed was 860.

2. Academic perspectives on the Catholic Charismatic Renewal

In academic literature, there are, aside from theological discussions about the charisms and Catholic Charismatic theology[3], three main perspectives on the Catholic Charismatic Renewal: empirical studies that explore certain aspects

---

2   https://www.erneuerung.de.
3   Although those debates are academic and important to understand the Charismatic Renewal Movement, they depict more internal debates and negotiations about the validity of Catholic Charismatic theology as well as their belonging to the Church. These debates are not included into the overview on academic literature about the CCR; they are, however, an important element of the negotiation of the place of the CCR in the Catholic Church.

of the CCR in specific contexts, scholarly research on 'EPC Christianity'[4], and the German theological discourse.

Empirical studies, mainly anthropological or sociological case studies, usually focus on the CCR in one specific (often national) context or explore one specific aspect of Charismatic Catholicism. Oftentimes, these studies are set in contexts where Charismatic practices are a strong factor in local Catholicism (which is not the case in Germany). In this area, mainly psychological studies about conversion and religious experience of Charismatic Catholics have been conducted (e.g. Halama/Halamová 2005; Siekierski 2012; Zarzycka et al. 2015). They found that, on the one hand, religious experience plays an important role in religious actors' self-conception as Charismatic Catholics, and on the other hand, conversion is perceived as a turning point in their religious biography that strengthens their connection to the Catholic Church. Anthropological studies have focused more on local forms of Charismatic Catholicism and its relation to Catholic hierarchy and structure (e.g. in Italy: Pace 2006) or the relation between local and global forms of Charismatic Catholicism (e.g. Theije/Mariz 2008; Hoenes del Pinal 2017; Lado 2017; Pace 2020). One aspect that surfaces again and again in these studies is that Charismatic Catholics have a strong sense of belonging and a generally positive attitude toward the Catholic Church. Furthermore, they aspire to attain institutional recognition by Church authorities (Turco 2016).

The Catholic Charismatic Renewal is also a focal point in the context of Pentecostalism research or research on EPC Christianity. In these approaches, the Charismatic Movement in the Catholic Church is usually subsumed under Charismatic movements, although it is a special form of Charismatic Christianity. EPC research usually focuses on the transnational and transdenominational entanglements of EPC Christianity. The history and development of global EPC Christianity is narrated as "one of the great success stories of the current era of cultural globalization" (Robbins 2004). The perspective on Charismatic Christianity as one form of EPC Christianity, and on Catholic Charismatics as one type of Charismatic Christianity, is characterized by two premises: the narrative of growth and the concept of Pentecostalism as a global phenomenon.

---

4   Evangelical, Pentecostal and Charismatic Christianity. As distinctions between those forms of Christianity are difficult, EPC Christianity is used for the whole spectrum.

> Pentecostalism in all its multi-faceted variety, including the 'Pentecostal-like' independent Churches and the Catholic Charismatics, is one of the most significant forms of Christianity in the twentieth century. According to oftquoted but controversial estimates, there may have been over five hundred million adherents of these movements worldwide in 2000, found in almost every country in the world and spanning all Christian denominations. In less than a hundred years, Pentecostal, Charismatic and associated movements have become a major new force in world Christianity. (Anderson 2006: 106)

While Charismatic Catholicism is frequently mentioned as the largest Charismatic movement, especially active in Latin America and the Philippines (Johnson/Zurlo 2020), the focus usually lies on non-denominational EPC Churches.

While the core narrative in the discourse on global EPC Christianity is one of growth and globalization, the discourse on the Catholic Church in Germany is characterized by the narrative of the decline of Catholicism in times of decreasing membership and increasing secularization (Gabriel 1996: 11). The GCCR is discussed mainly in two contexts: first, as a new community and a sign of pluralization of Catholicism – these perspectives on the GCCR are mostly sociological – and second, as a connecting point between the Catholic Church and EPC Christianity – usually with more practical theological implications.

The earlier, mostly sociological studies on the field saw new communities as alternative forms of Catholicism that are partly independent from traditional parish structures and parish priests. They offer what is perceived as new and appealing forms of spirituality, theology, and religious practice (Hochschild 2005). Their sociological interest was to formulate a Sociology of Catholicism. These new communities therefore were seen as examples of non-traditional social forms of Catholicism in Germany; the GCCR, in this context, serves as a case to discuss whether it is a movement or not (Lehmann 2003).

More recently, the second debate has become more prominent: there have been several publications on Charismatic Catholicism as a Catholic form of Pentecostalism and the dogmatic and theological questions that arise in this context (e.g. Krämer/Vellguth 2019). The aim of these publications is twofold: on the one hand, they try to find solutions as to how to attract people to Catholicism and stop membership decline; on the other hand, they discuss the dogmatic and practical implications of Charismatic Catholicism and its place in the Catholic Church.

Overall, the academic discussion of Charismatic Catholicism is characterized by the tension between being Catholic while at the same time being Charismatic. The question of belonging is asked and answered on two different levels. First, on the individual level – do individual actors in the Catholic Charismatic Movement perceive themselves as members of the Catholic Church? Second, on the level of the local groups – do they identify more as Catholic or Charismatic, and what does this mean for the Catholic Church? The goal of these debates is to categorize the GCCR and solve the question of belonging. I, however, will not try to sort them into one box or the other but rather take a closer look at how they themselves maintain this two-fold positioning. The abovementioned social forms, between which members of the GCCR move frequently, serve as lenses through which their oscillation between these two positions can be observed.

3. Strategies of positioning and two logics of legitimization

While the position and belonging of the GCCR is debated in the literature, there seems to be no struggle for the actors themselves. They see themselves as belonging to both the Catholic Church and the Charismatic Movement. By belonging, I refer to the actors' understanding of being part of a group. Positioning, on the other hand, refers to social practices to explicate, reinforce, change, or claim affiliation to a social form and, therefore, make belonging socially visible. Positioning and belonging therefore are tightly connected. In order to defend their belonging to the Catholic Church and the Charismatic Movement, the GCCR and its members must develop positioning strategies, that is, a set of practices and narratives to legitimize their strategies, claims, and values. The recognition of belonging as well as the strategies of positioning need to be negotiated internally, among the members of the GCCR, as well as externally, with regard to other groups, namely the Charismatic Movement and the Catholic Church. In order to legitimize actions and practices, actors of the GCCR refer to elements from both interpretative frames, the Charismatic Movement and the Catholic Church. They apply two different logics: a Catholic logic on the one hand and a Charismatic logic on the other.

In the following, I will explore Catholic Charismatics' strategies of positioning themselves in the Catholic Church and the Charismatic Movement and the two different logics of legitimization which actors apply to legitimize and reinforce their positions and thereby negotiate belonging. Additionally, the social forms in which the examples take place speak to these logics of legitimization and serve as markers of belonging.

3.1 Strategies of positioning the GCCR in the Catholic Church

The GCCR firmly positions itself within the Catholic Church. To underline this claim of being Catholic, members and texts frequently reference elements of the Catholic symbol system and interpretive framework, such as Catholic theology, structure, and ecclesial hierarchy, but also doctrine, tradition, Catholic literature, liturgy, and the sacraments. Furthermore, the Catholic Church as an institution is referenced. Although the reference to the Catholic Church as an institution implies the notation of the Church as established by God on one hand, while being a societal institution on the other, these implications are not discussed in the data. It seems that the status, form, and nature of the Catholic Church are not seen as topics of debate in the GCCR. At a time when the status of the Church in society is repeatedly discussed and questioned, this lack of debate hints at a strong loyalty towards the institution in both aspects.

The GCCR's fundamental positioning in the Catholic Church is first of all expressed in the explicit statement to be part of the Church and the understanding that there is a mission that the GCCR – and the CCR in general – must fulfill: to renew the Catholic Church in the name of the Holy Spirit. The Church in its current state is seen as "dried up" and "not on fire." It is perceived as the GCCR's task to "bring the flame of the Holy Spirit back into the Church." Florian[5] explains how people who experienced the Holy Spirit change and bring that change back into the Church:

Florian: And then there are these charisms, of which we can read a lot in the Bible, and which we have experienced again and again in our movement, that they come from God, that a life with these charisms is possible [...].

I: hmhm. That would mean that the change would come from the roots, so to speak, right? So it is always people...

Florian: A change of the humans' inner nature. Like, people have a personal encounter with God, experience God's work in their own life, in their own inner being, in their everyday life, and with that they change themselves,

---

5   The names of all interview partners and field contacts have been changed for anonymity.

but they also change their environment, their family, and with that also the Church. Yes.[6]

The "renewal" that is aimed for in the GCCR, however, is expected to take place purely on a spiritual level. It explicitly does not result in any demands for changes at the structural or hierarchical level of the Catholic Church. Neither structure, hierarchy, nor Catholic doctrine is questioned in the GCCR's publications and articles at any point. On the contrary, one strategy to position the GCCR within the Catholic Church is to explicitly subordinate it to the Church and its structures. In one interview, Manfred, a leading member of the GCCR, described the strategy in the early days of the CCR in Germany:

> So in the early days of the Charismatic Renewal, Herbert Mühlen was very significantly involved, they tried to integrate it very well into the Catholic Church. Therefore, good statutes were quickly established, and a good theological policy paper was quickly written, which was then also recognized by the bishops, so much effort was made. I think in other movements, they just developed over time, and at some point, someone looked at what they had become and put it into papers. These papers were drawn up very, very quickly and quite uncharismatically. However, perhaps also out of fear that it is so new, and we do not want to be seen as a cult and we want to be Catholic, so that they made such papers very quickly. And then they said, OK, so let's have a diocesan structure.[7]

What Manfred points out here is a) that for the GCCR, it was and is very important to be acknowledged as being part of the Catholic Church and b) that the GCCR tried to achieve this goal by developing a "good" theological position (meaning a position that holds up to Catholic standards) and structure, as affirmed by the Catholic hierarchy (meaning the bishops and the pope), and integrating their structure and organization into the Catholic structure of dioceses. This integration can also be seen in the fact that the Catholic Charismatic Bible reading and prayer groups I attended during my fieldwork took place in local Catholic parishes with the agreement of local priests and parish leaders. Thus, they were firmly embedded in Catholic institutional contexts.

Another strategy to strengthen the GCCRs claim of being part of the Catholic Church, while at the same time practicing charisms, was to for-

---

6   Interview (I#7) with Florian, member of the GCCR leaderboard, March 08, 2016.
7   Interview (I#8) with Manfred, member of the GCCR leaderboard, March 09, 2016.

mulate a Catholic theology of charisms. In the Charismatic Movement or in Pentecostalism, the formulation of a theology of charisms in an academic sense did not play a major role for a long time (Chan 2020: 39). In the circles of the CCR there were efforts from the 1970s onwards to classify the experiences of the actors theologically and to have them recognized by the Church. Such attempts were made (and partly successfully so) by leading CCR members such as Kilian McDonnell, Edward O'Connor, and Kevin and Dorothy Ranaghan (Anderson 2014: 166). The formulation of a distinct Catholic Charismatic theology began as early as the 1960s and early 1970s in the USA (Ciciliot 2019), but from the mid-1970s, it was advanced locally, especially in Germany (Hocken 1999, 406). With the establishment of the Theological Committee of the GCCR, a body was set in place to accompany developments within the GCCR theologically. Peter Zimmerling notes that "given the Protestant counterpart [...] the *theological clarification* of the Charismatic spiritual experience in the Catholic sphere is significantly more advanced" (Zimmerling 2018: 25, original emphasis). In this context, Zimmerling identifies the professors of Catholic theology Heribert Mühlen, Norbert Baumert, and Otto Knoch, the theologians Lucida Schmieder and Michael Marsch, as well as "a number of pastors and retreat masters known in the Catholic field" (ibid.) as formative figures of the GCCR. In their publications, they firmly based Catholic Charismatic practice on Catholic tradition and theology. The writings were directed not only toward the members of the GCCR themselves but especially toward Catholic externals and critics. Parallel to and partly interwoven with this more academic-theological debate, leaders of the GCCR constantly reflect on and discuss their own theology and practice, their foundation in Catholic Theology and Tradition, and communicate those debates to GCCR members and groups at meetings, in books, faith courses, and seminars. The multiple platforms and ways of communication within the GCCR reflect, like the multitude of social forms, its fluidity. There is not one medium through which to stay theologically and religiously informed, but many; there is not one social form to practice faith and have religious experiences, but many. It is the individuals' responsibility to pick and choose the subjectively most adequate one. Though in this sense, the GCCR is an individualistic, post-modern phenomenon, the individual's choices are not arbitrary but rooted in their faith and shared interpretive frame.

Like structural integration and the theology of charisms, sacraments play an important role in the GCCR's positioning within the Catholic Church, especially Eucharist and Confession. Frequent emphasis on the importance of the sacraments implies and enhances the acknowledgment of the Catholic hierarchy, as sacraments can only be given by ordained priests. For example, the Eucharist can only be granted by ordained Catholic priests. While there are ordained priests among the members of the GCCR, most of the members of the GCCR attend the usual Catholic Mass to receive the Eucharist. Therefore, the Holy Mass is a Catholic social form in which members of the GCCR participate. Especially in the context of GCCR events, mass is either held by GCCR priests or by non-Charismatic priests or bishops, making this a distinctly Catholic social form in which the GCCR gathers.

3.2 Strategies of positioning the GCCR in the Charismatic Movement

The GCCR's positioning in the Charismatic Movement is as firm as in the Catholic Church, though it manifests very differently; while its positioning in the Catholic Church occurs in the dimensions of structure, hierarchy, theology, and tradition, its positioning in the Charismatic Movement takes place at the individual level of personal experience. Therefore, it is characterized by fluid, individual patterns of attribution and justification in specific situations. Members frequently refer to personal and subjective experiences and the work of the Holy Spirit. The social forms in which these experiences take place are also more fluid and individualized, such as weekend seminars, irregular worship services, or Charismatic prayer conferences or events.

The unifying element across denominational boundaries in the Charismatic Movement is the shared emphasis on the experience of the Holy Spirit, the "baptism in the Holy Spirit", and charisms as the most visible and obviously distinguishing Charismatic features.

Another aspect that connects the GCCR with the Charismatic Movement is its attitude towards the Bible. In the interviews and during field research, it became clear that most of the actors read the Bible for themselves, both in a weekly prayer group and at home on their own. In doing so, the Bible or selected biblical passages are repeatedly referenced as a guide and instruction for questions of everyday life and for shaping one's own life. In prayer group meetings, reading the Bible together takes a lot of space, with the focus on relating the Bible passages to one's own questions and individual needs:

> When we have concrete questions about life, we may look for corresponding answers in the Bible. It is an ingenious guide to life, as God intended

and willed it to humans. Thus, God can speak into our lives through his written word. (Hemberger 2012: 34)

The Bible, from the GCCR's point of view, is not to be understood primarily as a historical text, but as the "Word of God" and a guide for everyday life. Thus, there are many actors within the GCCR who distance themselves from a hermeneutical approach to the Bible, which is present in German Catholic theology and the Church, and instead push for a more personal and literal understanding of the Bible, which is characteristic of the Pentecostal and Evangelical context (Buchard 2014: 141).

Many members and also the GCCR as a group are committed to ecumenism, especially in the form of joint events and projects. Ecumenical cooperation is not without tension, for example regarding theology or the role of the Pope. Personal experience, however, is regarded as being at a different level than the debate between Catholic and non-Catholic Charismatic Christians. The underlying religious experience is identified as the same in all Charismatic groups:

> The Holy Spirit works in all Christian Churches and ecclesial communities, and often in the same way, despite their different and sometimes contradictory theologies. (ThO#5, p. 30)

Against the background of a similar experience, the GCCR sees itself simultaneously as part of the interdenominational Charismatic Movement and as different from the others, as something "special." Florian points out:

> So, what I find quite exciting is that the Charismatic Movement exists in all denominations, all over the world, and we are the only movement that exists in all denominations. Sometimes that makes us special, but sometimes it is [...] that it becomes normal, so you can be interdenominational and always meet someone who thinks similarly. And then there are still differences. And you notice them again and again.[8]

This ambivalent attitude between affirmation and demarcation fundamentally characterizes the positioning of the Catholic Charismatic Renewal in the Charismatic Movement. It allows members of the GCCR to draw a line towards

---

8   Interview (I#7) with Florian, member of the GCCR leaderboard, March 08, 2016.

Charismatic and Pentecostal theology and doctrine, while still recognizing their experience as being the same. At gathered events, Catholic Charismatics do not regularly meet as a subgroup, but just take part, pray, listen, worship, etc. In reports about such events in the CE-Info, the quarterly journal, the denominational affiliations of organizers, speakers, and participants are usually mentioned. No judgement is attached; it is more of a contextualization, which again leaves the interpretation to the individual actors.

Subtle commonalities between the GCCR and the Charismatic Movement can be found with regard to positions on everyday religious life and the surrounding society, where the statements of members of the GCCR show strong links to EPC patterns of interpretation. In the GCCR's publications, topics such as gender roles and family values, as well as immigration, Christian values, and the "right" way to deal with Islam, are explicitly addressed in only a few programmatic texts (Grünenthal 2021). However, in more informal discussions, they are a recurring theme and are addressed and discussed, for example, at prayer meetings in connection with biblical passages. However, the leadership of the GCCR is reluctant to make public statements on socially controversial issues.

The GCCR positions itself in the Charismatic Movement mainly through religious practices and attitudes in daily life, such as worship, the charisms, the significance of prayer as a form of communication with God, a vibrant Bible study practice, an emphasis on personal relationships with God, and the importance of God in everyday life.

3.3 The double logic of legitimization: Catholic and Charismatic

The strategies of legitimization that have been discussed above are, however, not effective in themselves, but have to be enacted, applied, and maintained by concrete members in concrete situations. In encounters with other Catholics, as well as other Charismatic and Pentecostal Christians, members of the GCCR need to explain themselves and demarcate and justify their position on a regular basis. In these statements, they draw on the strategies of legitimization that are established within the GCCR and apply them to the situation at hand. They thereby switch between two different modes of legitimization, the Catholic and the Charismatic modes of legitimization.

I argue that in the positioning of the GCCR, but also in the everyday religious life of its members, there are two basic logics at work at the same time: on the one hand, the Catholic logic, which is based on the institution and hierarchy of the Catholic Church, and on the other hand, the Charismatic logic, which is based on the experience of the Holy Spirit. Depending on situation and context, actors within the GCCR use either one or the other logic to legitimize their positions, actions, and principles and substantiate them within the Catholic Charismatic framework.

As shown above, the Catholic logic is characterized by references that are assumed to be valid for actors in the Catholic Church. These include not only references to theology, structure, and ecclesial hierarchy, but also doctrine (represented, for example, in publications of the bishops or the papal Congregation for the Doctrine of the Faith), tradition (e.g., saints or mariology), historical situations (such as the Second Vatican Council), Catholic literature (e.g., the Book of Hours or other pious literature), liturgy and sacraments, and the Catholic Church as an institution with all its implications: the organizational aspects as well as the understanding of the Church as a holy, perennial, and eschatological body.

The Charismatic logic, on the other hand, is characterized by references that relate to and are validated through the experience of the Holy Spirit. Therefore, it is characterized by fluid, individual patterns of attribution and justification. The validity of the references and their position in the GCCR's shared frame of reference are actively negotiated, with the basic standard of evaluation being the individual experience of the actors.

Within the GCCR, both logics are available at the same time within the same shared interpretive framework. They can be used flexibly, depending on the context and situation. For example, a decision by the bishop of Passau to raise the age of Confirmation to sixteen years can be argued to be legitimate because he is the leader of the diocese who made the decision, or because it is presumed that Confirmation at an older age means that the candidates for confirmation are more likely to be ready for a personal relationship with Jesus. However, the application of the logic is not arbitrary: which references can be made in which situation by whom is subject to constant negotiation processes within the GCCR. These negotiation processes take place all the time when actors of the GCCR meet as such. Their shared framework is negotiated in informal conversations as well as in religious seminars, theological guidelines, articles in the quarterly journal and reading recommendations, the implementation of expected behavior as well as forms of organization and meetings. Of course, there are cases where it is clear which mode to apply, but more interesting are cases where it is not clear, where ascriptions are contradictory or in conflict. In two examples, I will analyze how actors apply one or both modes of legitimization in the discussion of topics in the example of the negotiation of religious authority.

3.4 Sacraments and charisms

When asked about what was special about being Catholic in a Charismatic context, one participant at a regional prayer meeting answered:

> In contrast to the independent Churches, where you also sing and also experience the Holy Spirit, Catholicism is more serious, and more grounded, deeply rooted in tradition and the sacraments. Especially in the sacraments. It's not just worship, but it is also confession and eucharist. (FP#4)

The importance of the sacraments, especially the Eucharist and Confession, also becomes apparent when looking at reports about events at Holy Mass and who celebrated it. The emphasis on sacraments is one of the most prominent distinguishing traits of Catholic Charismatics in the EPC Christianity, as are the charisms in the Catholic Church.

Regarding sacraments, the GCCR is interested in proving that the Charismatic understanding of the works of the Holy Spirit does not contradict the Catholic understanding of the sacraments. In the Catholic Charismatic understanding, the charisms are considered to be worked by the Holy Spirit, but unlike the sacraments, no universality or generality is assumed. While the charisms in the GCCR's view are dependent on the respective person and concrete situation, i.e. "subjective", the sacraments are "objective" in the sense that they work independently of the person and situation. Accordingly, in the Catholic Charismatic view, the sacraments are "superior" to the charisms. At the same time, "one reckons that the sacraments themselves can also become places of spontaneous and spectacular spiritual experience" (Zimmerling 2018: 133–134). The coexistence and parallel use of the two logics mentioned above become evident in the GCCR's discussion about sacraments and charisms.

In the publications of the Theological Committee of the GCCR, the practice of charisms is clearly restricted and subordinated to Catholic doctrine and structure. As charisms are understood as "gifts of the Holy Spirit" to individuals, Charismatic practices elude external control: neither "prophetic impressions" nor the "baptism in the Holy Spirit" nor the personal experience of God can be objectively verified. When talking about the charisms, the GCCR consistently applies the Catholic logic and subordinates personal experience under the rules and hierarchy of the Catholic Church. For example, in the area of "prophecy", where actors claim to receive impressions or images sent by the Holy Spirit, the GCCR emphasizes the need for examination and refers, among other things, to the teaching of the Church as an important standard:

> Received impressions are always subject to examination: Do they agree with the Word of God, with the commandment of love, with the teaching of the Church, and with the criteria of the discernment of spirits? (CE-Info#330)

Elsewhere it is clearly stated that:

> If something violates the commandments of God, the standards of Holy Scripture, or the doctrine of faith and morals of the Church, then it is not of God. (ThO#2, p. 14)

The teachings of the Church are thus mentioned – along with the Bible – as the decisive standard against which "prophecies" would have to be measured in order to test their authenticity and validity. If statements are marked as prophetic that are not compatible with the teaching of the Church, then from the GCCR's point of view this is an indication that the corresponding impression does not come from God. The "spontaneous working of the Spirit", which is emphasized again and again in the GCCR, is thereby subordinated to the teaching of the Church. Here, the Charismatic logic of legitimization is subordinated to the Catholic logic: if the Catholic logic is not applicable, it is not legitimate.

The case is a little bit different when it comes to "baptism in the Holy Spirit". According to Catholic doctrine, the sacraments of Baptism and Confirmation confer to the recipient a "stamp" of belonging to Christ and his Church when they are administered. In the Catholic understanding, this imprint is unrepeatable and cannot be changed, which is why these two sacraments can only be received once. According to Catholic dogmatic understanding, renewed baptism – and therefore, "baptism in the Holy Spirit" – is impossible. Narratives of baptism in the Holy Spirit are, however, one fundamental pillar of Pentecostal and Charismatic spirituality. There is an entire genre of literature on testimonies and the experience of conversion. Catholic Charismatic theologians dealt with this conceptual problem already in the early days of the GCCR. As a result of these disputes, the understanding of the "baptism in the Holy Spirit" as a "reactivation" or "actualization" of the sacraments of baptism and confirmation has become established in the GCCR:

> Theologically, the main effect of the educated leaders was to help integrate the CCR into existing ecclesial structures and to argue that baptism in the Spirit was a "release" of the Spirit or, at any rate, functioned in a way that was compatible with the sacramental theology of Christian initiation. The argument was that the Holy Spirit is first given at infant baptism but subsequently released at the time of Spirit baptism. (Kay et al. 2011: 330)

This integration of the Charismatic experience into the Catholic doctrine of the sacraments, which was pushed by early leaders and theologians, was an essential prerequisite for the recognition of the GCCR in the Catholic Church by the bishops and the Pope. In today's GCCR the matter of baptism in the Holy Spirit does not play a role, though nearly everybody has their own narrative of personal conversion, albeit slightly different: While the Pentecostal narrative typically describes life before the experience of the Holy Spirit as sinful, in German Catholic Charismatic narratives life before conversion is described in terms of membership in the Catholic Church, but still missing 'something'; that missing 'something', i.e. the personal experience of the Holy Spirit and the personal relationship with God, is filled through conversion. Here, the Charismatic logic is applied while the subject of legitimization is moved out of reach of the Catholic logic.

Similar mechanisms are at work in cases where members of the GCCR implement Charismatic alternatives to priestly or sacramental practices, for example the "prayer for deliverance" as an alternative to exorcism or "pastoral conversation with lay people" as a Charismatic alternative to confession. In all three examples, laypersons assume tasks and roles that are functionally similar to those reserved for priests in the Catholic Church without questioning priestly actions or their importance. Formally and theologically, the Charismatic, spirit-given alternatives are strongly demarcated from priestly practices. However, in practice, there is a great overlap in terms of content and function. Although it seems natural that the different practices take place in different social forms, this is not always the case. Prayers for deliverance take place in the context of Charismatic faith courses as well as in Holy Mass organized by GCCR members; confession is taken in the context of large prayer events, even interdenominational events. Again, the social forms are fluid and reflect the fluidity of the logics of legitimization.

In the first example, the case of exorcism and the "prayer for deliverance", the Theological Committee of the GCCR, formed of elected priests and theologians with the role of supervising and supporting theological developments in the GCCR, published a *Theologische Orientierung* ('Theological Orientation') with the title *Gebet um Befreiung. Ein Beitrag zum innerkirchlichen Gespräch* ('Prayer for Deliverance. A contribution to the debate within the Church'). The authors distinguish clearly between the responsibility and authority of the layperson and those of the priests:

> For laypeople [who enact the prayer of deliverance], the following applies: According to the law of the Catholic Church, insight into the actions of evil or evil powers does not automatically lead to a vocation to the exorcist ministry. This is reserved for some priests who are expressly called to it by their respective bishop. Exorcism is a special case of the Church's liberating actions. (ThO#2, p. 34)

From the perspective of the GCCR, laypeople may have insight into the "action of evil powers", but the exorcistic ministry is explicitly reserved for specific priests who are called to it by their bishop. Thus, the exorcistic ministry is integrated into the ecclesiastical hierarchy and marked as inaccessible to laypeople. The "prayer for deliverance", on the other hand, is distinguished from exorcism and thus available for non-priests. The lines drawn indicate that, in contrast to exorcism, Satan is not directly addressed, but conspicuous annoyances are met without directly addressing invisible powers. In the Theological Orientation "Prayer for Deliverance" (ThO#2), the Theological Committee sets out to show in detail how to deal with "demonic activity" and the practice of "prayer for deliverance", and discusses not only biblical foundations, systematic-dogmatic considerations, Church tradition, and magisterium, but also describes various forms and causes of "demonic activity", possibilities of "anamnesis and diagnosis", and "healing methods". In doing so, the text constantly refers, on the one hand, to Catholic tradition and doctrine, and, on the other, to the spiritual effects of "prayer for deliverance", thus separating the formal framework from the practical application in concrete situations.

A rather pragmatic approach to questions of spiritual competence becomes clear in the following interview excerpt:

Manfred: I can also consciously say in prayer, 'Power of evil, depart from me,' if I feel somehow attacked, why not. [...] And then there's always this discussion, may non-priests command demons directly.

I: hmhm

Manfred: Well. I also find it to be a bit of an idle academic discussion. I mean, the form can be quite different. If someone does not want to say: 'Spirit of lies, leave me!', then he should pray the Lord's Prayer and 'Deliver me from evil'. I think you shouldn't be so anxious.[9]

Without fundamentally questioning the meaning of an exorcism or the separation between "exorcism" and "prayer for deliverance", Manfred bases his evaluation on the question of the concrete effectiveness of spiritual action. He attributes such effectiveness both to a direct address, for example, of the "spirit of lies" within a prayer, and to the formula "Deliver us from evil" in the Lord's Prayer, which anybody can pray at any time. In the further course of the interview, Manfred emphasizes that he is not talking about explicit "demonic possessions", which, according to Catholic doctrine, require an exorcism, but rather about "nuisances", which, in his view, can arise in everyday life and which he understands as an expression of the "spiritual struggle" between God and the devil.

A similar evaluation, based on the effect of spiritual action, is also found in relation to spiritual and pastoral support and, in particular, "pastoral conversation with lay people" as an alternative to confession. The *'Theological Orientation' 'Receiving Forgiveness. Repentance and forgiveness of sins in pastoral conversations with lay people'* describes the following:

Spiritual accompaniments are being increasingly valued and sought. Christians look for believers as companions with whom they can talk about their lives. [...] Trust, grown from common spiritual experiences, opens a space for fearless personal encounters. Weakness, guilt and sin are given a name. One believer confesses his sins to another. There are people with a pronounced pastoral charism. One goes to them. It is all like confession. What happens here in terms of spiritual consummation must be recognized and named in its true value. [...] What is 'missing' in the sense of the sacrament of penance is an authorized minister of the sacrament. The 'absence'

---

9 Interview (I#8) with Manfred, member of the GCCR leaderboard, March 09, 2016.

can have several reasons. Sometimes a priest is simply unavailable. Or the priest may well have the official authority to administer the sacrament, but not the conversational and contact skills. A space of trust as a prerequisite for the free opening of oneself does not exist. (ThO#3, p. 3, emphasis H. G.)

As a prerequisite for the sacrament of penance, that is, confession, a personal prerequisite is addressed here in addition to the "official authority to administer the sacraments" with the "ability to talk and make contact", which creates a "space of trust". For cases in which this personal requirement is not fulfilled by the priest, the GCCR points out the alternative of conducting conversations about guilt and atonement with laypeople who fulfill these personal requirements. Although they are not ordained and therefore have no "official authority", they are endowed "with a pronounced pastoral charism". Even if it is not a confession in the sacramental sense, there is a "spiritual consummation" that must be "recognized and named in a true value". The importance of the priest and the sacramental confession is not disputed, but a "Charismatic alternative" of equal value is pointed out. The legitimation of the people in question takes place firstly via an authorization by God or the Holy Spirit, secondly via the personal prerequisite, and thirdly via the effect, i.e. the "success" of the spiritual act. These aspects are closely connected to the question of authority, which in turn is connected to the question of the organization of the social, and therefore with social forms.

3.5 Legitimizing and questioning religious authority

Authority, as understood here, is not a quality that people 'have', nor can authority be taken away from them. Rather, authority takes place where actors take into account the positions of others and consider them in their own decisions, actions, attitudes or opinions (Sofsky/Paris 1991). Authority, therefore, is ascribed by actors to authority figures, acknowledged, and can be withdrawn. However, the attribution of authority in social contexts is a matter not merely between two actors – the one that ascribes authority and the one authority is ascribed to – but is negotiated within social groups with recourse to a common frame of reference. Thus, both recognition and denial of authority are closely linked to the negotiation of group identity and, moreover, to the relation of the group to its environment (ibid.; cf. Grünenthal 2021). Therefore, religious authority is also ascribed or denied in connection with the social form in which a specific practice takes place.

In the case of the GCCR, the ascription and recognition of religious authority are tightly connected to processes of legitimization. As the GCCR needs to argue for its belonging to the Catholic Church as well as to the Charismatic Movement, the recognition of authority that is also recognized by other actors in the respective fields indicates the GCCR's belonging to the field. By acknowledging the authority of, for example, the Pope, Bishops or Catholic priests, members of the GCCR indicate that they acknowledge the shared Catholic frame of reference and thus belong to the Catholic Church. By not opposing recognized authorities, they indicate that they do not oppose the Catholic frame of reference. In the Charismatic setting however, that same acknowledgment of the Pope's and the Bishops' authority sets them apart from non-Catholic Charismatics. For example, at the interdenominational Charismatic Congress 'pfingsten21', which took place in 2016 in Würzburg and was organized by Catholic, Protestant, and non-denominational Charismatic Christians, there were specifically Catholic activities, such as a Holy Mass on Sunday morning.

In the media discourse of the GCCR, there are quite often references to especially Catholic authority figures, such as bishops or cardinals, or the popes, that merely mention them without further elaborating or substantiating their authority. This indicates that their authority is not up for debate, but rather set. References to Charismatic leaders are more often accompanied by an explanation or elaboration; for example, their expertise on the topic at hand, their deep connection with the Holy Spirit, their religious affiliation, or their reputation in the Charismatic field.

At first glance, it seems clear that Catholic clergy is legitimized in the Catholic mode and that Charismatic actors are legitimized in the Charismatic mode. At a second glance, however, it is not quite that simple. In the negotiation of religious authority, that is, whether and to what extent views, positions, and opinions are considered for one's own decisions, one or two modes of legitimization are applied depending on the situation at hand. In some cases, the person's authority is legitimized in one mode but delegitimized in the other. In some cases, both modes of legitimization are applied to support a person's authority. I will illustrate this using three examples.

The first example is how a member of the GCCR talks about a German Baptist leader. Asked whom he considers an authority, Florian answers, after a moment's thought:

> [T]he former leader of the Spiritual Renewal in the Baptist Church, Dr. Heiner Rust, he is someone, a very sought-after speaker, really competent theologian, and an extremely gifted, prophetic man. So his main focus is really the prophetic gift, so the charisma of prophecy, and how to deal with it, and so on. And he also is a totally humble person. So, he impressed me very much recently. We were in a group, before an event which was to start soon, and we simply prayed before, as a preparatory prayer, prayed the Lord's Prayer. I asked, is there anything else? Does anyone want to say anything here? And then he answered tersely, "yes, well, I have the impression that God wants to say something to you, and to you..." That was so very clearly prophetic as I have experienced it very rarely in someone. [...] He really spoke into their lives. And into mine, too. And deep truth that he could not know. But he spoke things with a determination and courage, though he could not know if they were right or wrong. Just out of God's impulse Yes.[10]

In narrating this episode, Florian first characterizes Rust with reference to his affiliation and position, outreach, and theological expertise, but also as a "humble man", thus characterizing him as a man of Christian values. The actual basis for the ascription of authority, however, are not these traits, but the subjective acknowledgment of Rust's Charismatic, i.e. spiritual, actions when he utters prophetic words in an unexpected situation that were experienced as being 'real,' that is, as indeed coming from God. In this case, a Charismatic leader doing charisms is legitimized in the Charismatic mode.

That it is not always so simple will be shown in the second example, where a Catholic local priest's authority, although not questioned in principle, is implicitly questioned by the application of the Charismatic mode of legitimization. Rüdiger, a GCCR group leader and part-time deacon, describes his experiences in trying to establish specific Charismatic social forms in his local parish:

> I thought at some point, just a few years ago, now it's time, now I would like to offer a new possibility and have a Charismatic worship service, not in the Church, but next door in the parish hall... No, our pastor didn't want that. He somehow got cold feet, like that something could happen that slipped away from him, where he no longer had any control over it... and, no, he did not allow it. [...] He also did not allow for a course of faith. Our

---

10   Interview (I#7) with Florian, member of the GCCR leaderboard, March 08, 2016.

pastor saw that as competition to his faith course, which he didn't even hold personally, but invited someone from the vicariate general. Hmmm, no, that did not go very well.[11]

The pastor's structural authority in prohibiting – or permitting – the worship service as well as the faith course is not at all questioned in this account: No Charismatic worship service took place, and the faith course was chosen to the pastor's preferences. The Catholic mode of legitimization is applied. At the same time, however, the Charismatic mode of legitimization was applied, in which his authority was highly questioned: Rüdiger attributes the refusal of Charismatic social forms to a fear of losing control, which from a Charismatic perspective can be interpreted as the pastor not trusting the work of the Holy Spirit. His formulation that the pastor "got cold feet" stands in a strong contrast to the "determination and courage" which was ascribed to the Baptist leader in the first example. Furthermore, by pointing out that the pastor had not even held the faith course he chose himself but had invited someone from the vicariate general to do so, Rüdiger suggests that the pastor could not or did not want to give testimony of his own faith but retreated to hierarchies and formalities.

The third example shows how authority is negotiated and legitimized within the GCCR: The ecclesiastic office of leadership, which is reserved for the clergy, is contrasted by the charism of leadership, an equally "spiritually based" leadership competence, which is not bound to ordination or clerical status. Norbert Baumert, priest and former chairman of the GCCR, addresses this in an interview on the occasion of the CCR's 50th anniversary:

> I always resisted the tendency that – typically Catholic – the priests would have the say. Leadership should be given to those who have the charism of leadership, including some priests. And I noticed that women in particular often received this charism. So I saw my task rather in discovering and supporting such vocations. (CEInfo#246)

Not only is the charism of leadership attested to laypeople, it is also separated from priesthood. This means that from the GCCR's perspective, there can be priests who are ordained but do not have the charism of leadership. Baumert

---

11 Interview (I#2) with Elisa and Rüdiger, diocesan spokespersons for the GCCR, March 21, 2014.

explains that he had often experienced this "charism of leadership" especially in women, who are systematically excluded from priesthood in the Catholic Church. He continues that he himself withdraws to the status of a promoter of these charismatically gifted women. With respect to leadership roles and decision making, no difference is made between ordained priests and laypeople.

It is, however, considered very useful to have ordained priests within the movement. Thomas, who is a priest himself, explains:

> It does not matter so much that I am a priest. It's practical, because we can celebrate the Eucharist together when we come together, which of course is not possible without a priest, but… yes. Also, the first […] sacrament is baptism, that's the most fundamental of all. Without baptism there is nothing. We also need priests, and I would also still ask people to pray for priestly vocations, but above all we need people who let themselves be addressed by God, let themselves be addressed by Christ, and who are ready to follow him.[12]

Thomas defines his role as priest in terms of its usefulness for the community – namely, that it is "practical" because it allows celebrating the Eucharist together – and otherwise emphasizes the equality between all members of the GCCR. When he emphasizes that the first and most fundamental sacrament is baptism, he implies that after being baptized, every human being is called by God, one of the possible vocations being that of a priest. Thomas thus presents his vocation – and his status as priest – as equal to other vocations and relativizes the special status of priests in the Catholic Church, which is expressed, for example, in their authority for spiritual (sacramental) action and access to resources and ministries.

Another practical aspect of having priests in the group was brought up in a conversation over lunch during a diocesan election meeting. Two members of the GCCR, laypeople, talked about a Charismatic priest they knew who had lived in the area but had moved away. They said it was a shame because they could really do with a priest like him. When I asked why, they explained that priests are beneficial because they represent GCCR ideas in the priests' councils and the higher bodies to which the laity has no access (FP#4). Here it becomes clear that the hierarchical position of priests, also of priests in the GCCR, by no means goes unnoticed, but that it is considered not to be important with

---

12   Interview (I#5) with Thomas, member of the GCCR leaderboard, October 15, 2015.

regard to GCCR religious life, other than representing the GCCR in the Church structure and administering the sacraments.

On the other hand, personality very much adds to the ascription of authority, as the following interview segment illustrates:

Julia: this course, it's so beautiful. Have you ever heard of Hans Buob?

I: I have a CD, yes, where he talks about the Gospel of Mark, I think. I think he has a pleasant way of speaking, right, so very, vividly.

Julia: Yes, exactly. Very simple. And when he celebrates Mass... Well. That's... There, really, heaven and earth connect. Heaven and earth are one. He also conveys that well. He also has humor. He is matter-of-factly. He always says it doesn't depend on feelings. It doesn't depend on feelings. God is real, you can believe that, he is there, it doesn't depend on feelings. [...] Because the feelings pass away. And he's totally right about that.[13]

What is remarkable about this interview is that Julia hardly responds to the suggested legitimization of his authority – namely that he speaks well and can convey things vividly. Instead, she highlights another aspect: the experience she associates with his services. Buob's authority is also based on his qualities and abilities ("can communicate well", "has a sense of humor", "matter-of-factly"), but her focus is on the content he conveys and his actions, for example, the way he celebrates Mass and how this affects her.

To tie these three examples of the construction of religious authority back to the question of social forms, some observations need to be made. First, Charismatic leaders are usually referred to in a Charismatic context. Their authority is acknowledged and negotiated in the Charismatic mode of legitimization. The social forms in which charismatic leaders' authority is enacted are workshops, events, lectures, and social forms that are characteristic of the Charismatic Movement. Second, the Catholic clergy's authority is not negotiated or questioned when it comes to the sacraments or their office in the Church. The Catholic mode of legitimization is applied whenever it comes to sacraments and Church hierarchy. Third, the Catholic clergy's authority is subject to negotiation in questions of experience. When GCCR members discuss a priest's or bishop's impact on their personal faith and experience,

---

13   Interview (I#6) with Julia, member of a GCCR prayer circle, February 02, 2016.

they discuss their authority in the Charismatic mode of legitimization, but without questioning their authority in the Catholic mode of legitimization.

4. Conclusion

How do members of the GCCR position themselves and the GCCR in the Catholic Church as well as in the Charismatic Movement? How do they negotiate their belonging in concrete situations and topics? And what does that mean for the social forms the GCCR takes?

As I have shown, members of the GCCR negotiate their position in both contexts, the Catholic Church and the Charismatic Movement, by applying both a 'Catholic' logic – a logic that is oriented to the Catholic Church, its hierarchies, structures, theology, and practices – and a 'Charismatic' logic – a logic that is oriented towards personal experiences. These two logics, although independent of each other in principle, are often combined or, in some cases, played off against each other. While in official texts the Catholic logic is often stressed, in private religious practice there are more pragmatic solutions. The basis for this flexible construct of legitimization is the wide range of social forms in which Charismatic Christianity in Germany takes place: the simultaneity of Holy Mass and Worship Weekends, weekly Bible groups, EPC events, seminars, and community meetings. In these different events, members of the GCCR negotiate their positions and arguments and thus establish a shared frame of reference that consists of both Charismatic and Catholic elements, which can be referenced in the Catholic as well as in the Charismatic logic to legitimize actions and arguments. The religious experience, the experience of the Holy Spirit, is explicitly not tied to one social form or the other in GCCR practice but can occur in different situations and contexts. The wide variety of social forms found in the GCCR reflects the emphasis on subjective beliefs and the individual experience of the Holy Spirit within the GCCR.

Bibliography

Anderson, Allan H. (2014): An Introduction to Pentecostalism. Global Charismatic Christianity, Cambridge: Cambridge University Press.

Anderson, Allan H. (2006): "The Pentecostal and Charismatic movements." In: Hugh McLeod (ed.), The Cambridge History of Christianity. Volume 9: World Christianities, Cambridge: Cambridge University Press, pp. 89–106.

Baumert, Norbert (1998): "Anstößig oder Anstoß? Zur Charismatischen Erneuerung." In: Stimmen der Zeit 216, pp. 594–606.

Buchard, Emmanuelle (2014): "Autoritätsausübung: Figuren und Mechanismen." In: Jörg Stolz/Olivier Favre/Caroline Gachet et al. (eds.), Phänomen Freikirchen. Analysen eines wettbewerbsstarken Milieus, Zürich: Pano Verlag, pp. 139–165.

Chan, Simon (2020): "Introduction to the Special Theme: Pentecostalism and Spiritual Formation." In: Journal of Spiritual Formation and Soul Care 13, pp. 39–43.

Ciciliot, Valentina (2019): "The Origins of the Catholic Charismatic Renewal in the United States: Early Developments in Indiana and Michigan and the Reactions of the Ecclesiastical Authorities." In: Studies in World Christianity 25, pp. 250–273.

Gabriel, Karl (1996): Christentum zwischen Tradition und Postmoderne, Freiburg i. Br.: Herder Verlag.

Grünenthal, Hannah (2021): Verortungsprozesse und die Konstruktion religiöser Autorität. Eine Untersuchung am Beispiel der Charismatischen Erneuerung in der Katholischen Kirche in Deutschland, Bremen: Universität Bremen.

Halama, Peter/Halamová, Júlia (2005): "Process of Religious Conversion in the Catholic Charismatic Movement. A Qualitative Analysis." In: Archive for the Psychology of Religion 27/1, pp. 69–91.

Hemberger, Christof (2012): Lebendige Charismatische Gruppen. Handbuch zum Baustein 1 der CE-Leiterausbildung, Grünkraut: D&D Medien.

Hochschild, Michael (2005): "Zukunftslaboratorien. Soziologische Aspekte der Neuen Geistlichen Gemeinschaften." In: Christoph Hegge (ed.), Kirche bricht auf. Die Dynamik der Neuen Geistlichen Gemeinschaften, Münster: Aschendorff, pp. 11–34.

Hocken, Peter (1999): "Charismatic Movement." In: Erwin Fahlbusch/Geoffrey W. Bromiley (eds.), The encyclopedia of Christianity, Grand Rapids, MI.: Eerdmans, pp. 404–408.

Hoenes del Pinal, Eric (2017): "The Paradox of Charismatic Catholicism. Rupture and Continuity in a Q'eqchi'-Maya Parish." In: Kristin Norget/Valentina Napolitano/Maya Mayblin (eds.), The Anthropology of Catholicism, Oakland: University of California Press, pp. 170–183.

Johnson, Todd M./Zurlo, Gina A. (2020): World Christian Encyclopedia, Edinburgh: Edinburgh University Press.

Kay, William K./Slijkerman, Kees/Pfister, Raymond et al. (2011): "Pentecostal Theology and Catholic Europe." In: Anne E. Dyer/William K. Kay (eds.), European Pentecostalism, Leiden, Boston: Brill, pp. 313–331.

Krämer, Klaus/Vellguth, Klaus (eds.) (2019): Pentekostalismus. Pfingstkirchen als Herausforderung in der Ökumene, Freiburg, Basel, Wien: Herder.

Lado, Ludovic (2017): "Experiments of Inculturation in a Catholic Charismatic Movement in Cameroon." In: Kristin Norget/Valentina Napolitano/Maya Mayblin (eds.), The Anthropology of Catholicism, Oakland: University of California Press, pp. 227–242.

Lehmann, David (2003): "Was trennt die katholische Charismatische Erneuerung von den Pfingstkirchen? Dissidenz und Konformismus in religiösen Bewegungen." In: Concilium 39, pp. 361–378.

Pace, Enzo (2006): "Salvation Goods, the Gift Economy and Charismatic Concern." In: Social Compass 53, pp. 49–64.

Pace, Enzo (2020): "The Catholic Charismatic Movement in Global Pentecostalism." In: Religions 11, pp. 1–19.

Robbins, Joel (2004): "The Globalization of Pentecostal and Charismatic Christianity." In: Annual Review of Anthropology 33, pp. 117–143.

Siekierski, Konrad (2012): "Catholics in the Holy Spirit. The Charismatic Renewal in Poland." In: Religion, State and Society 40/1, pp. 145–161.

Sofsky, Wolfgang/Paris, Rainer (1991): Figurationen sozialer Macht. Autorität – Stellvertretung – Koalition, Opladen: Leske und Budrich.

Theije, Marjo de/Mariz, Cecília L. (2008): "Localizing and Globalizing Processes in Brazilian Catholicism. Comparing Inculturation in Liberationist and Charismatic Catholic Cultures." In: Latin American Research Review 43, pp. 33–54.

Turco, Daniela (2016): "Religious forms in secularized society: Three Catholic groups in comparison." In: Social Compass 63, pp. 513–528.

Zarzycka, Beata/Pietruszka, Rafał/Śliwka, Jacek (2015): "Religiosity as a source of comfort and struggle in members of religious movements. A comparative analysis of the Neocatechumenal Way and the Catholic Charismatic

Renewal." In: Journal for Perspectives of Economic Political and Social Integration 21/1-2, pp. 91–114.

Zimmerling, Peter (2018): Charismatische Bewegungen, Stuttgart, Göttingen: UTB GmbH; Vandenhoeck & Ruprecht.

Primary Sources

CEInfo#246. Fleddermann, Josef (2017): "50 Jahre Charismatische Erneuerung – Interview mit Prof. Dr. Norbert Baumert SJ." In: CE-Info 2017(2), pp. 6 + 11.

CEInfo#330. Hemberger, Christof (2018): "Charismen in der Gebetsgruppe." In: CE-Info 2018(1), pp. 11–13.

FP#4. Field Protocol of election of diocesan spokespeople, 16. 01. 2016.

I#2. Interview with Elisa and Rüdiger, diocesan spokespersons for the GCCR, March 21, 2014.

I#5. Interview with Thomas, member of the GCCR leaderboard, October 15, 2015.

I#6. Interview with Julia, member of a GCCR prayer circle, February 02, 2016.

I#7. Interview with Florian, member of the GCCR leaderboard, March 08, 2016.

I#8. Interview with Manfred, member of the GCCR leaderboard, March 09, 2016.

ThO#2. Theologischer Ausschuss der Charismatischen Erneuerung in der Katholischen Kirche (2011): Gebet um Befreiung. Ein Beitrag zum innerkirchlichen Gespräch. Theologische Orientierung.

ThO#3. Theologischer Ausschuss der Charismatischen Erneuerung in der Katholischen Kirche in Deutschland (2008): Vergebung empfangen. Umkehr und Sündenvergebung im seelsorgerlichen Gespräch mit Laien. Theologische Orientierung.

ThO#5. Theologischer Ausschuss der Charismatischen Erneuerung in der Katholischen Kirche in Deutschland (2005): Zu auffallenden körperlichen Phänomenen im Zusammenhang mit geistlichen Vorgängen. Theologische Orientierung.

Web References

Charismatische Erneuerung. "Charismatische Erneuerung in der Katholischen Kirche." Accessed December 1, 2018. https://www.erneuerung.de/.
Charismatische Erneuerung. "Wer wir sind." Accessed December 1, 2018. https://www.erneuerung.de/wer-wir-sind/.

"I am happy to be Catholic"
The Catholic Charismatic Renewal and the Dynamics of the Religious Field in Brazil

Astrid Reuter

Abstract *Since the 1970s and increasingly since the 1990s, Charismatic movements have experienced an unexpected boom in Brazilian Catholicism. This development can be interpreted as resulting on the one hand from the dynamics of the religious field in Brazil as a whole, and on the other from the dynamics of the Catholic sub-field. The paper aims to situate the rise of the Catholic Charismatic Renewal in Brazil in this dual context. I will argue that the rise of Pentecostalism since the 1950s and 1960s has set in motion a previously unknown dynamic of competition both in Brazil's overall religious field and in its various sub-fields. This competitive dynamic, it is claimed, coincides with converging religious beliefs and needs: beliefs in spiritual beings (be they good or evil) and aspirations for deeply personal spiritual experiences (of "baptism in the Spirit", possession, exorcism, deliverance). Competition and convergence are thus interconnected, which fosters a dynamic of 'mimicry' (isomorphism) in the religious field: mimicry in relation to both styles of piety and those religious social forms that facilitate personal spiritual experiences. Particular attention will be given to social forms within Charismatic Catholicism; it will be argued that these provide a flexible new type of institutional access to the traditional infrastructure of the church.*

Keywords *Brazil, Catholic Charismatic Renewal, community, event, mimicry, neo-Pentecostalism, organization, religious field, singing priests, spiritual warfare*

1. Introduction[1]

"Eu Sou Feliz por Ser Católico" ('I am happy to be Catholic') – this is the title of a book by the Brazilian priest Marcelo Rossi which was published in 2000 (Rossi 2000). Marcelo Rossi is one of the most prominent figures of the so-called Catholic Charismatic Renewal (CCR) in Brazil: He is considered not only a fascinating priest but also famous as a singer and songwriter and is omnipresent in both church and private media (Carranza 2011; Clarke 1999). Thus, to give an example, the renowned weekly journal *Veja* featured a long report on him entitled "Uma estrela no altar" ('A star at the altar'; Junqueira 1998).

The Renovação Carismática Católica (RCC) has since experienced an unforeseen boom, especially since the 1990s. As part of this boom, it has produced quite a number of such "singing priests", who – as "stars at the altar" and on the stage – have contributed significantly to the movement's success (Carranza 2011; Clarke 1999; Fernandes 2005; Souza 2005). All of them praise the happiness of being Catholic.[2] Now, happiness is not what we would readily identify as the core message of Catholicism. However, the slogan 'I am happy to be Catholic' sums up what distinguishes Charismatic Catholicism from other styles of Catholic piety: Charismatic Catholics enjoy their faith!

What is the status of Charismatic Catholicism within the religious field in Brazil in general and in the Catholic sub-field in particular? What is its role in the religious dynamics and what social forms are set up to live Charismatic Catholicism? In the following, I will explore these questions.

My conceptual approach is based on Pierre Bourdieu's field theory. While not reconstructing it in detail here (Reuter 2018), I will however clarify some of its central features. In fact, when Bourdieu (inspired by his reading of Max Weber) conceptualized the religious field (Bourdieu 1987 [1971]; 1991 [1971]), he did not have in mind the plurality of different religions in a given context – which is how his concept is mostly applied today. Rather, Bourdieu was concerned with the dynamics of competition and conflict within religions or denominations. His prototype of the religious field was the French Catholic field. Still, Bourdieu's approach can be also applied to contexts of religious diversity. In this

---

1   I thank David West and Paula König for their thorough editorial assistance.
2   To give another example besides Pe. Marcelo Rossi: João Carlos Almeida, better known as Padre Joãozinho, also sings about the happiness of being Catholic. His song "Sou feliz por ser Católico", which he composed in 2009, became the *leitmotif* of a successful CD (Pe. Joãozinho SCJ 2009).

contribution, I try to intertwine both perspectives: I will look at the dynamics of Brazil's very diverse religious field as a whole as well as (and specifically) at the dynamics of its Catholic sub-field.

In the first part, I will identify the main actors in the overall religious field in Brazil, namely Catholicism, Protestantism (or, rather, Pentecostalism), and Afro-Brazilian religions, providing somewhat more detail about the Protestant and the Afro-Brazilian sub-fields (1.). The second part focuses on the Catholic sub-field, and in particular on the role of the Charismatic Renewal in its internal dynamics (2.). In my final considerations (3.), I will again zoom out to look at the broader religious field of Brazil: The point here is to show how the rise of Pentecostalism since the 1950s has set in motion a previously unknown dynamic of competition in this field (cf. Chesnut 2003). But what is this competition about? I will argue that this competitive dynamic coincides with a cross-religious and cross-denominational converging of religious beliefs and needs: beliefs in spiritual beings of whatsoever character (good or evil) and intense aspirations for personal spiritual experiences ("baptism in the Spirit", possession, deliverance, exorcism). Taking up an expression from R. Andrew Chesnut (2003: 64), I will refer to this as an "option for the spirit[s]". I will argue further that this interconnectedness between competition and convergence of religious beliefs and needs fosters a dynamic of 'mimicry' between religions and denominations. Thus, I claim that there are isomorphic tendencies both in relation to styles of piety and in relation to social forms that enable much-longed-for personal spiritual experiences. Particular attention will be given to social forms within Charismatic Catholicism; I will argue that these provide a new, flexible type of institutional access to the Catholic Church (cf. Hero 2009).

2. The religious field in Brazil: Main actors

Brazil has always been considered a Catholic country *par excellence*. Although this is not completely incorrect, it doesn't show the whole picture. After all, while 92 per cent of Brazilians still self-identified as Catholic in 1970, that figure had dropped to 65 per cent by 2010, and to 54 per cent by 2017. Remarkably, during the same period, the proportion of Protestants rose substantially from 5 to 27 per cent, this growth obviously being mainly at the expense of the Catholic Church. Among the remaining 19 per cent who are neither Catholic nor Protestant, the largest and fastest-growing group comprises the non-religious (at 14 per cent). The remaining 5 percent are made up of Jehovah's Witnesses, Jews and Muslims, Hindus and Buddhists, indigenous and other religions (at 2.7 per cent), and, not least, Afro-Brazilian religions, including Spiritism (at 2.3 per cent) (Chesnut 2016: 77, 80; da Silva 2016: 490; Engler/Schmidt 2016: 5; Latinobarómetro 2017; Pew Research Center 2013: 2; 2014: 27; Schmidt 2016).

If we now look for the main players in this field, two are obvious immediately: Catholicism and Protestantism. The third is less evident: It is the Afro-Brazilian religions, including the many variants of Spiritism. In terms of statistics, Afro-Brazilian religions are marginal players. But statistics in this case are misleading since they hide the common practice of many Brazilians to identify as Catholic while practicing Afro-Brazilian religions alongside Catholicism. Afro-Brazilian religions thus play a far more important role than the data suggest.

To achieve a better understanding of the competitive dynamics in Brazil's religious field, we must first take a closer look at these main actors. Following Pierre Bourdieu's conceptualization, we can speak of a 'Catholic field', a 'Protestant field', and an 'Afro-Brazilian field' as 'sub-fields' within the broader religious field.

Protestantism was of minor importance in Brazil for centuries (Campos 2016; Dove 2016; Dreher 2016). It was only in the early 19th century that Protestantism succeeded in gaining a foothold in Brazil. At that time, Lutherans (predominantly Germans) settled in southern Brazil, where they founded rather 'closed' religious-ethnic communities. As they largely refrained from proselytizing, Brazilian Protestantism at that time basically kept its European character. Missionary ambitions were first developed by North American Protestants (Presbyterians, Methodists, Baptists, members of the Episcopal Church, and others), who started to proselytize in Brazil in the middle of the 19th century. Their success remained modest – and yet their endeavors represent a turning point in the history of Protestantism in Brazil. Since they successfully recruited converts among local people, the growth of Protestantism became ever more independent of immigration. The constant expansion of Protestantism since the early 20th century is thus due not to immigration but to conversion. However, so-called historical Protestantism (i.e. mainly Lutheranism and Calvinism) did not profit from this 'turn', but remained a minor segment within Brazil's Protestant sub-field. Instead, it was the Pentecostal churches that benefitted from the high conversion rates and were consequently able to establish themselves permanently in Brazil.

The Pentecostal movement emerged in the United States at the beginning of the 20th century (Anderson 2014: 40–70) and reached Brazil soon afterward

(Anderson 2014: 78–83; Chesnut 1997; 2003: 39–63; Rivera 2016). The first Pentecostal church in Brazil, Assembléia de Deus ("Assembly of God"), was founded by Swedish-American missionaries in Belém (in the northern state of Pará) in 1911 (de Alencar 2019 [1998]; Correa 2020 [1998]). The many, mostly small local Pentecostal churches that emerged at this junction did not achieve high conversion rates in the first half of the 20th century. In the second half, however, they experienced rapid growth. Crucially, this growth was mainly on account of Brazilian converts who themselves now founded new churches. As a consequence, the prevailing North American influence gradually diluted. Moreover, the spread of the movement was accompanied by its internal diversification, and this led to the emergence of a new variant, called "neo-Pentecostalism", in the 1970s. Unlike the mostly small, independent local churches of the first Pentecostal "wave", neo-Pentecostalism tends to organize itself in megachurches (Chesnut 2016; Freston 1998; 1999; 2016), which claim theological dominance and rule by means of strict church control and, not least, at great financial expense. The most important neo-Pentecostal church in Brazil is the Igreja Universal do Reino de Deus (IURD; 'Universal Church of the Kingdom of God'; UCKG), founded in 1977 in Rio de Janeiro by Edir Macedo. Managed like a business, the Universal Church conducts evangelization with marketing strategies. Thus, it has invested an enormous amount of money to gain public influence, especially through mass media: At great financial expense, it has established successful media groups of its own, including TV and radio stations, publishing houses, and so forth. Moreover, immense efforts have been taken to be visible in the public sphere, not least through prestigious church buildings – which are in sharp contrast to the predominantly very modest local Pentecostal churches throughout the country. The best example is the so-called Templo de Salomão in São Paulo ('Solomon's Temple'). Built according to what is thought to be known about the plans of the first Jewish temple in Jerusalem, this oversized church can seat 10.000 people.[3]

Neo-Pentecostalism sees evangelization in terms of what is called "spiritual warfare". And this concept has greatly influenced not only Pentecostalism itself or the Protestant sub-field but the dynamics of the religious field as a whole (Chesnut 2003). "Spiritual warfare" has a double meaning: On the

---

[3] The 2014 inauguration, which was broadcast nationwide on the private channel TV Globo, was attended by Brazil's entire political leadership, including then-President of the Partido dos Trabalhadores (Workers' Party), Dilma Rousseff; cf. the official version distributed on the church's own Youtube channel: Igreja Universal 2014.

one hand, it concerns inner conversion, i.e. the fighting against one's inner demons. On the other (and above all), it relates to proclaiming the exclusivity of (neo-)Pentecostalism with regard to other religions and other Christian denominations. The Universal Church thus stigmatizes certain practices of folk Catholicism as superstitious (such as the very popular cult of the Virgin Mary[4]). Most of all, however, spiritual warfare aims its sights at Afro-Brazilian religions, whose deities and spirits it labels as demons and which it fights aggressively (Macedo 2019 [1989]; da Silva 2007; 2016).

The term 'Afro-Brazilian', examining this sub-field now, denotes a number of heterogeneous religious groups that are institutionally autonomous and often compete with each other (da Silva/Brumana 2016; Engler 2016; Engler/Brito 2016; Engler/Isaia 2016; Prandi 2010). It is a spectrum which stretches from Candomblé groups (that claim to be firmly committed to the African religious heritage) and Umbanda groups (integrating new elements into the Afro-Brazilian religious matrix) to groups that hardly differ from Spiritism, which came to Brazil from France in the 1860s and very quickly found great success (Aubrée/Laplantine 1990).

Despite these differences, most Afro-Brazilian groups share basic features, first and foremost the cult of African deities and spirits that came to Brazil during the transatlantic slave trade from the 16th to the 19th century. In Brazil, these deities are included in a common 'pantheon' together with Catholic saints, indigenous spirits, and other spiritual beings of different origins. Another common feature of the many Afro-Brazilian religions is their focus on healing practices: Indeed, Candomblé and Umbanda groups, as well as Spiritist centers, serve as points of contact for people seeking help with regard to everyday health, family, or work problems.

Over the course of centuries, the Catholic side, despite its dogmatic condemnation, has developed a rather pragmatic 'tolerance of ambiguity' towards

---

4   Cf. as an example the incident "Chute na Santa" („Kicking the Saint'). It took place in a religious TV program broadcast nationwide by Rede Record (the TV station of UCKG) on October 12, 1995, which is a national holiday in honor of Brazil's patron saint Nossa Senhora Aparecida. A UCKG bishop, Sérgio von Helder, who had brought a statue of Nossa Senhora Aparecida along, led through the program; he walked around the statue and made remarks about how ugly it was, questioning how anyone could believe that such a figure could even have anything to do with God. He then insulted those beliefs as idolatry and kicked the statue repeatedly. The incident set off a large controversy about religious tolerance. Cf. the report on the incident on Jornal Nacional (1995).

the widespread habit of merging Catholic and Afro-Brazilian practices and beliefs. On the Protestant side, such pragmatic tolerance is found less with Pentecostal and neo-Pentecostal churches strongly rejecting Afro-Brazilian religions. Their special offer of salvation is, as previously stated, strictly exclusive, and in addition acts increasingly aggressively towards competing religions, especially those of African provenance (da Silva 2007; 2016; Oro 2005).

This concludes our brief look at the Protestant and Afro-Brazilian subfields and the emerging competitive dynamics in the overall religious field. In the next part, I focus on what is still the most important religious sub-field in Brazil, at least in terms of statistics, namely Catholicism.

3. The Catholic field in Brazil with a special focus on the Catholic Charismatic Renewal

Brazilian Catholicism is remarkably diverse. We can distinguish (at least) four currents: Folk Catholicism, Romanized Catholicism, Liberation Theology, and Charismatic Catholicism.

Folk Catholicism developed since the beginning of the colonial period in the 16th century. It is a particular Catholic culture rooted in the Iberian Catholicism of the early modern period and shaped by the counter-reformatory ideas of the Tridentine Council (1545–1563). Its central feature is the worship of the saints – first and foremost: the Virgin Mary – which is expressed in shrines, offerings, pilgrimages, belief in miracles, etc. This specific devotional culture was, in a sense, the first religious 'export' from Europe to Latin America. Once there, however, it developed a life of its own, merging with local religious (and non-religious) customs and profane festive culture (González 2016; Larkin 2016; Steil 2016).

Towards the end of the 19th and the beginning of the 20th century, the impact of European Ultramontanism also took hold of the non-European branches of the Catholic Church. Brazil was no exception: Here, too, a Roman Catholic culture based on the European model would be established. The main characteristics of this Romanized Catholicism (as Ultramontanism came to be called outside of Europe) are prioritizing the magisterium and the clergy (first and foremost the Pope) as well as focusing pastoral care on providing the so-called holy sacraments (de Roux 2014; Steil 2016). An entirely different pastoral concept was favored by the third current in Brazil's Catholic sub-field: Liberation Theology.

Influenced by Marxism and other anti-capitalist theories, Liberation Theology emerged in various Latin American countries in the early 1960s and gained wide influence in the 1970s. Among its core tenets is the conviction that there is a preferential divine "option for the poor" (Hartch 2014: 57–72, 73–82, 134–136), i.e. the idea that God loves the poor, the deprived, those who suffer, more than the rich and privileged and that he empowers the poor to fight in solidarity for their rights in order to overcome oppression, poverty, and hunger. Liberation theology thus radically challenged clerical Romanized Catholicism. Priests and lay people in this movement founded so-called local base communities, the idea being to come together to read and interpret the Bible in the light of the "option for the poor". Instead of focusing on providing the holy sacraments, these base communities aim at empowering the poor, both religiously and socially: religious practice is thus combined with social work (with the landless, the illiterate, street children, prostitutes, industrial workers, etc.). Liberation Theology was supported by the Latin American bishops (Consejo Episcopal Latinoamericano; CELAM) at their conferences in Medellín (1968) and Puebla (1979) before it was systematically (and effectively) suppressed by Rome, especially since the pontificate of John Paul II (since 1978).

Much more successful than Liberation Theology is the Catholic Charismatic Renewal. Launched in the US with the so-called "Duquesne Weekend" in 1967 (Ciciliot 2019: 252f.; 2020: 131f.), the Charismatic wave spilled over to Brazil soon afterward. In a pioneering study, Brazilian sociologist Brenda Carranza (2000) identifies 1969 as the founding year of Brazil's Renovação Carismática Católica (RCC). In 1969, a US Jesuit, Harold Rahm, who had been working in Brazil since 1964, initiated Brazil's first Catholic Charismatic prayer group in Campinas (São Paulo state) – a group which should become the nucleus of a highly successful movement. In 1971, alongside Harold Rahm, two other priests became involved in establishing the RCC in Brazil: Eduardo Dougherty, also a US Jesuit, and Jonas Abib, a Brazilian Salesian priest of Lebanese origin. Both contributed to the rapid growth of the movement in the following years by encouraging the creation of many such local prayer groups (Carranza 2000; Chesnut 2003; 2016; Cleary 2011: 96–151; Prandi 1997).

How did the surrounding Catholic sub-field react to the charismatic "awakenings"? Actually, the pioneers of the movement were invited to a first meeting with the Brazilian bishops in May 1973. The bishops declared that the Charismatic movements were "um novo modo de ser Igreja" (Carranza 2000: 37; 'a new way of being church'). On the one hand, with this phrasing the movement's claim to renew the church as a whole was taken up and, in a sense, legitimized; at the same time, however, the bishops thereby also verbalized their expectation for the Charismatic Movement to take its place within the institutional structure of the Church and to submit to the magisterium. And this is what happened in the following years.

The further organizational development of the movement took place rapidly; in the course of 1974, starting from local prayer groups and regional prayer meetings, transregional coordination groups were established. In the same year, the RCC held its first national congress in Itaicí (São Paulo state); a nationwide representation, the Conselho Nacional da Renovacão Carismática Católica, was created to support the movement's further development. Organizational units and "ministries" with specific tasks were established at different ecclesiastical and political levels (parish, diocese, federal states) – in short, the movement institutionalized and professionalized.

The fact that after initial hesitation, both the 'National Conference of Brazilian Bishops' (Conferência Nacional dos Bispos Brasileiros; CNBB) and the Vatican[5] eventually gave their "blessing" to the RCC might partly be due to the fact that they finally saw it as an opportunity to "save" Catholicism from its leftist politicization represented by Liberation Theology. But it was clearly also motivated by the rapid rise of an efficient competitor outside the Catholic sub-field: namely, Pentecostalism. Supporting the Charismatics thus seemed to be a good strategy to fight both competitors, inside and outside the Catholic sub-field. And it was effective – certainly relatively effective, for statistics are clear about one point: the RCC has not succeeded to any significant extent in winning back former Catholics (who converted to Pentecostal churches or opted for non-religion). Instead, its success so far remains limited to the shrinking Catholic sub-field, which is witnessing 'conversions' from Romanized or Folk Catholicism or from base communities to Charismatic Catholicism.[6]

In terms of geography, the RCC has spread all over Brazil since the 1970s, and particularly since the 1990s, with a focus in the southeast (namely São

---

5   The Vatican supported the Charismatic Renewal through the establishment, of a central service unit called International Catholic Charismatic Renewal Service (ICCRS) in 1978, which changed its name to Catholic Charismatic Renewal International Service (CHARIS) in 2019. For the development of the CCR from its beginnings in the US, its global spread and the changing attitude of the Vatican cf. Ciciliot 2020.

6   Chesnut (2016: 77) estimates that at least 50 percent of Brazilian Catholics belong to the Charismatic spectrum.

Paulo) and south. In the following, a few examples from the extremely broad spectrum of Catholic Charismatic communities in Brazil shall be presented (for the following: Cleary 2011: 96–131).

I start with a preliminary remark: After the first spillover of the Charismatic impulse from the US at the end of the 1960s, it was initially Charismatic communities operating internationally that gained a foothold; nevertheless, soon after Brazilian Charismatics themselves began to establish a variety of new communities of their own. Among them, we can distinguish between "life communities" and "covenant communities". The members of life communities are expected to share their entire lives with each other, which often includes giving up their private property for the benefit of the community to which they have bound themselves by certain vows. The members of covenant communities, in contrast, usually carry on with their lives outside the community where they gather exclusively for specific communal activities. Some communities combine both types.

One of the first international communities to take root in Brazil is the Comunidade Emanuel.[7] Founded in France in the early 1970s, it is also successful in Europe (cf. Dolbeau's chapter in this volume). Its Brazilian branch was founded by the Benedictine Father Cipriano Chagas in Rio de Janeiro in 1976. The Comunidade Emanuel combines life community with covenant community features. It counts diocesan priests as well as married people among its members, and likewise lay people who feel called to celibacy and to placing their lives at the service of the community. As the name of the community suggests ('Emanuel' means 'God is with us'), members see their specific vocation in joyfully proclaiming and praising God's presence in the world.

Canção Nova ('New Song'), one of the most successful Charismatic communities in the country, was founded by the above-mentioned Jonas Abib in Cachoeira Paulista (São Paulo state) in 1978 (Cleary 2011: 106–109, 120f.; de Oliveira 2009).[8] At the center of this covenant community's vocation is – as its name indicates – music, which Jonas Abib identified as a special instrument of evangelization and mission. Canção Nova thus promotes composers and singers and the production and dissemination of popular Christian music. Starting in its early days, the community established its own radio station, and today runs one of the largest Catholic media groups in the world, including radio and television stations that broadcast around the clock, a publishing house

---

7 Cf. https://emanuelnobrasil.com.br/.
8 Cf. https://www.cancaonova.com/.

and, unsurprisingly, a professionalized internet presence, naturally including social media. Cancão Nova also sells a wide range of products, from books, CDs, and DVDs to clothing, devotional objects, and merchandising items. At its headquarters in Cachoeira Paulista, the construction of one of the largest religious meeting places (called Centro de Evangelização) in Latin America (seating 30.000 people plus 44.000 standing) was completed in 2004. Canção Nova is successful not only in Brazil, but worldwide; it also has branches in Europe, especially in Portugal (Gabriel 2009).

One of the first communities active in northern Brazil is Shalom, which was founded in 1982 in Fortaleza (state of Ceará) – and not, like the two previously mentioned communities, by a priest, but by a layman: Moyses Louro de Azevedo (Cleary 2011: 112f.; Mariz/Aguilar 2009).[9] Azevedo was influenced by Jonas Abib and the Canção Nova community. It is thus no surprise that Shalom also draws on music as a central missionary tool. It runs more than 50 community houses in Brazil, which organize religious orientation days and summer camps; it is also present on the radio and television with its own programs and has spread internationally, including to France, Italy, Switzerland, Canada, and Israel (Cleary 2011: 112f.). Once a year, it organizes the annual music festival Halleluya (cf. below).

Very successful is also the community Toca de Assis, which again originated in the southeast of the country, in Campinas (São Paulo state) (Cleary 2011: 113f.; Portella 2009).[10] Founded in 1983 by a priest (Roberto José Lettieri), its members see their specific vocation in following the footsteps of Francis of Assisi, i.e. in a simple lifestyle and in caring for the poor, especially the homeless; accordingly, they call themselves "filhos da pobreza" ('sons of poverty'). Toca de Assis is a lay congregation that maintains more than 100 houses throughout Brazil, with a focus on the state of São Paulo.

The boundaries between the numerous Charismatic communities, of which only a few have been mentioned here, are blurred; membership is often not formalized and specific cross-community events contribute to the emergence of an overarching Charismatic sense of community. Among them are the large-scale worship services for which stadium-like meeting places have been created (modeled on Pentecostal megachurches, though mostly less representative). The best-known example is the Santuário Theotókos – Mãe de Deus ('Shrine of the God-bearer – Mother of God') in São Paulo, initiated by

---

9   Cf. https://shalombrasil.com.br/.
10 Cf. https://tocadeassisirmaos.org.br/.

the aforementioned singing priest Marcelo Rossi.[11] The Santuário Theotókos is Brazil's second largest church in the country; it can accommodate about 25.000 people inside and 100.000 people outside.[12] The Holy Mass is read here several times a week and broadcast by both church-owned and private TV stations.[13] When celebrated by Marcelo Rossi, it resembles a staging that alternates between pop concert and Sunday service, i.e. secular pop cultural forms are adopted and embedded in a Catholic context. I shall come back to this further on.

This melting of Catholic elements with pop-cultural ones is also the recipe for the success of religious music festivals such as those hosted by Canção Nova or Shalom. Shalom organizes an annual five-day festival of Catholic music called Halleluya in Fortaleza (northern Brazil): more than a million people gathered for more than 40 individual events as part of this festival in pre-COVID years. On the professionally designed website, the festival is advertised with the slogan "Mais que um Festival. Uma experiência!" ('More than a festival. An experience!').[14] A similar three-day event – named Hosana Brasil – is organized annually by Canção Nova in Cachoeira Paulista (in the southeast; São Paulo state) and brings together hundreds of thousands religious 'fans' from numerous different communities and local prayer groups.[15]

Within Brazil's Catholic sub-field, the RCC provides an alternative to the other styles of Catholic devotion: Its dynamic and emotional approach to liturgy, which is focused on a belief in the actual presence of the Holy Spirit, is in sharp contrast with the rigid clerical culture of Romanized Catholicism as well as with the rather ascetic liturgical style practiced in Liberationist base

---

11   Cf. https://padremarcelorossi.com.br/ and the Facebook and Instagram accounts of the Santuário Theotókos.
12   The largest being the Sanctuary of the national patron Santa Maria Aparecida (São Paulo state). The Santuário Theotókos was financed exclusively by donations and the proceeds from the sale of CDs, DVDs, books, etc. Its 2012 inauguration was broadcast by Brazil's largest TV-station Rede Globo (cf. the report: https://www.youtube.com/watch?v=ZHZAYyFuFXw&t=47s).
13   According to the website "Horários de Missa em todo o Brasil" the Holy Mass is read at the Santuário Theotókos twice on Sundays (5:45 a.m.; 8:45 a.m.) and once on Wednesdays (7:45 p.m.) and Saturdays (3:00 p.m.); all four masses are broadcast either by the private TV- and radio-station Rede Globo or by the Catholic TV station Rede Vida or by Web TV; cf. https://www.horariodemissa.com.br/igreja.php?k=Ag7U9.
14   Cf. https://www.festivalhalleluya.com/festival.
15   Cf. https://eventos.cancaonova.com/edicao/hosana-brasil-17/.

communities (Oro 1996: 89–119; Prandi 1997: 97–157). What distinguishes the RCC from other currents in Brazilian Catholicism, however, is not just its expressive, enthusiastic style of piety (which strongly resembles Pentecostal forms), but also the social forms that Charismatic spirituality takes on. It is noteworthy that, in terms of social structure, the basic social form of Charismatic Catholicism – the usually small local prayer group ("grupo de oração") – resembles the base communities and thus the social form invented by Liberation Theology, the main competitor of Charismatic Catholicism in the Catholic sub-field (Prandi 1997: 97–121). However, Charismatic prayer groups and base communities fill their respective basic social forms, which are similar in some regards, with fundamentally disparate religious messages and completely different devotional styles: The primarily sober spirituality observable in base communities reflects experiences of suffering and oppression. Base communities apply the biblical message to the living conditions of the poor in order to obtain religious guidelines for social action – social action that aims at changing those unjust social conditions. Charismatic prayer groups, in contrast, concern personal experiences of the Holy Spirit ("baptism in the Spirit") and thus individual spiritual renewal. Charismatic religiosity is joyful, its focus is on praising God and on the personally (not socially) liberating experience of the Holy Spirit. 'I am happy to be Catholic' – this slogan, brought to life by singing priests like Marcelo Rossi, sums up what Charismatic Catholic piety is about, and how it differs from all other types of Catholicism in Brazil: While Romanized Catholicism is experienced as ritually petrified, Folk Catholicism is marked by magical ideas, and Liberation Theology takes a rather rational approach to religion, while Charismatic piety simply makes Catholics happy!

In Charismatic prayer groups, the "baptism in the Spirit" as an experience of being personally called, is longed for, prayed for, and sung for together. It is experienced as spiritual empowerment to cope with the given life conditions and thus acknowledged as a path to healing. Healing is understood both in a concrete sense, as recovery from physical or psychological suffering, and in a figurative sense, e.g. as turning away from alleged sexual or religious aberrations, namely homosexuality, promiscuity, or the practice of Afro-Brazilian religions (Maffi 2019). The experience of being "baptized in the Holy Spirit" is also interpreted as a divine calling for further commitment – commitment both in the sense of developing one's own faith (inwardly) and of actively engaging in missionary work (outwardly). This is far from trivial: In a country where not long ago (as recently as the early 1970s) more than 90 per cent of the population still identified with Catholicism, both concerns point to a profound religious change. The Renovação Carismática Católica is both part of that change and a response to it. This unprecedented zeal for evangelization and mission challenged the established pastoral praxis, which could not rely on approved models. The Charismatics thus first had to invent practices and build up social forms appropriate to their evangelization and mission goals – or borrow them from other contexts.

In this regard, the RCC's representatives proceed methodically. An example of this is a document entitled "Planejamento Estratégico de Evangelização" ('Strategic Planning of Evangelization'), authored by the National Council of the RCC in 2014.[16] The document, which was presented at a national meeting of RCC leaders, unfolds a general agenda to be implemented nationwide in anticipation of the (then upcoming) 50th anniversary of the global Catholic Charismatic Renewal in 2017. It displays a range of activities based on seven pillars: evangelization, pastoral care, spirituality, formation (of multipliers), communication, administration, and mission. These pillars are in turn structured according to the criteria (general) intention, (concrete) objective, (possible) action, and responsibility. In addition, a structure for self-assessment is provided (not yet implemented; ongoing implementation in per cent; already implemented). It should not be considered a coincidence that this seven-part spectrum is framed by the pillars evangelization and mission, since one's own anchoring in the faith is considered the prerequisite for effective missionary activity.

Besides, the document exemplifies how a religious renewal movement which began from below might gradually become controlled from above. Here, we can observe the particular tension between microsocial religious community building and meso- or macrosocial religious organization: While it is correct that organizational logics risk inhibiting the dynamics of spontaneous Charismatic experiences and community building, especially those based on eruptive experiences such as the "baptism in the Spirit", this is only one side of the story. The other is that religious organizations might also create conditions that make Charismatic experiences and subsequent processes of community-building possible in the first place. This somewhat paradoxical effect can be observed in the case of the RCC.

---

16   Cf. https://novoportal.rccbrasil.org.br/blog/planejamento-estrategico-de-evangelizacao/.

For instance, the RCC's website[17] provides not only general information on the movement and its organizational structure, but also contains interactive pages that allow committed adherents to register their prayer groups,[18] and, as a result, interested people to find a prayer group in their neighborhood. The RCC thus uses its organizational structure (which is supported by the church hierarchy) to promote grassroot activities, i.e. to encourage local people to start Charismatic prayer groups or to participate in existing ones. At the same time, it also channels this process by providing general explanations about the religious purpose of prayer groups and offering suggestions for prayer or communal activities as well as pictures and videos visualizing such activities.[19] As a result, a certain standardization of piety is being pushed: The RCC as a well-structured organization (on the macro-level) provides a model that individuals and local Charismatic prayer groups (on the micro- and meso-level) are supposed to follow.

In contrast to Max Weber's line of argumentation, who assumed that the Charismatic character of a movement would be lost (by routinization) when the movement is transformed into an organization (Weber 1968 [1922]: 246–254), the RCC exemplifies that setting up professional organizational structures does not necessarily slow down the initial Charismatic impetus, but might even promote further Charismatic experiences and initiate processes of Charismatic community-building – because of and not despite efficient church organization. Thus, typical events which can only take place with a great deal of professional organizational effort, such as the abovementioned music festivals Halleluya and Hosana Brasil, transregional or national prayer meetings ("cenáculos"), local 'Jesus bars' ("barzinhos de Jesus") or 'Christotheques' ("cristotecas"), or the alternative carnival ("Carneval

---

17 Cf. https://novoportal.rccbrasil.org.br/.
18 Cf. https://novoportal.rccbrasil.org.br/cadastre-um-grupo-de-oracao/; https://novopo rtal.rccbrasil.org.br/o-que-e-grupo-de-oracao/. In this way, data on the spread of the RCC is collected. At the beginning of 2022, a total of 14.313 prayer groups were listed on this website, broken down by states; according to this, the greatest density was found in the south and southeast. These numbers were no longer publicly accessible in August 2023; the call to register groups and the possibility to find groups in one's neighborhood are still in place.
19 Cf. the websites "O que é Grupo de Oração e como participar?" ('What is a prayer group and how can I take part?') and "Grupo de oração – Formação" ('Prayer group – Formation'): https://novoportal.rccbrasil.org.br/o-que-e-grupo-de-oracao/; https://novoporta l.rccbrasil.org.br/grupo-de-oracao-formacao/.

de Jesus"), open up new social spaces for Charismatic experiences for both individuals and groups.

What is more, these events bring something else to light that is typical of the social forms that Charismatic Catholicism in Brazil takes on: they are hybrid. We can observe a mingling of (1) distinct Catholic practices, symbols and social forms (such as the Eucharist, the rosary, the Virgin Mary, reverence for the pope, etc., and, not least, the social structure of base communities) with (2) historically successful social forms from other religious origins (especially from Pentecostalism, such as prayer groups or the camp meetings) and (3) social frames drawn from pop culture (discotheque, bar, concert, camping, even sports, etc.). For instance, "cenáculos" ('prayer meetings') typically take place in large sport arenas or as camp meetings and resemble, for one thing, the Great Awakenings that took place in the US in the 18th and 19th centuries; at the same time, however, they make use of basic social elements from present-day pop culture (just think of music festivals). Even the Holy Mass with its core ritual of the Eucharist is not exempt from this hybridization. The singing priest Marcelo Rossi actually stages the Holy Mass like a pop show.[20] The point here is that we are dealing with highly organized religious events that facilitate individual as well as communal Charismatic experiences.

Music plays an important role in (almost) all of this. In Brazil, Charismatic Catholicism has developed its own style of music, which is popularized by the "barzinhos de Jesus", the "cristotecas", and not least the festivals of religious music, and has become successful on the commercial music market. In fact, music is at the heart of the dynamic process of Charismatic community-building in Brazil today, and this dynamic is driven by a figure exclusive to Charismatic Catholicism, namely, the singing priest.

Singing priests are key figures for the movement's success (Cleary 2011: 1–29, 96–151; Clarke 1999; Chesnut 2003: 64–101; Souza 2005). One reason might be their ability to perform smoothly in highly different social fields: they are big names in the pop-cultural scene and renowned personages in the religious field. They perform proficiently both at the altar and on the stage; they turn Holy Mass into an event that oscillates between show and Sunday service; they run daily radio and television programs, sell their own CDs, DVDs, and books, stream their music, maintain personal websites, Instagram, and Facebook accounts, etc. And they are successful. In 2002, the most famous

---

20 His latest videos can be watched via his personal website: https://www.padremarcelorossi.com.br/WebTV.php.

of Brazil's singing priests, Padre Marcelo Rossi, received a nomination for the Latin Grammy.

The singing priests represent a style of joyful piety that is compatible with the modern world and its 'well-being' ideals. They act as ambassadors of a renewed Catholicism whose core message is that Catholicism is about being happy, and moreover about being happy in *this* world!

To conclude this part: The reason that the RCC does quite well in gaining followers among Catholics might be that Charismatic Catholicism (in Brazil) has created a joyful culture of piety that combines traditional Catholic elements with new non-Catholic practices, ideas, and social forms. Popular elements from outside the Catholic sub-field are thus embedded within a Catholic framework and invested with a Catholic meaning. Particularly important in this regard is not least the devotion to Mary, which connects the Charismatic current with the other three currents in the Brazil's Catholic field. This is most evident in the case of Marcelo Rossi. Not only did he name the huge religious arena that he founded in São Paulo after Maria Santuário Theotókos ('Shrine of the God-Bearer'); Mary is also iconographically omnipresent there as well as on his website and in his books. She is a constant point of reference in his songs, and the prayer of the rosary is a preferred and recommended devotional practice, streamed every day through his personal website, thus creating a virtual community of praying believers.[21]

4. Final considerations: 'Option for the spirits': Dynamics of competition and convergence in the religious field in Brazil

Now that we have taken a closer look at the heterogeneous Catholic sub-field and especially the role of the Charismatic Renewal in its dynamics, I will again 'zoom' out of the Catholic sub-field and cast a glance at the dynamics of the entire religious field of Brazil. Let's take a quick look back: Even though Pentecostal churches had begun growing in the 1950s, the Catholic Church only started taking other religious actors seriously in the 1970s, and even then, only

---

21 Cf. https://www.padremarcelorossi.com.br/IndiceDoRosario.php. In a 2003 film entitled "Maria, Mãe do Filho de Deus" ('Mary, Mother of God's Son') Rossi even participated as an actor; cf. Moacyr Góes (dir.) 2003.

reluctantly. As a result, the church was late in realizing that it had come under competitive pressure in the religious field and, consequently, was late in actually taking care of the faith and inner devotion of Catholics themselves.

As 'newcomers' in the religious field, Pentecostal churches, in contrast, have presented themselves from the beginning as an alternative to Catholicism, thereby triggering a dynamic of competition in the overall religious field. They did so not only by offering alternative beliefs, but also by introducing alternative social forms of religion, with Pentecostalism organizing itself into 'sect'-like social forms rather than 'churches'. By 'sects', I understand (in line with Max Weber's and Ernst Troeltsch's definition; Weber 2011 [1920]; Troeltsch 1960 [1912]; cf. the Introduction to this volume) exclusive communities whose members are expected to be deeply devout and to live a life that consistently pleases God. Pentecostal sects thus represent a social alternative to the 'church' and thus to the dominant social form of Catholicism in Brazil until at least the mid-20th century. Unlike sects, churches (still according to Weber and Troeltsch) follow an inclusive model of membership, i.e. membership does not necessarily require an inner commitment. Religious communities that follow the sect-type and its corresponding devotional style (which in the case of Pentecostalism consists of a combination of emotional religiosity and strict lifestyle) proved to be very successful in Brazil. It is therefore not surprising that Catholics should have imitated sect-like social forms, based on the personal calling as experienced in the "baptism in the Spirit", the key moment in the religious life of Charismatics.

Yet, to fully comprehend the religious dynamics in Brazil we must realize something else: All three main actors share a fundamental conviction, namely a belief in the power of spirits – be it the (one and only) Holy Spirit of Christians or the many spirits of African, indigenous, or other provenance that are worshipped in the Afro-Brazilian religions. Just as important as this shared belief in the existence of powerful spirits, however, are the differences in the background beliefs about the character of these spirits. While the Holy Spirit of Christians (as an aspect of the divine trinity) is imagined as unambiguously good, the African, indigenous, and other spirits, for their part, are without exception highly ambiguous, i.e. neither good nor evil, or both good and evil at the same time. Christianity, by contrast, has split off all evil from the idea of God and transferred it to the figure of the devil.

This is no theological hair-splitting. Rather, it is crucial if we want to understand how (neo-)Pentecostalism and Charismatic Catholicism relate to Afro-Brazilian religions: They imagine the African spirits as demons, and therefore see ritual trance as demonic possession, as the bestseller *Orixás, Caboclos e Guias: Deuses ou Demônios?*[22] ('Orixás, Caboclos and Leaders: Gods or Demons?') authored by Edir Macedo (2019 [1989]), founder of the neo-Pentecostal Universal Church of the Kingdom of God, testifies; this highly aggressive bestseller was first published in 1989 and relaunched in 2019. Neo-Pentecostal churches, in particular, are highly aggressive towards Afro-Brazilian religions, even physically attacking their centers and their adherents (da Silva 2007; 2016). There are no reports yet of Catholic Charismatic groups behaving in a similar way, but Charismatic Catholics are also increasingly distancing themselves from Afro-Brazilian religions (Maffi 2019), interestingly much more so than representatives of Romanized Catholicism and in contrast to Folk Catholicism and Liberation Theology.

We can thus state that there actually is a dynamic of competition in Brazil's religious field – a dynamic that emerged with the rise of Pentecostalism, and that has since then impinged upon other actors.

What determines this competition? In his book *Competitive Spirits* (2003), R. Andrew Chesnut noted the prevalence in the Catholic sub-field in Brazil of what he calls a "Preferential Option for the Spirit" (ibid.: 64–101) – "Spirit" in the singular, referring to the Holy Spirit. What he (alluding, needless to say, to the liberation theologists' phrase of a 'preferential option for the poor') describes as the basic logic within the Catholic sub-field, however, seems to apply to the religious field as a whole: it is the search for personal spiritual experiences that determines the religious dynamics in Brazil – whether these experiences can be traced back to the one and only Holy Spirit or to the many other spirits of any origin. The logic of the religious field in Brazil is thus dominated by an 'option for the spirits' – this time in the plural.

As a result, religious 'providers', so to speak, will do their best to make such experiences available. The convergence of religious beliefs (in powerful spirits) and demands (the search for personal experiences of those spirits) thus leads to competition among religious providers. Convergence and competition are mutually dependent. And this – which is what I am getting at – favors a dynamic of 'mimicry' (or 'isomorphism') in Brazil's religious field: styles of piety and their corresponding social forms (actually, social forms that allow for spiritual experiences) are being reproduced across religious and denom-

---

22 "Orixá" is the name for the deities of African origin; a "caboblo" is an indigenous spirit; "guia" is an umbrella term for a variety of spirits that are worshipped in Umbanda.

inational boundaries, namely across Pentecostalism, Catholicism, and Afro-Brazilian religions. I shall explain this a little further.

I will start with the 'mimicry' of devotional styles: actually, trance experiences, possession – and its counterpart: exorcism – are at the center of the devotional culture of all successful religious providers in Brazil. They are accompanied by certain patterns of bodily expressions, such as glossolalia, physiognomic changes, falling, clumsy movements or spasms, etc. (which usually turn into harmonized body performance after a while). Significantly, a positive tone underlies this style of piety: It is not only 'I am happy to be Catholic' – we could replace Catholic with Pentecostal, Spiritist, or Afro-Brazilian to obtain a motto which concisely expresses the basic attitude of those who, to refer to Chesnut, 'opt for the spirit(s)' and corresponding devotional styles. Successful religion in Brazil is thus about being happy and healthy, namely: being happy and healthy in *this* world – not primarily about eternal 'salvation' (such as preached by both 'Romanized Catholicism' and historical Protestantism, the two 'losers' in Brazil's religious field).

The mimicry of devotional styles is accompanied by a second form of 'mimicry': mimicry of social forms of religion. This becomes obvious when we compare the social structure of Charismatic Catholicism with that of Pentecostalism: both have developed a scheme of religious social forms and activities that ranges from the micro- to the meso- to the macro-level, i.e. from small local groups (with high interactive commitment) to regional worship gatherings (with medium commitment) to, eventually, large transregional or even national religious events (with only loose personal commitment). Unsurprisingly, the macro-level receives the greatest recognition in Charismatic Catholicism: the RCC has gradually adapted to the hierarchical organizational structure of the Brazilian church, thus securing the Vatican's approval as well. This, however, has set off its own dynamic: the more Rome has supported the Charismatic "awakenings" in Brazil (and worldwide), the more the movement and its social forms have come under the control of the papal magisterium and thus have been standardized.

I will conclude: In Brazil, those religious 'providers' that respond to the prevalent 'option for the spirit(s)' are most successful. These are: Afro-Brazilian religions, Pentecostal and neo-Pentecostal churches – and Charismatic Catholicism. The latter, as we have seen, is prospering, but its success remains limited to the (otherwise shrinking) Catholic sub-field. Despite the backing of the Brazilian bishops and the Vatican, the RCC has so far failed to win back former Catholics. Instead, it has succeeded in gaining ground among

Catholics themselves. The number of Catholics identifying with Charismatic groups is currently estimated as being as high as 50 per cent (Chesnut 2016: 77). Whether the trend towards Charismatic piety will stop the ongoing erosion of the Catholic sub-field is almost impossible to predict. Yet, one observation persists indisputably: The Charismatic Renewal has significantly changed the social forms of Catholicism in Brazil.

Bibliography

Anderson, Allan Heaton (2014): An Introduction to Pentecostalism: Global Charismatic Christianity, Cambridge: Cambridge University Press.

Aubrée, Marion/Laplantine, François (1990): La Table, le livre et les esprits: Naissance, évolution et actualité du mouvement social spirite entre France et Brésil, Paris: J.C. Lattés.

Bourdieu, Pierre (1987 [1971]): "Legitimation and Structured Interests in Weber's Sociology of Religion." In: Sam Whimster/Scott Lash (eds.), Max Weber: Rationality and Modernity, London: Allen & Unwin, pp. 119–136.

Bourdieu, Pierre (1991 [1971]): "Genesis and Structure of the Religious Field." In: Comparative Social Research, pp. 1–44.

Campos, Leonildo Silveira (2016): "Traditional Protestantism." In: Steven Engler/Bettina E. Schmidt (eds.), Handbook of Contemporary Religions in Brazil, Leiden and Boston: Brill, pp. 95–116.

Carranza, Brenda (2000): Renovação Carismática Católica: Origens, mudanças e tendências. Aparecida, SP: Editora Santuário.

Carranza, Brenda (2011): Catolicismo Midiático, Aparecida, SP: Idéias & Letras.

Carranza, Brenda/Mariz, Cecilia/Camurça, Marcelo (eds.) (2009): Novas communidades católicas: Em busca do espaço pós-moderno, Aparecida, SP: Idéias & Letras.

Chesnut, R. Andrew (1997): Born Again in Brazil: The Pentecostal Boom and the Pathogens of Poverty, New Brunswick, New Jersey, and London: Rutgers University Press.

Chesnut, R. Andrew (2003): Competitive Spirits: Latin America's New Religious Economy, Oxford and New York: Oxford University Press.

Chesnut, R. Andrew (2016): "The Spirit of Brazil: Charismatic Christianity among the World's Largest Catholic and Pentecostal Populations." In: Steven Engler/Bettina E. Schmidt (eds.), Handbook of Contemporary Religions in Brazil, Leiden and Boston: Brill, pp. 76–94.

Ciciliot, Valentina (2019): "The Origins of the Catholic Charismatic Renewal in the United States: Early Developments in Indiana and Michigan and the Reactions of the Ecclesiastical Authorities." In: Studies in World Christianity 25/3, pp. 250–273.

Ciciliot, Valentina (2020): "From The United States to the World, Passing through Rome: Reflections on the Catholic Charismatic Movement." In: PentecoStudies 19/2, pp. 127–151.

Clarke, Peter B. (1999): "'Top-star' Priests and the Catholic Response to the 'Explosion' of Evangelical Protestantism in Brazil: The Beginning of the End of the 'Walkout'?" In: Journal of Contemporary Religion 14/2, pp. 203–216.

Cleary, Edward L. (2011): The Rise of Charismatic Catholicism in Latin America, Gainsville: University Press of Florida.

Correa, Marina (2020 [1998]): Assembleias de Deus: Ministérios, carisma e o exercício do poder, 3rd ed., São Paulo: Recriar.

da Silva, Vagner Gonçalves (2007): "Neo-Pentecostalism and Afro-Brazilian religions: Explaining the Attacks on Symbols of the African Religious Heritage in Contemporary Brazil." In: Mana 13/1, pp. 207–236.

da Silva, Vagner Gonçalves (2016): "Crossroads: Conflicts between Neo-Pentecostalism and Afro-Brazilian Religions." In: Steven Engler/Bettina E. Schmidt (eds.), Handbook of Contemporary Religions in Brazil, Leiden and Boston: Brill, pp. 489–507.

da Silva, Vagner Gonçalves/Brumana, Fernando Giobellina (2016): "Candomblé: Religion, World Vision and Experience." In: Steven Engler/Bettina E. Schmidt (eds.), Handbook of Contemporary Religions in Brazil, Leiden and Boston: Brill, pp. 170–185.

de Alencar, Gedeon Freire (2019 [1998]): Matriz Pentecostal Brasileira: Assembleias de Deus 1911 à 2011, 2nd ed., São Paulo: Recriar; Unida.

de Oliveira, Eliane Martins (2009): "A 'vida no Espírito' e o dom de ser Canção Nova." In: Brenda Carranza/Cecilia Mariz/Marcelo Camurça (eds.), Novas communidades católicas: Em busca do espaço pós-moderno, Aparacida, SP: Idéias & Letras, pp. 195–221.

de Roux, Rodolfo R. (2014): "La Romanización de la Iglesia Católica en América Latina: Una Estratégia de Larga Duración." In: Pro-Posições 25/1, pp. 31–54.

Dove, Stephen C. (2016): "Historical Protestantism in Latin America." In: Virigina Garrard-Burnett/Paul Freston/Stephen C. Dove (eds.), The Cambridge History of Religions in Latin America, New York: Cambridge University Press, pp. 286–303.

Dreher, Martin H. (2016): "Immigrant Protestantism: The Lutheran Church in Latin America." In: Virigina Garrard-Burnett/Paul Freston/Stephen C. Dove (eds.), The Cambridge History of Religions in Latin America, New York: Cambridge University Press, pp. 304–318.

Engler, Steven/Schmidt, Bettina E. (eds.) (2016): Handbook of Contemporary Religions in Brazil, Leiden and Boston: Brill.

Engler, Steven/Schmidt, Bettina E. (2016): "Introduction." In: idem (eds.), Handbook of Contemporary Religions in Brazil, Leiden and Boston: Brill, pp. 1–29.

Engler, Steven (2016): "Umbanda." In: Steven Engler/Bettina E. Schmidt (eds.), Handbook of Contemporary Religions in Brazil, Leiden and Boston: Brill, pp. 204–224.

Engler, Steven/Brito, Ênio Brito (2016): "Afro-Brazilian and Indigenous-Influenced Religions." In: Steven Engler/Bettina E. Schmidt (eds.), Handbook of Contemporary Religions in Brazil, Leiden and Boston: Brill, pp. 142–169.

Engler, Steven/Isaia, Artur Cesar (2016): "Kardecism." In: Steven Engler/ Bettina E. Schmidt (eds.), Handbook of Contemporary Religions in Brazil, Leiden and Boston: Brill, pp. 186–203.

Fernandes, Sílvia Regina Alves (2005): "Padres cantores e a mídia: representações da identidade sacerdotal." In: Ciências Sociais e Religião 7, pp. 131–155.

Freston, Paul (1998): "A igreja universal do Reino de Deus e o campo protestante no Brasil." In: Estudos de religião 12/15, pp. 9–19.

Freston, Paul (1999): "'Neo-Pentecostalism' in Brazil: Problems of Definition and the Struggle for Hegemony." In: Archives de Sciences Socailes des Releligion 105, pp. 145–162.

Freston, Paul (2016): "History, Current Reality, and Prospects of Pentecostalism in Latin America." In: Virigina Garrard-Burnett/Paul Freston/Stephen C. Dove (eds.), The Cambridge History of Religions in Latin America, New York: Cambridge University Press, pp. 430–450.

Gabriel, Eduardo (2009): "Expansão da RCC brasileira: a chegada de Canção Nova em Fátima-Portugal." In: Brenda Carranza/Cecilia Mariz/Marcelo Camurça (eds.), Novas communidades católicas: Em busca do espaço pós-moderno, Aparacida, SP: Idéias & Letras, pp. 223–240.

Garrard-Burnett, Virginia/Freston, Paul/Dove, Steven C. (eds.) (2016): The Cambridge History of Religions in Latin America, New York: Cambridge University Press.

González, Douglas Sullivan (2016): "Religious Devotion, Rebellion, and Messianic Movements: Popular Catholicism in the Nineteenth Century." In: Virigina Garrard-Burnett/Paul Freston/Stephen C. Dove (eds.), The Cambridge History of Religions in Latin America, New York: Cambridge University Press, pp. 269–285.

Hartch, Todd (2014): The Rebirth of Latin American Christianity, Oxford; New York: Oxford University Press.

Hero, Markus (2009): "Das Prinzip 'Access'. Zur institutionellen Infrastruktur zeitgenössischer Spiritualität." In: Zeitschrift für Religionswissenschaft 17, pp. 189–211.

Junqueira, Eduardo (1998): "Uma estrela no altar." In: Veja, November 4, 31/44, pp. 114–120.

Larkin, Brian (2016): "Tridentine Catholicism in the New World." In: Virigina Garrard-Burnett/Paul Freston/Stephen C. Dove (eds.), The Cambridge History of Religions in Latin America, New York: Cambridge University Press, pp. 107–132.

Macedo, Edir (2019 [1989]): Orixás, Caboclos e Guias: Deuses ou Demônios, São Paulo: Unipro Editora.

Maffi, Bruno (2019): "Pois a Promessa á para Vòs..." 1969–2019: Os anos das Renovacão Carismática Católica no Brasil, n.p.: RCC Brasil.

Mariz, Cecília Loreto/Aguilar, Luciana (2009): "Shalom: construção social da experiência vocational." In: Brenda Carranza/Cecilia Mariz/Marcelo Camurça (eds.), Novas communidades católicas: Em busca do espaço pósmoderno, Aparacida, SP: Idéias & Letras, pp. 241–266.

Oro, Ari Pedro (1996): Avanço pentecostal e reacão católica, Petrópolis: Vozes.

Oro, Ari Pedro (2005): "A demonologia da Igreja Universal do Reino de Deus." In: Debates no NER 6/7, pp. 135–146.

Portella, Rodrigo (2009): "Medievais e pós-modernos: a Toca de Assis e as novas sensibilidades católicas juvenis." In: Brenda Carranza/Cecilia Mariz/Marcelo Camurça (eds.), Novas communidades católicas: Em busca do espaço pós-moderno, Aparacida, SP: Idéias & Letras, pp. 171–194.

Prandi, Reginaldo (1997): Um sopro do espírito: a renovação conservadora do catolicismo carismatico, São Paulo: Editora da Universidade de São Paulo.

Prandi, Reginaldo (2010): "African Gods in Contemporary Brazil." In: Robin Cohen/Paola Toninato (eds.), The Creolization Reader: Studies in mixed identities and cultures, London; New York: Routledge, pp. 207–218.

Reuter, Astrid (2018): "Praxeologie: Struktur und Handeln (Pierre Bourdieu)." In: Detlef Pollack/Volkhard Krech/Olaf Müller/Markus Hero (eds.), Handbuch Religionssoziologie, Wiesbaden: Springer VS, pp. 171–202.
Rivera, Paulo Barrera (2016): "Pentecostalism in Brazil." In: Steven Engler/Bettina E. Schmidt (eds.), Handbook of Contemporary Religions in Brazil, Leiden and Boston: Brill, pp. 117–131.
Rossi, Pe. Marcelo (2000): Eu Sou Feliz por Ser Católico, n.p.
Schmidt, Bettina E. (2016): Contemporary Religions in Brazil, Oxford Handbooks Online (https://doi.org/10.1093/oxfordhb/9780199935420.013.50. Accesed April 2, 2024).
Souza, André Ricardo de (2005): Igreja in concert: Padres cantores, mídia e marketing, São Paulo: Annablume; Fadesp.
Steil, Carlos Alberto (2016): "Traditional Popular Catholicism in Brazil." In: Steven Engler/Bettina E. Schmidt (eds.), Handbook of Contemporary Religions in Brazil, Leiden and Boston: Brill, pp. 60–75.
Troeltsch, Ernst (1960 [1912]): The Social Teaching of the Christian Churches, 2 vol., New York: Harper.
Weber, Max (1968 [1922]): Economy and Society: An Outline of Interpretive Sociology, ed. by Guenther Roth/Claus Wittich, New York: Bedminster Press.
Weber, Max (2011 [1920]): The Protestant Ethic and the Spirit of Capitalism, revised 1920 edition, New York and Oxford: Oxford University Press.

Web References

Canção Nova. "cancaonova.com." Accessed September 13, 2023. https://www.cancaonova.com/.
Canção Nova. "Eventos." Accessed September 13, 2023. https://eventos.cancaonova.com/edicao/hosana-brasil-17/.
Comunidade Emanuel. "Communidade Emanuel." Accessed September 13, 2023. https://emanuelnobrasil.com.br/.
Horários de Missa em todo o Brasil. "Santuário Theotokos – Mãe de Deus." Accessed September 13, 2023. https://www.horariodemissa.com.br/igreja.php?k=Ag7U9.
Igeja Universal. "Vídeo Completo da Inauguração Oficial do Templo de Salomão." YouTube. July 31, 2014. Accessed September 13, 2023. https://www.youtube.com/watch?v=eYprcb5Jg3U.

Jornal Nacional. "Chute na Imagem Da Santa." YouTube. October 12, 2016 [1995]. Accessed September 13, 2023. https://www.youtube.com/watch?v=QiNJ8mQU6g8.

Latinobarómetro 2017, quoted from: Forschungsgruppe Weltanschauungen in Deutschland (fowid). "Religion in Lateinamerika." fowid. January 10, 2018. Accessed September 13, 2023. https://fowid.de/meldung/religion-lateinamerika.

Padre Marcelo Rossi. "Padre Marcelo Rossi." Accessed September 13, 2023. https://www.padremarcelorossi.com.br.

Padre Marcelo Rossi. "Vídeos que Edificam Nossa Fé." Accessed September 13, 2023. https://www.padremarcelorossi.com.br/WebTV.php.

Padre Marcelo Rossi. "Rosário Nossa Senhora. Mistérios do rosário". Accessed April 2, 2024. https://www.padremarcelorossi.com.br/IndiceDoRosario.php.

Pew Research Center. "Brazil's Changing Religious Landscape." Pew Research. July 18, 2013. Accessed September 13, 2023. https://www.pewresearch.org/religion/2013/07/18/brazils-changing-religious-landscape/#trends-within-brazilian-protestantism.

Pew Reserach Center. "Religion in Latin America." Pew Research. November 13, 2014. Accessed September 13, 2023. https://www.pewforum.org/2014/11/13/religion-in-latin-america/.

Rede Globo. "A inauguração do Santuário Mãe de Deus por Padre Marcelo Rossi em São Paulo." YouTube. November 2, 2012. Accessed September 13, 2023. https://www.youtube.com/watch?v=ZHZAYyFuFXw&t=47s.

Renovacão Carismática Católica. "RCCBRASIL." Accessed September 13, 2023. https://novoportal.rccbrasil.org.br/.

Renovacão Carismática Católica. "O que é Grupo de Oração?" Accessed September 13, 2023. https://novoportal.rccbrasil.org.br/o-que-e-grupo-de-oracao/.

Renovacão Carismática Católica. "Cadastre um Grupo de Oração." Accessed September 13, 2023. https://novoportal.rccbrasil.org.br/cadastre-um-grupo-de-oracao/.

Renovacão Carismática Católica. "Planejamento estratégico de evangelização." Accessed September 13, 2023. https://novoportal.rccbrasil.org.br/blog/planejamento-estrategico-de-evangelizacao/.

Renovacão Carismática Católica. "Grupo de Oração – Formação." Accessed September 13, 2023. https://novoportal.rccbrasil.org.br/grupo-de-oracao-formacao/.

Shalom. "Shalom Brasil." Accessed September 13, 2023. https://shalombrasil.com.br/.
Shalom. "Halleluya." Accessed September 13, 2023. https://www.festivalhalleluya.com/festival.
Toca de Assis. "Toca de Assis." Accessed September 13, 2023. https://tocadeassisirmaos.org.br/.

Discography/Videography

Pe. Joãzinho SCJ (2009): Sou feliz por ser Católico. CD: MC Produções e Eventos.
Moacyr Góes (dir.) (2003): Maria, Mãe do Filho de Deus. DVD: Sony Pictures.

Everyday Familialism in the Emmanuel Community

Samuel Dolbeau

Abstract *Familialism is generally understood as a conceptual framework aimed at organizing political life, manifesting through mobilizations in the public sphere. Recent Catholic mobilizations in Europe, focusing on issues related to sexuality and gender, have brought attention to the importance of familialist networks that intersect with religious, associative, and political spheres. Within the French context, several researchers have underscored the pivotal role played by the Emmanuel Community, the largest Catholic Charismatic community in Europe. This paper aims to direct attention to the development of familialism within the Emmanuel Community, from a sporadic form of activism to the scaffolding serving for the construction of social forms within the Emmanuel Community. Referred to as everyday familialism, this phenomenon can be identified through the dissemination of religious resources that specifically target families, as well as through organizational dynamics and the promotion of a distinct clerical gender regime. This article builds upon broader doctoral research that examined the institutionalization of the Emmanuel Community. The materials used here consist primarily of semi-structured interviews conducted with members of the organization, as well as archival sources from the movement and its publications. All interviews were conducted in French; quotes were translated into English by the author.*[1]

Keywords *Catholic Charismatic Renewal, Catholicism, Community, familialism, New Ecclesial Movements, Sociology of Religion*

---

1   Many thanks to Petre Maican for reviewing and refining my English. I also thank Maren Freudenberg and Astrid Reuter for their suggestions.

1. Introduction

The Emmanuel Community originated as a Catholic Charismatic prayer group that was established in Paris in 1972 by two lay individuals: Pierre Goursat (1914–1994) and Martine Laffitte-Catta (1942). Currently, the Emmanuel Community is present in approximately 60 countries and boasts a membership of around 12.000 individuals.[2] It is regarded as one of the most vibrant New Ecclesial Movements[3] in Europe (Landron 2004). Of the 12.000 members of the Community, most of whom are from upper social classes, approximately half reside in France. Out of the total membership, 275 individuals are priests, while 225 are "consecrated in celibacy".[4] Notwithstanding, the Community's activities extend beyond these numbers, encompassing various associations and affiliated companies. The influence of the Emmanuel Community can also be noticed in the ways of expression of mainstream Catholicism. For instance, Emmanuel hymns are sung on a weekly basis in numerous French-speaking European parishes.

In the 2010s, during the period of heightened politicization of gender and sexuality issues, in which religious groups, especially Catholics, actively engaged, the organization gained public prominence in France (Béraud 2020: 241). During the Catholic mobilizations against same-sex marriage (2012–2013), several researchers highlighted the significant political role played by the Emmanuel Community, particularly through its yearly gatherings in Paray-le-Monial, Bourgogne[5] (Brustier 2014; Béraud and Portier 2015; Dolbeau 2021). Through a range of rhetorical strategies and repertoires of action (Stambolis-Ruhstorfer and Tricou 2018), these Catholics sought to

---

[2] Source: https://emmanuel.info/qui-sommes-nous/ (accessed on September 5, 2023).
[3] Broadly speaking, this term refers to communities that emerged in the wake of the Second Vatican Council (1962–1965). Catholic Charismatic communities are integral components of these New Ecclesial Movements.
[4] In the 1970s, the concept of 'consecrated celibacy' gained significant traction among New Ecclesial Movements, encompassing a diverse array of commitments that variously approximate a religious lifestyle. Individuals committed to this path undertake to live by the evangelical counsels of poverty, obedience, and chastity – expressed through continence – via vows whose canonical status can differ markedly from one movement to another. Often, these individuals wear distinctive attire and generally live in communal settings. Beyond this basic definition, the lifestyle is marked by a notable degree of heterogeneity. For further reading on the subject, cf. van Lier 2022.
[5] Organized since 1975.

defend a concept of 'family' (nuclear, heteronormative, and often large), that can be aligned with the category of familialism.

In a 1999 article, French sociologist Rémi Lenoir provided the following definition of familialism: "[familialism is] the totality of political movements and actions primarily carried out through the mobilization of local and national elites (lobbying, orchestrated press campaigns by private associations, occasionally recognized as having public utility), with the objective of 'defending the family'" (Lenoir 1999: 77). Lenoir distinguishes two sources of this familialism within the French context: one stemming from the state, which the Third Republic relied upon starting from the late 19th century (the family as a means of "preserving political order through morality" in response to the issue of "depopulation"[6]), and the other originating from the Catholic Church, which, during the late 19th and early 20th centuries, emerged "in the form of various philanthropic movements associated with social Catholicism" aiming to "reinstate a Catholic moral order" by promoting "large families" (ibid.: 77).

The objective of my contribution is to slightly shift the focus of familialism from a form of Catholic activism in the public sphere on issues related to marriage, sexuality, and gender, towards a form of everyday activism. Following Sylvie Ollitrault's work on environmental activists (Ollitrault 2008), I propose to study everyday familialism as a central driver of the construction of social forms within the Emmanuel Community. Although everyday familialism is not a social form in itself, it operates as an interpretive model of pre-existing social forms (cf. Introduction to this volume). Indeed, everyday familialism operates both at the local level, where the dominant social form is that of the group, and within the overarching governance of the Emmanuel Community, where the dominant social form is that of the organization. Furthermore, across the various tiers of the Emmanuel Community, the pronounced centrality of the married couple underscores the significance of the dyad.

In order to study these different levels, I first will demonstrate how everyday familialism manifests in the religious offers targeted at families (e.g.

---

[6] "The concept [of familialism] was indeed part of a movement aimed at promoting natality. Following the defeat against Germany in 1870, depopulation was construed as both the cause of this calamity and a calamity in its own right. Terms such as 'declining birth rates' and 'depopulation' were reflective of a prevailing sentiment among certain sectors of the French elite at the time, who viewed France as a nation in decline" (ibid.: 76).

printed materials, specific events), as well as from an organizational perspective. To do so, I will focus on the parish level. I will illustrate how the practical organization of parishes and the process of couples' commitment, shaped by everyday familialism, influence local group dynamics. In the second section, focusing on a more meso-social level, I will delve into the internal governance of the Emmanuel Community. I will illustrate how the governance model of this organization, predicated on the dyad of the married couple, leads to a distinct division of religious work. Lastly, I will demonstrate how everyday familialism is also manifested in the priestly masculinity promoted among the clergy members, which aligns quite closely with the 'spousal' model described by sociologist Josselin Tricou (Tricou 2021: 349).[7]

2. "You don't feel like creeps who bring in their bawling kids": The parish and the family

The first aspect, which is arguably the most immediately apparent, is the emphasis placed on the nuclear family and marital relationships in the discourse promoted by the Emmanuel Community, both internally and externally, at the group level (e.g. parish, prayer group) or the organization level (the Community as a whole). This emphasis is manifested through the regular publication of prescriptive materials on marital relationships and the upbringing of children and teenagers. It is important to note that this promotional effort should be understood within the broader context of the Catholic Church's increasing emphasis on family and marital relationships since the 1980s.[8] However, following Anthony Favier's observations (Favier 2021: 57–58), it is worth mentioning the Catholic Church's historical influence on family and couples counseling prior to the 1980s, particularly through the development of the profession of marriage counselor.[9] The involvement of Catholics, particularly women

---

7   In his doctoral thesis, Josselin Tricou examines the four main regimes of "clerical gender" at play in contemporary Catholicism. The spousal regime is one of these regimes.
8   Especially following the 1980 Synod on the Family, from which the apostolic exhortation *Familiaris Consortio* was derived.
9   Anthony Favier draws upon the work of Geneviève Valla-Chevalley in this context. In her book on the history of marital and family counseling, she elaborates: "Even though it has been institutionally developed in France since the 1970s, marital and family counseling gradually emerged in France, as well as in other American and European countries, in the first half of the 20th century. It has been constructed from several

working in the healthcare sector, in promoting "integral education for couples" (ibid.: 58), represents a significant aspect of the forms of activism observed in my field. This promotion extends beyond printed material. For instance, the family sessions organized annually since 1983 are consistently the most popular weeks during the summer gatherings in Paray-le-Monial. These religious offers, which are open to a broad Catholic audience, are also accessible in local parishes through a series of courses affiliated with an Emmanuel association called "Amour et Vérité" ('Love and Truth'[10]).

The second point worth mentioning pertains to the organization of parishes entrusted to community priests. These priests place a primary focus on the families within the parishes (whether members of the Emmanuel Community or not), offering specific activities for parents (e.g. dinners, courses), teenagers and young adults (e.g. prayer groups, weekends), and children (e.g. dedicated liturgy of the Word during Mass, nurseries). This family-oriented religious approach, reminiscent of the tailored group approach observed in Evangelical Protestantism[11], is not exclusive to the Emmanuel Community. Similar tendencies can be found in other New Ecclesial Movements as well as numerous ordinary urban parishes (Aubourg 2016). However, in the case of the Emmanuel Community, the emphasis on the family dimension emerges as a significant factor influencing the choices of the interviewed parishioners, whether they are members of the Community or not. Sophie, a woman in her

---

more or less ancient roots, both Anglo-Saxon and French, among which are two main 'parents', quite different in nature, one being Catholic religious and the other secular feminist. [...] One of these 'parents' has been the Catholic lineage of marriage preparation, which offered – and later mandated for the religious celebration of marriage – a period of reflection with clergy members and other couples. This movement reflected as early as the 1920s a growing awareness of the importance of marital life, particularly through the Association of Christian Marriage (founded by Abbé Jean Violet in 1918)" (Valla-Chevalley 2009: 13–14).

10 Founded in 1981, this association is dedicated to the pastoral care of couples and family. Source: https://emmanuel.info/france/amour-et-verite/ (accessed on September 5, 2023).

11 "From this array of activities emerges the impression of mass sociability, yet tailored to meet a multitude of individual needs. [...] One must be cautious of appearances: the megachurch is not a train station or a supermarket where individuals can get lost in the crowd without ever being called to account for their motivations. Megachurches uniformly emphasize the identification of newcomers and underscore the importance of directing them towards groups and activities that are likely to suit their needs." (Fath 2008: 39)

forties from an aristocratic background, describes how she transitioned from a parish led by another New Ecclesial Movement to joining a parish under the guidance of the Emmanuel Community:

> *Sophie:* That was also one of the very strong reasons for me, because when I found this parish [run by Emmanuel], I arrived six and a half months pregnant, so I quickly had a little girl, then we had a second one after that, and the way the children are looked after is brilliant. So that already allows... already there are lots of other parents with children, so you don't feel like creeps who bring in their bawling kids. And that's it. There were structures. [...] It wasn't a pretentious thing at all, people came, there were lots of families with lots of children, there was a little explanation of the Gospel for the children during mass. There was even a nursery, and at first, I used to take them to the nursery. So that helped me to live my faith more serenely on Sundays and to be a bit cooler during mass. [...] The priests have a way of talking... and I think it's linked to the Emmanuel approach, which is that it's very grounded in reality. In other words, they don't give you moralistic speeches about the fact that you're really sinners, that "you've got to get a move on", well if "you've got to get a move on" they tell you differently.
>
> *I:* And that was a difference from what you'd experienced [in your former parish]?
>
> *Sophie:* Well completely... so [the New Ecclesial Movement in charge of this parish], I don't believe I stayed there long enough to... I thought it was not bad musically, but it was still very elitist as... I think I had to go to this parish for two years and never speak to anyone. No one ever spoke to me.
>
> *I:* Elitist, in what sense do you mean that?
>
> *Sophie:* Well, like... I wasn't married, I was a student, I was too old for youth groups, and so maybe I didn't do enough, but I really met... unlike what I have here [...] where there's a community beyond the community people I mean, we have a parish community.[12]

In Sophie's remarks, it is evident that the emphasis on families goes beyond the tangible structures mentioned earlier, such as the liturgy of the Word for

---

12   Interview with Sophie, layperson, January 29, 2020.

children. This focus creates a pervasive sense of familiarity nurtured by an inherent *entre-soi* dynamic that already exists within the Community (reinforced by the recruitment of members from high social classes). This familiarity is also fostered through a close relationship with the priestly team, which is then contrasted with the group experiences from the previous parish settings, where there may have been a perceived distance between clergy and laity, or disapproving looks directed towards parents with noisy young children during Mass.

This sense of familiarity within the group is accompanied by a rapid process of entrusting couples with responsibilities by the parish team. New parishioners, as a couple, are quickly given the task of managing the courses they themselves have previously taken, such as baptism preparation or marriage preparation. This circular model, at times resulting in an accumulation of commitments, reflects the internal functioning of the Emmanuel Community. The process is primarily based on an affinity between marital/family commitment and religious commitment, as expressed more or less explicitly in the interviews with my respondents. Several devoted women parishioners establish a connection between the expectations associated with the different roles they undertake in the parish and their role as mothers. They emphasize the nurturing and caring aspects inherent in their tasks, often describing them as acts of "motherly care". Devotion, solicitude, and compassion for others are all regarded as "feminine attributes" (Béraud 2007: 306) and are consistently required in these different contexts. Françoise, a woman in her fifties from an aristocratic background, is actively involved in a parish run by the Emmanuel Community in Belgium, despite not being a member herself:

> I've always been very touched by children, it's always been… my field has always been children more than anything else. What touched me was to see this [parish] team that was completely dedicated to children, with tools that I didn't know, songs with gestures, very gentle words, very touching in fact, and very oriented towards their daily lives. […] And so I said to myself "I would have liked to have had this when I was a child too. And so, I want this for my children". Because there's a dimension in the Gospel, Jesus often talks about children. And then, little by little, that led me to meet people who were involved in [an activity aimed at mothers]. So there too, I said to myself "this is fantastic, I can be myself, I can have my time […] with these people".[13]

---

13 Interview with Françoise, layperson, January 30, 2020.

It is important to note that this affinity between marital/family commitment and religious commitment should be understood in parallel with the "processes of reinvesting professional skills in activist activities" (Rétif 2013: 418), which is particularly notable among the men. However, it is noteworthy that the "social function of mothers" (ibid.: 421) continues to be of paramount importance for my respondents in the perception and self-perception of the qualities they bring to the religious sphere. The frequent use of a dual vocational framework, encompassing both motherhood and Christian vocation, serves to reinforce this phenomenon.

In summary, at the group level, the Emmanuel Community promotes a religious offer specifically tailored to families, which is evident both through direct means such as publications and events, as well as in more subtle ways, including the practical organization of parishes and the process of couples' commitment. These commitments, typically following a circular model, are shaped by gender dynamics that emphasize a correspondence between family and religious commitment, particularly for women. However, to gain a deeper understanding of how everyday familialism shapes social forms within the Emmanuel Community, further explorations of the internal dynamics of the Community are necessary, particularly the central role of conjugality in its governance.

3. Governing through the couple: A dyad-based organization

Apart from the general moderator[14] and those responsible for specific branches (i.e. for priests and consecrated celibates), most decision-making bodies

---

14   While the position of moderator is canonically defined and cannot be shared by two individuals, it is worth noting the ambiguous status of the moderator's wife, which can be loosely compared to the role of the "first lady" within the Emmanuel Community. In the context of Ghanaian Charismatic movements, British anthropologist Jane E. Soothill has studied the phenomenon known as the "first lady syndrome" (drawing on the works of political scientist Lisa Aubrey), which pertains to the wives of pastors (Soothill 2007: 154–163). The concept of the "first lady syndrome", originally conceptualized by Amina Mama, is thus defined by Lisa Aubrey: "There are those in the state and in alternative civil society that are able to reconcile greater democratic space for *men only* in public life, while women ingratiate themselves to men and the state through organizational arrangements that promote various forms of state feminism, such as 'femocracy' or the first lady syndrome [...], both of which are systems in which female autocracies parallel and serve male dictatorships while advancing conserva-

within the Emmanuel Community – regardless of the level of governance: weekly household, sector, province, summer session at Paray-le-Monial – are led predominantly by married couples, with occasional temporary exceptions.[15] While a mix of individuals in different 'states of life' is also common in these bodies (i.e. priests, consecrated individuals, and laypeople), the couple constitutes the fundamental unit of governance within Emmanuel. This organizational characteristic is not entirely unique within the landscape of New Ecclesial Movements. However, the extent to which the Community implements this approach is noteworthy. By way of comparison, the second largest Charismatic community in France, Chemin Neuf[16], follows a somewhat similar structure by entrusting responsibility to couples at local and regional levels. Nevertheless, at the international level, clerics and consecrated celibates tend to occupy the majority of positions of high responsibility. Beyond French Charismatic Renewal, the Focolare Movement[17] adopts a governance model based on dyads, typically consisting of a single consecrated woman and a man (either a cleric or a consecrated man). Here, the woman holds the preeminent position of president, with the man acting as co-president. These various configurations aim to promote, to varying extents, "a certain equality between men and women, while respecting complementarity" (Tricou 2021: 349). Although this emphasis on equality and complementarity is also evident within the Emmanuel Community, the dyadic governance model employed does lead to a certain gendered division of religious work.

To gain insight into this division, let us delve into the narrative of Nicole, a woman in her fifties. Nicole comes from a middle-class background, is married, primarily a homemaker, and has been a member of the Emmanuel Community for approximately twenty years. Alongside her husband, she has held several positions of responsibility within the organization. In an interview conducted separately from her husband (who participated in an initial interview), Nicole reflects upon her involvement in the Emmanuel Community and the division of religious work within her own relationship. I provide a

---

tive gender ideologies to the detriment of democracy and gender equality" (Aubrey 2001: 105, original emphasis).
15   There are in certain countries where the Emmanuel Community has a relatively small presence, only one individual serving as a manager or coordinator. This is the case in countries such as Cuba, Haiti, Chile, and Ireland.
16   Founded in 1973 in Lyon by the Jesuit Laurent Fabre (1940).
17   Founded in Trento by Chiara Lubich (1920–2008).

substantial excerpt from the interview below, as it sheds light on a recurring pattern within the Community.

> *Nicole:* In our relationship, clearly, I have a [master's level] education, but I chose never to work because it didn't work out that way, because he [her husband] had his career, and given the direction his career was taking [...] it was incompatible with my job. And in the early years, with young children, I couldn't do much. But I didn't have any problems with it. And then we met the Community and got involved. The problem for a lot of women is that they don't feel useful if they don't work. I didn't feel that way because we devoted ourselves fully. And I had the impression that it was for something useful, even if it wasn't necessarily socially recognized, but it was useful. So, I was satisfied with that. That solved a problem of identity, let's say. Secondly, we're very complementary. He [her husband] is very self-confident, likes to take responsibility, and when he makes a decision, he sticks to it. That's not my style at all, I'm not used to that. As a result, I'm reassured to be able to take steps, knowing that he's not going to collapse before I do. So, I'm pretty conscientious, I'm not afraid of working, but I need to be second rather than first, so all in all I've found my place in this shared service. [...] So I see that with experience, this year in particular, I'm the one writing the teachings, I'm the one drawing up the plans, and he fits in, and it's worked really well like that. And it's really me who's taken over the teachings. [...] I travel a lot with him [her husband], not all the time because I can't, but quite a lot because our job is to liaise with local leaders who are also couples. And if they only talk to him [her husband], he is the salaried employee [...] and I'm a volunteer [...]. But I think it's important to be there. I can't keep track of all the files here [...]. But when I'm there, I can see that it's very important for me to go. And when I'm not there, the wives say, "but Nicole isn't here". So, it's a lot about the fraternal bond, because this communion between us for the mission has to be embodied at every level of the chain of responsibility. Otherwise, people say "well, that's not true".
>
> *I:* Was there some sort of division of labor between you?
>
> *Nicole:* Yeah, we're not really like that by nature. I think that's because I find it a bit difficult to really take responsibility. Because I doubt myself a lot (laughs). And especially because I'm actually quite involved in the family and household responsibilities, and we have seven children. I had to do a lot of work when they were little, but I still have to pay a bit of attention to them. He [her husband] is asking me to take on more of the support issues

[in their community mission]. But I can see that in fact I still find it hard to do it seriously, to make the contacts I need to... So, all the administrative stuff as well, that's not really my temperament, I'm not very methodical by nature, and I easily put a lot of myself into human relationships. I'm prepared to give a lot of my time. But I don't necessarily have to put it in writing, it's difficult for me to make files and all that. But I'm only representative of myself here. I know that there are couples where things are much more organized. She does this, he does that. Sometimes it's more the women who are going to be in contact, in community pastoral service responsibilities, so provincial or sector responsibilities. That requires a lot of contact with people. So, it's often telephone contact or personal contact. And it's often the women who generally have a bit more time, but it really depends on the temperament of the couple.[18]

One notable aspect to highlight is Nicole's perception of her involvement in the Emmanuel Community as a source of personal fulfillment. For her, being part of the Community compensates for the sense of social uselessness that she believes housewives can sometimes experience ("I didn't feel that way because we devoted ourselves fully. [...] So I was satisfied like that. That solved a problem of identity, let's say"). As previously mentioned in the case of the parish volunteer, this sense of fulfillment does not stem from the reinvestment of professional skills, acquired through higher education, within the Emmanuel Community. Instead, it revolves around "essentially domestic skills" (Rétif 2013: 421), primarily relational in nature, tied to her social role as a mother and wife.

The asymmetry in gender relations (with men associated with technical or political skills oriented outward, and women associated with relational skills oriented inward) reinforces the affirmation of sexual difference, thus justifying the emphasis on a certain division of labor within the Community ("[her husband] is very self-confident, likes to take responsibility, and when he makes a decision, he sticks to it. That's not my style at all, I'm not used to that"). The difference is even more pronounced given that Nicole's work, as mentioned in the interview, is voluntary, whereas her husband's work is paid.

Nonetheless, it is important to acknowledge that the configuration of the Emmanuel Community heavily relies on the "privatization of sociability" (Bozouls 2021: 110) which is fostered through the regular and discreet maintenance of relational capital. Within this context, Nicole's role and agency are far from

---

18   Interview with Nicole, layperson, member of the Emmanuel Community, November 18, 2019.

incidental. In fact, she epitomizes this phenomenon towards the end of the quotation when she discusses her presence in the "field" alongside her husband. Beyond the Catholic context, the significance of this relational work, particularly in fostering a sense of camaraderie, is akin to the role played by the wives of soldiers or diplomats (Loriol 2009).

However, it is important not to reduce this gendered division of religious work to a static configuration where women in these couples are forever confined to exclusively relational tasks. On the contrary, it seems that the agency developed by these women through their commitments in the Emmanuel Community encourages certain forms of "transgression of gendered assignments" (Rétif 2013: 434). In this regard, while Nicole emphasized in the interview her perceived lack of organizational and decision-making skills (considered masculine), she acknowledges that in practice she has the lead in many decisions ("I'm the one writing the teachings, I'm the one drawing up the plans, and he fits in, and it's worked really well like that. And it's really me who's taken over the teachings").

This type of discrepancy between the gender representations associated with a particular form of gendered division of religious work and the actual day-to-day management of commitments appeared regularly in my fieldwork. While reproducing a 'traditional' asymmetry in gender relations, the women in these relationships acquire an agency which in practice goes beyond most of the conventional avenues for commitment offered by the Catholic Church (e.g. involvement in associations, parishes, or service to the diocese). My research corpus shows that in those cases where couples decide to join the Emmanuel Community, the initiative mostly stems from the women. This sexual dimorphism, to some extent reflecting a classic phenomenon within Catholicism (Langlois 1995), is also evident in the interviews conducted with their husbands. Women often take the lead, even interrupting their husbands.

The everyday familialism manifested within the Emmanuel Community is reflected in its governance. While the organization promotes a certain level of equality between women and men, the governance structure centered around the dyad of the couple is influenced by gender representations that result in a gendered division of religious work. Men, who tend to reinvest their professional skills, are assigned more frequently to management tasks, while women, utilizing their relational skills, are primarily responsible for the discreet maintenance of relational capital. However, the agency acquired by women within the Emmanuel Community tends to complicate this traditional pattern. In addition to governance, which I have chosen to focus on, everyday familialism also influences various aspects of marital life, including sexuality, through the promotion of "natural methods" of birth control within the Community (Dolbeau 2021).

Nonetheless, as noted by British sociologist Jon Bernardes, "'family ideology' comprises, among others, the ideologies of masculinity, femininity, motherhood, fatherhood, and many more" (Bernardes 1985: 278). Within the Emmanuel Community, everyday familialism extends beyond models of masculinity and femininity for married couples. The case of the priests serving in the Community, who are themselves affected by these dynamics, deserves particular attention.

4. Community priests shaped by everyday familialism

The following excerpt from an interview with a former high official of the Emmanuel Community (now in his fifties and a member for about thirty years), carries significant implications and will serve as a guiding principle for my analysis.

> I see priests who live all alone in presbyteries [...]. They have a lifestyle of old bachelors; they go to bed at such and such an hour. So of course, you have to pay attention to the lifestyle, but it's almost a kind of imprisonment on their lives, and in fact, who is attracted to this priestly way of life? [...] I met a young priest, well a young priest... in his forties, who said to me "you know, I haven't given any vocations, I don't have any children" he said, in the professional sense of course, and it was so sad... And in fact, of course, I didn't dare tell him because it was too violent, but when I saw his way of life, I said to myself: "but what young person, normally constituted, is going to want to go through that?" In any case, I wouldn't want my children to go through that. So, he said to me, "But I've put on a cassock" and so on (*laughs*). "Do you think the cassock will attract young people? That's not what's going to attract, lad". I didn't tell him like that, obviously. [...] So I'm not saying that Community life is a bulwark against all faults because I can tell you that [since the start of his involvement] I've seen a lot. But I think it's a more solid bulwark, stronger, with dikes that are stronger against rising waters. [...] In fact, we have quite a strong life. And I see in particular the priests, the seminarians [...] I see they have something different, they have a life of closeness, very, very strong, and then they are brought together by lay people, the lay people say things to them, encour-

age them, say "well have you seen how you're dressed there?" or "you smell of sweat" or I don't know things like that. "Are you getting enough sleep?" and stuff like that. You can say that to a guy, or a girl for that matter if you know that you love him. Otherwise, you're a dull old bore.[19]

Firstly, this excerpt clearly illustrates how the figure of the Emmanuel Community priest is constructed in constant relation to the concept of the "communion of states of life". This concept, which is disseminated within several Charismatic communities, emphasizes a certain equality (in complementarity) between clergy and laypeople. Members of the Emmanuel Community are considered "brothers" and "sisters" of the Community before their clerical or lay status is mentioned. This "communion of states of life" is evident at the group level of the Emmanuel Community, through the promotion of family life, with a particular emphasis on the figure of the father. This emphasis on fatherhood draws inspiration from the ideal of priestly masculinity that is promoted within the Emmanuel Community. In addition to the weekly household, which serves as the primary setting for the dissemination of this "gender project"[20] within the group, the influence of the family can be observed at various levels of Community life, particularly in the training of seminarians. Frédéric, a cleric of the Community, discusses the importance of the figure of the father as a reference point for seminarians, positioning them to mature from "retarded teenagers" into future "fathers" after their ordination:

> It's also a danger for seminarians to have their own little armchair, their own little timetable, their own little life balance, to put their feet under the table, the dishes are brought to them, and then they wipe the dishes. It's a real danger. These are young people aged 27/28... Our friends at the same age are engaged in life. So, we have to avoid turning seminarians into retarded teenagers, through a suitable system. It's a vision to have. [...] Well, here we have a generation that comes from divorced families for the most part, and I remember at one point in my seminary there were a good number of young people whose parents were divorced. So how do we deal with this kind of issue? It's not easy. But I think we still need to improve on the quality of support, but support that is appropriate for today's young

---

19 Interview with Philippe, layperson, member of the Emmanuel Community, November 7, 2019.
20 This concept, originally coined by Australian sociologist Raewyn Connell (Connell 1995), is employed by Josselin Tricou in his research (Tricou 2021: 47).

people. So, I've just mentioned the question of seminarians whose parents are divorced. So how do we help them to become 'fathers' themselves?[21]

This observation aligns with the findings of Josselin Tricou's doctoral research, where he identifies various clerical gender regimes operating within contemporary Catholicism. Specifically, Tricou refers to a "spousal" model promoted by several Charismatic communities, including the Emmanuel Community:

> In Charismatic communities that bring together individuals from various states of life [...], the heterosexual married couple often assumes a central role and is presented as a sacramental model of the Church, symbolizing the bride of Christ. This gender regime, which I will refer to as "spousal", [...] draws on nuptial symbolism and gained theological prominence with the influence of John Paul II. Within the context of the Church's increasing emphasis on "heterosexual culture" [...], the term "spousal" is used to signify God's plan, drawing an analogy between divine love and conjugal love. [...] These communities, through their practices, prioritize the image of the traditional couple (faithful and procreative) while incorporating modern elements such as expressive culture and a negotiated balance between investment within and outside the family. They also strive for a certain equality between women and men while respecting the concept of complementarity, with Christ remaining the head and the Church his body. (Tricou 2021: 349)

As evident from the statements made by the first interviewee of this section, the spousal model serves as a safeguard against the unappealing image of the "old bachelor" priest that is seemingly favored within the traditional diocesan circuit. François, a cleric in his fifties, discusses how he manages his celibacy, employing the figure of the "old bachelor" priest (and, conversely, the "family man") in his reflection.

> For us in the Community, the people in charge have always been couples. That hasn't been a problem for us, and I can see the human balance that it brings. I mean as a seminarian, as a young priest, this contact with families... For celibacy, it's super important. I think it gives you a real balance. It prevents us from becoming old bachelors (*laughs*), clearly. And above all, it also avoids, well I mean living with families, we realize that it's not any

---

21   Interview with Frédéric, cleric, member of the Emmanuel Community, February 21, 2020.

easier to be married [...], that married life, family life, is not easy. So, we're there to help each other. When I see a father who gets up very early every morning to take his time in worship before going to work. And I find it hard to get up? There you go. There's an emulation, a mutual support.[22]

The invocation of the figure of the "old bachelor" priest reflects a dual criticism: first, it critiques a perceived flawed priestly masculinity characterized by challenges in managing celibacy, emotional isolation, and immature behavior, among others. Secondly, it critiques pastoral and ecclesiological choices considered outdated, such as the priest as the sole manager of the parish and tendencies towards "clericalism". Furthermore, my respondents' embrace of the spousal model helps distance themselves from competing local gender regimes.

In the initial excerpt from the interview, the seemingly innocuous remark made by my respondent about the priest's cassock illustrates this phenomenon ("Do you think the cassock will attract young people? That's not what's going to attract, lad."). This criticism of the cassock, often expressed in a humorous manner, alludes to the imagery associated with a gender regime described by Josselin Tricou as "neo-sacerdotal":

> The restitutionist communities, on the other hand, have largely embraced the idealized image of the "good priest" from the nineteenth century. This image repositions the priest not as an equal, but as a superior to lay women and men. In this sense, I would categorize them as a neo-sacerdotal gender regime. Within these communities, the reaffirmation of the distinction between clergy and laity (based on the clerical monopoly over the management of salvation) is practically achieved through the resacerdotalization of the cleric. This involves the revival of priestly attributes such as the cassock and the sense of separation from the laity. As for the laymen and women who gravitate towards these communities and draw inspiration from them, they are expected to embody a traditional family and conjugal ideal. (ibid.: 285–286)

In France, the Saint-Martin Community[23] is perhaps the most prominent example of this regime. Jean-Joseph and Solène, who have been committed for

---

22 Interview with François, cleric, member of the Emmanuel Community, September 3, 2020.
23 Founded by Jean-François Guérin (1929–2005) in 1976, in Genoa.

over thirty years in the Emmanuel Community and are in their seventies, spent several years in a parish run by priests from the Saint-Martin Community. In an interview, they discuss the differences they perceive between the Saint-Martin Community and the Emmanuel Community.

> *Solène:* In the Emmanuel Community, a priest is a priest, of course, but he's also a brother, and that's a strong concept that's not known in many places. And in the Saint-Martin Community, they are fathers. There's no notion of brothers... I mean of being close as brothers. The priests of the Emmanuel Community are also fathers, but they are first and foremost brothers. [...] In the Emmanuel Community, you're in a household with priests, for example, so they share something profound. If they share the Word of God, what does it do in their lives? The priests of the Saint-Martin Community, well if you're in contact with a priest maybe, but it's not the same thing.
>
> *Jean-Joseph:* Their community time is very important, and certainly brings a lot to priests in general. It's a way of life that we envy in our community. They set an example for us in that respect, and then we set an example for them in other ways. [...]
>
> *I:* Any other differences?
>
> *Jean-Joseph:* Oh well, they have Latin for example. They like to have one Gregorian mass a week. Well, I went to a monastery when I was a kid and I'm delighted. But from a pastoral point of view, I wonder, do people understand? Do they like it? So, statistically, they have a lot of vocations to the priesthood, so there's something about Latin, about the sacred, about I don't know what. There's something there. But for me, for us I think, Latin was rejected. We found that all the texts we could read in French, the luck we had, didn't exist. So, we discovered that. [...]
>
> *Solène:* If only to experience mass. We used to experience it differently. Now that it's in French, we understand what's going on better. Well, we never understand much. We experience it better. And when we have to go back to Latin, it's a bit hard. In a monastery [...] it's fine, I don't know how to put it, but in the middle of the city, it seems more difficult. But that's the way they do things. [...]
>
> *Jean-Joseph:* And their all-black look (laughs).

Solène: No, it doesn't matter.

Jean-Joseph: Oh it does...[24]

It is important to highlight the interconnection between pastoral and ecclesiological choices and the clerical gender system for Jean-Joseph: the relationship between clergy and laity, the use of Latin, the distinctive "all-black look". This deliberate departure from a neo-sacerdotal gender regime carries particular significance, especially considering the relatively competitive context between New Ecclesial Movements (ibid.: 360–365). Indeed, several of these groups, including the Saint-Martin Community, share a similar socio-religious background with the Emmanuel Community.

Furthermore, within the Emmanuel Community itself, some young priests have started wearing the cassock. This change in attire, which extends beyond the Community's context, is often met with a slight sense of mistrust, usually accompanied by humor, from older Community priests who view it as a sign of "clericalization". It is worth noting that the criticism of the clericalization of younger generations of priests also extends to the laity, with older members accusing them of maintaining an excessive reverence for the clerics of the Community. In an interview, a former member in his sixties, who is a layman, expressed his observations: "I've noticed that laypeople today show more deference to priests than we did back in our days [with the Emmanuel Community]. A priest was first and foremost a brother. But I see the new generations referring to them as 'Father so-and-so'".[25] This apprehension of clericalization underscores, in negative, the centrality of everyday familialism in shaping the Emmanuel Community as a group. Finally, it should be acknowledged that the egalitarian representation associated with the "communion of states of life", similar to the gendered division of religious work mentioned earlier, needs some qualification due to the diverse situations experienced by my interviewees in the field. In practice, interviews occasionally reveal a certain competition for authority between the couples in leadership positions and the Community priests.

---

24 Interview with Solène and Jean-Joseph, laypeople, members of the Emmanuel Community, June 11, 2019.

25 Interview with Pierre-Henri, layperson, former member of the Emmanuel Community, February 12, 2019.

5. Conclusion

In summary, everyday familialism serves as a significant driving force for the construction of social forms within the Emmanuel Community. It is primarily based on the (re)production of a particular lifestyle prevalent among the upper classes, which constitutes the background of the majority of its members. This lifestyle fosters a sense of communal familiarity among Catholics from a similar background. Central to this lifestyle is the promotion of a "privatization of sociability" where the discreet maintenance of relational connections is primarily the responsibility of women within Community couples (Bozouls 2021). This form of couple-to-couple sociability is accompanied by a religious homogeneity that encourages a strong ethos of commitment. This everyday familialism permeates all aspects of Community life, ranging from the organization of Community parishes to the governance of the organization, and even influences the model of masculinity promoted among clerical members.

Outside the boundaries of the Emmanuel Community, everyday familialism sheds light on the transformations occurring in contemporary Catholic social dynamics. While there are partial overlaps with other typologies of Catholicism, such as "observant" (Raison du Cleuziou 2019) or "identity" Catholics (Dumons and Gugelot 2017), everyday familialism stands out through several specific characteristics. One of these features is the emphasis on catering to the nuclear family through the provision of services and the dissemination of discourses related to the nuclear family. This focus on the family unit is accompanied by a promotion of increased responsibility for laypeople, particularly married couples, supported by the idea of a certain equality with the clerics. Moreover, everyday familialism fosters a form of privatization of sociability, where social engagement is primarily channeled within the confines of the family. Furthermore, within the framework of familialism, specific sexual practices are often propagated, notably the adoption of "natural methods" of birth control. This reflects a broader interest in promoting a particular approach to sexuality and reproduction within the context of family life.

However, it is crucial to acknowledge that this everyday familialism within the Emmanuel Community is not free from internal contradictions. One noteworthy example is the complex and challenging question of the lifelong engagement with the Community and of the children raised in it. This issue has posed significant challenges and generated debates and discussions among Community members for an extended period. Starting from the second half of the 1990s, the first generation of members, who possessed strong personal charisma, gradually stepped back from leadership positions within the organization. However, in addition to high-profile departures of long-standing members, the abandonment of religious practice among several children of these first-generation community members raises concerns within the organization. Faced with the relative failure of passing down the Catholic faith within several families, an unprecedented internal reflection took place regarding the status of children inside the Emmanuel Community. In this context, and as part of a broader sequence of relaxing the prerequisites for community engagement, several adjustments have been implemented since the 2000s. These include improvements in the "children's service" during Community weekends and sessions in Paray-le-Monial as well as a moderation of the internal discourse on the primacy of Community commitment. However, in practice, tensions between community life and family life are not entirely resolved and persist to this day. These tensions are particularly complex to address and grasp for the researcher. Indeed, the dissemination of rhetoric emphasizing the proper transmission of these Catholics, aligning with discourses on the proper reproduction of socioeconomic elites, contributes to establishing a form of community silence (or at least discomfort) regarding failures in transmission. Although examples of successful Community dynasties are regularly highlighted by my interviewees (and in the organization's literature), narratives of the failures in transmission, are less frequently and indirectly publicized. This observation aligns with the findings articulated by historian Claude-Isabelle Brelot regarding the lack of research on the phenomenon of social downward mobility among the elite. According to Brelot, "visibility of notoriety imposes itself [on historians], while social memory requires concrete evidence, and the downwardly mobile become invisible" (Brelot 2000).

Bibliography

Aubourg, Valérie (2016): "L'Oraison des mamans: Un nouvel entre-soi religieux" In: Ethnologie française, 46/2, pp. 323-334.

Aubrey, Lisa (2001): "Gender, Development, and Democratization in Africa" In: Journal of Asian and African Studies, 36/1, pp. 87-111.

Béraud, Céline (2007): Prêtres, diacres, laïcs: révolution silencieuse dans le catholicisme français, Le lien social, Paris: Presses Universitaires de France.

Béraud, Céline (2020): "The Catholic Opposition to Gender and Sexual Equality in France: Reviving the Traditional Condemnation of Homosexuality During the Debates on Marriage for All?", In: Marco Derks/Mariecke Van Den Berg (eds.), Public Discourses About Homosexuality and Religion in Europe and Beyond, Cham: Springer International Publishing, pp. 241-260.

Béraud, Céline/Portier, Philippe (2015): Métamorphoses Catholiques, acteurs, enjeux et mobilisations depuis le mariage pour tous, Paris: Éditions de la Maison des sciences de l'homme.

Bernardes, Jon (1985): "'Family Ideology': Identification and Exploration" In: The Sociological Review, 33/2, pp. 275-297.

Bozouls, Lorraine (2021): "Travail domestique et production d'un style de vie. Les femmes au foyer de classes supérieures" In: Travail, genre et sociétés, 46/2, pp. 97-114.

Brelot, Claude-Isabelle (2000): "Introduction Conflits et déclassement: La légitimité de l'histoire des Élites en question", In: Cahiers d'histoire, 45/4, unpaginated. http://journals.openedition.org/ch/391.

Brustier, Gaël (2014): Le mai 68 conservateur: que restera-t-il de la Manif pour tous?, Paris: Cerf.

Connell, Raewyn (1995): Masculinities, Berkeley: University of California Press.

Dolbeau, Samuel (2021): "The Politicisation of French Catholics on Intimate Issues Through the Promotion of Lay Expertise: A Case Study Based on the Emmanuel Community's Magazine *Il est vivant!* (1975–2018)" In: Claude Proeschel/David Koussens/Francesco Piraino (eds.), Religion, Law and the Politics of Ethical Diversity: Conscientious Objection and Contestation of Civil Norms, Routledge Studies in Religion and Politics, Abingdon, Oxon and New York, NY: Routledge, pp. 175–192.

Dumons, Bruno/Gugelot, Frédéric (2017): Catholicisme et identité: regards croisés sur le catholicisme français contemporain (1980–2017), Signe des temps, Paris: Karthala.

Fath, Sébastien (2008), Dieu XXL: la révolution des megachurches (= Frontières), Paris: Autrement.

Favier, Anthony (2021): "Avec l'aide et aux frontières de la médecine: L'accompagnement pseudo-médical des homosexuels catholiques en France (des années 1960 au moment de la Manif pour tous)" In: Émulations 38, pp. 49-67.

Landron, Olivier (2004): Les communautés nouvelles: Nouveaux visages du catholicisme français, Histoire, Paris: Cerf.

Langlois, Claude (1995): "'Toujours plus pratiquantes'. La permanence du dimorphisme sexuel dans le catholicisme français contemporain" In: Clio 2, unpaginated. http://journals.openedition.org/clio/533.

Lenoir, Rémi (1999): "La Question Familiale: Familialisme d'Église, Familialisme d'État." In: French Politics, Culture & Society 17/3-4, pp. 75–100.

Loriol, Marc (2009): "La carrière des diplomates français: entre parcours individuel et structuration collective." In: SociologieS, unpaginated. http://journals.openedition.org/sociologies/2936.

Ollitrault, Sylvie (2008): Militer pour la planète: Sociologie des écologistes, Rennes: Presses Universitaires de Rennes.

Raison du Cleuziou, Yann (2019): Une contre-révolution catholique: Aux origines de La Manif pour tous, Paris: Seuil.

Rétif, Sophie (2013): Logiques de genre dans l'enseignement associatif: Carrières et pratiques militantes dans des associations revendicatives, Nouvelle bibliothèque de thèses. Science politique, Paris: Dalloz.

Soothill, Jane E. (2007): Gender, social change and spiritual power: Charismatic Christianity in Ghana, Studies of religion in Africa, Leiden and Boston: Brill.

Stambolis-Ruhstorfer, Michael/Tricou, Josselin (2018): "La lutte contre la 'théorie du genre' en France: pivot d'une mobilisation religieuse dans un pays sécularisé" In: Roman Kuhar/David Paternotte (eds.), Campagnes anti-genre en Europe: des mobilisations contre l'égalité, Lyon: Presses Universitaires de Lyon, pp. 143-166.

Tricou, Josselin (2021): Des soutanes et des hommes: Enquête sur la masculinité des prêtres catholiques, Paris: Presses Universitaires de France.

Valla-Chevalley, Geneviève (2009): Le conseil conjugal et familial, Trames, Toulouse: Erès.

van Lier, Rick (2022): "Forces et fragilités au sein des communautés nouvelles catholiques." In: Laval théologique et philosophique 78/2, pp. 269-292.

Sources

Interview with Pierre-Henri, layperson, former member of the Emmanuel Community, February 12, 2019.

Interview with Solène and Jean-Joseph, laypeople, members of the Emmanuel Community, June 11, 2019.

Interview with Philippe, layperson, member of the Emmanuel Community, November 7, 2019.

Interview with Nicole, layperson, member of the Emmanuel Community, November 18, 2019.
Interview with Sophie, layperson, January 29, 2020.
Interview with Françoise, layperson, January 30, 2020.
Interview with Frédéric, cleric, member of the Emmanuel Community, February 21, 2020.
Interview with François, cleric, member of the Emmanuel Community, September 3, 2020.

Web References

Communauté de l'Emmanuel. "Qui sommes nous?" Accessed September 5, 2023. https://emmanuel.info/qui-sommes-nous/.
Communauté de l'Emmanuel. "Amour&Vérité." Accessed September 5, 2023. https://emmanuel.info/france/amour-et-verite/.

The Capital of Closed Churches
Heritage Buildings as Social Entrepreneurship in Quebec

Hillary Kaell

Abstract *Across North America, historic churches are rapidly closing. The problem is especially acute in urban areas where these buildings often house community organizations. Graham Singh, an Anglican pastor and non-profit CEO in Montreal, is promoting a solution: remake churches into community hubs. For Singh and his team, hubs are an opportunity for Christians to leverage their primary asset – tax-free land – and become full partners in the public sphere. Based on anthropological fieldwork, this chapter argues, first, that more scholarship should consider social entrepreneurship as a key area where religion and market meet, beyond much-studied neo-Pentecostal growth churches and prosperity gospel. Instead, Singh and his team are working to define entrepreneurship as social by dint of its physical embeddedness in historic churches. Doing so, they consciously adapt cutting-edge financial trends by positioning hubs as a smart real estate investment for private investors with social purpose goals. In this view, church property, supported by private investment, becomes central to reinvigorating Christian influence in the public sphere. In keeping with the theme of this volume, this chapter's second contribution is to suggest that community hubs might therefore be considered an intriguing new social form within North American Christianity, which derives value from its location at the border of historically religious forms (heritage churches), economic forms (corporate investment), and the public sphere.*

Keywords Christianity, economy, finance, heritage, material religion, public sphere, Quebec, social entrepreneur

1. Introduction

Montreal is a city of churches. While many religious congregations meet in storefronts or suburban new builds, the city is best known for large neo-gothic structures graced with steeples and stained-glass. Those are the churches to which Mark Twain (1881: 3) referred when, upon visiting Montreal, he famously quipped: "This is the first time I was ever in a city where you couldn't throw a brick without breaking a church window." Ever the satirist, Twain was exaggerating. But he was right in identifying this feature as particular to an urban environment that had been built by French Roman Catholics and expanded by British Anglicans. Both groups prized the construction of ornate stone churches that, once ritually consecrated to God, were pictured as eternal.

More than a century later, many such churches now figure in a growing crisis across North America and Western Europe. Historic churches are rapidly closing as dwindling congregations cannot afford to maintain them. Across Canada, ten thousand churches are slated to close within the next decade, which comprises more than a third of the churches currently owned by denominations; the situation is especially acute in Quebec (Okesson 2020: 207).

Enter Graham Singh. He is Rector of St. Jax, a Montreal Anglican Diocese plant in a church inaugurated as St. James the Apostle in 1864. Since Singh arrived in 2015, St. Jax has grown, by his estimation, into the largest Anglican parish east of Toronto with about 250 weekly worshippers. More importantly for Singh, the building is now a community hub run by a non-profit called Centre St. Jax – a system he believes will contribute to making churches financially solvent and socially vital. In 2018, Singh founded another non-profit, Trinity Centres Foundation (TCF), to support innovative financial solutions along the St. Jax model. His work is thus divided into three overlapping branches in which several people, including Singh, circulate: St. Jax, the parish where he serves as pastor; Centre St. Jax, an autonomous administrative organization that manages rentals and the community hub; and TCF, where Singh serves as CEO.

In their introduction to this volume, Maren Freudenberg and Astrid Reuter position "social forms" as a key conceptual framework in sociological studies of religion. At base, these forms refer to structures of social interaction, which, as they note, derive from a heuristic proposed at the turn of the twentieth century, initially by Max Weber (1958 [1905]) and elaborated by his friend, theologian Ernst Troeltsch (1931 [1912]). Troeltsch's model identified three forms of organization: church, sect, and mysticism. Over the intervening century, sociologists have refined, rejected, and reclaimed the typology. For example, sociologist of religion Lorne Dawson applauds its universal applicability, which he sees as the goal of any (social) science "with its regulatory ideals of generalization, theory construction, empiricism, and even prediction" (2009: 534). Other contemporary sociologists, wrestling with how the legacy of these ideal analytical types correspond with empirical realities, have responded by multiplying variants of the social form to include aspects such as community, event, and market exchange. Sociologists have also studied how social forms blend, especially in organizations that, as Freudenberg and Reuter put it during a workshop on social forms in Bochum, Germany, in March 2023, are located on the border between social fields, such as religious charity organizations where economic logics compete with religious ideas and semantics.

While as an anthropologist I have little at stake in this debate, it provides an opening to examine Graham Singh's model of overlapping churches and non-profits, which is certainly located on the border between social fields. More particularly, Freudenberg and Reuter's invitation to think about the competition between economic logics and religious ideas provides an opportunity for me to reflect on the economic component of Singh's work. Sociologists have pioneered an approach to economics that, paraphrasing Freudenberg and Reuter at the workshop in Bochum, is the quantification of an originally economic idea that is religiously reinterpreted. What they mean is that sociologists have taken statistical data about churches and interpreted it through the lens of free-market competition. As an example, they note sociologist Robert Wuthnow's metaphor of "church shopping" in U.S. Christianity (2007) referring to how people seek out churches that suit them rather than retaining membership in the same institution as their parents. Another example, especially prevalent among sociologists of North American religion, is the market exchange metaphor introduced and widely circulated as a "new paradigm" in the 1990s (Jelen 2002) to explain how denominational churches differ from historic and state-funded churches across much of Europe. This metaphor-come-theory of religion proposed that denominationalism created free-market church competition, which resulted in more choices (supply) that has led to higher rates of attendance (demand). I am certainly not the first to express reservations about this model (for example, Gauthier and Martikainen 2016). Like other critics, I find troublesome the assumption that capitalist competition strengthens socio-religious commitments and, further, that one can quantify church 'health' based on the number of members or attendees.

Singh and his team likely agree with me on the first point and, as I discuss below, they certainly agree with me on the second.

Instead of using economic metaphors as an analytical tool, therefore, I am interested in studying empirically through anthropological field work how Christians, like Singh, consciously adapt market logics to the religious sphere. And this process is not one-way; it speaks to cutting-edge trends within investment circles too, as funders and private investors seek to prioritize "impact investing" and "social purpose" goals. This chapter offers a preliminary discussion of Singh's work based on research being carried out in Montreal by myself and post-doctoral researcher Sam Victor, along with our graduate student assistants Alexandre Duceppe-Lenoir and Sophie Ji. We began preliminary fieldwork in autumn 2022 and more focused fieldwork in March 2023. In this article, which I am writing in August 2023, I mainly draw on my early field notes related to TCF, some of Victor's field notes about St. Jax (as cited in the text), and my review of the St. Jax/TCF team's quite prodigious output on social media and the web.

More generally, I make the case that scholars of religion should devote more attention to social entrepreneurship as a key area where the blurred edges of religion and market meet. Positioning Singh as entrepreneur serves to expand the category beyond what anthropologists and other scholars of contemporary Christianity have called the "pastorpreneur" (Jackson 2004, 2011; Klaver 2015; Jennings 2017). The neologism, which combines "pastor" and "entrepreneur", refers to a (nearly always) male pastor who valorizes risk-taking individualism in his quest to build a mega-church. It fits snugly within a broader emphasis on neo-Pentecostals, growth churches, and the prosperity gospel that is typical of how scholars of religion discuss money and faith. Such ministries generally either operate without owning a building or they construct one in a hyper-modern style (Lehto 2020). A heritage building like St. Jax has no place in this literature, which is understandable since pastorpreneurs, as they have been defined, view attachments to such structures as irrelevant or even a problematic sign of stagnation. Clearly, then, neither the pastorpreneur nor metaphors of market competition are sufficient to capture the less intuitive kind of economic logic Singh's project suggests. As I show, his entrepreneurship is embedded in neoliberal capitalism, but it rejects a growth or prosperity model. Nor is it place-agnostic. Instead, Singh and his fellow travelers are working to define innovation and entrepreneurship as social by dint of its physical embeddedness in place. In keeping with the theme of this volume, I suggest that community hubs might therefore be considered an intriguing new social form within North American Christianity.

2. Introducing St. Jax

I borrow the phrase in my title – "the capital of closed churches" – from Graham Singh, who used it with respect to Montreal in a newspaper profile on his work (Schwartz 2021). Capital can refer to a primary location, which is what Singh meant, but it also refers to wealth in the form of money or other assets. This intersection of location, money, and assets is at the heart of Singh's work to address a church crisis in Canada.

Like most historic Anglican churches, a decade ago St. James the Apostle had a small standing congregation of older parishioners. The building was grand – a relic of a period when 80 per cent of Canada's wealth was controlled by people living in the neighborhood – and it is legally designated as a heritage site. While this designation adds social value, it creates an added economic burden as maintenance is more difficult and expensive. The congregation repeatedly asked Montreal's Bishop Mary Irwin-Gibson to fund repairs. The Bishop was unwilling to continue draining Diocesan coffers, yet she saw value in retaining the church and its land because of its location in one of the busiest sections of downtown. The area is characterized by shopping, tourism, and high-rises housing thousands of students, especially new arrivals from Asia. The land itself, the primary asset for most historic churches in Canada, is worth millions and the church benefits from a full property tax exemption.[1]

In 2015, Bishop Irwin-Gibson temporarily suspended operations at St. James and recruited Reverend Graham Singh, a Canadian working in England, to pastor a new church. Singh is deeply influenced by Holy Trinity Brompton (HTB), the UK church where he was trained at the cutting edge of the Anglican missional movement. Its ethos celebrates historic buildings but does not shy away from closing them if they cease to serve a congregation's mission. Besides being an expert in church planting, Singh also has a strong interest in social finance, having participated in Oxford Business School's

---

[1] Properties designated for religious use are exempt from taxation in Canada. Historic churches are grandfathered into this system but newer congregations in Montreal often fail to qualify because they do not own their own property or because city officials are unwilling to authorize exemptions for storefronts and other spaces.

Impact Innovations program. A year later, under Singh's guidance, St. James re-opened as St. Jax, a zippier and more bilingual name recalling "Jacques" (the French version of James). Most of the old congregants left and St. Jax, the parish, now shares its space with multiple partners, notably a circus troupe that performs in the sanctuary. Post-doctoral researcher Sam Victor vividly describes his first impression of the space in his fieldnotes:

> The vaulted wooden ceilings, the wooden paneling and ornamental carving, the storied engravings of the names of notable figures dating back to the nineteenth century, all contributed to what Graham likes to call the "wow effect." [...] The absence of pews (folding chairs instead) and the black plywood stage juxtaposed the weighty historic feel of the rest of the space with a [sense] of temporariness, informality, dynamism, incompleteness, etc. Also, circus rigging was affixed to the wooden beams in the center of the ceiling...further adding to the porousness between backstage/production and front stage/performance.

In many ways, Singh embraces the ambiguity between a historic building with a "wow" factor and that informal and dynamic feel. It bespeaks his larger ethic.

Church sharing is hardly novel, and many congregations rent or donate space so it can be used by other congregations, charities, and non-profits (Alcoholics Anonymous is ubiquitous). Yet Singh's model differs from the norm in a few ways. First, he emphasizes the value of high-end profit-generating renters, not just the non-profits that church congregations normally identify as the ethically correct target group for their space. St. Jax rents space on a sliding scale, with events hosted by banks, for example, helping to subsidize other groups' use. Singh's ultimate goal is not that the host congregation essentially underwrites other groups' use of the space, but that the church itself – as a collective hub – becomes self-sustaining. For Singh, a hub does more than generate money: it serves a spiritual purpose by making the church accountable to the needs of the wider public. As he sees it, Christians have an important spiritual message to contribute to society but, because of the dismal recent history of the (mainly) Catholic Church in Quebec, all historic churches need to be given "permission", as Singh often puts it, to re-enter the public sphere.[2] Remaking churches into shared hubs responds to the community's needs and therefore

---

2   I have heard Singh use this word multiple times in conversation as well as in more formal sessions at TCF over the course of fieldwork.

gives Christians a license to become full partners in reimagining how to right societal wrongs, such as colonization (in which Singh recognizes Christian culpability), urban blight, and social isolation. Singh views hubs as an ethical imperative if churches are going to share their privileged status as major landholders, compounded by their exemption from property tax.

Shortly after reopening St. Jax, Singh founded Trinity Centres Foundation. As a non-profit, TCF aims to make land and buildings into positive assets for communities – both for the church congregations that own them and for the communities around them. Not surprisingly, one of TCF's favored solutions for historic churches with economic woes is the community hub. However, Singh and his team are not only speaking to Christian congregations. They also position community hubs as a smart real estate investment for private individuals and funders who want to broaden their portfolios to include "social impact" investments. In sum, Singh views Christian real estate, supported by private investment, as integral to retaining (or creating) Christian influence as an ethical guide in the public sphere. In this respect, the community hub, as a new social form, derives its value from its surprising location at the border of historically religious forms (heritage churches), economic forms (corporate investment), and the public sphere. Just *how* Christians will guide the public seems to be of less importance to Singh at this point than beginning the process of gaining permission, as he puts it, to sit at the table again.

3. Entrepreneurship, including that which is social

A social entrepreneur is usually defined as someone who meets people's needs through the marketplace, including generating income for shareholders, but with the primary goal of doing "good" rather than turning a profit. While this category of activity would seem to lend itself to analysis through studies of religion, very little recent social scientific work unites religion and entrepreneurship. Most relevant studies come from the fields of sociology, economics, management, and business. Scholars of religion, including anthropologists, have written little on the subject, and there is criticism of their as-yet "unreflective use of the term social entrepreneurship" (McVea/Naughton 2021).

Based on my survey of recent articles on religion and entrepreneurship, this critique is correct.[3] Most relevant studies define entrepreneurship as an individual's "predisposition" and "skills to create a business" and/or be self-employed (Paiva et. al. 2020: 2). In adding "social" to their analysis, they make the basic point that entrepreneurial work should be better framed in socio-cultural contexts, which includes religion (Dana 2010). As "depositories of values" (Dana 2009: 87), religions help complicate the classical economic assumption that rational individuals always maximize profits amid mechanical market forces. Though I concur with the general sentiment, this literature creates a confusion of terms: because it considers religion to be *ipso facto* "social", it assumes that religiously motivated entrepreneurship is always 'social entrepreneurship'. Thus, most studies I surveyed simply asked how an individual's beliefs (a "social factor") helped or hindered their economic activity, mainly small-scale businesses (Rundle/Lee 2022).[4]

Only 15 per cent (n=7) of studies in my survey used the definition of social entrepreneurship that is widely accepted in other fields, referring to balancing "business viability" (Kimura 2021) with socially useful outcomes (McVea/Naughton 2021). This definition accords with Graham Singh's goal to create self-sustaining and even profit-generating church buildings. Some studies also suggest that to be considered a "religious" entrepreneur, one must manifest one's beliefs at work (Roudy et al. 2016; Kimura 2021). A more intriguing definition, via a study of Belgian Catholicism, sees social entrepreneurship less as integrating a pre-existing set of beliefs into one's work and instead defines it as a set of personal qualities that can be developed much like spiritual expertise: it is "the capacity to deal skillfully with uncertainties, to experiment on a small scale, to collaborate in a co-creative way, to gather scarce resources, to allow failure, and to dare to draw critical lessons" (Vandewiele 2021: 133–34). The emphasis on small-scale experimentation, co-creation, and failure is very

---

3   Based on my analysis of a database compiled by my research assistant Alexandre Duceppe-Lenoir. It contains 48 social scientific articles published from 2018–2022 he found with the search terms "social entrepreneur*" and "religion" (Scopus, EBSCO, ATLA, Google Scholar). Nine other articles date from 2010–2017. The earliest, from 2009, corresponds with the first wave of studies on social entrepreneurship in business and associated fields.

4   Most studies conclude that religion motivates entrepreneurship by building networks, creating hope and confidence, and justifying economic actions (Agarwal/Jones 2022; Tovar-García 2022; Paiva et. al. 2020).

much in keeping with the St. Jax ethos adapted from the Anglican missional movement.

Neo-Pentecostal and Charismatic Christians are of significant interest to scholars; nearly a third of the articles (n=14) in my survey focused on these groups and many others mentioned them in passing. No other religious group appears as often. As (often) independent congregations focused on growth, these churches fit easily with discussions of branding, marketing, and the sociological 'marketplace' metaphor, noted above, that is structured largely on Evangelical forms of Christianity proliferating in a 'market' of religious choices. CEO pastors who build growth-oriented megachurches become the "obvious" example of the "market logic" of North American Christianity (Gorski 2022). The subset of this literature that emphasizes entrepreneurship focuses on economic self-determination and risk-taking, especially among pastors who plant, market, and grow new churches (Foppen et al. 2017).[5] Religious Studies scholar Mark Jennings (2017: 243), using the neologism "pastorpreneur", criticizes these pastors as celebrating "the risky neoliberal individual" to valorize innovation, creativity, and economic risk as a godly model of leadership in service of church growth. In this literature, African case studies dominate (Agyeman/Carsamer 2018; Nyamnjoh/Carpenter 2018; Gusman 2021; Resane 2022), which anthropologist Séraphin Balla (2021) suggests is due to the rise of Pentecostalism during a continent-wide economic collapse in the 1990s: the pastors' success seemed so remarkable in this context that it prompted scholarly interest.

While St. Jax is not an Evangelical or Pentecostal church, its model shares aspects of the neoliberal economics that characterize these "personalised and embodied" ministries (Klaver 2015: 149). By neoliberalism, I mean the idea that everything is potentially marketable, including oneself as a personal brand and "human capital" (Brown 2015: 36). A gifted leader who emphasizes collaboration, Singh is nevertheless highly attuned to how his qualities – young, non-White, bilingual – represent St. Jax and TCF, especially in the media. He prizes professional-quality photos and good marketing. He leverages

---

5 In the case of pastors, scholars imply that 'entrepreneurship' is social because it builds religious institutions. Studies on lay people imply it is social because religious values and networks support their (non-church) economic activities. In contrast to studies of Christianity, relevant work on Islam rarely focuses on leaders. It emphasizes laypeople, often those with little formal economic power, notably women (Karimi 2018; Ouragini 2019; Senda 2019) and/or migrants (Hüwelmeier 2013; Gusman 2021).

his personality – gregarious, entrepreneurial, innovative – to grow the St. Jax/TCF brand (my word, not his). Beyond Singh's personal style, however, his model is sharply differentiated from how scholars describe the "CEO pastor" and pastorpreneur. These paradigmatic types are often associated with digital platforms, emphasize church growth without limit, and are place agnostic. The last point refers to how places, let alone a specific building, are rarely viewed as integral to the work. As one guide to church planting puts it, "steeples and stained glass" merely burden Christians with costs and the weight of history (Ringdal 2022: 56). Innovation and entrepreneurship are about being modern, nimble, digital, and constantly growing out of one building and into another – if one has a building at all. Theologically, this model is adapted to independent Evangelical churches, especially to those that are newly established. It is much less compatible with historic congregations where church buildings are an important legacy and, as Singh argues, a key asset for social and financial innovation. Thus, Singh suggests an economic logic that is less intuitive, at least for social scientists studying Christianity.

4. The St. Jax Model of Social Entrepreneurship

The St. Jax and TCF model adapts components of social entrepreneurship to suit the challenges faced by many traditional mainline churches in North America. The TCF website described its goal as "applying a new social business model that generates both societal and economic value…enabling church properties to continue to facilitate positive change, while maintaining a secure financial future."[6] Church properties are essential in this process. Economically, Centre St. Jax generates value in part by renting church space for high-end activities at market rates to generate a self-sustaining financial system. Because church congregations often lack the expertise to negotiate in the real estate market, TCF also creates economic value through its consultancy arm: congregations in financial crisis can hire TCF to guide them through negotiations with buyers. These services are not free (initial assessments run from $15.000 to $20.000), but the promise is that professional consultants will help congregations attain their goals. One TCF recommendation is that congregations and denominations retain the land as an income-generating asset, even if the church building is sold. Working through TCF, Singh is also trying

---

6   Cf. https://trinitycentres.org/en/about-us.

to create a market for private investment. His hope is that high-end investors and philanthropic foundations will invest in historic church buildings as part of diversified "social impact" portfolios. This strategy exists more generally – it is sometimes called "purpose-driven property investment" – but Singh wants to include churches as a viable, and even crucial, generator of social impact.

As TCF's website notes, economic viability is twinned with societal value. For example, when Centre St. Jax rents at market rates, it provides deep discounts for renters, such as other churches and non-profits, that it sees as generating social value (what it calls its "Robin Hood policy").[7] When private investors make profits on their social impact portfolios, it provides infusions of capital so churches can carry on as community hubs, which, as I noted, Singh views as part of churches' ethical responsibility to share their space with a wider public. Ironically, then, private real estate investors become the key to saving churches from being sold and made into private real estate, which (for Singh) negates the building's capacity to act for the public good. Selling churches to developers is an outcome so frequent for buildings in lucrative urban areas, like St. Jax, that I have heard TCF members refer to condominium developers as "wolves circling their prey."

The St. Jax/TCF model is rooted in the social goals typical of social entrepreneurship. It also accords with how entrepreneurship values innovation, audacity, and risk-taking. This factor deserves more scholarly attention. For example, a recent study of Silicon Valley argues that its entrepreneurial culture replaces more traditional religious commitments by providing analogous feelings and attachments (Chen 2022). However, while it discusses the 'pastoral' model of leadership in Silicon Valley where entrepreneur CEOs inspire devotion from "faithful disciples" (ibid.: 42), it only implies that innovation might have spiritual value in these circles. Scholars have more directly discussed innovation and risk-taking – gendered as masculine virtues – in the context of studies of Evangelical/Charismatic Christian pastors cited above. In TCF's case, it emphasizes church communities rather than individual leaders, promising to help groups find "innovative new ways of delivering services, while advancing social inclusion and revitalizing communities and local neighbourhoods."[8] At TCF's eight-week introductory course for church board members, which I attended, Singh and his co-convenor Dave Harder repeatedly made explicit the link between innovation and risk taking. In every

---

7   Cf. http://stjax.org/our-story.
8   Cf. https://trinitycentres.org/en/about-us.

session, they pushed participants to forget the "fears" holding them back from taking the risks required to think "outside the box" about the future of their church buildings.

Sam Victor, post-doctoral researcher on this project, first alerted me to the importance for Singh of Holy Trinity Brompton's missional approach. His insight is useful in the context of entrepreneurship as well. Being "missional" is an orientation that developed among British Anglicans in the 1980s and spread to North American Evangelicals (Bielo 2011: 269). Holy Trinity Brompton, where Singh trained, is a flagship of this approach and it lists "audacity" as its first value.[9] St. Jax is also positively referred to as "audacious" by missional Christians with ties to Singh (Okesson 2020: 207). At a basic level, this orientation refers to being a missionary in one's own society, which missional Christians define as a secular, post-modern one. In North America, this view translates into harsh criticism of conservative, (often) suburban white Evangelicalism and its megachurches for being inauthentic and ineffective (Bielo 2011: 278). Missional Christians hold innovation in high regard, which leads to the idea that one must sometimes reject received norms and rules to make an impact. The main purpose is evangelism; one "breaks the rules" of secular society by creating clever communication strategies to spread the Gospel. These strategies – "ambient" forms, as per Matthew Engelke (2012) – aim to meet people where they are (that is, outside church buildings). They are often irreverent and fun, but their main distinguishing feature is how they generally avoid talking directly about God or church. For example, in one of his first acts as St. Jax pastor, Singh dressed up in a blue bunny suit and frolicked with spectators at the St Patrick's Day parade, posing for photos with a sign that read "#More Than The Bunny / #Plus qu'un lapin." As coverage in the local news noted, he did this "without bringing in notions of church or Jesus" – which Singh would argue is precisely why it did, in fact, succeed in drawing people for Easter Sunday worship (Schwartz 2021).

In our conversations, Victor applied this basic concept from missional Evangelicalism to the less intuitive realm of heritage governance. For Singh and his team, the same positive valuation of cleverness and innovation helps structure their approach to managing relations with bureaucratic partners in the municipality and government-funded heritage councils. The St. Jax team often view these partners as stifling creativity since pragmatic bureaucrats rarely share their visionary plans for revitalizing religious heritage across

---

9   Cf. https://htb.org/story.

North America. More specifically, the Quebec heritage council often manages the local projects it funds by imposing strong restrictions, such as mandating that churches work with approved, and more expensive, contractors for repairs.[10] Clever ways around some of these systems include, for example, partnering with a circus that can apply for government arts grants for which religious organizations are not eligible. In 2023, these funds paid for improvements to the church, including new bathrooms. Another workaround was how the team slotted the bathrooms into a preexisting hallway that did not significantly alter the church's interior, allowing them to skirt the need for a building permit which is a difficult bureaucratic undertaking in a heritage building.

Innovative solutions also serve missional teams well within their denominations where pastors fall under the aegis of larger structures, such as an Anglican Diocese.[11] Singh demonstrated this ethos at a luncheon with leaders from Montreal's Catholic Archdiocese.[12] In response to one of the invitees, he suggested that Catholic Canon Law was unduly restricting churches from becoming community hubs. "We need to find workarounds", he urged, with "a package of short cuts" through which "clever" Catholic leaders could find ways "to bend Canon Law". He illustrated with an example from his work in the UK where, as church planters, they faced an Anglican rule to prevent removing the pews. Missional church planters dislike pews since they view them as too 'churchy' and less open to mixed uses (Singh immediately removed all the pews when he arrived at St. Jax). In the UK case, the clever workaround consisted of relying on Archdeacons' capacity to grant a temporary license to remove 20 per cent of a church's pews at one time.[13] Singh and his fellow church planters would request a license, remove 20 per cent of the pews, then wait six weeks and approach the archdeacon to authorize another temporary

---

10   The Federal government is more hands off and private foundations can be flexible negotiation partners. Singh hopes to grow the latter funding stream, which is more amenable to tackling innovative society-scale questions.
11   The current Montreal Bishop supports Singh completely and it is she who recruited him. The situation could shift with a new Bishop, which points to the tensions of operating within an episcopal system. That said, it is a fiction that any entrepreneur acts alone; there are always social pressures and opportunities (Dana 2009).
12   The lunch, which I attended as part of my fieldwork, took place at St Jax church on May 11, 2023.
13   An archdeacon is a senior Anglican clergy member responsible for the buildings in multiple parishes.

license until the church was emptied. It took longer, but they were able to skirt the official Diocesan rule. Thus, a certain amount of subversion is a virtue if it accomplishes what Singh and his team view as socially productive ends.[14] At the luncheon, however, Singh's suggestion did not resonate: the Catholic leaders – likely because they lacked the missional esteem for audacity – responded that Canon Law posed no problem as far as they were concerned.

5. Land as Privilege and Asset

The most important aspect of social entrepreneurialism is the 'social', which as I have noted in my brief literature review is severely undertheorized in studies of religion. Perhaps a reason for this lacuna derives from emic – that is, Evangelical Christian – perspectives on the social: from this vantage point, all Christian activities related to Evangelism are 'social' insofar as it addresses a pressing societal need for salvation. Singh agrees that salvation is important, but he defines his project in keeping with more widely accepted views that the "social" in social entrepreneurship refers to something other than Christian witness. Singh also distinguishes his model from more typical "church sharing" where congregations rent out space merely to pay the bills. Instead, he views property as a privilege and an asset for historic congregations, through which they can make social impacts.

Singh's emphasis on property derives partly from his training at Holy Trinity Brompton (HTB), where missional Anglicanism orients it toward historic buildings. By contrast, the missional movement adapted by non-denominational Evangelicals, as is most typical in North America, values physical places insofar as they create opportunities for Evangelism but does not value historic buildings per se (Bielo 2011). Of its church planting mission, HTB writes, "Historically significant and beautiful Anglican churches – often facing closure – have been restored and are now home to vibrant, growing, worshipping communities that have significant impact on their local areas."[15] With HTB, Singh shares an emphasis on historic buildings as the impetus for vibrant communities that impact the wider culture. However, HTB's goal of "evangelizing the nation and transforming society" takes place in a country where it is the established and majority church (represented on the same webpage by photos of a

---

14   Wording in this sentence drawn from Sam Victor's fieldnotes.
15   Cf. https://htb.org/story.

visit from none other than King Charles).[16] For Anglicanism in Canada the situation is complicated. It was never the established church and it always catered to a privileged minority. In Montreal, this is especially true. Singh is highly aware that he speaks within a historic French Catholic-majority culture that has traditionally viewed the English as its colonizers. He is also explicit about representing a colonial system that divested indigenous people of land, which is a key public issue in Canada. As a result, Singh creatively adapts HTB's focus on churches in a Canadian context to emphasize justice and access as social values.

Singh views societal ills, including power differentials between white settlers and indigenous people or more recent immigrants, as being partly redressed if historic churches, like St. Jax, come to think of their access to untaxed and centrally located space as a privilege that it is incumbent upon them to share. These privileges are not available to more recently arrived religious groups that cannot afford to buy land or qualify for property tax exemptions under restrictive government policies (on similar difficulties in Europe, cf. Cao 2022: 4). Singh also recognizes that historic churches stand because of the land and labor of others, including indigenous people, who were never part of the historically white, affluent, Anglophone congregation at St. James. Justice is making sure others now have access to the space, which, for Singh, makes real estate into a medium through which a traditional Anglican (and Catholic) concern with place can become a cross-denominational, and non-religious, Canada-wide issue about justice. It also signals another difference from missional Evangelicals who emphasize access to leadership for people traditionally excluded – for example, women, recent immigrants, or African Americans. The purpose is to make congregations internally stronger in order to, ultimately, focus outward on attracting more adherents. Singh agrees on the need for more diverse leadership, but his focus is not on growing a congregation; it is on reorienting church buildings outward as a widely usable resource. As a result, TCF rejects classic indicators of church 'health' based on the number of members or attendees. It also rejects the church growth model that scholars often criticize as a "market logic" (Gorski 2022). In TCF's investing school, for example, Singh and Harder urge church board members to change what they call the "limiting" or "doom" mindset that merely equates church success with questions such as, how do we get more families and how do we grow our numbers? Instead, they urge a "wonder" or "delight" mindset

---

16 Cf. ibid.

that asks, how can we serve our neighbors' needs, especially in terms of space? With this mindset, church health and success are measured according to how well congregations share their land and buildings with others.

However, land is not only a privilege: it is also churches' main financial and social asset. TCF calls for "the development of inclusive social ecosystems, leveraging the land wealth of Canada's faith communities as a foundation."[17] The website describes one impetus for Centre St. Jax as a "new way [...] to revive an older idea of a church's role in society, which is to provide for the temporal needs of the community, but to do so in a radically open and inclusive manner."[18] Scholars are often less sanguine. For example, sociologist Danièle Hervieu-Léger bases her analysis of France on the Weber/Troeltsch triad from which Freudenberg and Reuter derive the concept of 'social form' in this volume. Hervieu-Léger (2002: 102) contrasts newer 'sect-type' religious groups in France with an established 'church-type' (Catholicism) that uses its inherited hold over territory to magnify "the fiction of being all-encompassing". Power is obviously at stake in the context I have been discussing as well. After all, Christians are not proposing to give over land and walk away. In fighting privatization, they are reviving the foundational role of church in "social ecosystems", as TCF puts it. By retaining historic structures *in situ*, Christian iconography, history, and presence remain vital in the urban landscape. By opening the building to those who have been traditionally excluded – albeit without asking them to join the congregation – these users are interpolated into a Christian story.

However, unlike Hervieu-Léger's model that sees the main source of tension as intra-religious (that is, between 'sects' and a dominant 'church'), St. Jax demonstrates how 'church' itself may in fact be a shifting constellation of churches, non-profits, diocesan actors, private investors, and philanthropic foundations – all of which become stakeholders by dint of their social and/or financial investments in a single building. In his assessment of St. Jax, pastor and missiologist Greg Okesson calls it "a place with multiple expressions of church" (2020: 215).[19] If we think in terms of social forms, it is a constellation on the border of many social fields. With such a complex structure, it is

---

17 Cf. https://trinitycentres.org/ecosystem.
18 Cf. http://stjax.org/en/home.
19 Singh recommended Okesson's book to me as largely reflecting his own point of view. The two are also close colleagues, Singh having started a ThD at Asbury Seminary where Okesson serves as Provost.

no surprise that St. Jax is unlikely to solve the tension between property as social justice and church asset. In fact, leaving room for ambiguity is how the St. Jax model succeeds. It can become multiple things for multiple people and – in good entrepreneurial fashion – embraces change as a constant.

6. Concluding Thoughts

The St. Jax model is located on what this volume calls the border between social fields. Historic church buildings are the tangible remnants of an era when 'church' (the ideal type in Troeltsch/Weber's sense) was not far from the empirical reality in Quebec. The community hub might thus be considered a new social form that aims to reconfigure 'church' as a constellation of people and projects in response to contemporary society's negative valuation of religion's public role in Quebec. Hubs also address a pragmatic issue at the heart of the church building crisis in North America: these historic structures benefit from central locations and tax exemptions yet are enormously expensive for dwindling congregations to maintain, especially if they are heritage sites. Sociological models that assume North American religious success mimics economic supply and demand ('strong' churches are defined by the number of individuals seeking membership) would dismiss these historic churches as moribund relics. By contrast, Singh's entrepreneurial model recruits the market – mainly in terms of real estate rentals and private investment – to fund heritage churches and thus secure historic Christianity's enduring, but evolving, public influence.

Devoting more attention to social entrepreneurship, and more carefully defining the 'social' in this context, offers a novel way for scholars of religion to explore the permeable border of religious and economic social forms. Identifying Singh as an entrepreneur helps broaden the category beyond the current emphasis in studies of Christianity on what scholars have called "CEO pastors" and "pastorpreneurs". As noted, the St. Jax model harnesses market logics embedded in neoliberal capitalism, most obviously in terms of private investment, but rejects the church growth and prosperity gospel movements to which anthropologists and sociologists so often turn to study Christianity and the market. Singh's entrepreneurial embrace of audacity and innovation colors his outreach as a pastor, his work with partners in the heritage sector, and his integration of cutting-edge trends where private investors seek "impact investing" or "social purpose" goals. Singh's ambition for TCF is to position it as "one of Canada's most significant social purpose real estate investment offerings."[20]

The St. Jax/TCF model foregrounds property as a key privilege and asset of historic Christian congregations. In this respect, it contributes to the sociological project of identifying how new social forms emerge in response to changes in thinking about religion. In Quebec, such changes have been drastic since the 1960s, resulting in a massive reorganization of institutional religious forms. The St. Jax/TCF model also contributes to the ongoing interest among anthropologists of Christianity to understand how historic churches, notably Anglicanism and Catholicism, reposition themselves as publicly relevant within the countries where they are historically rooted by using material spaces and objects in ways that are "ambient" (Engelke 2012; Kaell 2017) and "banal" (Oliphant 2021). Singh's model adds a new twist to this ongoing conversation as it makes private rentals and investment into a major basis for retaining church buildings as public spaces. Another twist lies in how it counsels congregations to devolve control over their buildings to the larger community in order to reinvigorate the power of Christianity as a partner for social good within the putatively secular city.

Bibliography

Agarwal, Ruchi/Jones, William J. (2022): "Social Media's Role in the Changing Religious Landscape of Contemporary Bangkok." In: Religions 13/5, pp. 1–17.

Agyeman, E. A./Carsamer, E. (2018) "Pentecostalism and the Spirit of Entrepreneurship in Ghana: The Case of Maame Sarah Prayer Camp in Ghana." In: Journal of Contemporary African Studies 36/3, pp. 303–318.

Balla, Seraphin (2021): "Pentecostal Pastors in Cameroon as Social Success Stories: An Anthropological Perspective." In: Africa Today 67/2, pp. 41–61.

Bielo, James (2011): "Purity, Danger, and Redemption: Notes on Urban 'Missional' Evangelicals." In: American Ethnologist 38/2, pp. 267–280.

Brown, Wendy (2015): Undoing the Demos: Neoliberalism's Stealth Revolution, Brooklyn NY: Zone Books.

---

20 "About Us", Accessed 20 March 2023 (https://trinitycentres.org/en/about-us).

Cao, Nanlai (2022): "Merchants and Missionaries: Chinese Evangelical Networks and the Transnational Resacralization of European Urban Spaces." In: Global Networks, pp. 1–16.
Chen, Carolyn (2022): Work Pray Code: When Work Becomes Religion in Silicon Valley, Princeton, NJ: Princeton.
Dana, Leo Paul (ed.). (2010). Entrepreneurship and Religion, Cheltenham, UK: Edward Elgar.
Dana, Leo Paul (2009) "Religion As an Explanatory Variable for Entrepreneurship." In: The International Journal of Entrepreneurship and Innovation, 10/2, pp. 87–99.
Dawson, Lorne L. (2009): "Church-sect-cult: Constructing Typologies of Religious Groups." In: Clarke, Peter B. (ed.), The Oxford Handbook of the Sociology of Religion, Oxford: Oxford University Press, pp. 526–544.
Engelke, Matthew (2012): "Angels in Swindon: Public Religion and Ambient Faith in England." In: American Ethnologist 39/1, pp. 155–170.
Foppen, Annemarie/Pass, Stefan Paas/van Saane, Joke W. (2017): "Personality Traits of Church Planters in Europe." In: Journal of Empirical Theology 30, pp. 25–40.
Gauthier, François/Martikainen, Tuomas (2016 [2013]): Religion in Consumer Society: Brands, Consumers and Markets, New York and London: Routledge.
Gorski, Philip (2022): "Fragmentation of the Sacred or Disenchantment of the World? An Alternative Narrative of Western Modernity." In: Social Science Historical Association conference, Chicago, IL.
Gusman, Alessandro (2021): "'We Make the Voice of These People Heard': Trajectories of Socioeconomic Mobility among Congolese Pastors in Kampala, Uganda." In: Africa Today 67/23, pp. 85–102.
Hervieu-Leger, Danièle (2002): "Space and Religion: New Approaches to Religious Spatiality in Modernity." In: International Journal of Urban and Regional Research 26/1, pp. 99–105.
Hüwelmeier, Gertrud (2013): "Bazaar Pagodas – Transnational Religion, Postsocialist Marketplaces and Vietnamese Migrant Women in Berlin." In: Religion & Gender 3/1, pp. 76–89.
Jackson, John (2004): Pastorpreneur: Pastors and Entrepreneurs Answer the Call, Friendswood, TX: Baxter Press.
Jackson, John (2011): Pastorpreneur: Creative Ideas for Birthing Spiritual Life in Your Community, Westmont, IL: InterVarsity Press.

Jelen, Ted, ed. (2002): Sacred Markets, Sacred Canopies: Essays on Religious Markets and Religious Pluralism, Lanham, MD: Rowman & Littlefield.

Jennings, Mark Alan Charles (2017): "Great Risk for the Kingdom: Pentecostal-Charismatic Growth Churches, Pastorpreneurs, and Neoliberalism." In: Ana-Maria Pascal (ed.), Multiculturalism and the Convergence of Faith and Practical Wisdom in Modern Society, Hershey, PA: IGI Global, pp. 236–249.

Kaell, Hillary (2017): "Seeing the Invisible: Ambient Catholicism on the Side of the Road." In: Journal of the American Academy of Religion 85/1, pp. 136–167.

Karimi, Hanane (2018): "The Hijab and Work: Female Entrepreneurship in Response to Islamophobia." In: International Journal of Politics, Culture, and Society 31, pp. 421–435.

Kimura, Rikio (2021): "What and How Hybrid Forms of Christian Social Enterprises Are Created and Sustained in Cambodia? A Critical Realist Institutional Logics Perspective." In: Religions 12/8, pp. 1–30.

Klaver, Miranda (2015): "Pentecostal Pastorpreneurs and the Global Circulation of Authoritative Aesthetic Styles." In: Culture and Religion, 16/2, pp. 146–159.

Lehto, Heather Mellquist (2020): "Designing Secularity at Sarang Church." In: Journal of Korean Studies 25/2, pp. 429–454.

McVea, John F./Naughton, Michael (2021): Enriching Social Entrepreneurship from the Perspective of Catholic Social Teaching." In: Religions 12/173, pp. 1–17.

N.N. (1881) "Mark Twain: The Great Humourist Dined at Montreal." *The Globe*, 9 December, p. 3.

Nyamnjoh, F.B./Carpenter, J.A. 2018. "Religious Innovation and Competition in Contemporary African Christianity." In: Journal of Contemporary African Studies 36/3, pp. 289–302.

Okesson, Greg (2020): A Public Missiology: How Local Churches Witness in a Complex World, Grand Rapids, MI: Baker Academic.

Oliphant, Elayne (2021): The Privilege of Being Banal: Art, Secularism, and Catholicism in Paris, Chicago, IL: University of Chicago Press.

Ouragini, I. B. A. (2019): "The Impact of Islamic Religion on Women's Entrepreneurship." In: Khaled Tamzini/Anis Ben Salem (eds.), Understanding the Relationship between Religion and Entrepreneurship, Hershey, PA: IGI Global, pp. 214–229.

Paiva, Luis E. B./Sousa, E.S./Lima, Tereza C.B./D. Da Silva (2020): "Planned Behavior and Religious Beliefs as Antecedents to Entrepreneurial Intention: A Study with University Students." In: RAM, 21/2, pp. 1–27.
Resane, Kelebogile T. (2022): "From Small Country Churches to Explosion into Megachurches: A Modern Pentecostal Cultural Fit for the Assemblies of God in South Africa." In: Verbum et Ecclesia 43/1, pp. 1–9.
Ringdal, Bethany (2022): "Money and Mission Starts: Funding New Churches for God's Mission." In: Word & World 42/1, pp. 56–66.
Roudy, Philip/Taylor, Valerie/Evans, Randy (2016): "Founded by Faith: Social Entrepreneurship as a Bridge between Religion and Work." In: Journal of Ethics and Entrepreneurship, pp. 1–33.
Rundle, Steve/Lee, Min-Dong P. (2022): "The Motivations, Backgrounds, and Practices of Business as Mission Practitioners: Insights from an International Survey." In: Missiology 50/4, pp. 420–441.
Senda, B. K. (2019): "Is Islam Associated with Business Success?" In: Khaled Tamzini, Anis Ben Salem (eds.), Understanding the Relationship between Religion and Entrepreneurship, Hershey, PA: IGI Global, pp. 51–78.
Tovar-García, E. D. (2022) "Religiosity and Entrepreneurship in Post-Soviet Russia." In: Journal for the Academic Study of Religion 35/3, pp. 271–297.
Troeltsch, Ernst. (1931 [1912]): The Social Teachings of the Christian Churches, London: George Allen & Unwin.
Vandewiele, Wim (2021): "The Post-Secular Society. Desert or Oasis for Social Entrepreneurship in Religious Communities and Organizations?" In: Louvain Studies 44/2, pp. 131–151.
Weber, Max (1958 [1905]): The Protestant Ethic and the Spirit of Capitalism, trans. T. Parsons, New York: Charles Scribner's Sons.
Wuthnow, Robert (2007): After the Baby Boomers: How Twenty- and Thirty-Somethings are Shaping the Future of American Religion, Princeton, NJ: Princeton University Press.

Web References

Centre St Jax. "Our Story." Accessed May 21, 2023. http://stjax.org/en/home.
Centre St Jax. "Our Story." Accessed October 4, 2023. http://stjax.org/our-story.
Holy Trinity Brompton. "Our Story." Accessed May 28, 2023. https://htb.org/story.

Susan Schwartz. "What if Montreal's shuttered churches became 'centres of gravity for joy'?" Montreal Gazette. February 19, 2021. Accessed October 16, 2023. https://montrealgazette.com/news/local-news/what-if-montreals-shuttered-churches-became-centres-of-gravity-for-joy.

Trinity Centres Foundation. "About Us." Accessed March 20, 2023. https://trinitycentres.org/ecosystem.

Trinity Centres Foundation. "Ecosystem Development." Accessed May 21, 2023. https://trinitycentres.org/ecosystem.

God Is Not at Church
Digitalization as Authentic Religious Practice in an American Megachurch

Ariane Kovac

Abstract *In this article, I analyze how increasing digitalization changed the organizational structure of an Evangelical megachurch in the US and how the church theologized and idealized this transformation. My case study Churchome switched from a multisite megachurch model to what I call a 'click-and-mortar church'. It reduced in-person events and worked on making all aspects of church life available online, enabling people in other cities or countries to not only passively consume content but to become active and committed long-distance church members. I show that this transformation in the church's membership structure led to a diversification of how members relate to the church and an eventization of church life. Churchome presents its digitalization as a bold and possibly inconvenient but necessary move to make mission work more efficient and church life more authentic. I argue that Churchome uses its digital approach to emphasize the ideal of communitization and to present itself as an authentic and exciting organization. Through this, Churchome can counter internal and external criticism against megachurches per se and its move into the digital in particular. Churchome's self-presentation thus is an example of how a church theologizes its social forms or, in other words, for a congruence of religious semantics and social forms.*

Keywords *American religion, authenticity, digital religion, Evangelicalism, megachurches, organizational studies*

1. Introduction: Empty pews, full Zoom calls

I had been researching Churchome, a global megachurch based in the Pacific Northwest of the US, digitally for more than a year before first attending an in-person service. More than excited, I made my way to the church on Sunday morning – only to find the large auditorium almost empty. Shaking off the thought that I might have chosen the wrong case study, I returned the following Sunday. This time, the church was packed and excitement was in the air. I quickly learned why: Head pastor Judah Smith was in the house. Whereas the week before, visitors had followed a pre-recorded sermon by Smith on the large screens towering over the stage, we would now get to watch him preach in person. The previous week's solemn tranquility was replaced with a noticeable buzz.

This pattern – a full auditorium when Smith preached live, empty pews on all other Sundays – repeated itself throughout my stay in Seattle. As the video shown in the church is also streamed online, many of Churchome's followers enjoy the flexibility and convenience of staying home when Smith is not present and only visit the church on special occasions. Churchome not only tolerates this, but even encourages its members not to come to church and to attend digitally instead. In fact, in a sermon he preached at the time of the 30th anniversary of the church, Judah Smith announced that he would also stay home at some point in the future:

> I don't expect any of you to be here 30 years from now. I hope you're following Jesus wherever he takes you. Now, if you are still here, I won't be, but that's awesome, seriously, that's great. I won't. But, I mean, I'll still be practicing with Churchome. It'll be hopefully through the technology and it'll be wonderful.[1]

Churchome did not focus on digital technology for its church growth from the beginning. What was founded as "City Church" in 1992 first grew into a local multi-site megachurch until it was relaunched as "Churchome" in 2017. This move was primarily justified as an efficient evangelization strategy. While a local church building was always limited, with digital technologies the church

---

[1] Sermon by Judah Smith. "God Pursues You." https://www.youtube.com/watch?v=UixDJthl7dU, 29:40-30:06.

could potentially reach millions. The portmanteau of "church" and "home" symbolized how the church's new approach was supposed to restructure followers' religious practice: Churchome intended to make every aspect of church life available online. As the church reduced in-person events, members were encouraged to watch live-streamed or recorded services from home, preferably together with fellow believers in small groups. The differences between services with live preaching and video recordings are just one example of how digitalization changed the organization of religious practice at Churchome and the self-presentation of the church as an organization.

From an organizational perspective, megachurches are an interesting case. Scholars have generally considered religion and organization to have a problematic relationship. In this perspective, religious entities strive toward close emotional bonds between members. The pragmatic decisions and economic entanglements that come with a higher level of organization run counter to this ideal of communitization. Megachurches, however, have not only been compared to businesses by outsiders but consciously present themselves as organizations that follow economic alongside religious logics. They appoint CEOs, publicly speak about having applied marketing strategies to grow their audience, and take membership numbers as the primary marker for success. Still, megachurches are religious entities and thus follow ideals that go beyond those of business organizations. If their organizational structures contradict their religious ideals, they risk being perceived as inauthentic by their followers.

In this article, I analyze how the digitalization of my case study Churchome changed the megachurch as an organization and how these changes have been religiously interpreted and idealized. I am interested in how digitalization has altered the social forms with which Churchome as an organization provides its followers and how Churchome uses its "going online" for its self-presentation. I argue that digitalization reinforces existing organizational developments of megachurches. While all megachurch services are events, digitalization at Churchome has led to an eventization of church life in which in-person services are specifically advertised as "church experiences".[2] Megachurches offer their followers both the option for passive, occasional as well as active, committed membership. Through digitalization, member roles become even more diverse. At Churchome, digitalization has led to a new membership category:

---

2   Churchome: Churchome Experiences. https://www.churchome.org/monthly-experiences (accessed November 8, 2023).

Long-distance members are committed members who follow the church digitally. Lastly, while megachurch attendees are known to be "promiscuous worshippers" (Abraham 2018: 39), digitalization makes it even easier for believers to follow several churches at the same time. Long-distance members at Churchome tend to approach their faith practice with a "mix-and-match" attitude and use different churches and other institutions for different services.

Churchome understands streaming from home as a means to integrate faith into everyday life and to build up an authentic religious practice that does not depend on spectacular in-person events. Churchome's digitalization thus not only altered the church's social forms and the relation of members to the organization but also the church's self-presentation. I argue that Churchome uses its digital approach to emphasize the ideal of communitization and to present itself as an authentic and exciting organization. Churchome's self-presentation thus is an example of how a church theologizes its social forms or, in other words, for a congruence of religious semantics and social forms. First, Churchome presents itself as boldly going to new places for evangelizing by developing a digital missional identity, which allows it to counter common stereotypes and critiques against megachurches and to distance itself from other churches. Second, as it relocates religious practice from a church building into members' homes, Churchome presents its approach to faith as particularly authentic. In this perspective, by embedding faith into everyday life, Churchome's followers do not depend on an impressive building or an emotional worship performance for their religious experience.

The following analysis draws on material collected for research on my dissertation which focuses on Evangelical boundary maintenance and identity work. I worked with an ethnographic approach and designed my study according to Grounded Theory Methodology (Corbin/Strauss 2015). In the first research phase in 2021, I participated in a digital small group set in Europe, conducted interviews with international Churchome members, and listened to live-streamed Churchome services. This was not a conscious decision, as COVID-19-related travel and contact restrictions made it impossible for me to enter the field in person (Kovac 2021). My second phase, in 2022, when travel restrictions had been lifted, consisted of an in-person field research stay in Seattle and Los Angeles, where I participated in in-person small groups, services, and other church events, and conducted interviews with pastors at Churchome. Later in 2022, I concluded my data collection with several digital interviews with Churchome members in the US and analyzed relevant sermons by Judah Smith from between August 2021 and November 2022. Going back and forth between digital and in-person ethnography allowed me to follow my interlocutors, whose religious practice takes place in both online and offline spheres (Laughlin 2022: 2). One important limitation of my research, particularly for this article, is that I started researching Churchome after the church's rebranding and digitalization. Thus, I did not personally witness the church's development and transition from City Church to Churchome. For this article, I instead rely on interviews and conversations with long-time members.

In the following, I first explore the particular case of social forms and economic logics at play at megachurches (2). After turning to my case study Churchome and shortly recounting how the local City Church has become the digital and global Churchome (3), I analyze how digitalization has changed Churchome's social forms, in particular events, groups, and the relation of members to the organization (4). My last subchapter aims at how Churchome uses its digital strategy for its self-presentation (5).

2. The laughter of megachurch pastors: Megachurches' religious and economic logics

Scholars on megachurches usually define megachurches according to the criteria of the Hartford Institute for Religion Research, that is, a megachurch is a Protestant church that has 2000 or more weekly attendants, possibly across multiple campuses.[3] Although individual large churches had of course existed earlier, megachurches emerged as a distinctive form of organizing Christian faith practice in the US in the 1970s and 1980s, following suburbanization and the surge in privately owned vehicles. Megachurches have been compared to shopping malls (Ritzer 2005: 23), but in contrast to their secular counterparts, they apparently do not see any sign of decline. Wellman et al. (2020: 5) have argued that megachurches have now become "the way Americans 'do' religion".

The success story of megachurches cannot be understood separately from societal and religious developments in the past fifty years. Megachurches, which are usually nondenominational or only have loose ties to a denomination, both profited from and advanced the declining importance of denominations (Wuthnow 1989) and the emergence of a generic Evangelical subculture (Du Mez 2020). Megachurches spread at the time when an Evangelical media market was established, and many megachurches and their pastors became

---

3   http://hirr.hartsem.edu/megachurch/definition.html.

successful media producers. Starting with the televangelists of the 1970s and 1980s, megachurches were often headed by famous media personalities. Many churches succeeded in marketing their media products, such as music or books, not only to their members but to a more general Christian or even non-Christian audience. This way, megachurches' ideas and theologies traveled far beyond their pews. The idea that congregation size is an indicator for a church's success and vitality, for example, can also be found in smaller churches (Maddox 2012).

Moreover, the trend towards a concentration of faith practice and the extension of auditorium sizes not only influenced theology but also created a distinctive aesthetic and organizational style: Megachurches can usually be found in car-friendly locations in the suburbs of big cities. Often, they congregate in nondescript buildings that have little to no markers of their being a church. Services are multi-media events centered around a charismatic head pastor and contemporary Christian worship music performed by a band of professional musicians. Most megachurches hold several services per week and have a wide array of different ministries and groups that provide members with services and activities. Worship ministries, for example, produce media products to be circulated and sold beyond the church's membership.

Megachurches usually have a highly differentiated and hierarchical organizational structure and rely on a host of staff that is not only trained in theology but also in areas such as finances, media production, or marketing. Often, these structures resemble those of businesses in name or function, such as when megachurches appoint a CEO to oversee the church's operational side. Arguably, the larger a megachurch gets and the more economic transactions it is involved in, the more it needs to function like a business. Examples would be those megachurches that are at the same time global media empires whose albums reach the tops of Billboard charts, such as the Australian Hillsong or Bethel and Elevation Church in the US. However, functioning like a business is not only a necessity that comes with higher membership numbers. Maddox (2012) and Sanders (2016), among others, have argued that an economic logic is inherent to megachurches, whose primary goal, however theologically framed, is to grow their audiences.

Scholars of organizations usually argue that religious entities do not voluntarily engage in economic endeavors and that, when they have to, this leads to tensions (Petzke/Tyrell 2012). In this perspective, churches do not understand themselves as businesses and are oriented toward otherworldly goals that run counter to the logics of the economic field. According to Bourdieu

(1998: 113), actors in the religious field have a "double consciousness". Like all agents, they cannot avoid following an economic logic. However, to the outside world, they must pretend that economic rationales play no part in their decision-making, or, in Bourdieu's words, play the "religious game". If not, they risk being perceived as unauthentic by their followers. In other words, churches are businesses that deny and conceal that they are businesses. When the Catholic bishops that Bourdieu observed spoke about economic matters of the church or used economic terminology, laughter served to alleviate the tensions surrounding the gap between what the church actually did and what the church was supposed to do.

Megachurches, however, do not only often openly associate themselves with businesses and a corporate culture but also bring together economic and religious rationales. Thus, on the one hand, one could argue that megachurches solve the tensions of organized religiosity by completely blending into the economic sphere. Some scholars of religion, like Berger (1990 [1967]), have predicted that the increasing organization of religion contributes to the secularization of society. On the other hand, megachurches can be understood as an example of how a high degree of organization and vital religiosity do not need to be mutually exclusive (Schlamelcher 2018: 499). Chang (2003: 127) has rejected a clear-cut dichotomy between organizational and religious spheres as an outdated assumption that goes back to Weber's church-sect typology. According to her, in perceiving organization, including economic rationales, and religion as antithetical, scholars make implicit assumptions about what it means to be religious and project these onto the churches they study. Instead, the relationship between religious and economic logics must be understood to be complex and intertwined. For example, when a religious organization wants to change the secular world, including its economy, its involvement in the economic field cannot be understood as entirely secular (ibid.: 129). Similarly, when megachurches interpret a high number of followers as a God-given sign of being on the right theological path, a decision to hire a marketing expert is not exclusively grounded in economic logics.

Megachurches' economic involvement, however, is subject to criticism both inside and outside Evangelicalism. While some critics perceive megachurches as soullessly commodified and suspect pastors to exploit their audience for their fame and fortune (Wellman et al. 2020: 216), others do not have problems with megachurches per se but closely monitor how their church spends its money or makes decisions. In my own research on Churchome, I got the impression that most people had no problems with the church orienting itself toward fame and fortune but voiced criticism in those instances when they felt like this negatively influenced congregational life. For example, Churchome has many celebrity members (among them, most notably, pop singer Justin Bieber) and some of my interviewees argued that sometimes the pastors cared for them at the expense of "normal" congregants.

Thus, instead of understanding megachurches as simply reacting to contradictory sets of logics, scholars should be aware of the entanglements of religious and economic logics inherent in megachurches and their theology and faith practice. Rather than asking whether megachurches lean more on the economic or the religious side, it is therefore more promising to closely examine the intersections of the two, or in other words, which economic rationales are consciously presented and which are concealed, what members accept without question and what leads to internal criticism, or how megachurches react to such criticism.

3. From multi-site to click-and-mortar: Churchome as a case study

Churchome did not start with an emphasis on digital media or even an overt intention of global outreach. The name the church was founded under in 1992, "City Church", reflected its rootedness in the Seattle metropolitan area. City Church's founder Wendell Smith grew the nondenominational church into one of the largest churches in the region with several campuses in and around Seattle. In 2009, Wendell's son Judah Smith took over the church as head pastor together with his wife Chelsea because of the declining health of Wendell, who suffered from cancer and died one year later. This second generation of pastors stylistically adapted the church for a younger audience. Judah and Chelsea Smith started doing outreach in Hollywood, opening a church location in Los Angeles and befriending celebrities such as Justin Bieber. Regarding what was preached, Judah Smith accentuated grace theology, a theological view that believes salvation to solely depend on faith, not on actions or repentance. These innovations turned out to be fruitful, as the church continued to grow and Judah Smith became an Evangelical celebrity with a large social media following.

In 2017, however, the church changed its strategy and City Church was rebranded as "Churchome", a portmanteau of "church" and "home". Instead of planting further church buildings, Churchome intended to bring the church to peoples' homes by digitally streaming services. Members were called to gather in small-group settings (called "church at home") and to watch live-streamed or recorded sermons together. The church started several digital small groups in which people gathered via Zoom. Additionally, Churchome launched an app intended to replicate other aspects of church life in the digital sphere. Through a "pastor chat", anyone interested in the church can seek pastoral care or find answers to their questions. A prayer function in the app enables believers to publicly request prayers from fellow congregants and to react to these requests. Daily "guided prayer" exercises and recorded worship performances help people new to the church to align with Churchome's theology and practice their faith online. Congregants can also give and tithe online, without ever being physically present in church. While online campuses and live-streamed services have become staple in most Christian churches since the COVID-19 pandemic, at the time, Churchome's approach was unusual if not pioneering, and prepared the church well for what happened later. In 2020, when contact restrictions were issued and large gatherings prohibited, Churchome had not only already successfully set up digital options for participation but these had become a normal and much-used part of church practice.

Churchome's digitalization led to an increasing internationalization of the church. Judah Smith claims that services reach people in over 80 countries.[4] There are digital small groups hosted by people from all continents. Churchome, however, did not adapt much to integrate its international following. Sermons are, for example, exclusively in English, and YouTube videos do not come with subtitles other than automatically generated English ones. Many of Judah Smith's examples and anecdotes only make sense in a US context and require an understanding of the country, its politics, and its culture. In my interviews, it became clear that Churchome relies on the small groups and especially the group hosts to adapt the church's content to their respective local culture. As a result, internationally, the church mainly attracts people who are mobile, globally oriented, and highly educated.

At the same time, Churchome sold or demolished the buildings they had owned, keeping only the Kirkland church campus, and reduced the number of in-person services. When large events were prohibited from happening during the height of the COVID-19 pandemic, Churchome already had all technological necessities in place and ceased in-person services. When in-person services started again, as congregants told me, the pews were not as full as before the pandemic. Many Churchomians who had previously attended services in

---

4   Field notes, May 8, 2022.

person enjoyed this enforced participation in digital church and did not want to go back to "regular" church. In May 2023, Churchome offered one in-person service weekly at their Kirkland campus and one service per month in a rented location in Los Angeles. At the Kirkland campus, one service a month featured Judah Smith preaching live on stage. The other three Sundays, visitors watched a pre-recorded sermon on the auditorium's huge screens or listened to an in-person sermon by a local pastor, followed by a live worship performance. The services featuring a live in-person sermon by Smith are called "church experiences" and are specifically advertised. In addition to their regular services in Kirkland and Los Angeles, Churchome at times organizes services in other U.S. cities.

With its rebranding of the City Church to Churchome, Churchome has switched from a multi-site megachurch to a church model I designate, in parallel to the business administration term, *click-and-mortar church*. A click-and-mortar church provides its members with both digital and in-person opportunities for participation. It does not understand its digital campus as solely an optional add-on or a lesser alternative to in-person church attendance but instead sees both modes of participation at least equally justified and works on making all aspects of in-person church and faith life available in the digital realm. As seen in the sermon excerpt at the beginning of this article, Churchome plans to rely even more on technology in the future. It will be interesting to see whether the church will at some point give up its Kirkland campus and focus on irregular events throughout the country, or even become a fully digital church.

4. Digital and hybrid social forms at Churchome

In going from a multi-site to a click-and-mortar church, Churchome not only replicated offline social forms for an online audience but also saw changes in its existing, in-person social forms. In the following, I analyze these developments regarding events, groups, and membership in the organization.

4.1 Events

In May 2023, Churchome still held weekly services at its main campus in a Seattle suburb. Head pastor Judah Smith, however, was only present once per month. These services were specifically advertised as "church experiences".[5] During other Sunday services at the Kirkland campus, Churchome would either show a pre-recorded sermon by Smith or have a local pastor preach the sermon. In both cases, sermons took up the largest part of the service, usually lasting between forty minutes and over one hour. Announcements and pleas for giving and tithing took place either before or after the sermon. At the end of the service, a live worship band played several songs. While church experiences were livestreamed directly and fully from the Kirkland auditorium, on other Sundays those who joined digitally saw the same recording as the church visitors, usually followed by music videos of worship songs.

This similarity of the online and offline experience on regular Sundays explains why "church experiences" draw many more visitors than regular services. While it did not make much difference for my interviewees whether they watched a video recording in church or at home, the experience of participating in a "church experience" could not be replicated in the same way by attending online. "Church experiences" not only feel different than regular Sunday services, but Churchome also markets them as such. Digitalization for Churchome goes hand in hand with and provides a basis for an eventization of church life. In-person services are not simply services but "experiences", made special precisely because of their infrequency. In promoting these events, Churchome draws both on pastor Smith's popularity and the live and in-person aspect of the services. Attendees of a "church experience" can be sure to see pastor Judah Smith live on stage and come specifically to see him. At least in my own experience as a participant observer, Smith's live preaching is not only longer but also more enthusiastic, emotional, and agitated. During church experiences, Churchome also puts more of an emphasis on the parts of a church service that are hard to replicate online, like the worship performances. Instead of having an anonymous worship band, for example, the church invites musicians and uses their names for the promotion of its events. Whether or not attendees have heard of them before, the mention of a special act makes the event seem even more extraordinary.

Hitzler (2011: 39) has argued that in parallel to a tendency to eventization in general society, believers increasingly concentrate their faith practice on special events. By "eventizing" regular church services and marketing them as something special, Churchome enables its followers to experience such events while engaging in the conventional practice of church attendance. Moreover,

---

5   Cf. https://www.churchome.org/monthly-experiences.

attending services monthly and not weekly appeals to the busy demographic of young professionals and young families that Churchome mainly attracts, and provides an incentive for people who live in the wider surroundings of Kirkland and would not travel to Churchome every Sunday.

By livestreaming its services, Churchome enables all its members, spread out all over the globe, to have a shared experience. Klaver (2021: 95) has argued that the livestreaming of services can contribute to a shared sense of belonging of a globally spread out megachurch. Similarly, Campbell and DeLashmutt (2014: 276) and Hutchings (2017) have observed that churches explicitly reference online visitors to make them feel included. At Churchome, this sense of belonging is encouraged by frequent references to the global membership of the church. When pastors Judah and Chelsea Smith address their audience directly, they often add the phrase "wherever you are" and sometimes list possible cities from where people might be watching. Also, they use many occasions to mention that people all over the world are listening to Churchome's sermons digitally and present Churchome as a "church scattered all over the world".[6]

4.2 Groups

Small groups or house groups have been a fundamental feature of Evangelical church practice at least since seventeenth-century Pietism. Especially in megachurches, they are a means to counter large, possibly anonymous services and to differentiate between occasional visitors and committed members. Usually, these groups meet either in one of the members' homes or in a designated church space. While some groups discuss Bible passages, others speak about how to apply the content of the previous week's sermon to their current struggles in life, read Christian self-help books together, or pray for and with each other (Bielo 2009). At Churchome, small groups are asked to watch the service together. Churchome staff provide group hosts with discussion questions related to the sermon. However, as Churchome employee Philipp[7] explained in an interview with me, whether they use these questions and "what they do before or after [...] is really up to them", as is the meeting location and the length of the meeting. With this flexibility, small group hosts are

---

6   Sermon by Chelsea Smith. "Let Jesus Serve You." https://www.youtube.com/watch?v=ewoVnnVMh08, 02:04.
7   All names of interviewees in this article are pseudonyms.

expected to create a group that "serves their community the best", or in other words, that appeals to as many people as possible.[8]

Both in sermons and interviews with me, Churchome's pastors continually emphasized the importance of watching the digital recordings of sermons not alone but with a group of fellow believers. Conversely, small groups were hardly ever mentioned concerning in-person services. Churchome staff believes digital participation to lead to a lack of togetherness and community that can be countered by watching together instead of alone. "Finding community" is an omnipresent goal at Churchome, often aimed toward people Churchome suspects must be watching the sermons alone. If someone watches from a place in the world where there is no small group, they are encouraged to start their own group. Since 2022, Churchome has also been producing a video series featuring mostly small group hosts outside of Seattle who speak about how they practiced "community" with Churchome from afar.[9] The emphasis on small groups especially for online participants might stem not only from the desire to combat the isolation of digital participation but also from an intention to draw occasional visitors into the church. Those who watch online are "free-riders" (Thumma/Travis 2007: 50) even more than those who occasionally visit a service. By integrating digital members into small groups, Churchome not only expands its number of loyal (and loyally giving) members but also gets insights into and control over the anonymous number of YouTube and app viewers. Thus, groups help counter the anonymity of the megachurch crowd both for individual members, who can get to know fellow worshippers, and for the church as an institution, for whom digital attendees are hard to grasp.

4.3 Organization and membership

Digitalization at Churchome has diversified the possible ways of relating to and engaging with the church. All megachurches offer a variety of possible modes of interacting with the church, some of them more distant and others more active (Thumma/Travis 2007: 50). In megachurches, "low-cost" attendance (Wellman et al. 2020: 20) is tolerated more easily than in smaller, more tight-knit congregations, as megachurch services tend to be anonymous events that attract a lot of infrequent visitors and many megachurches encourage people to consume their media products without ever attending a

---

8   Interview with Philipp, Churchome pastor, January 14, 2022.
9   Cf. https://www.youtube.com/playlist?list=PLicUMmdCSpPjuC4NFk-JRzSlOxks5Z-eJ.

service. Membership is usually not formalized but based on participation in church activities, giving and tithing to the church, and a feeling of belonging. In a local, non-digital megachurch, being an active church member usually depends on physical presence. Active members attend services regularly, are part of a small group, and might even take on volunteering roles. In a click-and-mortar church, defining active membership becomes complicated: Can someone be considered an active member who regularly watches services on YouTube but has never gotten in contact with anyone at the church? Is in-person participation a sign of greater commitment than following the church digitally?

Churchome has, through digitalization, attracted a category of followers I call *long-distance members*. Long-distance members live too far from a church campus to regularly attend in-person services but extensively use the church's digital offers and consider themselves active and committed church members. While some of them visit infrequently, others have never been to a physical location of the church, be it for financial, visa-related, or other reasons. Some of them might have been local members before but moved away. Others stumble upon a sermon or book by coincidence and decide to follow from afar. At Churchome, the long-distance members I interviewed either took note of Churchome when they heard pastor Judah Smith speak at an event[10] or when, after watching other faith-related videos, YouTube's algorithm recommended one of Smith's sermons. All of them followed Churchome for a while, watching services online and using the church's app, before reaching out to the church, usually via the pastor chat function in Churchome's app. The pastors referred them to digital small groups or groups that met in their region or encouraged them to start their own group. One example of such a trajectory is Diane, who lives on the US East Coast and had been following Churchome digitally for about ten years before "getting involved".[11] What nudged her to reach out to the church was that someone at Churchome explicitly mentioned that they were looking for people to host small groups outside the West Coast area. While all of the long-distance Churchomians I interviewed were enthusiastic about the

---

10   Some large megachurches regularly organize events called conferences to which they invite several pastors to give a "guest sermon". Judah Smith gained much of his fame from preaching at conferences organized by the Australian global megachurch Hillsong.

11   Interview with Diane, long-distance member, pastor, and small group host, December 22, 2022.

church, some also reflected on having a limited perspective from afar. Sophia, a long-distance member from Europe, noted that, as an online participant, she did not get insights into church life beyond the digital small group she attended.[12] Thus, she could not know for sure whether the lived-out church culture reflected Smith's preaching.

For some of my interviewees, attending a church digitally was a matter of personal preference. Two of my interviewees, for example, told me that they felt socially anxious and experienced video calls as a relief. Others felt called to Churchome and their missionary vision of reaching people through technology. Some of my interviewees traveled or moved a lot and found it practical to be able to access the church from wherever they had an internet connection. Long-distance member Carmen, for example, had worked as a flight attendant and considered Churchome to be "right in her wheelhouse", as she identified as a "global traveler".[13]

Most of the long-distance members I spoke with, however, simply did not find a church they liked as much as Churchome where they lived. Particularly those living in countries where Evangelical Christianity is a fringe phenomenon explained that they found local churches to be too conservative, services neither lively nor dynamic, and the overall atmosphere not as "unique" or "special" as at Churchome.[14] This resonates with the fact that most of my interviewees emphasized purposely choosing a church that fit their convictions and lifestyle. The internet made it easier for them to design their faith practice, as they can choose from a broad array of church offers and religious content from around the world. In other words, digitalization enormously expanded their "spiritual marketplace" (Roof 1999). Sophia explained that she closely followed three US churches online because each of them focused on a different aspect that was important to her character and faith. In her view, "people are complex, and we all need quite a few things to kinda feed us [...] [spiritually]".[15]

---

12   Interview with Sophia, long-distance member from Europe, October 15, 2021.
13   Interview with Carmen, long-distance member and small group host, December 15, 2022.
14   Interestingly, some of my non-American interviewees connected their fondness for Churchome with the physical location of the church. Sophia, who lived in a predominantly Catholic area, laughingly mentioned that she might move to Seattle one day because it "seems like it might be my town" (interview with Sophia, October 15, 2021).
15   Interview with Sophia, October 15, 2021.

Long-distance members are often "promiscuous worshippers" (Abraham 2018: 39): Usually, they listen to sermons by several pastors online, and many of them are members of and attend in-person services at a local church. Digitalization has simplified and expanded the possibilities of such "split loyalties" (Coleman 2003: 19). While "church hopping" (Wuthnow 2007: 116), or spending one's Sundays in various churches, is a common practice encouraged by large, anonymous megachurch services, digitalization makes it possible to quite literally be in several places and engage in several activities at once. Followers do not even need to commit to a single church on any given Sunday but can easily close the browser window if they do not like the digital service they are watching and try out something different.

Thus, long-distance Churchomians approached both their membership at Churchome and their religious affiliation more broadly with a "mix-and-match" mentality that led them to consciously design their religious practice drawing on several sources. This resonates with Campbell's (2012) concept of "networked religion", which intends to grasp how believers assemble their religious practice from both online and offline aspects. Churchome's long-distance followers flexibly make use of what the church offers and listen to sermons on other days of the week if they do not find time on any given Sunday or listen to sermons while doing household chores, as one of my interviewees told me. "Mixing and matching" one's faith practice is, however, not only done out of preference or curiosity but also because there are things that Churchome just does not provide its followers with. Especially for long-distance members, but also for those who come to in-person services, Churchome is not a "full-service church" (Roof 1999: 94). Carmen, for example, missed live worship and attended a local church to experience it.[16] One of my interviewees got baptized in a local church, although he was more actively involved in Churchome than the local church he chose for his baptism. Apparently, some of Churchome's attempts to relocate religious rituals into the digital sphere, such as recordings of worship performances or Zoom baptisms, do not satisfy all long-distance members. There are also some important Christian rituals that Churchome does not offer to its members, neither digitally nor in person, such as weddings. Not being able to meet pastors in person, however, was not an issue to any of my interviewees, many of whom were experienced followers of global

---

16   Interview with Carmen, December 15, 2022.

megachurches with celebrity pastors. To Sophia, for example, it was clear that she "will never have a conversation with [the] pastors that I'm listening to".[17]

5. More digitalization, less organization: Churchome's digital self-presentation

In the following, I will turn to how Churchome religiously interprets and idealizes its digital practices and show how Churchome presents its digital approach as not only efficient and bold but also more authentic than religious practice at other megachurches.

5.1 Digital missional identity

The emergence and popularization of megachurches cannot be explained without their suburban locations and embeddedness in suburban lifestyles. Bielo (2011: 168) notes that the "organizational invention" of the megachurch was a result of a link between conservative Evangelicalism and suburbia that solidified in the second half of the 20th century. Due to their size and car-friendly location, megachurches, like the shopping centers they were often compared to, could draw masses of people who were already used to driving long distances for their daily chores (Loveland/Wheeler 2003: 117). Correspondingly, megachurches designed their buildings to fit the habits and preferences of middle-class suburbanites (Laughlin 2022: 26–27).

This 'suburbian-ness' of megachurches, however, evoked a range of criticism from inside and outside the Evangelical subculture. Due to their isolation from their surroundings and lack of any religious or denominational markers, megachurches have been described as interchangeable "religious non-places" (Sanders 2016). The high level of maintenance (and thus the large amount of money, usually through tithes and donations) needed to uphold megachurch infrastructure has been criticized as inefficient and excessive. Evangelical critics, in particular, accuse megachurches of being inefficient evangelizers, more interested in filling their buildings than in bringing people closer to faith or in building up sustainable relationships with attendees. For representatives of the inner-Christian reform movement Emerging Church, for example, megachurches were a symbol of the conservative Evangelical conviction that

---

17   Interview with Sophia, October 15, 2021.

it was enough to plant a building and wait for people to come through the door (Bielo 2011: 118). To counter this, Bielo's Emerging Church interviewees initiated church activities in the urban, low-income areas they had chosen to be their mission fields and sometimes even fully relocated there. What they described as "being missional" was not only an ideal but also an identity acted out in everyday life (ibid.: 119).

At Churchome, such criticisms against megachurches are taken up and countered with reference to digital technology. Presenting its technology-focused approach as a way to overcome the isolation of a suburban megachurch campus, Churchome has developed a digital missional identity that works as an add-on to the conventional megachurch model of the church.

In a sermon Judah Smith preached around the time of Churchome's thirtieth anniversary, titled "God Pursues You", he laid out several arguments as to how digital technology was not only more efficient but also meant being able to bring faith to people instead of waiting for them to come. In the months prior, Smith had already begun advertising new "technologies" the church was planning to develop and asking for donations, arguing that a little money put into creating an app or launching a website could go a long way. In "God Pursues You", Smith condensed this to the formula that "we're gonna spend thousands to reach millions" by technology "instead of spending millions to reach thousands", as would be the case with planting a new church campus.[18] Spending money on digital technologies meant that "we're going to spend more money on people than buildings, [...] we're going to spend more money on people than events".[19] Thus, Smith directly counters criticism against the inefficiency of megachurches. Churchome might own a physical campus, but it did not plan to build another one. Instead, the money that members donated would be used toward "reaching millions" via technology.

By regularly emphasizing that church, to Churchome, is not a building, Judah Smith can refute accusations that he as a megachurch pastor is primarily interested in filling his pews. Moreover, in his sermons, Smith often mentions that not everyone needs to find their home at Churchome. He wants to bring people to Jesus, and if another church helps them strengthen their faith more than Churchome, so be it. In "God Pursues You", Smith explicitly states that

---

18   Sermon by Judah Smith. "God Pursues You." https://www.youtube.com/watch?v=Uix DJthl7dU, 1:02:13-1:02:18.
19   Ibid.: 1:02:18-1:02:32.

"this isn't about your allegiance to Chuchome".[20] Carmen, a long-time Churchomian who has experienced both living in Seattle and attending what was then called City Church and being a long-distance member of Churchome, was passionate about Churchome not tying members to the church. She explained to me that when Judah Smith took over as head pastor, the church dropped a lot of conservative ideas. One of the changes was letting go of the idea that "you're committed to this house and you need to stay in this house, this is where you're fed, and this is where you're tied".[21]

Smith not only allows or even encourages attendees to get input from various churches or to find their luck somewhere else if they do not like Churchome's approach, but also calls on church members to stay home and not physically come to church. In his "God Pursues You" sermon, Smith argues that God is not at church, either:

> Everyone thought that God would come and have church friends, but all of his friends didn't go to the synagogue, so that really annoyed people, because they're like, no, God should be in a robe in church putting little Wafers on everyone's tongue for communion, right, it's our picture of God. But instead, he's up late [at] night with knuckleheads [and] drug dealers.[22]

According to Smith, God cares about people, and for that reason, he joins people who would not set foot into or have been excluded from a church. With this quote, Smith makes an analogy to Churchome's approach: With technology, Churchome can also reach people 24/7 and be everywhere at once, similar to God. By not focusing on gathering everyone in a specific building, Churchome can meet people in need instead of waiting for them to come to church. Diane, a long-distance member on the US East Coast who had recently come on the staff of Churchome at the time of our interview, was enthusiastic about this possibility. Her job position included attending conversations on "pastor chat", a function in the Churchome app and website that connects people to Churchome pastors for spiritual care or more general questions. According to Diane, the availability of pastor chat enabled people to reach out in moments of crisis:

---

20   Ibid.: 29:34-29:40.
21   Interview with Carmen, December 15, 2022.
22   Sermon by Judah Smith. "God Pursues You." https://www.youtube.com/watch?v=Uix DJthl7dU, 49:14-9:46.

> [Before], there was nothing like that. There was nothing like that at all. Except, maybe you could call your pastor, but how many times are you gonna call your pastor at night? And when you're broken, [...] you [need] someone to be there [...].[23]

Smith's idea of Churchome, like God, being awake at night helping "knuckleheads and drug dealers", however, is not only directed at external criticism against a perceived ignorance of megachurches. By comparing the effects of Churchome's mission to God's omnipresence, Smith showed his congregation the utmost importance of focusing on digital technologies. In his sermons, Smith regularly mentions that some congregants are not happy about the church's transition from City Church to Churchome and especially the cutback on in-person preaching, and counters such criticism by pointing to the significance and uniqueness of Churchome's approach. Smith presents Churchome's decision to focus on digital technologies as a bold and risky move that people only criticize because they are too comfortable to try out new ways. Just like God's work is excitingly unpredictable, according to Smith, Christians need to be open to trying out new things. In "God Pursues You", Smith declared that God had called Churchome and its members to follow him, even if this meant giving up things they had come to know and love, such as in-person services. In a particularly energized and emotional part of the sermon, Smith presented this need to let go of the familiar as a "prophecy" from God:

> Some of you need to hear that tonight, I'm talking to you, and this just went from sermon to, like, prophecy. Your word is "go" and you know it. You gotta go, you got to do what God told you to do, you got to step out. [...] The goal is not that we all stay together, the goal is that we go with him wherever he takes us. [...] This church was not set up to stay, this church was set up to go. 30 years ago, we started with a goal. We're not ending with the word safe or stay or convenient or comfortable or predictable, we're going to keep going. [...] People are worked up that Churchome doesn't have a service every week where they can hear a live preacher. The word is go. The church is not an event where we come [to] hear a preacher, it's a romance and a journey and you follow Jesus wherever he takes you to. Go! It's unpredictable, it's wild, it's fierce, it's beautiful, it is painful, it's won-

---

23   Interview with Diane, December 22, 2022.

derful, it's called your journey with Jesus. It's not meant to be the same, it's gonna be new challenges and new days and new seasons.[24]

The Churchome members I spoke with mostly embraced Churchome's focus on digital technologies. When they mentioned that they missed in-person services or meetings, they often framed this as a sacrifice they were willing to make to support Churchome's vision. Diane, who had only been to in-person Churchome events twice, called technology a "miracle" that God was able to use for good, and compared it to the long history of media use for Christian evangelizing:

> I mean, being in person, you know, being able to hug people, [...] that's great, but even if we look at, like, you know, the original disciples, right? A lot of what they had to do was write letters, like, they would go out as much as they could, but it was hard to travel back then. [...] And they didn't have the internet, you know. [...] We just happen to have the ability now to reach people all over the world [...].[25]

Being a worship musician, Diane, however, not only missed "being able to hug people" but especially the live music during in-person services. After listening to her passionate recount about reaching people through technology, I asked her whether she didn't miss live worship. In her response, Diane subordinated her preferences to the larger vision of Churchome:

> I am. [...] I'm missing it. But I don't think there's anything wrong with missing something. I'm, you know, I'm a worship leader, I would love to be leading worship. It isn't about me, though.[26]

Churchome's digitalization thus allows members to be part of something bigger than themselves. By using digital media, they can reach people all over the world and be part of a new and exciting endeavor that is still ongoing and constantly changing. Like this, Churchomians can counter the egoism and suburbian-ness that megachurch-goers are often associated with.

---

24 Sermon by Judah Smith. "God Pursues You." https://www.youtube.com/watch?v=UixDJthl7dU, 38:18-40:04.
25 Interview with Diane, December 22, 2022.
26 Ibid.

5.2 Streaming as the path to authenticity

Churchome not only presents its technology-focused approach as an efficient evangelizing strategy and as proof of it caring about people instead of profit but also as a means for people to practice their faith more authentically. Authenticity is a classic Protestant value. Lindholm (2008: 4) argues that the modern aspiration to authenticity was significantly shaped by Protestantism's emphasis on introspection and modesty. For Protestants, salvation could not be attained by performing rituals or following religious rules but through faith alone. Believers thus needed to constantly make sure that their faith was genuine (Scheer 2012: 180).

Striving for authenticity fueled a Protestant reluctance to rely on media or other tools when evoking religious experiences or emotions (Scheer 2014). Believers who attend megachurches, which have been carefully designed to create an atmosphere enabling intimate religious experiences (Rakow 2020), seem to have overcome such skepticism. As my interviews show, however, megachurch services are an ambiguous activity for many attendees. My interviewees were aware of how the architecture of megachurches and the presence of large crowds of other worshippers influenced their emotions. Even though they were not critical of megachurches and their strategic usage of media and architecture per se and found live worship to be an important part of their religious practice, many of them emphasized that their faith should not and did not depend on "putting on a show every weekend".[27] According to pastor Kevin, while a building might draw people in for the show, church at home groups attracted people interested in the same goal as the church, namely building a sustainable and authentic community:

> [...] I'm hosting church in a donut and coffee shop [...] and people aren't turning up because we have this amazing building with lights and all the things, they're turning up there because they actually wanna meet genuine people [...].[28]

Fittingly, to the Churchomians I spoke with faith practice is more authentic when it takes place in locations not usually associated with Christianity. This is true for digital spaces but even more so for in-person meetings in

---

27   Interview with Natalia, long-distance member, December 16, 2022.
28   Interview with Kevin, local pastor, December 5, 2022.

unorthodox environments such as Kevin's donut and coffee shop, whose usage the livestreaming of services makes possible. The church at home group that was most frequently highlighted in my interviews and conversations with Churchome members was a group that met in a CrossFit gym and watched the service together after their workout.[29]

To Churchomians, staying at home to stream services and connecting with other people outside of a church building in church at home groups was not only more authentic because it lacked the dubious showiness of a megachurch service, but because it integrated faith into everyday life. As Kevin put it, "we see a limitation in only gathering in a church building on Sunday morning. There's just so much more to following Jesus than that".[30] This "so much more", at Churchome, takes on the form of building up a personal relationship with Jesus and involving him in all life decisions. As Luhrmann (2012) has shown, in much of present-day Evangelicalism, God is perceived to be an always available friend, and practicing one's faith means working on this friendship. Churchome's sermons often center around the idea that God wants people to include him in their everyday lives, not only because he is desperately interested in every single human being but also because he

> wants to get in your dirt with you, [...] he wants to be involved with [...] all of the things that you're facing, that you're struggling, that you're ashamed of, maybe the things you don't even like about yourself.[31]

Building up a relationship with God is so central to Churchome's message that the people I spoke with often used this idea to contrast Churchome with other Evangelical churches. Both my interviewees and Smith in his sermons constructed a binary of churches that focused on relationships and churches that focused on rules. The latter, "legalistic"[32] rule-focused churches that thought behavior to be more important than belief, served as a negative other whom Churchomians could differentiate themselves from. In his sermon "Fruit Over Works", Smith made this binary explicit and explained that integrating faith into everyday life was the basis for a relationship with Jesus:

---

29 E.g. Interview with Philipp, January 14, 2021.
30 Interview with Kevin, December 5, 2022.
31 Sermon by Chelsea Smith. "Let Jesus Serve You." https://www.youtube.com/watch?v=ewoVnnVMh08, 10:56-11:12.
32 Interview with Carmen, December 22, 2022.

> [...] I'm a fruit over works person, [...] I am relationship over rules. [...] Our focus isn't supposed to be our moral code or the rules we keep or the disciplines we practice, it is to be [in] a relationship with the person of Jesus. I believe someone who focuses on the fruit of the spirit as opposed to the works of the flesh is someone that truly believes that the person of Jesus is far more important than the principles of Jesus. Your focus isn't about disseminating or even assimilating [to the] principles of Jesus, it's about staying close and following the person of Jesus every day.[33]

Integrating God into everyday life, to Churchomians, also means not being able to hide anything from him. Smith's sermons advise listeners to be completely honest with God and my interviewees strove toward opening up to him in prayer. Transparency and vulnerability are important values at Churchome that are regularly acted out both in conversations between followers and in Smith's self-presentation, as he often touches upon his faults and failures in his preaching. In this perspective, reducing one's faith practice to a Sunday service impedes honesty and transparency, and driving to a designated building for religious practice provides an opportunity for pretense. Practicing one's faith from the intimacy and privacy of one's home instead made it more difficult to hide one's shortcomings from oneself, other believers, and, ultimately, God. At Churchome, this was seen as not only intensifying believers' relationships with God but also with each other. Judah Smith's wife and co-pastor Chelsea Smith mentioned in a sermon that when she thinks about the "significant change" from City Church to Churchome, "what comes to mind is the quality of relationships".[34] This resonates with the emphasis Churchome puts on small groups, particularly for those who digitally stream services.

Many of my interviewees, and I argue that this observation can be extended to Churchome's followership more generally, have grown up in Evangelical churches, often ones that were more conservative than Churchome and, in their perspective, belonged to the "rule-focused" side of the binary. Rachel lived in Seattle but enjoyed the freedom of only driving to church for the monthly "church experiences" and streaming the services from home on the other Sundays. For her, Churchome's approach of integrating faith into everyday life via technology opened a whole new perspective on Christianity. Rachel told me

---

[33] Sermon by Judah Smith. "Fruit Over Works." https://www.youtube.com/watch?v=ElrUXVabrz4, 16:42-17:48.

[34] Sermon by Chelsea Smith. "A Gift From Jesus." https://www.youtube.com/watch?v=I6qLNIbFOZ8, 2:26-2:32.

that, having grown up in a rule-focused church, she had always experienced Sunday services as a time when she and her family had to pretend to be happy and pious and to hide their family's "dysfunctionality". Not "having to go to church to have a relationship with God" helped her understand that she did not have to hide her everyday struggles because "Jesus wants to meet you in all of that". As she could be more honest with Jesus, she also allowed herself to take off the "mask of perfection" she had previously worn to all church-related activities.[35]

6. Conclusion: An "authentic" and "exciting" organization

Going online profoundly changed Churchome as an organization: The church diversified possible membership roles and integrated long-distance members, many of them from outside the US. Also, it differentiated between regular and in-person services and framed the latter as special events. The church's followers increasingly consider Churchome as one tile in the mosaic of their religious practice and combine their participation in Churchome with options from other churches and services. Going "beyond a building" also helped Churchome define its identity as an authentic megachurch. By presenting its digital approach as bold and unusual for a megachurch, Churchome can react to critique against the commodification and isolation of megachurches. Paradoxically, for Churchome and many of its members, digital religious practice is more authentic than in-person church attendance.

As they have emerged from modern consumer and event cultures, megachurches arguably depend more than other religious institutions on offering their followers an exciting, unusual, and continuously new experience. As Wellman et al. (2020: 73) put it, at megachurches, "whenever things become too comfortable, too stable, too predictable, the jig is up". Megachurches have been a relevant part of the religious landscape of the US at least since the 1980s. Having church services in large auditoriums can hardly be considered a wow factor anymore. Churchome's digital approach, however, is something new and unique. As Evangelicals have become used to megachurches, they have also become used to thoroughly structured religious organizations that often make decisions according to market logic. At the

---

35 Interview with Rachel, Churchome member and small group host in Seattle, December 5, 2022.

same time, megachurches have received lots of criticism from believers and nonbelievers alike. Churchome, thus, does not see a need to generally conceal its high degree of organization. Instead, it uses its digital approach to combine organization and communitization, to specifically counter criticism against megachurches, and to present itself as an authentic and exciting organization.

As it religiously justifies and idealizes its digitalization strategy, Churchome can stand as an example of how religious entities seek to bring the social forms they choose in alignment with their beliefs. By presenting its "church at home" approach as what God has intended, Churchome can counter criticism from church members unhappy with the church's increasing digitalization and from outsiders accusing the church of not being authentic. According to Churchome, God is not at church, and neither do humans need to be. When more and more of the church's followers are not at church, however, there is of course a risk of anonymity. Churchome's emphasis on "community" for those who follow digitally and the creation of in-person meetings for long-distance members show the fragility of the church's technology-focused approach and a longing to complement digital with in-person participation.

Bibliography

Abraham, Ibrahim (2018): "Sincere Performance in Pentecostal Megachurch Music." In: Religions 9/6, pp. 38–58.

Berger, Peter Ludwig (1990 [1967]): The Sacred Canopy. Elements of a Sociological Theory of Religion, New York: Anchor Books.

Bielo, James S. (2009): Words Upon the Word. An Ethnography of Evangelical Group Bible Study, New York: New York University Press.

Bielo, James (2011): Emerging Evangelicals. Faith, Modernity, and the Desire for Authenticity, New York: New York University Press.

Bourdieu, Pierre (1998): Practical Reason. On the Theory of Action, Stanford: Stanford University Press.

Campbell, Heidi (2012): "Understanding the Relationship between Religion Online and Offline in a Networked Society." In: Journal of the American Academy of Religion 80/1, pp. 64–93.

Campbell, Heidi/DeLashmutt, Michael (2014): "Studying Technology and Ecclesiology in Online Multi-Site Worship." In: Journal of Contemporary Religion 29/2, pp. 267–285.

Chang, Patricia (2003): "Escaping the Procustean Bed: A Critical Analysis of the Study of Religious Organizations, 1930–2001." In: Michele Dillon (ed.), A Handbook of the Sociology of Religion, Cambridge: Cambridge University Press, pp. 123–136.

Coleman, Simon (2003): "Continuous Conversion? The Rhetoric, Practice, and Rhetorical Practice of Charismatic Protestant Conversion." In: Andrew Buckser/Stephen Glazier (eds.), The Anthropology of Religious Conversion, Lanham: Rowman & Littlefield, pp. 15–27.

Corbin, Juliet/Strauss, Anselm (2015): Basics of Qualitative Research. Techniques and Procedures for Developing Grounded Theory, Thousand Oaks: SAGE.

Du Mez, Kristin Kobes (2020): Jesus and John Wayne. How White Evangelicals Corrupted a Faith and Fractured a Nation, New York: Liveright Publishing Corporation.

Hitzler, Ronald (2011): Eventisierung. Drei Fallstudien zum marketingstrategischen Massenspaß, Wiesbaden: VS Verlag für Sozialwissenschaften.

Hutchings, Tim (2017): Creating Church Online. Ritual, Community and New Media, New York: Routledge.

Klaver, Miranda (2021): Hillsong Church. Expansive Pentecostalism, Media, and the Global City, Cham: Palgrave Macmillan.

Kovac, Ariane (2021): "Forschen im Lockdown-Blues. Methodische Reflektionen zum wissenschaftlichen Arbeiten in der Pandemie." In: Zeitschrift für junge Religionswissenschaft 16.

Laughlin, Corrina (2022): Redeem All. How Digital Life Is Changing Evangelical Culture, Oakland: University of California Press.

Lindholm, Charles (2008): Culture and Authenticity, Malden: Blackwell Publishing.

Loveland, Anne/Wheeler, Otis (2003): From Meetinghouse to Megachurch. A Material and Cultural History, Columbia: University of Missouri Press.

Luhrmann, Tanya Marie (2012): When God Talks Back. Understanding the American Evangelical Relationship With God, New York: Vintage Books.

Maddox, Marion (2012): "'In the Goofy Parking Lot': Growth Churches as a Novel Religious Form For Late Capitalism." In: Social Compass 59/2, pp. 146–158.

Petzke, Martin/Tyrell, Hartmann (2012): "Religiöse Organisationen." In: Maja Apelt/Veronika Tacke (eds.), Handbuch Organisationstypen, Wiesbaden: Springer VS, pp. 275–306.

Rakow, Katja (2020): "The Light of the World. Mediating Divine Presence Through Light and Sound in a Contemporary Megachurch." In: Material Religion 16, pp. 84–107.

Ritzer, George (2005): Enchanting a Disenchanted World. Revolutionizing the Means of Consumption, Thousand Oaks: Pine Forge Press.

Roof, Wade (1999): Spiritual Marketplace. Baby Boomers and the Remaking of American Religion, Princeton: Princeton University Press.

Sanders, George (2016): "Religious Non-Places: Corporate Megachurches and Their Contributions to Consumer Capitalism." In: Critical Sociology 42/1, pp. 71–86.

Scheer, Monique (2012): "Protestantisch fühlen lernen. Überlegungen zur emotionalen Praxis der Innerlichkeit." In: Ute Frevert/Christoph Wulf (eds.), Die Bildung der Gefühle, Wiesbaden: Springer VS, pp. 179–193.

Scheer, Monique (2014): "Von Herzen glauben: Performanzen der Aufrichtigkeit in protestantischen Gemeinden." In: Anja Schöne (ed.), Religiosität und Spiritualität. Fragen, Kompetenzen, Ergebnisse, Münster: Waxmann, pp. 111–130.

Schlamelcher, Jens (2018): "Religiöse Organisation." In: Detlef Pollack/Volkhard Krech/Olaf Müller et al. (eds.), Handbuch Religionssoziologie, Wiesbaden, Heidelberg: Springer VS, pp. 489–506.

Thumma, Scott/Travis, Dave (2007): Beyond Megachurch Myths. What We Can Learn From America's Largest Churches, San Francisco and Chichester: Jossey-Bass; Wiley.

Wellman, James/Corcoran, Katie/Stockly, Kate (2020): High on God. How Megachurches Won the Heart of America, New York: Oxford University Press.

Wuthnow, Robert (1989): The Restructuring of American Religion. Society and Faith Since World War II, Princeton: Princeton University Press.

Wuthnow, Robert (2007): After the Baby Boomers. How Twenty- and Thirty-Somethings Are Shaping the Future of American Religion, Princeton: Princeton University Press.

Primary Sources

Interview with Philipp, pastor, January 14, 2021.
Interview with Sophia, long-distance member from Europe, October 15, 2021.
Interview with Kevin, pastor and small group host, December 5, 2022.
Interview with Rachel, small group host in Seattle, December 5, 2022.

Interview with Carmen, small group host and long-distance member, December 15, 2022.
Interview with Natalia, small group host and long-distance member, December 16, 2022.
Interview with Diane, small group host and long-distance member, December 22, 2022.

Web References

Churchome. "Churchome Experiences." Accessed November 8, 2023. https://www.churchome.org/monthly-experiences.

Churchome. "Churchome Stories." YouTube. Accessed October 13, 2023. https://www.youtube.com/playlist?list=PLicUMmdCSpPjuC4NFk-JRzSlOxks5Z-eJ.

Hartford Institute for Religion Research. "Definition Megachurches." Accessed October 4, 2023. http://hirr.hartsem.edu/megachurch/definition.html.

Chelsea Smith. "A Gift From Jesus." YouTube. November 20, 2022. Accessed October 4, 2023. https://www.youtube.com/watch?v=I6qLNlbFOZ8.

Chelsea Smith. "Let Jesus Serve You." YouTube. November 13, 2022. Accessed October 4, 2023. https://www.youtube.com/watch?v=ewoVnnVMho8.

Judah Smith. "Fruit Over Works." YouTube. October 16, 2022. Accessed October 4, 2023. https://www.youtube.com/watch?v=ElrUXVabrz4.

Judah Smith. "God Pursues You." YouTube. November 17, 2022. Accessed October 4, 2023. https://www.youtube.com/watch?v=UixDJthl7dU.

Shapeshifting the Christian Right
The Moral Majority as a Faith-Based Organization and the Immanent Turn of Evangelicalism in the Late 20th Century

Sebastian Schüler

Abstract *Without organizations, religious movements would unlikely survive or achieve social and political influence. This article therefore looks at nonprofit organizations as a specific religious social form. It uses the Moral Majority as an example of how the Christian Right evolved from a loose network of church organizations into a politically successful movement by adopting new forms of organization. These nondenominational faith-based organizations arose in part in response to tax regulations imposed by the government. The Christian Right thus underwent an immanent turn, increasingly adapting its social forms and semantics to secular forms of organization and legal discourse.*

Keywords *Christian Right, faith-based organization, Moral Majority, nonprofit organization*

1. Introduction

On June 24, 2022, the US Supreme Court overturned the 1973 Roe v. Wade legal ruling that granted women the federal right to make a personal choice on abortion. Since then, it has been up to individual states to decide whether and how to grant this right. Twenty-two states have already banned abortion or placed more significant restrictions on it than before. What makes this ruling so unique is that for nearly half a century, conservative Christians in the US not only ceaselessly fought the 1973 decision but also managed to turn this private matter into a public issue to morally charge and politicize it. Many Christian campaigns, rallies, and even physical assaults in front of abortion clinics have taken place since then. Yet, all these local protest actions would not have had such an impact on public discourse and politics had it not been for the emergence of larger organizations of conservative Christians that have since engaged in targeted political lobbying (Hertzke 1988). As a 2012 study by the Pew Research Center for Religion and Public Life showed, not only have religious organizations begun to open offices in Washington and engage in political lobbying since the 1950s, but their numbers and diversity have also grown tremendously in the 20 years preceding the study, and have nearly quadrupled since the 1970s.[1] One reason for this increase, according to the study, is the "growing reach of the federal government in economic, environmental, and social policy", which acts like a magnet and "draw[s] religious groups to the nation's capital" (ibid.: 26). However, the rise of the Christian Right and its political lobbying cannot be explained quite so simply. Historian Randall Balmer (2021), for instance, has even argued that the beginning of the Christian Right lies not in Roe v. Wade but in segregated schools, an argument I will discuss later. Scholarly research on the beginnings of the Christian Right shows one thing above all: astonishment at its sudden success. How could isolated churches and preachers with few connections swiftly mobilize the broad masses and conquer the political stage? Different answers have been given to this question.

My purpose in this paper is not to add yet another answer to the question about motives that gave rise to the Christian Right. Instead, I want to shift the focus away from motives and toward changing organizational forms. I thus endorse the theses of Markus Hero (2010), who points towards the importance of the "productivity of mediation structures" for religious change and assumes an "inherent logic of institutional arrangements" (35). The turn toward Evangelical political activism in the late 1970s was spawned by several organizations that had a lasting impact on public opinion and party politics. Among the best-known of these were Focus on the Family (founded 1977), Christian Voice (founded 1978), The Religious Roundtable (founded 1979), and Moral Majority (founded 1979). By this time, Evangelical leaders such as Jerry Falwell, Robert G. Grant, Paul Weyrich, and James Dobson had established solid networks. They forged a plan for Evangelical Christians to exert more influence on Washington politics. These organizations, most notably the Moral Majority, were their first genuinely successful instruments for doing so.

---

1   Cf. https://www.pewresearch.org/religion/2011/11/21/lobbying-for-the-faithful-exec/.

Two aspects of these organizations are of particular interest: First, they are not ecclesiastical or denominational organizations, as was typical in the US for a long time, but rather supra-denominational organizations whose religious character is only sometimes immediately apparent. Second, they often consist of several component organizations with different tax statuses. They were usually founded as tax-exempt religious nonprofit organizations but, at the same time, established sub-organizations that are not tax-exempt but enable political lobbying. As I will argue in this contribution, the differentiation and diversification of organizational forms in the US has provided new opportunities for the Christian Right, and these two organizational strategies helped the Moral Majority, in particular, to achieve its success and influence.

For a long time, research into religious social forms was based on the classic distinction between church and sect; it was not until the 1970s that other terms, such as movement, cult, or network, were added (see the introduction to this volume for a detailed discussion). More recently, religious organizations have been considered as well, but rarely in their function as a social form. In the last 30–40 years, there has been an enormous increase in religious organizations, leading to a transformation of religious social forms. Religious organizations – be they so-called religious nongovernmental organizations (RNGOs), religious nonprofit organizations (RNPOs), or faith-based organizations (FBOs)[2] – are exerting significant influence on social and political processes and, at the same time, becoming more and more like secular organizations because they have to translate their religious motives into secular language. I therefore speak of an 'immanent turn' in US Evangelicalism based on this change in religious social forms. However, I do not claim that religions or Evangelicalism have transformed into mere organizations. Instead, I argue that several social forms of religion exist side by side and that religious organizations have changed the face of religion in the US significantly in more recent decades. Therefore, I will take a closer look at religious organizations as particular social forms of religion to address the transformation of US Evangelicalism.

---

2   These terms for religious organizations are sometimes used synonymously. While RNGOs are often more internationally active, RNPOs tend to operate at a local or national level. The term FBO is more recent and often used in the context of social welfare or development discourses. There is no adequate typology (Jeavons 2004). I do not see it as my task to solve this problem here, but rather to address the role of religious organizations as religious social forms, regardless of the definitional problem. For this purpose, I will use the more general term FBO and, in the context of US tax law, RNPO.

First, I will review some of the central arguments for the success of the Christian Right to argue that so far, mainly substantive motives have been discussed and less attention has been paid to the social forms of the religious organizations that make up the Christian Right. Secondly, after reviewing recent literature on religious nonprofit organizations and explaining the differences between the various 501(c) types of organizations based on the United States Internal Revenue Service, I argue that they, as particular social forms of religion, play a crucial role in explaining religious change. Building on this, I will further argue that the rise of the Christian Right is closely intertwined with tensions between Evangelical organizations and the US's Internal Revenue Service (IRS) about tax exemption. Finally, and against the background of this tension, I will show that the social forms of Evangelicalism have shifted from church-based to faith-based organizations, giving the Religious Right its success and paved the way for the 'immanent turn' of US Evangelicalism. By this, I mean replacing its rhetoric of redemption with nationalist and legal rhetoric and establishing advocacy groups. I understand my contribution as a cautious sketch of some implications of this development while providing references to relevant literature to acknowledge previous work and further stimulate the debate.

2. Out of the blue? Explaining the success of the Moral Majority

The Moral Majority (1979–1989) is considered one of the most influential Christian conservative organizations and lobby groups of the Christian Right in the United States. It was founded in 1979 by Rev. Jerry Falwell (1933–2007), the well-known best-selling author, televangelist, founder of a megachurch, and founder of the Evangelical Liberty University. Falwell actually has a Baptist background, in which religion and politics are traditionally strictly separated (Allitt 2005: 152). By the 1970s at the latest, and in the wake of the counterculture movement as well as rising unemployment, the attitude of many conservative Christians changed, and they now increasingly blamed the government for social and moral decay. In a series of rallies entitled "I love America", Falwell traveled the country intending to awaken patriotism, morality, and cohesion among Christians and make them aware of their opportunity to exert political influence and to get them out of their self-imposed bubble, which until then had resulted primarily in missionary work to save souls. In his view, there was a moral majority in the country that was not (yet) visible and needed to be mobilized to exert real political influence. The term "moral majority" in this context goes back to Paul Weyrich, who co-founded the Heritage Foundation and Moral Majority, Inc. with Jerry Falwell. By 1980, the Moral Majority already had state chapters in 18 states, and at its peak, it had more than 4 million members.

The rapid success was astonishing to many contemporary observers. For several decades, it seemed that the activities of Evangelical Christians were limited exclusively to saving souls and planting new churches. After the Scopes Trial in the 1920s, Christian fundamentalists were particularly critizied, and it was not until the 1950s that Bible-believing Christians were given a new social stage on which to publicly express their devout faith, most notably through the famous preacher Billy Graham. In the following years, Evangelical training and education centers, radio stations, and televangelists also increasingly emerged. Still, most activities served missions. Politics in Washington was far too distant for many Evangelicals to be closely involved, and local campaigns had little reach because there was no organization to focus activities (Liebman 1983b: 227).

It came as all the more of a surprise – in the perception of the media public and among scholars – that an organization like the Moral Majority should achieve a meteoric rise seemingly out of nowhere and begin exerting enormous political influence. Through the media prominence of Jerry Falwell (he reached some 15 million viewers every week through his television program "Old Time Gospel Hour"), mass letters, and an ideological program, it succeeded in mobilizing Evangelicals and bundling their votes. This way, the Moral Majority managed to cast itself as the conservative and moral conscience of the nation. However, even in the years before the Moral Majority's founding and in the wake of Jimmy Carter's presidential candidacy, the power of Evangelicals as a constituency became clear. Carter, a representative of the Democratic Party, officially declared himself a "born-again Christian" and received the full support of Jerry Falwell for his candidacy. On October 25, 1976, *Newsweek* magazine ran the headline "Born Again! The Evangelicals", and *Christianity Today*, the largest Christian magazine in the US, programmatically proclaimed 1976 as "The Year of the Evangelical" (Kucharsky 1976), followed by the *Time Magazine* titling "The Evangelicals: New Empire of Faith" on December 26, 1977. It was only when Carter did not come out firmly in support of conservative causes such as school prayer or a ban on abortion that the mood tilted. Falwell turned his back on Carter and in the next presidential campaign supported Republican Ronald Reagan with the help of his newly formed Moral Majority. The Moral

Majority was not the first Evangelical lobby group. Still, it was certainly one of the most influential, and its unexpected success drew a lot of attention to this movement, which led scholars to take up the phenomenon of the Christian Right. Over the years, much has been written about its sky-rocketing appearance and much research done to seek explanations for this surprising development. Initially, Moral Majority attracted the interest of political scientists, sociologists, and also communication scientists. Some contributions attempted to explain the religious and political support for Moral Majority using demographic evaluations and analyses of voter behavior. For example, Clyde Wilcox (1989) points to such diverse factors as geography, religious values, social status, party identification, alienation, and symbols, and argues that support for the Christian Right was primarily a reaction to political symbols rather than a reaction to social problems. Sociologists Johnson and Tamney (1984; 1988), on the other hand, examined the voting behavior of Christians in several quantitative studies and found that older, less educated people predominantly voted for the Moral Majority, but also that Christian media possessed a great deal of influence (televangelism, radio stations, etc.) (Lienesch 1982; Roberts 1983; Shupe/Stacey 1983).

Since many also attributed the success of the Moral Majority to the prominence of its leader Falwell, several publications initially focused on Falwell's rhetoric. Between 1983 and 1985 alone, at least five dissertations were written on this topic (Buckelew 1983; Brenner 1984; Jefferson 1984; Phipps 1985; Ray 1985). These works focus primarily on Jerry Falwell's sermons and public speeches, analyzing in particular the argumentative strategies of the Moral Majority in light of their political opposition. In addition, Snowball (1991) attempted an analysis of Falwell's use of war metaphors, which he considered significant for Moral Majority rhetoric. But this explains more about how Evangelicals perceived social tensions than it does about the success of the Moral Majority as a politically influential organization.

For many observers, especially sociologists, the success of the Moral Majority was at odds with modern America. They believed in the secularization of society and that Evangelical and fundamentalist Christians were a dying breed, to be found at most in the very rural areas of the United States. However, the opposite was true. While liberal churches lost members, conservative congregations experienced growth (Liebman 1983b: 234). The rural-urban divide played a role here, as did the establishment of Evangelical educational institutions in the 1970s. Susan Harding (2009), for example, argues that only liberal intellectuals (like herself) believed for too long that religion in general and

Christian fundamentalism in particular were on the wane as secularization progressed. In her view fundamental Christians never disappeared, which she attempts to demonstrate through her historical review going back to the 19th century. In doing so, she emphasizes that the "period between World War II and the birth of the Moral Majority hosted an unbroken series of politically active or politically inflected conservative Protestant mobilizations" (ibid.: 1281). Harding points out a historical thread of the Christian Right that has never been broken and argues that Evangelicals were already trying to bring moral issues into the public sphere before the 1970s to "legislate morality" (ibid.: 1282).

There is no question that the Moral Majority did not simply emerge out of thin air but built its success on various activities and diverse organizations. However, I argue that the success of the Moral Majority cannot be explained solely by the expression of its moral consciousness and social concerns. Before the 1970s, the issues were much more centered on anticommunism, a minor issue for the Moral Majority and only one of many it served. Moreover, the organizations Harding listed were not as successful as the Moral Majority, both in their expansion and reach or membership. Many Evangelical organizations at that time were almost exclusively registered as religious, tax-exempt organizations and, therefore, did not function much differently than church congregations. Their opportunity for political influence was limited if they did not want to risk their status. Accordingly, I argue that a closer look at the organizational form of the Moral Majority promises to shed a different light on the question of its political success.

Robert C. Liebman and Robert Wuthnow made an initial foray in this direction as early as 1983 in their anthology *The New Christian Right: Mobilization and Legitimation*. They also express their astonishment at the rapid success of the movement by opening the volume with the following words: "Scarcely anyone expected it. For more than 50 years Evangelicals kept studiously aloof from American politics" (Liebman/Wuthnow 1983b: 1). They also emphasize that while there had been Evangelical activities before, against communism, for example, these had been exceptions and for many conservative Christians politics was "an evil of the flesh, an exercise in futility" (ibid.: 1). To better understand the Evangelicals' sudden turnaround, they propose a movement-sociological perspective, first noting that social and political movements are often short-lived and that it was therefore uncertain how long the Christian Right movement would last. Today, 30 years later, it can be said that they were right, as the Moral Majority lasted only about 10 years. On the other hand, the authors also emphasize that social and political movements can have a lasting effect on society, which is also true for the Moral Majority.

The main concern in their volume is to show that common interpretations of the sudden success of Evangelicals have too often been attributed solely to the social discontent of Evangelicals and the popularity of pastors like Jerry Falwell, with less consideration of the actual activities and strategies of the movement.[3] Moral protest and burgeoning ideological visions alone might explain a movement's beginnings and motivation, but not necessarily its societal triumph. Every movement consists of various protagonists, lobbyists, and, most importantly, organizations that provide an infrastructure to make the protest permanent and gain political influence. In the new Christian Right, several organizations can be found with financial resources, technical capabilities (such as computerized direct mail solicitation), media publicity, targeted lobbying, and particular organizational forms (Liebman/Wuthnow 1983b: 4). Robert Liebman compared four of the most successful of these new Christian Right movement-organizations and found that Moral Majority's advantage over the others was its experience in fundamentalist political activity as well as its access to a widespread fundamentalist network (1983a: 49). Although the anthology on the Christian Right focused on social and political movements and their organizations, the aspect of particular social and organizational forms, especially regarding the Moral Majority, was not pursued more deeply. The fact that the Moral Majority consisted of various organizational forms sheds a different light on its success, a point to which I return in the next section.

In more recent years, however, historian Randall Balmer (2021) has brought a very different reading of the success of the Christian Right into the debate. Balmer argues that its success was not (solely) due to the abortion issue, but that the real motive was to be found in a dispute over segregated schools (see also Marti 2020). Balmer even claims that the narrative of the Christian Right's success triggered by Roe v. Wade is a fiction served by scholars as much as by Evangelicals themselves. The historical facts would prove that Falwell did not prominently feature the abortion issue in his speeches until the late 1970s. Moreover, he emphasizes that the real key figure was not Jerry Falwell, but

---

3   The editors emphasize that the contributions in the anthology argue quite differently. While some emphasize the role of ideology in the rise of the new Christian Right, others do not see it as a central factor. The volume deliberately unites different positions (Liebman/Wuthnow 1983b: 6).

Paul Weyrich, who tried out various themes to mobilize the Christian Right. Balmer's reading goes like this: In 1970, public schools in seven federal states were still racially segregated, which had been illegal since the US Supreme Court's 1954 Brown v. Board of Education decision. In response to that decision, white students left public schools to enroll in private, racially segregated schools, so-called segregation academies. These schools not only were funded by churches, but also enjoyed tax-exempt status. In a legal trial in 1971 (Coit v. Green), the Supreme Court ruled that nonprofit segregation academies could not be eligible for tax exemption based on the IRC 501(c)(3) definition of public charities. In reaction, the Internal Revenue Service (IRS) withdrew the tax-exempt status of segregation academies, sparking an outcry among white conservative Christians. According to Balmer, Paul Weyrich found this a common ground for Evangelical leaders and approached Jerry Falwell with this issue, which both now turned into a conversation about government interference. It took until 1976 for the United States Supreme Court to rule, in Runyon v. McCrary, that private schools implementing racial segregation violated federal law. Another famous case from the late 1970s was Bob Jones University v. United States (1983), in which Bob Jones University lost its tax exemption on the grounds of racial discrimination.

Balmer's discovery is very intriguing, even though I don't share his rather one-sided account of the Christian Right mobilizing solely on the grounds of segregated schools. Nevertheless, his studies highlight a central point in the emergence of the Christian Right, which I believe was also important for the strategic orientation of its organizational forms. Following Balmer's findings, I argue that it was not only abortion (nor was it only segregation) that gave rise to the Christian Right, and that the influence of Paul Weyrich on Jerry Falwell has probably been underestimated in most historical explanations. Given Weyrich's process of trial and error, it is convincing that abortion, even though it was already an important topic for some Evangelicals, was made a central issue not immediately after Roe v. Wade in 1973, but was publicly politicized only when the Moral Majority was in place. The success of the Moral Majority – in my opinion – therefore cannot be reduced to a single reason or contentious issue. The advantage of the Moral Majority over many other Evangelical organizations was that it served several issues simultaneously. In addition, I argue that past experiences of Evangelicals with the IRS prepared them to develop new ideas on how to build an organization per se. Evangelicals felt that they had long enough been castigated by the political arm from Washington with the IRS as its sharpest tool. The tax-exempt status of religious organizations such as churches or Christian schools has always been an important pillar for organized religion in the United States. It guarantees tax-free income via donations and donors' tax claims on their donations. In addition, tax exemption also means freedom from the state. However, the tax law for religious charities and their relationship with the US government has a checkered history. I will argue, therefore, that the trigger for Evangelicals' mobilization lay primarily in the perceived threat to their religious liberty from the government and the IRS. The mobilization of the Christian Right cannot be explained by motives alone but must consider the infrastructure and strategies involved in establishing new forms of organization. In the following, I will discuss these particular forms of religious organization in more detail.

3. Religious social forms: From nonprofit organizations to faith-based organizations

The Christian Right in general, as well as the Moral Majority in specific, are often casually classified as religious movements. The term movement seems a popular label for many religious social forms. However, religion has rarely been researched in its social form as a movement (Snow/Beyerlein 2019). Research on New Religious Movements (NRMs) from the 1960s onward has scarcely engaged with social science movement research. In contrast, older distinctions of religious social forms such as church, sect, and mysticism have been taken up repeatedly and supplemented by further terms such as cult, consciousness, or charisma (Ashcraft 2018). This has not helped to sharpen the concept of movement in the field of religion. On the contrary, it seems to be applied to any 'religious movement' that is not a church, denomination, or cultic community. While most NRMs are groups with a concrete and manageable following that turns to a charismatic leader, the term movement is more appropriate for collective mobilizations such as religious reform and protest. The Christian Right also rises from a position of protest against the state and the perceived moral decay of society and seeks divine reform of society and politics. Therefore, the movement concept often forms the overarching classification of such a social form, which consists of diverse groups, informal networks, and organizations (Diani 1992: 13).

To better understand the dynamics and structure of such movements as the Christian Right, it is necessary to distinguish between the substantive motives of collective dynamics and mobilizations on the one hand, and the formal strategies and organizational structures on the other that together form a movement. As such, movements like the Christian Right also consist of (movement-)organizations. While much has been written about the motives of the Christian Right, less is found about its organizational structures. However, without organizations the dynamics of the newly emerging collective consciousness would fizzle out shortly. Moreover, organizations must translate the (religious) ideological demands of the mobilized masses into secular policies and political action.

To become politically active, the Moral Majority had to adopt a different organizational form than most religious organizations in the US. All formally organized religions in the US are run as private nonprofit organizations (Hammack 1998). A religious nonprofit organization operates within legal parameters defined by the Internal Revenue Service (IRS) that allow it to receive tax-exempt status and engage in activities related to its mission.[4] For many decades, religions in the US were organized primarily as churches and congregations, legally registered as charitable nonprofit organizations and thus tax-exempt. However, this was to change from the 1970s at the latest. I argue that it was the Christian Right that initiated this change and became the forerunner of a new type of religious nonprofit organization, which on the one hand consists of a more complex organizational form to be able to become politically active, and on the other hand identifies itself less as a religious organization. From this perspective, the Moral Majority is one of the first so-called faith-based organizations (FBO). This transition from a denominational church-based loose network to a politically right-wing movement is grounded on creating faith-based organizations. It has allowed the Christian Right to take advantage of the benefits of this legal structure, such as fundraising, legal recognition, and targeted advocacy efforts, while continuing to address its core religious and moral concerns. To better understand this change in social form, the present section will provide an overview of different variants of nonprofit organizations and past research on religious nonprofit organizations to determine the specific character and appearance of FBOs.

For centuries, religions have seen charity and care for the poor as one of their most important tasks. In the US, it is primarily local churches and congregations that provide such social services. Legally, all organizations whose activities serve the general and public good are classified as charitable nonprofit or-

---

4   Cf. IRS Tax Guide for Churches & Religious Organizations: https://www.irs.gov/pub/irs-pdf/p1828.pdf (last accessed January 18, 2024).

ganizations.[5] In fact, the definition of a "charity" is determined by the requirements of state laws and the federal tax laws represented by the IRS. The IRS also distinguishes between several variants of charitable organizations, all of which are coded according to the internal IRS coding system. In total, there are 29 different 501(c) types, such as for Social and Recreational Clubs (501(c)(7)) or Veterans Organizations (501(c)(23)). Religious organizations such as churches are usually listed as 501(c)(3) organizations. All 501(c) corporations are exempt from corporate income tax, but donations to (c)(3)s are the only ones that are tax deductible. This makes it especially valuable for religious groups to be run as 501(c)(3) organizations. The label "nonprofit" also means that these organizations may take in more than they spend, but the income may not enrich individuals.

Most religious organizations fall under section 501(c)(3). Since at least the 1970s, there has been a shift of some religious organizations to establish one or more sub-organizations that have 501(c)(4) status. According to the IRS definition, a 501(c)(4) is a "social welfare" organization that is primarily engaged in promoting the common good and general welfare. This rather vague definition makes it difficult for the IRS to understand the exact intentions of an organization and classify it accordingly, thus allowing religious organizations to expand their activities. Social welfare organizations are also granted tax-exempt status, but one important difference is that donations to 501(c)(4) organizations are not tax-deductible for donors, unlike donations to 501(c)(3) charitable organizations. This is a consideration for both the organization and potential donors. What makes the status of a 501(c)(4) organization interesting for religions is that they have more flexibility in engaging in political activities and advocacy. This means they can actively influence legislation and public policy debates by supporting partisan campaigns and candidates. It's important to note that while 501(c)(4) organizations are allowed to engage in political activities, there are limitations on the extent of their political involvement. They are still required to primarily focus on social welfare rather than solely engage in partisan political activities. Unlike (c)(3) organizations, (c)(4) organizations do not have to disclose their donors, and a change from (c)(3) to (c)(4) is not always easy because various aspects are taken into account here. It is therefore

---

5   Nonprofit organizations and not-for-profit organizations are different legal forms. A NFPO must be distinguished from a nonprofit organization (NPO) because it need not be established expressly for the public good. In addition, NFPOs are considered recreational organizations, which do not generate revenue.

also noticeable that religious organizations do not usually switch to (c)(4), but establish further sub-organizations with (c)(4) status. This also means that the activities and finances of each sub-organization must be kept separate. In general, the vague boundaries and requirements of nonprofits have led to litigation, and there are now special nonprofit associations that provide legal advice to individual nonprofits on tax issues.[6]

The relevance of the 501(c)(3) status for religious organizations in the United States has evolved over the past 100 years, particularly as the legal and regulatory landscape surrounding nonprofit organizations and their activities has developed. The significance of the 501(c)(4) status for religious organizations became particularly pronounced during the latter half of the 20th century and into the 21st century. For instance, in the early 20th century, tax-exempt status was primarily associated with charitable organizations and there was less differentiation for social welfare activities. However, over time, amendments to the tax code allowed for recognizing other tax-exempt organizations, including 501(c)(4) social welfare organizations. The distinction between the two types of organizations began to take shape during this period. The Civil Rights Movement of the 1950s and 1960s prompted increased advocacy and activism from various groups, including religious organizations. While religious groups had previously engaged in social and political issues, the civil rights movement highlighted the potential impact of organized advocacy. This period marked a growing interest among religious organizations in participating in political and social advocacy efforts. During the latter half of the 20th century and into the 21st century, issues such as abortion, LGBTQI+ rights, family values, and other moral and social concerns gained prominence in public discourse. Many religious organizations sought to influence the outcomes of debates surrounding these issues. The 501(c)(4) status provided a legal framework for organizations to engage more directly in advocacy, lobbying, and political activities related to these issues. The rise of the Christian Right marked a significant period of political activism among conservative religious groups. Some of its organizations operated as 501(c)(4) entities to maximize their ability to engage in political activities.

---

6   As an example, see the California Association of Nonprofits, which lists the advantages of being a nonprofit organization and creating another 501(c)(4) sub-organization to exert political influence. Cf. https://calnonprofits.org/publications/article-archive/616-what-should-nonprofits-know-about-501-c-4-organizations-especially-in-an-election-year.

These developments have further underscored the relevance of the 501(c)(4) status for religious organizations. Accordingly, the IRS has published a *Tax Guide for Churches & Religious Organizations*, which at least attempts to distinguish between churches and other welfare organizations. Nevertheless, the overall situation remains rather confused. It poses practical challenges to religious organizations and the government in dealing with the tax conditions for religious and other welfare organizations (Scheitle 2010: 137).

Research on religious nonprofit organizations has been very limited, although the religious nonprofit sector has grown significantly in the US and globally in recent decades. One of the earliest explorations of the topic was written by Jeff E. Biddle (1992), who describes who benefits from the religious and social activities of religious NPOs. It is noteworthy, however, that Biddle focuses mostly on local congregations rather than larger parachurch organizations or faith-based organizations such as the Moral Majority. This shows that until the 1990s, religious NPOs were perceived primarily in their social form as churches.

In the first edition of the handbook *The Nonprofit Sector*, initiated by sociologist Walter W. Powell, which has already been published in three greatly revised and expanded editions, there is no entry on religion (Powell 1987). Only in the second edition is there an entry entitled "Religion and the Nonprofit Sector", in which the authors make clear: "Whereas religious organizations generally fit the profile of voluntary associations that involve membership and support from members, they do not so easily fit definitions of nonprofit organizations based on registration with tax authorities" (Cadge/Wuthnow 2006: 485). Therefore, to obtain tax-exempt status, religious organizations must demonstrate that a substantial portion of their activities are for charitable and benevolent purposes. In addition, they highlight that "the law and policies governing religious organizations in the United States are subject to differing interpretations and frequently contested" (ibid.: 489).

The complexity of religious nonprofit organizations has also increased since the 1980s. Brad R. Fulton's article "Religious Organizations: Crosscutting the Nonprofit Sector" notes that religious organizations have rarely been considered from an organizational sociology perspective and emphasizes: "Religious organizations are also the most prevalent type of organization in the nonprofit sector, encompassing not only congregations but also a wide variety of other faith-based organizations that provide a vast array of products and services" (2020: 579). In addition, some religious organizations have recently become active in non-religious areas of the nonprofit sector and tend to downplay their religious roots and intentions (ibid: 580). Ultimately, this makes the transition between religious and secular nonprofits increasingly fluid and difficult to define for administrative authorities. Fulton also notes the changing nature of religious organizations: While many scholars understand religious organizations to mean primarily churches and congregations, and even other religious traditions such as Buddhists and Hindus in the US organize themselves into congregations, it is also clear that not every religious organization is a congregation. He therefore makes an analytical distinction between congregations and faith-based organizations, which I adapt here.

The term faith-based organization (FBO) is not a legal term and is understood more broadly than the category of a religious organization. Thus, FBOs do not necessarily have to be of or affiliated with a particular religion or denomination. Most FBOs are social service organizations that run soup kitchens and care for the poor. The term emerged in the late 1990s, after President Bill Clinton initiated the welfare reform of 1996 that took control over welfare away from the federal government and gave it to the states. As a result, they were now to decide whether to allow religious organizations funding for their charitable work (this state degree is therefore also known as charitable choice program, cf. Nagel 2006). This was pushed even further when President George W. Bush launched the so-called Faith Based Initiative in 2001 that provided more infrastructure for the welfare reform and allowed FBOs to partake in federally directed social service programs to the same extent as any other group as long as they used the money only for their welfare activities and not for religious activities (Scheitle 2010: 155). This development has resulted in much more research literature on FBOs than on religious NPOs since the 1990s (cf. Bielefeld/Cleveland 2013). Usually, it addresses only the state's financial support of religious organizations and not attempts on part of religious organizations to influence the state through lobbying.

Although the term FBO refers principally to developments in the nonprofit sector since the 1990s, I think it is also fruitful for describing the transformation of religious social forms particularly within the Christian Right since the 1980s. Similarly, sociologist Christopher Scheitle has shown that parachurch organizations have been growing since the 1980s (2010). The term parachurch organization is used here synonymously with faith-based organizations that work across or outside of denominations. In an additional study of Evangelical mobilization in the nonprofit sector, Scheitle and McCarthy (2018) have shown that counties with more Evangelicals in the population are more likely to establish parachurch organizations than counties with more Catholics or Mainline

Protestants. Unfortunately, their analysis only covers the period from 1998 onwards. Nevertheless, this study highlights an important point in my argument: I suggest that since the late 1970s, Evangelicals in particular have begun to form FBOs that have changed the organizational landscape of Evangelicalism. These are characterized above all by the fact that, unlike other religious NPOs, they cannot be assigned to any particular church or denomination and are often – at least in terms of their name and appearance – hardly recognizable as religious NPOs. The Moral Majority fits that description. It was also open to other denominations, but was composed of and addressed primarily to Evangelical Christians, without the name Evangelical in its title.

Summing this up, traditional religious social forms such as church, sect, or cult have often been the subject of academic inquiry. In contrast, religious movement organizations such as religious parachurch organizations, nonprofits, and faith-based organizations received less attention as distinct social forms of religion. Nevertheless, they can help to explain the transformation of religious social forms in late modernity. The emergence of faith-based organizations from the 1980s onwards can therefore be understood both as a reaction to the demands and possibilities of the rule of law (like the IRS) and as a way of manipulating the rule of law (as in federal politics). In the case of the Christian Right, faith-based organizations like the Moral Majority not only gave opportunity for political activism, but also gave the Christian Right a whole new image and an integrative, mobilizing force beyond church organizations and denominations, as I will exemplify further in the next section.

4. From mobilization to lobbying and advocacy: The immanent turn of Evangelicalism

Since the founding of the United States, the religious nonprofit sector has been characterized by "an ethos of voluntarism or self-help and the development of a strong civic sphere that was only loosely associated with government" (Cadge/Wuthnow 2006: 488). During the 20th century, however, tensions between the state and religious service providers increased: "As the role of federal government has expanded, church-state rulings have also governed the extent to which tax, employment, and nondiscrimination policies that apply to other nonprofit organizations would apply to religious ones" (ibid: 488). These tensions culminated in the 1970s and repeatedly led to legal disputes.

The first mobilizations took place at the local and regional level, and interest in political activism arose around abortion laws, pornography, and gay rights legislation, most of which were fought in local courts or led to protest campaigns. Accordingly, from the 1970s onward, Evangelicals became increasingly politically aware. Local and regional networks and organizations became an important infrastructure for the later success of the Moral Majority. It quickly utilized its infrastructure to engage in advocacy, education, and mobilization efforts while remaining aligned with its religious foundations. In addition to all the motives that contributed to the mobilization, a general awareness developed among Evangelicals that religious liberty was threatened by state impositions and an overly liberal government (Marti 2020). The IRS became a symbol of governmental evil and suppression of religious liberty.

At the National Affairs Briefing Conference in Dallas on August 21, 1980, just a few weeks before presidential election day, Ronald Reagan held a well-known speech in front of thousands of Evangelicals. Some say this is when Evangelicals finally embraced the Republican Party. In his speech, Reagan makes direct reference to religious freedom under threat by the state (which he himself soon intended to represent): "If we have come to a time in the United States when the attempt to see traditional moral values reflected in public policy leaves one open to irresponsible charges, then the structure of our free society is under attack and the foundation of our freedom is threatened" (American Rhetoric Online Speech Bank). Of particular interest here is that for Evangelicals, political activism is part of their religious freedom, but political decisions should not limit their religious freedom: "When I hear the First Amendment used as a reason to keep traditional moral values away from policy making, I'm shocked. The First Amendment was written not to protect the people and their laws from religious values, but to protect those values from government tyranny" (ibid.). This tyranny he also sees in the IRS when he speaks against plans to "force all tax-exempt schools – including church schools – to abide by affirmative action orders drawn up by – who else? – IRS bureaucrats".[7] Evangelicals saw America in jeopardy of losing its identity as a Christian nation, and the Christian Right continuously spread the narrative that America was founded as a Christian nation, a myth that prevails until today.

The name Moral Majority was therefore also programmatic and had an inclusive rather than a denominational character. To target advertising and reach

---

7 Cf. https://millercenter.org/rivalry-and-reform/building-movement-party.

additional groups of people, the Moral Majority distributed a leaflet with the inscription *Your Invitation to Join The Moral Majority*.[8] The leaflet was intended to address pastors in particular, who were seen as multipliers for the organization's concerns: "Bible-believing churches of America constitute the largest single minority bloc of America. However, this bloc is, for the most part, uninformed and disorganized, to the point that politicians ignore them. The only persons who can lead this mammoth bloc are the pastors".[9] This top-down process also shows that the Moral Majority was less of a grassroots movement than it is sometimes portrayed. The movement was much more thought through structurally by a small circle of actors, and its organizational form is modeled on modern FBOs. On the back of this tri-fold leaflet one finds a quite revealing organizational chart of the Moral Majority. According to this chart, the Moral Majority is divided into four organizational units: the Moral Majority Foundation, the Moral Majority, Inc., the Moral Majority Political Action Committee, and the Moral Majority Legal Defense Foundation. All four suborganizations had their legal status.

According to the leaflet, the Moral Majority Foundation is a 501(c)(3) organization whose central mission is to educate "pro-moral citizens". Conferences, rallies, and seminars are to be offered for this purpose. The leaflet specifically points out that donations can be deducted from one's taxes. The reader also learns that Moral Majority, Inc. is a 501(c)(4) organization whose primary mission is to influence national, state, and local legislation. The organizational structure here is the most extensive and includes the production of print media, targeted seminars, and assistance for political candidates and their staff to win elections. It also mentions a network of 435 congressional coordinators who can recruit and train "pro-moral" candidates for all public offices. The Moral Majority Political Action Committee is listed as a separate sub-organization, but without specifying its legal status (regarding the IRS). This committee aims to coordinate moral activism between the Moral Majority and other "pro-moral" organizations and promote voter registration among church agencies. It also specifically states that donations to the committee are tax deductible. Finally, the Moral Majority Legal Defense Foundation is listed as a 501(c)(3) organization and described as a "pro-moral" counterpart to the "humanist" American Civil Liberties Union. The ACLU, founded in 1920, is an NGO advocating for civil rights such as freedom of speech and liberal positions such as the

---

8 Cf. https://cdm17184.contentdm.oclc.org/digital/collection/p17184coll1/id/22/rec/2.
9 Cf. ibid.

right to abortion and the separation of church and state. The so-called "promoral" counterpart of the Moral Majority therefore wants to help individuals and families with adequate legal defense "who are attacked by the godless, amoral forces of humanism". It also states as one of its goals to "legally establish Humanism as a religion and have it expelled from the public schools". Here, once again, the Moral Majority's perception as a group of citizens oppressed by the liberal state and the attempt to legally translate its concerns into secular language (humanism as a religion) becomes clear. This way, the Moral Majority also established another trend: the use of legal action in addition to political lobbying. For example, Evangelical law firms proliferated after the end of the Moral Majority, with the American Center for Law and Justice, founded by Pat Robertson in 1990, as one of the leading firms.[10]

The Moral Majority can generally be seen as an FBO with clear hierarchical structures to organize a centralized decision-making process, allowing for swift and coordinated responses to emerging issues. This hierarchical structure aligned with the organization's objectives of influencing public policy, particularly on issues like abortion, homosexuality, and school prayer. The Moral Majority effectively utilized media platforms and personal networks to communicate its message, showcasing the significance of organizational communication in promoting its cause and garnering support. Unlike classical churches and denominations, FBOs often operate within a complex network of stakeholders, including members, donors, and other advocacy groups. These interconnections influence the organization's activities, strategies, and effectiveness in achieving its goals. The Moral Majority's collaboration with other conservative groups such as Robert Grant's "Christian Voice" or the "Roundtable" demonstrated the broader social forms that emerged from shared values and objectives. The Moral Majority is thus not a typical (denominational) religious organization but can be considered one of the first faith-based organizations to use the creation of sub-organizations to obtain various legal and tax benefits and to operate at various levels. In this way, Evangelicalism has taken an immanent turn on its organizational side. By immanent turn, I do not mean the Moral Majority's attempt to be politically active, but to position itself as a secular organization that is no longer set up like a church-based nonprofit and is even barely recognizable as a religious organization. Moreover, this organizational shift also implies a semantic shift:

---

10   Cf. https://www.duo.uio.no/handle/10852/41063.

religious concerns are translated into secular, partly legal, language. The salvation of souls through faith and repentance, as preached by Billy Graham, is being transformed into the salvation of the nation through morally educated citizens whose rights must be secured by the courts. In this process, there have been many areas where Evangelicals have identified moral lapses. These may have been triggers for mobilization. But as I have shown, it was also the organizational choice that made the actual success of the Moral Majority and the Christian Right possible.

5. Conclusion

In conclusion, the paper argues that understanding the success of the Christian Right requires examining not just ideological motives but also the changing organizational forms that allowed these groups to exert significant political influence. The interplay between religious organizations, their legal status, and political strategies is seen as crucial in shaping the trajectory of the Christian Right and its transformational impact on US Evangelicalism. Therefore, I focused on the organizational forms of the Christian Right, emphasizing the importance of movement organizations like Focus on the Family, Christian Voice, The Religious Roundtable, and Moral Majority. These organizations, founded in the late 1970s, significantly mobilized Evangelical Christians for political activism. Notably, they were supra-denominational and utilized tax-exempt religious nonprofit status while establishing sub-organizations that allowed for political lobbying. This legal transformation began as a response to tax regulations imposed by the IRS and led to the adoption of new organizational forms. The rise of Evangelical political activism is thus attributed to the differentiation and diversification of organizational structures. I further argued that this shift from church-based to faith-based organizations and the strategic use of legal statuses like 501(c)(3) and 501(c)(4) organizations with varied tax classes provided new opportunities for the Christian Right and contributed to its success. To explain this process, I have introduced the concept of an 'immanent turn' in US Evangelicalism, through which religious concerns are translated into secular language and used to address legal and political challenges. The Moral Majority began the legalization of the Christian Right, which continues to fight its battles primarily in the courtroom. While the Moral Majority's direct influence may have waned, its organizational tactics and impact continue to resonate in contemporary Evangelical political activism. The text underscores the importance of understanding both the substantive motives and formal organizational structures to grasp the dynamics of movements like the Christian Right.

Bibliography

Allitt, Patrick (2005): Religion in America Since 1945, New York: Columbia University Press.

Ashcraft, W. Michael (2018): A Historical Introduction to the Study of New Religious Movements, 1st ed. London, New York: Routledge.

Balmer, Randall (2021): Bad Faith: Race and the Rise of the Religious Right, Grand Rapids, MI: Eerdmans.

Biddle, Jeff E. (1992): "Religious Organizations." In: Charles T. Clotfelter (ed.), Who Benefits from the Nonprofit Sector? Chicago, IL: University of Chicago Press, pp. 92–133.

Bielefeld, Wolfgang/Cleveland, William S. (2013): "Defining Faith-Based Organizations and Understanding Them Through Research." In: Nonprofit and Voluntary Sector Quarterly 42/3, pp. 442–467.

Brenner, Douglas F. (1984): The Rhetoric of the Moral Majority: Transforming Perceptions of Opposition. Ph.D., Lincoln, NE: University of Nebraska.

Buckelew, Roy E. (1983): The Political preaching of Jerry Falwell: A Rhetorical Analysis of the Political Preaching of Rev. Jerry Falwell on Behalf of the Moral Majority During the 1980 Political Campaign. Ph.D., Los Angeles, CA: University of Southern California.

Cadge, Wendy/Wuthnow, Robert (2006): "Religion and the Nonprofit Sector." In: Walter W. Powell/Richard Steinberg (eds.), The Nonprofit Sector: A Research Handbook, New Haven: Yale University Press, pp. 485–505.

Diani, Mario (1992): "The Concept of Social Movement." In: The Sociological Review 40/1, pp. 1–25.

Fulton, Brad R. (2020): "Religious Organizations: Crosscutting the Nonprofit Sector." In: Walter W. Powell/Patricia Bromley (eds.), The Nonprofit Sector, Stanford, CA: Stanford University Press, pp. 579–598.

Hammack, David C. (1998): Making the Nonprofit Sector in the United States: A Reader, Bloomington, IN: Indiana University Press.

Harding, Susan F. (2009): "American Protestant Moralism and the Secular Imagination: From Temperance to the Moral Majority." In: Social Research 76/4, pp. 1277–1306.

Hero, Markus (2010) Die neuen Formen des religiösen Lebens: Eine institutionentheoretische Analyse neuer Religiosität, Würzburg: Ergon.

Hertzke, Allen D. (1988): Representing God in Washington: The Role of Religious Lobbies in the American Polity, Knoxville, TN: University of Tennessee Press.

Jeavons, Thomas (2004): "Religious and Faith-Based Organizations: Do We Know One When We See One?" In: Nonprofit and Voluntary Sector Quarterly 33/1, pp. 140–145.

Jefferson, Patricia A. (1984): Spokesmen for a Holy Cause: A Rhetorical Examination of Selected Leaders of the New Religious-Political Right. Ph.D., Bloomington, IN: Indiana University.

Johnson, Stephen D./Joseph B. Tamney (1984): "Support for the Moral Majority: A Test of a Model." In: Journal for the Scientific Study of Religion 23/2, pp. 183–196.

Johnson, Stephen D./Joseph B. Tamney (1988): "Explaining support for the Moral Majority." In: Sociological Forum 3/2, pp. 234–255.

Kucharsky, David (1976): "The Year of the Evangelical '76." In: Christianity Today 21/2, pp. 12–13.

Liebman, Robert C. (1983a): "Mobilizing the Moral Majority." In: Robert C. Liebman/Robert Wuthnow (eds.), The New Christian Right: Mobilization and Legitimation. New York: Aldine Publishing Company, pp. 49–73.

Liebman, Robert C. (1983b): "The Making of the New Christian Right." In: Robert C. Liebman/Robert Wuthnow (eds.), The New Christian Right: Mobilization and Legitimation. New York: Aldine Publishing Company, pp. 227–238.

Liebman, Robert C./Wuthnow, Robert (eds.) (1983a): The New Christian Right: Mobilization and Legitimation, New York: Aldine Publishing Company.

Liebman, Robert C./Wuthnow, Robert (1983b): "Introduction." In: Robert C. Liebman/Robert Wuthnow (eds.), The New Christian Right: Mobilization and Legitimation. New York: Aldine Publishing Company, pp. 1–9.

Lienesch, Michael (1982): "Right-Wing Religion: Christian Conservatism as a Political Movement." In: Political Science Quarterly 97/3, pp. 403–425.

Martí, Gerardo (2020): American Blindspot: Race, Class, Religion, and the Trump Presidency, Lanham: Rowman & Littlefield Publishers.

Nagel, Alexander-K. (2006): "Charitable Choice: The Religious Component of the US-Welfare-Reform." In: Numen 53/1, pp. 78–111.

Phipps, Kim S. (1985): The Rhetoric of the Moral Majority Movement: A Case Study and Reassessment of Conservative Resistance. Ph.D., Kent State University: Kent, Ohio.

Powell, Walter (1987): The Nonprofit Sector: A Research Handbook, New Haven: Yale University Press.

Ray, Veronn O. (1985): Rhetorical Analysis of the Political Preaching of the Reverend Jerry Falwell: The Moral Majority Sermons 1979. Ph.D., Baton Rouge, LA: Louisiana State University.

Roberts, Churchill L. (1983): "Attitudes and Media Use of the Moral Majority." In: Journal of Broadcasting 27/4, pp. 403–410.

Scheitle, Christopher P. (2010): Beyond the Congregation: The World of Christian Nonprofits, Oxford and New York: Oxford University Press.

Scheitle, Christopher P./McCarthy, John D. (2018): "The Mobilization of Evangelical Protestants in the Nonprofit Sector: Parachurch Foundings Across U.S. Counties, 1998–2016." In: Journal for the Scientific Study of Religion 57/2, pp. 238–257.

Shupe, Anson/Stacey,William. (1983): "The Moral Majority Constituency." In: Robert C. Liebman/Robert Wuthnow (eds.), The New Christian Right, New York: Aldine Publishing Company, pp. 103–116.

Snow, David A./Beyerlein, Kraig. (2019): "Bringing the Study of Religion and Social Movements Together: Toward an Analytically Productive Intersection." In: David A. Snow (ed.), The Wiley Blackwell Companion to Social Movements, Hoboken: John Wiley & Sons Ltd.

Snowball, David (1991): Continuity and Change in the Rhetoric of the Moral Majority, New York: Bloomsbury.

Wilcox, Clyde (1989): "Evangelicals and the Moral Majority." In: Journal for the Scientific Study of Religion 28/4, pp. 400–414.

Web References

Randall Balmer. "The Real Origins of the Religious Right. They'll Tell You It Was Abortion. Sorry, the Historical Record's Clear: It Was Segregation." Politico Magazine. May 27, 2014. Accessed October 19, 2023. https://www.americanrhetoric.com/speeches/ronaldreaganreligiousliberty.htm.

California Association of Nonprofits. "What Should Nonprofits Know About 501(c)(4) organizations? Especially in an Election Year?" Accessed October 12, 2023. https://calnonprofits.org/publications/article-archive/616-what-should-nonprofits-know-about-501-c-4-organizations-especially-in-an-election-year.

Internal Revenue Service. "Tax Guide for Churches & Religious Organizations." Accessed January 14, 2024. https://www.irs.gov/pub/irs-pdf/p1828.pdf.

Miller Center. "Rivalry and Reform. Building a Movement Party. The Alliance Between Ronald Reagan and the New Christian Right." Adapted from Chapter Six of Rivalry and Reform, by Sidney M. Milkis and Daniel J. Tichenor. Accessed October 19, 2023. https://millercenter.org/rivalry-and-reform/building-movement-party.

Moral Majority. "Your Invitation to Join the Moral Majority." Liberty University Archives. Accessed December 18, 2023. https://cdm17184.contentdm.oclc.org/digital/collection/p17184coll1/id/22/rec/2.

Pew Research Center. "Lobbying for the Faithful: Religious Advocacy Groups in Washington, D.C." Pew Research. May 15, 2012 [2011]. Accessed October 19, 2023. https://www.pewresearch.org/religion/2011/11/21/lobbying-for-the-faithful-exec/.

Ronald Reagan. "National Affairs Address on Religious Liberty." American Rhetoric Online Speech Bank. August 22, 1980. Accessed October 19, 2023. https://www.americanrhetoric.com/speeches/ronaldreaganreligiousliberty.htm.

Hanne Amanda Trangerud. "Evangelical Law Firms and the Translation of Arguments: A Study of the Evangelical Movements Influence Through National and International Courts." Master thesis, University of Oslo. September 16, 2014. Accessed December 18, 2023. https://www.duo.uio.no/handle/10852/41063.

Social Forms in Neo-Pentecostal Prosperity Contexts
From Network to Market Exchange

Maren Freudenberg

Abstract *This chapter discusses the various social forms that play a role in prosperity contexts, a diverse yet distinct strain within neo-Pentecostalism whose adherents believe that God will reward them with health and wealth in return for generous gifts to their churches and other financial investments. The contribution focuses on group, event, organization, network, movement, and market exchange as the social forms through which individuals and groups coordinate their religious interaction and practice, and highlights market exchange as a particularly salient form due to its congruence with prosperity semantics. Prosperity theologies teach that investment not only in one's personal faith and one's congregation, but also, and importantly, on the secular market, will be rewarded by God, and these semantics are mirrored on a structural level by the market exchange as a form of transaction between two parties. Given the fact that financial risk-taking and success on the secular market are coded religiously as signs of depth of faith and divine grace, the market exchange complements these core tenets by translating semantics into structure, as it were.*

Keywords *group, market exchange, neo-Pentecostalism, network, organization, prosperity ethic, prosperity gospel, prosperity theologies*

1. Introduction

This chapter focuses on what has been called the prosperity gospel, prosperity theologies, or, more recently, the prosperity ethic, a diverse yet distinct strain within neo-Pentecostalism whose adherents believe that God will reward them with health and wealth in return for generous gifts to their churches and other financial investments (Attanasi 2016). Prosperity teachings have spread at an astounding pace in recent years, particularly in the Global South, where Pentecostalism continues to gain adherents in large numbers (Attanasi/Yong 2016). While a host of literature exists on the popularity and rapid dissemination of prosperity theologies (cf. below), little attention has been paid to how the content of these theologies might affect the ways in which believers come together to practice their faith – how they structure and coordinate religious interaction. It is the aim of this chapter to shed light on various social forms that play a role in neo-Pentecostal prosperity contexts; it is thus primarily a theoretical contribution, less an empirical one. To this end, it will draw from existing literature and use selected empirical examples to illustrate its theoretical arguments.

The chapter consists of four sections: The remainder of this introduction (1) will locate neo-Pentecostal prosperity teachings within the broader Pentecostal-Charismatic landscape as a general orientation for readers unfamiliar with this Christian tradition. Following a brief summary of the history and main tenets of prosperity teachings in section 2, which serves to sketch the most important religious semantics in the field, section 3 shifts the focus to religious structure and discusses a variety of social forms that are evident in prosperity contexts. It focuses on group, event, organization, network, movement, and market exchange as the main forms by way of which individuals and groups coordinate their religious interaction and practice, and highlights market exchange as a particularly salient social form due to its congruence with prosperity semantics. The chapter closes with some concluding reflections.

Pentecostal-Charismatic Christianity, an experiential strain that emphasizes the "gifts" of the Holy Spirit, such as speaking in tongues, prophecy, and healing, is the fastest-growing Christian current worldwide (Miller et al. 2013). With its ability to adapt to local contexts, absorbing instead of disregarding existing religious worldviews and 'translating' its core tenets to meet a range of cultural expectations, it has successfully spread around the globe and particularly taken root in the Global South (Afolayan et al. 2018; Robbins 2004). Observers generally distinguish three phases in the history of Pentecostal-Charismatic Christianity: (1.) 'Classical' Pentecostalism, which emerged at the beginning of the 20th century in different parts of the world, including in the United States in the context of the Asuza Street Revival (1906–1915) in Los Angeles; (2.) Charismatic Renewal movements, especially but not exclusively in the Roman Catholic Church, which gained momentum through contacts with Pentecostalism since the 1960s; and (3.) neo-Pentecostalism (or neo-Charismatic Christianity), a 'softer' reinterpretation of classical Pentecostalism that emerged starting in the 1980s and emphasizes healing and self-empowerment (Bowler 2013; Hunt 2002).

There are a number of different statistics and reports on how many people identify as Pentecostal-Charismatic Christians; a rough consensus seems to be that at least 500 million people worldwide exhibit some degree of self-identification with this broad tradition. The World Christian Encyclopedia's third edition counts 644 million members globally: 230 million in Africa, 195 million in Latin America, 125 million in Asia, 68 million in North America, 21 million in Europe, and 4.5 million in Australia and Oceania (Johnson/Zurlo 2020); other general sources count e.g. 450 million Pentecostals and Charismatics worldwide plus an additional 200 million Christians strongly influenced by Pentecostal-Charismatic Christianity, including Evangelicals with a focus on the Holy Spirit (Jacobsen 2021). In her extensive study on the Prosperity Gospel in the United States, Kate Bowler reports that 17% of all US Christians identify with prosperity teachings, while 31% believe that God increases the wealth of those who give (2013, 6).

Clearly, thus, Pentecostal-Charismatic Christianity is an influential tradition in the Americas and, to a lesser extent, in Europe, and prosperity teachings play an increasingly large role in Asia, Africa, the Americas, and beyond. Because the prosperity gospel originated in the United States and has become similarly popular in Latin America in recent decades, the empirical examples this chapter draws from are largely located in the Americas, also to match the present volume's geographical focus. The following section offers a brief overview of the history and main tenets of prosperity theologies before we turn to our discussion of social forms in neo-Pentecostal prosperity contexts in the remainder of the chapter.

2. Neo-Pentecostal prosperity teachings

At the heart of prosperity teachings lies the conviction that God will reward believers with health and wealth for generous gifts to their churches and for a variety of other monetary and spiritual investments. Adherents are taught to expect multiple returns on what they give: material wealth, physical and emotional health, and a generally prosperous, "abundant" life. For this reason, prosperity theologies are often called the "health and wealth gospel", although observers have long since emphasized the heterogeneous nature of prosperity teachings around the globe (Coleman 2017; Hunt 2002). Coleman suggests thinking of "Prosperity discourse as manifested less in a single Gospel per se, and more in a set of ethical practices that can be combined and reconstituted in very different cultural contexts, and which may in fact work through ambiguity and play as much as through the expression of apparently firm and exclusive religious convictions" (2016, 276–277). Very generally, he argues, "prosperity orientation is constituted by ritual activity that establishes links between forms of giving and the creation of value" (Coleman 2017, 62–63). In the prosperity framework, the believer becomes an investor with the goal not only of spiritual salvation but of access to the secular market as a sign of this-worldly divine election. As elaborated below, economic risk-taking is increasingly coded as conviction of God's power to change adherents' lives for the better, while success in the marketplace translates into an indicator of divine grace. The following overview of the origins and development of global prosperity theologies takes these assumptions as a point of departure to emphasize their wide variety at the same time as stressing core commonalities in order to focus, in the following section, on the various social forms, particularly the market exchange, that emerge in neo-Pentecostal prosperity contexts.

Prosperity theologies also run under the heading of "Word of Faith", the name of a Pentecostal current that was coined by American evangelist Kenneth Hagin (Coleman 2016, 279). According to Harrison, Word of Faith consists of three core elements: Believers must (1) learn "who they are in Christ" and (2) practice "positive confession" to (3) be rewarded with prosperity, divine health, and material wealth (2005, 8–12). They are taught that because the Bible promises a life of "abundance" for the faithful – "God loves a cheerful giver" (2 Corinthians 9:7); "Give and it will be given unto you" (Luke 6:38); "My God will supply every need of yours according to his riches of glory in Christ Jesus" (Philippians 4:19); etc. (cf. Yong 2016) –, they must fully accept this fact as a kind of contract between themselves and God, never calling it into doubt and thus not accepting poverty and suffering as their lot in life. Instead, they are to cultivate an optimistic mindset which focuses on how "blessed" they are and to affirm this attitude out loud wherever possible. The belief in the transformational power of words lies at the heart of positive confession: "Members are encouraged to always be vigilant concerning the power their words carry in shaping their thinking and their subsequent lives or realities. […] Mental discipline, mental 'hygiene,' or self-censorship, should be an ongoing practice as demonstration of one's faith" (Harrison 2005, 10–11). Through these means, adherents argue, health, wealth, and prosperity can be attained by anyone. This line of reasoning can be seen as the smallest common denominator of prosperity theologies, their broad variety notwithstanding.

Prosperity theologies began emerging in neo-Pentecostal congregations in the United States during the 1980s and 1990s, but their roots lie in certain ways of thinking about spiritual power and the power of the mind at the turn of the 19th to the 20th century. In particular, New Thought (an 1870s offshoot of Christian Science emphasizing the power of thought and speech), classical Pentecostalism of the early 20th century, and the pragmatism, individualism, and "mythology of uplift" that American society is known for, including African American spiritualism, shaped prosperity theologies as they exist today (Bowler 2013, 11). Norman Vincent Peale's 1952 book *The Power of Positive Thinking* is considered as influential a source as televangelist Oral Robert's "seed faith" concept, which laid the groundwork for more recent entrepreneurial, risk-taking varieties of prosperity discourse. Bowler argues that, in contrast to the biblically prescribed tithe of 10 per cent of one's income, which can be seen as a secure investment as it constitutes part of a larger amount one has already received, seed faith money presents an additional donation that adds risk in the hopes of increasing returns (Bowler 2013: 67; cf. also Coleman 2017: 56–57). This idea has led to increasingly risky financial investment on part of prosperity adherents in the last decades with the aim of overcoming material poverty, physical suffering, and spiritual self-doubt, including in the Global South (Hunt 2002; Coleman 2016; Chesnut 2016).

While the growing popularity of prosperity churches around the world – in countries such as Brazil, Guatemala, Colombia, and other Latin American contexts, but also in Sub-Saharan Africa, East Asia, Southeast Asia, and, to a lesser extent, Eastern Europe – can be interpreted against the backdrop of the global dissemination of American religious and secular (i.e. capitalist) values (e.g. Brouwer et al. 1997), it is crucial to realize that prosperity churches in the Global South have long become religious actors in their own right that shape not only their own local and regional contexts in distinct ways but also strongly influence the international neo-Pentecostal scene through worldwide missionizing (e.g. Afolayan et al. 2018; Hunt 2000). For instance, the Brazilian Igreja Universal do Reino de Deus, the Universal Church of the Kingdom of God (UCKG), Latin America's largest neo-Pentecostal denomination, has meanwhile established a visible presence in southern Africa (Freston 2005).

What is the worldwide appeal of prosperity churches? The promise of health, wealth, and "abundance" is obviously compelling to many, particularly but not exclusively the lower strata of global society (Attanasi/Yong 2016). It seems to resonate in contexts of both material (absolute) deprivation, such as in the Global South, and of relative (perceived) deprivation, such as in the more affluent societies of the Global North (Hunt 2002), promising access to "the secular market not only as an enabler of open commerce but also as a somewhat exclusive space to which access is restricted but desired" (Coleman 2017: 52). In fact, prosperity theologies are attracting an increasing number of middle-class adherents with their promise of upward social mobility, including better jobs, better pay, no more loans and debt, and so forth (Marti 2008; Harrison 2005). Its messages are aimed at individuals (not at families, congregations, or communities) and may also encompass typical middle-class issues such as ameliorating circumstances in the workplace as well as improving one's social or romantic life. Chesnut notes that prosperity theologies' focus on health and healing is especially welcomed in contexts where the majority of adherents perform hard labor and do not have access to basic medical benefits such as sick leave and health care, while neo-Pentecostal exorcisms to drive out sickness are increasingly popular in the Global South as they dovetail with indigenous beliefs (2016: 221).

Whether the context is one of absolute or relative deprivation, it is important to note that the individualist ethos of prosperity theologies is at complete odds with more communally oriented interpretations of Christianity, such as Catholic Liberation Theology with its focus on communal justice and fundamental systemic change. In contrast, prosperity theologies emphasize individual "empowerment" by offering believers, who are usually the receivers of charity and assistance, the opportunity to "become active investors often in the same institution that facilitated a miracle in their lives or even helped them turn their lives around" (Chesnut 2016: 219). They are clearly strongly materialist in orientation, promoting what has been called "a kind of consumer 'instantism' […] that prosperity and health is the automatic divine right of all bible-believing [sic] Christians" (Hunt 2002: 16). While prosperity teachings certainly perpetuate the global capitalist order, they are at the same time more complex than simply a 'neoliberalization of religion'; for better or worse, the prosperity framework arguably grants moral agency to believers to work towards alleviating their own poverty through the market. Adherents believe that they are empowered by God to change their own circumstances by way of vocalizing their convictions of the better life that is in store for them and demonstrating the depth of their faith by spending money with the firm expectation of a multitude of divine rewards. Although there is no statistical evidence of overall social benefits from prosperity teachings and practices, their popularity continues to remain high on a global scale (Ukah 2020; Soboyejo 2016; Chesnut 2016).

While early prosperity theologies were more miracle-based and otherworldly in orientation, observers are noting subtle shifts in current prosperity discourses around the globe that increasingly emphasize this-worldly salvation. Cornelio and Media argue that giving and positive confession are, to a certain extent, a thing of the past; now, adherents are expected to develop investment and financial management skills with the goal of increasing financial revenue and freedom from debt. This new "prosperity ethic", according to them, "promotes an individualized work ethic, backed by a religious conviction that promises financial returns" and is characterized by two main features: *"sacralizing self-help* and *celebrating consumption"* (Cornelio/Medina 2021, 65; italics in original). The first includes achieving individual prosperity through one's own means instead of waiting for God to intervene, while the second refers not only to financial prosperity but, quite explicitly, to spending and consuming as a marker of a happy, fulfilled life. They argue that the new prosperity ethic "has three dimensions: the morality of the market (believing right), the prescribed mindset (thinking right), and the practical skills to accumulate wealth (doing it right)" (ibid.: 72). Joel Osteen, senior pastor of America's largest megachurch, is a forerunner of the prosperity ethic in this sense (Freudenberg 2024; Freudenberg et al. 2020), which has meanwhile spread around the globe. Bartel (2021) has shown how spending and consumption – to the point of maximizing one's credit card and running high debts – is considered a sign of absolute faith and trust in God in Columbia, while Ijaola notes "a shift from the 'claim it and have it' prosperity formula to 'work it and have it' by faith" in Sub-Saharan Africa in recent years (2018: 153).

Analytical investigations of the development of prosperity theologies have focused, on the one hand, on the marketization of religion and society, and, on the other, on convictions regarding capacity for change on part of individuals (Medina/Cornelio 2021). This contribution understands itself as located in the former line of investigation, given its focus on social forms as an expression of religious structure and the market exchange as a particularly salient form of social interaction in prosperity contexts. The following section begins with a brief overview of the concept of social form, referring to the volume's introduction for a more detailed discussion, before presenting the various social forms that are evident in neo-Pentecostal prosperity contexts.

3. Social forms of religion in neo-Pentecostal prosperity contexts

The introduction to this volume defines social forms very generally as ways in which individuals coordinate social interaction, and social forms of religion subsequently as ways of coordinating interaction in the religious field. This includes not only religious interaction per se, as in during a worship service or group prayer, but also the 'background coordination' that makes religious interaction possible, such as maintaining a congregation or organizing an event. Social forms of religion are thus located at the meso level of society, between the macro and micro levels, where mediation between individuals and society at large occurs and the dynamics of communitization, of deepening interpersonal connections in the process of coordinating religious practice, come to the fore (Ludwig/Heiser 2014).

The introduction offers an overview of various typologies of religious social forms, including Max Weber's ideal types of *church* and *sect* (Weber 2011 [1905]); Ernst Troeltsch's (1960 [1912]) expansion of Weber's work and his addition of *mysticism* as a third type; H. Richard Niebuhr's (1929 [2005]) addition of *denomination* as an attempt to apply Troeltsch's typology to the American context; Howard Becker's (1940) alternative expansion of Troeltsch's work that includes *ecclesia, sect, denomination,* and *cult*; Bryan Wilson's (1970) sevenfold sub-typology of sects; Roy Wallis's (2019) distinction between world-affirming, world-rejecting, and world-accommodating cults; and Stark and Bainbridge's (1985) distinction between church, sect and cult. Instead of drawing on the typologies proposed by Weber and Troeltsch and subsequently expanded by other authors, however, this chapter draws from newer perspectives on social forms in the sociology of religion which also look toward organizational sociology for inspiration.

One of these is Beyer's distinction between organized religion, politicized religion, social movement religion, and communitarian/individualistic religion (Beyer 2003), which draws on organization, movement, and group as three types of social forms of religion. Following a slightly different approach, Krech et al. (2013) view group (or community), organization, and market exchange as the three main social forms of religion and add movement and event as two further sub-types. Similarly, Heiser and Ludwig (2014) present five social forms of religion: organizations, networks (including movements), communitization (or group dynamics), marketization, and eventization (the increasing importance of religious events). The following discussion on different social forms that are evident in neo-Pentecostal prosperity contexts draws from this and other literature to show that a range of social forms shape neo-Pentecostal religion and are in turn influenced by prosperity ideologies.

In neo-Pentecostalism, congregations and small groups (such as Bible studies, prayer groups, and a range of other groups) are crucial: It is here that people come together to affirm and celebrate their beliefs, strengthen their social relationships, provide mutual support, and find means of accessing the divine in community. While these characteristics apply to religious congregations in general, the *group* is inevitably an important social form in neo-Pentecostalism. Here, prosperity teachings are disseminated among members and legitimated by way of shared practices, such as worship as a central, formalized ritual with its elements of preaching, prayer, and testimony, on the one hand, as well as through informal personal ties and close emotional bonds, on the other. In addition, weekly worship as a communitizing and legitimizing ritual can be conceived of as an *event* as a spatially, temporally, and socially condensed form of communal religious experience which transports participants out of the realm of the everyday and offers an extra-ordinary, cathartic experience (Hitzler 2011; Gebhardt 2018). Again, this social form is not exclusive to neo-Pentecostalism, being characteristic of other emotional, ecstatic traditions in and beyond Christianity. In prosperity contexts, however, the worship service and especially the sermon have the important function of elaborating the prosperity message and driving it home through specific performative and rhetoric strategies (cf. Freudenberg 2024 for an example).

At the same time, neo-Pentecostal congregations are usually embedded in an organizational context that provides the necessary personnel, structures, and resources to offer worship services and other forms of service to the community as well as to maintain staff, a building, and so on. This social form of *organization* may take the shape of a denomination, such as the Assemblies of God in the United States or the Igreja Universal do Reino de Deus ('Universal Church of the Kingdom of God') in Brazil. But there are also a multitude of non-denominational neo-Pentecostal congregations, many of them megachurches with an attendance of thousands of participants per weekend (cf. Thumma/Travis 2007), that are small organizations in themselves. Besides providing structures and resources for congregations, these denominations or non-denominational church organizations also facilitate access to (or are themselves nodes in) larger networks as channels for the further dissemination of prosperity theologies worldwide. As Coleman observes on organizational features of neo-Pentecostalism the United States, a loosely knit organization called the International Convention of Faith Churches and Ministries (ICFCM) has provided some ideological unity in more recent years, alongside powerful educational establishments such as Oral Roberts University and Kenneth Hagin's Bible School, both based in Tulsa, Oklahoma. And yet, no single church form or organization has held definitive sway. For instance, the suburban, middle-class, post-denominational megachurch phenomenon of the late twentieth and early twenty-first centuries has provided an important venue for dimensions of prosperity teaching (2017: 57).

In a similar vein, Harrison calls the neo-Pentecostal Word of Faith movement "a contemporary American religious subculture made up of denominationally independent churches, ministries, Bible training colleges and other educational institutions, voluntary organizations and fellowships, information and entertainment production facilities, and mass media broadcast networks" (2005: 5).

So while organizational structures are clearly evident in neo-Pentecostalism as a broader field, it also exhibits the characteristics of a *network*, with flatter hierarchies, decentralized power structures, and a global range. The Brazilian denomination Igreja Universal do Reino de Deus ('Universal Church of the Kingdom of God') again serves as a good example: It is based in São Paulo but has spawned subsidiaries not only throughout the country and region, but overseas, including in the United States, the United Kingdom, India, and, most importantly, southern Africa (Freston 2005). These 'sister churches' around the world are connected with each other through various channels, including through international conferences to share the latest developments and best practice examples, by way of guest preachers to expose congregations to different styles of preaching and interpreting the prosperity message, but most importantly through the internet and social media. In this way, the UCKG is able to integrate a range of different social actors and roles on this basis of a common identity, all the while maintaining distinct yet porous boundaries to ensure flexibility in the many different contexts it has (and continues to) spread to. Other prominent examples of global neo-Pentecostal prosperity networks that operate similarly include the Nigeria-based Redeemed Christian Church of God (Adogame 2004) and the originally Australian Hillsong Church (Rocha et al. 2021).

As mentioned in the introduction, the social forms of network and movement are often understood as somehow related, albeit in different ways, in the literature (e.g. Ludwig/Heiser 2014; Williams 2003). Social (including religious) *movements* have been defined as networks consisting of group and organization elements assembled around a collective identity, common goals, and resource mobilization and aimed at bringing about social (or religious, or political) change (Kern/Pruisken 2018). Neo-Pentecostal prosperity settings have been described as taking the social form of "meeting combined with movement: coming together while never quite wishing to accept stasis and institutionalization" (Coleman 2016: 281). At the same time, observers argue that the designation of movement misses the mark, as the term implies more coherence than is actually apparent in the field (e.g. Coleman 2017). The breadth of variety found in global neo-Pentecostalism – also considering that many neo-Pentecostal congregations are non-denominational instead of being part of a larger denomination (Walton 2016) – should not be underestimated, particularly in terms of how it affects the development of its social forms. Hunt emphasizes that "the designation of this relatively new religious phenomenon as a 'movement' is a misnomer, since the distinctive Faith gospel is represented by hundreds of independent ministries which might depart, to one degree or another, in both practice and doctrine, from the core teachings. What cannot be doubted, however, is the global significance of these ministries." (2002: 2). I agree with this assessment; although neo-Pentecostalism is often described as a 'movement' even in academic literature, the term is not used in a sociological but more in a popular sense, implying development and innovation instead of stasis. While neo-Pentecostalism is certainly a dynamic field, it lacks the unity – shared identity, goals, and resource mobilization – that would render it a coherent movement from a sociological perspective.

In the context of prosperity theologies, the *market exchange* is a salient social form that deserves special attention considering the fact that believers are encouraged to actively invest in their faith, their congregations, and the secular market as a sign of their conviction that God will reward them with "abundance". The market exchange involves exchange partners – individuals or groups – that come together for a limited amount of time to negotiate and conduct a transaction. Krech et al. (2013: 55–56) argue that because the exchange is a rational form of interaction, the exchange partners are included in this social form based on their formal roles and functions, not on their personalities. In slight contrast, Ludwig and Heiser (2014: 6) point out that both rational cost/benefit analyses as well as communally negotiated norms and values establish the basis for market exchanges . From the perspective of microeconomics, negotiating norms and values in the process of the market transaction falls under the individual's cost/benefit analysis, which means, for a discussion of social forms, that the exchange partners are in fact included based on their formal roles in the exchange (cf. Freudenberg/Rezania 2023: 85–125 for an overview of basic assumptions in microeconomics).

In prosperity churches, then, who are the exchange partners? They may be conceived of as the believer, on the one hand, and the divine, on the other: The believer invests time and effort to learn "who they are in Christ" and attain the skill of positive confession (Harrison 2005: 8–11), and invests money in and beyond their congregation to ultimately sow the seeds of health, wealth, and prosperity. This is an inevitably tricky analytical construct from a social scientific perspective as the divine is of course not a concrete empirical social agent; but considering that it is the task of the sociology of religion to investigate the social consequences of individual and collective religious beliefs, prosperity theology adherents' conviction that God responds to and rewards their investments must be taken seriously, also from an analytical vantage point. This means conceptualizing the divine as one 'partner' involved in prosperity transactions. Another way of understanding the partners included in the market exchange in prosperity contexts is the believer, on the one hand, and their congregation, on the other. In return for the believer's spiritual and monetary investment, the congregation grants affirmation and legitimacy to the individual's conviction that God will reward them with a healthy, wealthy, and prosperous life. The same framework could be applied to the believer and the congregation's pastor: The pastor as preacher and spiritual guide but also as a main beneficiary of donations to the congregation encourages individual believers' investments in return for the promise that God will reward them abundantly. In this case, the pastor represents the rewards promised by the divine in the form of his (or, more seldomly, her) own prosperity.

However, prosperity teachings have consequences that extend beyond the realm of the congregation. As adherents are encouraged to "celebrat[e] consumption" (Cornelio/Medina 2021: 65) by spending money as a sign of a blessed, fulfilled life, by conducting risky financial investments, and even by taking on debt to show their absolute faith in divine rewards, the social form of market transaction in prosperity contexts also includes transactions between believers and agents in the secular market. The latter may or may not hold prosperity convictions of their own, but secular market transactions become part of a larger set of religious practices from an analytical perspective as soon as believers frame spending money in the secular realm as an act of faith. When a prosperity adherent is encouraged by their pastor as spiritual guide to invest in something as seemingly mundane as, say, new living room furniture to demonstrate their conviction that God will abundantly reward their positive, optimistic mindset with health and wealth, the seemingly 'secular' act of buying furniture is coded religiously, i.e. as a divine investment that will reap multiple returns (cf. Freudenberg 2024 and Freudenberg et al. 2020 for examples). It is in this sense that prosperity teachings create a kind of 'double value' through investment: On one level, the believer invests in new furniture, increasing the value of their home; on the other, they invest in their religious convictions, increasing their expectation of manifold returns (cf. Coleman 2017: 62–63).

We arguably see here the extent to which prosperity semantics correspond to the social forms prosperity practices take. The main tenets of prosperity teachings have come to include not only investments in one's personal faith and one's congregation, but also increasingly risky and debt-prone transactions on the secular market. The market exchange – conceived of as taking place between the believer and God, or the congregation, or the pastor, or, importantly, agents in the secular market as exchange partners – is evidently the social form of religion best suited to 'translate' the central prosperity tenets into concrete social practices, as it allows individuals to interact and coordinate with one another in a way that gives expression to those religious ideas they, for better or worse, hold most valuable.

4. Conclusion

This chapter has focused on neo-Pentecostal prosperity theologies as a distinct yet diverse tradition within Pentecostalism to show the range of social forms that are evident in the ways that adherents come together to coordinate their faith: group, event, organization, network, and market exchange. It has suggested that the social form of market exchange is particularly salient in this context due to its correspondence with prosperity semantics: Prosperity theologies teach that investment not only in one's personal faith and one's congregation, but also and importantly in the secular market, will be rewarded by God in multiple ways – especially with physical and emotional health as well as material wealth –, and these semantics are mirrored on a structural level by the market exchange as a form of transaction between two parties. Given the fact that financial risk-taking and success on the secular market are coded religiously as signs of depth of faith and divine grace, the market exchange complements these core tenets by translating semantics into structure, as it were.

This is not to render any of the other social forms discussed above less important; for other dimensions of neo-Pentecostalism, such as community cohesion or globally organized structures, they remain central. As analytical categories, all of them could (and should) be investigated in more depth against the backdrop of the congruence between form and semantics. It is necessary to keep in mind that religions always exhibit a mix of social forms, with important effects on how religions – especially their core ideas – develop over time. In this sense, a closer investigation of the tension between community and individualism in neo-Pentecostalism would further our understanding regarding the importance of the social form of group and the dynamics of communitization just as much as an investigation of the logistical structures that undergird neo-Pentecostal denominations and megachurches would further our understanding of the centrality of organization and network as social forms. The correspondence between semantics and structure is thus not limited to a single social form; this chapter has highlighted the market exchange in the effort of making an indent in the larger work on social forms to be done in and beyond the neo-Pentecostal field.

Bibliography

Adogame, Afe (2004): "Contesting the Ambivalences of Modernity in a Global Context: The Redeemed Christian Church of God, North America." In: Studies in World Christianity 10/1, pp. 25–48.

Afolayan, Adeshina/Yacob-Haliso, Olajumoke/Falola, Toyin (eds.) (2018): Pentecostalism and Politics in Africa, Cham: Palgrave Macmillan.

Attanasi, Katherine/Yong, Amos (eds.) (2016): Pentecostalism and Prosperity: The Socio-Economics of the Global Charismatic Movement, Basingstoke: Palgrave Macmillan.

Attanasi, Katherine (2016): "Introduction: The Plurality of Prosperity Theologies and Pentecostalisms." In: Attanasi, Katherine/Yong, Amos (eds.), Pentecostalism and Prosperity: The Socio-Economics of the Global Charismatic Movement, Basingstoke: Palgrave Macmillan, pp. 1–12.

Bartel, Rebecca C. (2021): Card-Carrying Christians: Debt and the Making of Free Market Spirituality in Colombia, Oakland, CA: University of California Press.

Becker, Howard (1940): "Constructive Typology in the Social Sciences." In: American Sociological Review 5/1, pp. 40–55.

Beyer, Peter (2003): "Social Forms of Religion and Religions in Contemporary Society." In: Michele Dillon (ed.), Handbook of the Sociology of Religion, Cambridge: Cambridge University Press, pp. 45–60.

Bowler, Kate (2013): Blessed: A History of the American Prosperity Gospel, New York: Oxford University Press.

Brouwer, Steve/Gifford, Paul/Rose, Susan D. (1997): Exporting the American Gospel: Global Christian Fundamentalism, New York: Routledge.

Chesnut, R. Andrew (2016): "Prosperous Prosperity: Why the Health and Wealth Gospel Is Booming Across the Globe." In: Katherine Attanasi/Amos Yong (eds.), Pentecostalism and Prosperity: The Socio-Economics of the Global Charismatic Movement, Basingstoke: Palgrave Macmillan, pp. 215–223.

Coleman, Simon (2016): "The Prosperity Gospel: Debating Charisma, Controversy and Capitalism." In: Stephen Hunt (ed.), Handbook of Global Contemporary Christianity, Leiden: Brill, pp. 276–296.

Coleman, Simon (2017): "Morality, Markets, and the Gospel of Prosperity." In: Daromir Rudnyckyj/Filippo Osella (eds.), Religion and the Morality of the Market, Cambridge: Cambridge University Press, pp. 50–71.

Cornelio, Jayeel/Medina, Erron (2021): "The Prosperity Ethic: The Rise of the New Prosperity Gospel." In: Jayeel Serrano Cornelio/François Gauthier/Toumas Martikainen/Linda Woodhead (eds.), Routledge International Handbook of Religion in Global Society, London: Routledge, pp. 65–76.

Dillon, Michele (ed.) (2003): Handbook of the Sociology of Religion, Cambridge: Cambridge University Press.

Freston, Paul (2005): "The Universal Church of the Kingdom of God: A Brazilian Church Finds Success in Southern Africa." In: Journal of Religion in Africa 35/1, pp. 33–65.

Freudenberg, Maren (2024): "Joel Osteen's Prosperity Gospel and the Enduring Popularity of America's 'Smiling Preacher'." In: Ruth Conrad/Roland Hardenberg/Hanna Miethner/Max Stille (eds.), Ritual and Social Dynamics in Christian and Islamic Preaching, London: Bloomsbury, pp. 105–126.

Freudenberg, Maren/Lutz, Martin/Radermacher, Martin (2020): "Gospels of Prosperity and Simplicity. Assessing Variation in the Protestant Moral Economy." In: Interdisciplinary Journal of Research on Religion 16, pp. 2–47.

Freudenberg, Maren/Rezania, Kianoosh (2023): Religionsökonomie, Stuttgart: utb.

Gebhardt, Winfried (2018): "Religiöse Szenen und Events." In: Detlef Pollack/Volkhard Krech/Olaf Müller/Markus Hero (eds.), Handbuch Religionssoziologie, Wiesbaden: Springer, pp. 591–610.

Harrison, Milmon F. (2005): Righteous Riches: The Word of Faith Movement in Contemporary African American Religion, Cambridge: Oxford University Press.

Hitzler, Ronald (2011): Eventisierung: Drei Fallstudien zum marketingstrategischen Massenspaß, Wiesbaden: VS Verlag für Sozialwissenschaften.

Hunt, Stephen (2000): "'Winning Ways': Globalisation and the Impact of the Health and Wealth Gospel." In: Journal of Contemporary Religion 15/3: pp. 331–347.

Hunt, Stephen J. (2002): "Deprivation and Western Pentecostalism Revisited: Neo-Pentecostalism." In: Journal for the Interdisciplinary Study of Pentecostalism and Charismatic Movements 1/2, pp. 1–29.

Ijaola, Samson O. (2018): "Pentecostalism, the Prosperity Gospel, and Poverty in Africa." In: Adeshina Afolayan/Olajumoke Yacob-Haliso/Toyin Falola (eds.): Pentecostalism and Politics in Africa, Cham: Palgrave Macmillan, pp. 137–158.

Jacobsen, Douglas G. (2021): The World's Christians: Who They Are, Where They Are, and How They Got There, Chichester: Wiley-Blackwell.

Johnson, Todd M./Zurlo, Gina (eds.) (2020): World Christian Encyclopedia, Leiden: Brill.

Kern, Thomas/Pruisken, Insa (2018): "Religiöse Bewegungen – Das Beispiel des Evangelikalismus in den USA." In: Detlef Pollack/Volkhard Krech/Olaf Müller/Markus Hero (eds.), Handbuch Religionssoziologie, Wiesbaden: Springer, pp. 507–524.

Krech, Volkhard/Schlamelcher, Jens/Hero, Markus (2013): "Typen Religiöser Sozialformen und ihre Bedeutung für die Analyse religiösen Wandels in Deutschland." In: Kölner Zeitschrift für Soziologie und Sozialpsychologie 65/1, pp. 51–71.

Ludwig, Christian/Heiser, Patrick (2014): "Zur Mesoebene Von Religion. Eine Einführung." In: Patrick Heiser/Christian Ludwig (eds.), Sozialformen der Religionen im Wandel, Wiesbaden: Springer, pp. 1–16.

Marti, Gerardo (2008): Hollywood Faith: Holiness, Prosperity, and Ambition in a Los Angeles Church, New Brunswick: Rutgers University Press.

Medina, Erron/Cornelio, Jayeel (2021): "The Prosperity Ethic." In: Pneuma 43/1, pp. 72–93.

Miller, Donald E./Sargeant, Kimon H./Flory, Richard (eds.) (2013): Spirit and Power: The Growth and Global Impact of Pentecostalism, Oxford: Oxford University Press.

Niebuhr, Helmut Richard (1929 [2005]): The Social Sources of Denominationalism, Whitefish: Kessinger Publishing.

Pollack, Detlef/Krech, Volkhard/Müller, Olaf/Hero, Markus (eds.) (2018): Handbuch Religionssoziologie, Wiesbaden: Springer.

Robbins, Joel (2004): "The Globalization of Pentecostal and Charismatic Christianity." In: Annual Review of Anthropology 33/1, pp. 117–143.

Rocha, Cristina/Openshaw, Kathleen/Vokes, Richard (2021): "'Middle-Class' Africans in Australia: Choosing Hillsong as a Global Home." In: Culture and Religion 22/1, pp. 25–45.

Soboyejo, Josephine Olatomi (2016): "Prosperity Gospel and Its Religious Impact on Sustainable Economic Development of African Nations." In: Open Access Library Journal 3/11, pp. 1–13.

Stark, Rodney/Sims Bainbridge, William (1985): The Future of Religion: Secularization, Revival, and Cult Formation, Berkeley, CA: University of California Press.

Thumma, Scott/Travis, Dave (2007): Beyond Megachurch Myths: What We Can Learn from America's Largest Churches, San Francisco, CA: Jossey-Bass.

Troeltsch, Ernst (1960 [1912]): The Social Teaching of the Christian Churches: Vol. I and II, New York: Harper.

Ukah, Asonzeh (2020): "Prosperity, Prophecy and the COVID-19 Pandemic." In: Pneuma 42/3-4, pp. 430-459.

Wallis, Roy (2019): The Elementary Forms of the New Religious Life, Ann Arbor: Routledge.

Walton, Jonathan L. (2016): "Stop Worrying and Start Sowing! A Phenomenological Account of the Ethics of 'Divine Investment'." In: Katherine Attanasi/Amos Yong (eds.), Pentecostalism and Prosperity: The Socio-Economics of the Global Charismatic Movement, Basingstoke: Palgrave Macmillan, pp. 107–130.

Weber, Max (2011 [1905]): The Protestant Ethic and the Spirit of Capitalism. The Revised 1920 Edition. Translated and edited by Stephen Kahlberg. New York: Oxford University Press.

Williams, Rhys H. (2003): "Religious Social Movements in the Public Sphere: Organization, Ideology, and Activism." In: Michele Dillon (ed.), Handbook of the Sociology of Religion, Cambridge: Cambridge University Press, pp. 315–330.

Wilson, Bryan R. (1970): Religious Sects: A Sociological Study, London: Weidenfeld & Nicolson.
Yong, Amos (2016): "A Typology of Prosperity Theology: A Religious Economy of Global Renewal or a Renewal Economics?" In: Katherine Attanasi/Amos Yong (eds.), Pentecostalism and Prosperity: The Socio-Economics of the Global Charismatic Movement, Basingstoke: Palgrave Macmillan, pp. 15–33.

Pentecostal Social Engagement in Contemporary Guatemala

Virginia Garrard

Abstract *This essay explores emerging social forms in the context of Pentecostal social engagement in the Central American nation of Guatemala. It explores why in this specific context, evangélicos and Pentecostals in particular have begun to develop new social forms and hermeneutics of social transformation. Guatemala has undergone a tectonic epistemological shift from a post-temporal, apocalyptic orientation to one that is presentist and instrumentalist in its outlook. Pentecostals in recent decades have transitioned from an eschatological hermeneutics of separation from the world to one that embraces social and political participation, cohering, in the process, into social forms that emphasize collective mobilization and participation. This evolution of religious social forms corresponds to a shifting emphasis in religious ideals and theologies that become self-reinforcing logics within the vertical and horizontal networks of the church. Pastors build strong vertical patriarchal relations with their congregants, and they purposefully encourage strong lateral networks within "small groups," formed around different affinities, such as geography, interest, age, marital status, or demographic, that strengthen the group cohesion of the church as both a community and as an institution As these social relationships evolve, they transform the role of the church as an organization to one of increased, outward-facing social action. This chapter posits that this transition evinces an evolution of evangélico social forms. These differ in fundamental ways from classical Pentecostalism, which reified insularity, to modern social forms that adhere to religious values that they believe compel them to action.*

Keywords *Guatemala, hermeneutics, Latin America, Pentecostalism, social forms, social groups, social mobilization, theology*

1. Introduction

In 1990, the US anthropologist David Stoll published an early study on the rapid expansion of Protestantism, and specifically Pentecostalism, in Latin America entitled *Is Latin America Turning Protestant? The Politics of Evangelical Growth* (1990). The book's subtitle exposed an expectation as to the implications of religious conversion that pervades much of the literature to the present day. Both scholars and popular observers of Pentecostalism in Latin America have often defined the religion's function as one that is or should be, fundamentally political and socially engaged.

This work will explore how and why in the specific context of the Central American nation of Guatemala, *evangélicos* (used here in the Spanish sense to describe all Protestants, not only 'Evangelicals,' as the term means in English), and Pentecostals in particular, have begun to shift their individual and group religious understandings, as well as their own and institutional expectations, from staunch apoliticism to a new hermeneutics of social engagement. During what the noted British-Brazilian sociologist Paul Freston (1994) designated as the 'first wave' of wholesale conversions in Guatemala – roughly, the 1970s and 1980s, during the nation's civil war – these 'Classical' Pentecostals were perhaps the least likely of any sector to get involved in politics or political action of any kind. In sharp contrast, many of today's Pentecostals believe that their beliefs *compel* them to action (cf. Garrard-Burnett 2012). Pentecostals in recent decades have transitioned from an eschatological hermeneutics of separation from the world to one that embraces social and political participation, cohering, in the process, into social forms that emphasize collective mobilization and participation. This evolution of religious social forms corresponds to a shifting emphasis in religious ideals and theologies. As these social relationships evolve, they transform the role of the church as an organization – which previously prioritized insularity – to one of increased, outward-facing social action.

I posit that this transition evinces an evolution of *evangélico* social forms. These differ in fundamental ways from Classical Pentecostalism. Concepts of personhood and theological concerns throughout Latin America, even as recently as the 1980s, were fixated upon end times prophecies and the centrality of the salvation narratives within a social universe that they called "the church," but in practice, consisted of many disaggregated denominations and individual congregations. These religious groups were connected only by a shared embrace of key charismatic theological beliefs and somatic practices, specifically, an emphasis on "baptism in the Holy Spirit", manifest by "gifts", such as faith healing and speaking in tongues.

Classical Pentecostalism was extraordinarily atomized and highly individualized, as believers established their bona fides not by joining a specific church, but in their individual abilities to performatively manifest Charismatic virtues such as offering individual conversion stories and engaging in ecstatic behavior during worship services. A third characteristic of Classical Pentecostalism was its centrifugal tendency, as any individual member who had a unique Charismatic vision or heterodox theological perspective, regardless of his or (less commonly her) training or experience as a pastor, could and often did break off to start their own church, taking sectors of their home congregation with them. These factors all conspired to make Classical Pentecostalism in Latin America dynamic, but also very fragile in terms of social cohesion, and the churches weak in their collective efficacy as social organizations.

All this has changed over the past three or four decades, as the dynamism of Pentecostalism has generated new theologies that are presentist rather than eschatological in orientation, and which emphasize new technologies of self (self-improvement, capacity-building, education, wealth acquisition, and consumerism, leadership training) instead of focusing on the imminent Second Coming of Christ, the prophetic vaticination that animated their predecessors. The scholarly literature refers to this orientation as 'neo-Pentecostalism', an etic designation that few believers or pastors would utilize or even recognize; nevertheless, it is the dominant religious strain in Guatemalan Pentecostalism, as it is in most of Latin America.

Neo-Pentecostalism encourages and flourishes in large mega-churches. These types of churches typically gravitate around the Charismatic leadership of a single pastor, who often presides with his wife or other close family members as leadership affiliates. Pastors build strong vertical patriarchal relations with their congregants, and they purposefully encourage strong lateral networks within "small groups" (a term of art used in the churches); some congregations call these *grupos celulares*, or cellular groups, reflecting the aspiration that the groups reproduce themselves like cells undergoing mitosis in a living organism. Small groups form around different affinities, such as geography, interest, age, marital status, or demographic, that strengthen the group cohesion of the church as both a community and as an institution. The groups function as a social formation designed to encourage strong horizontal interpersonal relationships among group members. At the same time, they reinforce horizontal, patriarchal relations between the groups and the church as an institution as embodied by the pastor; these horizontal and vertical relations stabilize the structure of the church and the authority of its leader.

This is especially crucial in a very large church such as Guatemala's Fraternidad Cristiana, for example, which boasts an average Sunday attendance of 12.000 at services (cf. Célulares Fráter 2023).

In a congregation that is the size of a small town, many members may never otherwise have an opportunity to have a personal relationship with or even experience a one-on-one conversation with their pastor. But the small groups, as per Simmel, help to establish a relationship of super- and subordination that makes the believer predisposed to be bound by their pastor's mandates and teachings (1909: 289–322).

Horizontal groups encourage interpersonal relationships between friends and families, and small groups form close and coherent social groups; these connect and overlap with one another, thus reinforcing the church's hegemony across the totality of a member's life. These connections, at least in theory, provide for the believer and their family on every level of human need: friendship, career connections, financial education, leadership training, education, moral edification, support in life's sufferings, and, lest we forget, salvific assurances through involvement in the church. Churches, as organizations, typically allow members to come and go at will, but even deeply disillusioned members are socialized to such an extent that they often find it difficult to challenge the leadership or to leave the comprehensive world that the church provides, along with the social groups within it (Schmidt 2019; Alexander 2012: 1049–1078).

Neo-Pentecostal pastors typically have a higher degree of religious training than their Classical Pentecostal counterparts (although this is by no means a *sine qua non* to be a pastor, as charism and the ability to rally a congregation are the key qualifications for the job). They are usually connected to other pastors through regional, national, and even international Pentecostal nodes and networks. Through these, they are aware of and responsive to new currents and trends in their field. In this respect, Pentecostalism, displays elements that mark it as a religio-social movement, even as expressions within a belief and practice within a given congregation are locally derived and contextualized (Powe 1994).

2. Setting the political context

Guatemala has one of the largest *evangélico* populations, percentagewise, of any nation in Latin America. Just over 40 per cent of the population is Protestant and the vast majority of these – upwards of 80 per cent – are Pentecostals, the vigorous legacy of the conversion "boom" of the early 1970s.[1] The boom was concurrent with and in some respects a response to the 36-year-long armed conflict during which Guatemala's ferociously anti-communist military conducted deadly counterinsurgency campaigns against a small but tenacious leftist armed movement.

The violent nadir of the armed conflict took place in the early 1980s, when an idiosyncratic neo-Pentecostal general, Efraín Ríos Montt (1982–1983), headed up a full-throttle military campaign to defeat the leftist guerrillas and their indigenous supporters. A new convert to Pentecostalism, the general publicly advocated what he touted as Christian moral teachings on corruption and family values at the same time that he commanded a scorched-earth campaign in the rural countryside, which also killed, displaced, and terrorized many tens of thousands of Maya indigenous peoples (cf. Garrard-Burnett 1998). Although many urban elites, non-Mayas, and *evangélicos* admired Ríos Montt, subsequent revelations about the brutality of his regime did much to sully his name and his Pentecostal associations along with it for a time, and for good reason. The general was convicted of genocide and crimes against humanity in 2013. In the words of one Guatemalan pastor, "Like many of my generation, I was convinced that if the head of government were healthy (*sana*) [meaning *evangélico*], the social-political body would also become healthy. But history has shown us the irrationality of such ideas" (Cajas 2009: unpaginated).

Democracy returned to Guatemala in 1986, and the armed conflict concluded in 1996. However, Guatemala remains a country where what political scientists Guillermo Trejo and Camilo Nieto-Matiz term "criminal wars – armed conflicts by which states fight organized criminal groups and fight among themselves for control over illicit economies and territories – have emerged as one of the most lethal types of conflict in the world today, surpassing the death toll of the typical civil war of the second half of the twentieth century" (2022: 1328). Today, despite small signs of improvement, the nation

---

[1] https://www.statista.com/statistics/1067082/guatemala-religion-affiliation-share-type/

continues to struggle with many of the very same social and economic inequalities that militants in the 1970s and 1980s had sought to bring an end to in the first place.

Guatemala's earlier unresolved social, political, and economic problems in recent years have been augmented by an intractable array of new challenges, including endemic violent crime (the nation suffers some of the highest rates of homicide in the world), rampant narcotrafficking, corrupt and ineffective government, deeply engrained racism against the indigenous majority, widespread gang violence, the drain of productive human capital through emigration, and new inequities resulting from neoliberal economics (cf. Lessing 2017; Trejo 2020). The unexpected election of Bernardo Arévalo, a reformist and progressive, to the presidency in August 2023 – if Guatemalan's political elites actually allow him to assume power – promises what Guatemalans call a *nueva primavera*, or new spring, for the nation, but genuine progress, even under optimal circumstances, will remain a serious challenge for any government.[2]

3. From quiescence to mobilization: Shifts in the Pentecostal worldview

Notwithstanding the extremity of this context, Guatemala's *evangélicos*, until relatively recently, have kept themselves at a remove from social or political action, both for strategic and theological reasons. Subscribing to a *fugamundi* outlook (literally, 'flee the world'), they framed their moral constructs around a strict binary dividing "the church" and "the world" the former a safe haven of salvation, the latter dangerous and sinful. In Classical Pentecostalism, the only contact between these two spheres should be through prayer and evangelization.

By contrast, neo-Pentecostals, whose churches started to come of age in Guatemala in the late 1980s, embrace the notion of the manifestation of the Holy Spirit through temporal transformation: theirs is an instrumentalist theology that is very much of the here-and-now. Neo-Pentecostalism focuses not only on healing – a traditional Pentecostal preoccupation – but also promises faithful believers wealth and temporal success, a belief known as prosperity

---

2   https://www.bbc.com/news/world-latin-america-66569014.

theology. Not only in Guatemala but across the Global South, prosperity theology enjoys enormous appeal in places where urbanization, late-stage capitalism, and neo-liberalism in the late 20th and 21st centuries have eroded already fragile rural lifeways. In these settings, where traditional *saberes* (knowledge and ways of being) gave way, prosperity theology seemed to open up access to modernity's enchantments: consumer goods, lucrative employment, social stability, and respect (cf. Bowler 2018).

Neo-Pentecostals believe that God wishes them to have "life abundant" (John 10:10) in ways that are material and quantifiable: to ask God for less is not merely unwise, but unfaithful. They focus on the improvement of the individual through prayer and ascetic practices such as fasting; most importantly, they trust in God's power, which they believe flows to the individual, to his or her family, and then, almost by osmosis, permeates the church, the community, and beyond. God, in the neo-Pentecostal *imaginaire*, is a direct and negotiable agent in every matter of daily life, no matter how mundane or acquisitive.

For the proponents of this highly instrumentalist theology, as Daniel Míguez has noted, prosperity theology "inverts the moral value of acquisition and capitalism": money is no longer "the root of all evil," (1 Timothy 6:10) but tangible proof of God's sovereignty and grace (2001: 4). Pastors urge believers to give money and give again to the limits of their abilities and beyond, as a sign of their faith that God will provide, and do so abundantly, in the exchange. As a form of market exchange, prosperity theology reifies capitalist acquisition and serves as a heuristic through which religious 'consumers' enter into a symbolic marketplace where they are able to purchase, through their faith and tithing, both credence goods (as per Gill) as well as greater access to consumer materialism (cf. Gill 1998).

Thus is resolved the apparent paradox of Pentecostal pastors who display ostentatious wealth – well-tailored suits, expensive cars, fine homes, even private planes – purchased with believers' tithes and 'widow's mites.' Prosperity theology's devotees see these things not as signs of decadence, but rather as positive affirmation of blessing: it is a powerful signifier of the potential goodness available to every believer who seeks it. Within the world of prosperity theology, a well-coiffed pastor with an elegant wife clothed in designer apparel and a second home in Miami is a living testament to the good life abundant that awaits poor and aspiring Central American congregates, for whom economic and social access to capitalism's enchantments seem otherwise closed off. Believers understand prosperity theology to be a rational market interaction in which they exchange their time (via church attendance), talent (participation), and above all their treasure (donations), with every expectation that they will be able to maximize personal gain in return.

Within this matrix of understanding, there has not been any real theological space for social justice considerations, because prosperity theology *et in se* posits a market exchange that promises to bring those who suffer from poverty and inequality into the shining world of modernity and capitalism (cf. Freudenberg's chapter in this volume). However, it is important to remember that prosperity theology is also an actual *theology* –that is to say, it is a systematic method of relating to the divine. Because of this, access to the modality is, understandably, religious, through evangelization: spreading the message of the church and bringing others into the congregation. Evangelization is paramount to church growth, which is a trope within Guatemalan Pentecostalism, as for Pentecostals, church growth (*iglecrecimiento*, a neologism that combines the Spanish words for 'church' [*iglesia*] and 'growth' [*crecimiento*]) is a quantifiable measure of a church's vigor, prosperity, and favor in the eyes of God. It is, therefore, the critical obligation of all believers to bring individuals in from the cold of the soulless secular world to the warm and sanctified embrace of the church.

And the arms of the church are indeed expansive. Scholars such as Brusco, Mariz, Smilde, and Santos have demonstrated that there are many varieties of collateral social goods that can accrue from belonging to an Evangelical church – problems with alcohol diminish, *machismo* is tamed, family violence decreases, educational levels often increase. This said, after adopting these value-rational (*wertrational*) behaviors, *evangélicos* do not distinguish themselves from others in this regard to the degree that Max Weber, writing from his observations on the rise of capitalism in Western Europe, predicted in his work the Protestant ethic and on society and economy. Be that as it may, all these transformations continue to take place *within* the church and the church family, not outside of it (cf. Mariz 1994; Burdick 1993; Brusco 1995; Smilde 2007; Santos 2012).

A key aspect of this discourse is that neo-Pentecostal churches encourage self-improvement on all fronts, for which they mandate new technologies of the self (Garrard 2020: 191–236). These typically range from dictating mode of dress to personal comportment, to issues of health (often dealt with by spiritual rather than medical interventions), to the nature of daily interactions with friends and family, hobbies, and pastimes (members may attend church every single day and devote nearly all their free time to church-related activities). Danish sociologist Martin Lindhardt underscores the centrality of a Pentecostal identity to a believer's own personhood: "[T]he faith-drenched life of Pentecostals/charismatics and the ways in which notions of sacred agency and interference in human affairs pervades their life worlds shape their everyday experiences and interpretations of events, and enable them to cultivate a certain sense of agency," he writes. "[A]dherents live their religiosity on an everyday basis" (Lindhardt 2012: 7).

The church thus becomes an encompassing universe for a member, colonizing mind, body, and spirit for Christ. Churches encourage members to constantly read devotional and edifying texts and improve their spiritual education, and they provide training (often in the small groups) for leadership, economic stewardship, and general *capatación* (training and empowerment). Neo-Pentecostal churches demonstrably generate substantial amounts of human capital for their members, as evinced, for example, in the leadership skills they learn through the church. In the words of Lindhardt, "they create new practical skills and new ways of relating to oneself and the social world," (2011: 5) although that social world may, in fact, be only as large as the church itself.

The church produces a social universe in which interpersonal relations, personal networks, horizontal, and low-hierarchy relations built on a shared faith vision and *confianza* (trust and confidence: a coveted commodity of rare and inestimable value in Guatemala). This function is especially cohesive at the small group level, although the vertical linkages that membership provides farther up the hierarchy of the church can also be beneficial, not unlike the practice of *compadrazgo* (godparent relations) that bound patrons with reciprocal obligations to peasant families in earlier eras. Daniel Levine is one of several sociologists who have demonstrated that this is particularly true in leadership training and the teaching of executive function skills that men and especially women would likely not learn elsewhere (Levine/Stoll 1997: 63–103). But they can also make great *demands* on human capital, as the church can become a self-referential loop of meetings, services, small groups, and people that absorbs almost all the time, talents, emotions, and attention of its members.

In dealing with an outside "world" that they still largely regard as hostile and dangerous, Pentecostal and neo-Pentecostal churches have been more wary, even regarding charitable work. Even neo-Pentecostal churches, broadly speaking, do not share a common vision with Mainline Christians as to the meaning of Jesus' teachings about charity or the need to contribute to a worldly *summum bonum*, nor do they reify extending a helping hand to the poor and needy outside of their own communities. As Samuel Berberian, a leading Guatemalan Pentecostal educator, explained to me in a personal conversation: "We have simply not had the theology for that."[3]

4. Toward a Pentecostal hermeneutics of social engagement?

4.1 The Seven Mountains of Iglesia El Shaddai

There is a particular sector of neo-Pentecostalism, however, that claims this view reflects a limited view of God's potential to transform: for them, it is a short conceptual leap from believing that God wishes to upgrade the faithful believer's economic status to believing that He desires to improve the institutions, economic and social conditions, and governance in which one lives. The argument in favor of the church taking on these challenges is compelling in a place like Guatemala, where corrupt government, a nearly absent rule of law, a frail justice system, and the outsize roles played by illegal actors – narcotraffickers, gangs, and a venal political-economic elite – have all eroded civil society's ability to uphold its responsibilities to maintain the nation's public institutions and its people.

Guatemala's example par excellence of activist Pentecostalism is a Guatemala City-based pastor, Dr. Harold Caballeros, who has been willing to venture into this void. In the early post-war years, Caballeros envisioned a much larger role for himself and his church in transforming Guatemala, with the larger objective of bringing the entire nation into the Pentecostal fold. Caballeros was founder and pastor of a El Shaddai, a wealthy Guatemala City megachurch with a significant presence in other areas of the country. In the early 1990s, he launched his first large-scale crusade for national reformation, a campaign of prayer and revival called *Jesus es Señor de Guatemala*. In this national-wide public effort, Caballeros called upon *evangélicos* – even those who did not belong to El Shaddai – to pray and fast for the welfare of the nation, calling for the redemption of the nation and call to abundant life, by the grace of God.

The Jesus is Lord of Guatemala campaign was an aspirational social movement, built on Caballeros' initiative, but the ideas behind it grew out of an

---

3   Personal conversation, July 28, 2006.

emergent new current within global Pentecostalism known as the New Apostolic Reformation (NAR), of which Caballeros was an early proponent and later known as a "prophet." The NAR is an international Pentecostal/Evangelical network that promotes the notion that divine revelation is still unfolding in the contemporary world, and that God speaks directly to modern day prophets and apostles. These men, although there are a few women in the movement, believe they are specifically anointed to help bring their own nations, and indeed the whole world, under Christ's authority and governance. This they refer to as bringing "dominion": leading their nations into a new era where Christian leadership and values will rebuild fallen and sinful societies.

Dominion theology digresses from Classical Pentecostalism or even standard neo-Pentecostalism in its willingness – indeed its eagerness – to engage with the secular world and to flood it with a Christian message that advances very conservative and literally-defined "biblical values" (cf. Cowen 2021; Stewart 2020; Ingersoll 2015; Goldberg 2006; Hedges 2006; Diamond 1995). While the main arena for engagement is in politics, dominionism calls for Evangelical domination across seven key areas of influence that they believe form the bedrock of secular modernity. These are the so-called "Seven Mountains" (7M): 1) faith and religion, 2) politics and government, 3) family, 4) media and communications, 5) arts and entertainment, 6) education, and 7) business/economics. Dominionism calls upon Christians to "invade" and dominate each of these spheres in order to restore "godly" and "biblical" values to the world (Wallnau/Johnson 2013). By way of example, Paula White, a well-known North American pastor, advocate of 7M, and Christian nationalist, rationalized her support for Donald Trump' tendentious January 6, 2021 insurrection in the United States by framing it in the language of providential dominion. "We have God-given authority," she stated plainly, "to take over the world".[4]

The NAR also promotes the tenets of "spiritual warfare", a wide-spread practice in which Pentecostals pray and (literally) exorcise malign beings such as fallen angels, demons which have held people and places in their thrall, thus shutting them off from God's presence and goodness (O'Neill 2012). This is a Pentecostal practice that began in the 1980s and has spread rapidly through Pentecostal networks as a concrete ritual modality, although non-Pentecostals might consider it as a metaphoric resistance to social and moral changes that

---

4   Cf. https://www.cbc.ca/radio/day6/mrna-after-covid-19-blowing-up-trump-plaza-cro kicurl-history-of-swear-words-and-more-1.5874120/how-a-conservative-christian-m ovement-became-an-important-part-of-trump-s-political-strategy-1.5874143.

challenge traditional cultural and biblical values (such as abortion and same-sex marriage). In parts of Latin America, it is also strongly associated with Pentecostal enmity to indigenous- and African-spiritual beliefs and practices that remain active features on the religious landscape of the region. For example, spiritual warfare in Brazil is largely directed toward the exorcism of *exús* and *pomba giras* and other African spirits (cf. Reuter's chapter in this volume), while in places such as Guatemala, Peru, or Bolivia, where there are large indigenous populations, it highlights the targeting of native saints and gods. By contrast, in Argentina, which has the highest rate of psychologists per capita in the world, spiritual warfare combats mental illness as a spiritual disease.[5]

For believers themselves, however, these celestial struggles with evil are anything but symbolic: rather, they are physical and concrete. In 1990, for example, Guatemala's Caballeros claimed that workers on the El Shaddai church's new property unearthed an enormous pre-Columbian earthwork of a serpent, which he associated Mesoamerican god Quetzalcoatl. To Pastor Harold, this discovery provided both a soteriological explanation for Guatemala's troubled history and the opportunity for Caballeros to champion his theology, especially since the graven image's excavation happened to coincide neatly with the launch of the *Jesus es Señor* crusade (cf. Caballeros 2001). Declaring that "our entire country was dedicated [in 300 BC] to Satan," Caballeros used the *Jesus es Señor* platform to call upon all Guatemala to pray fervently for their country to deliver it at last from the power of malevolent Mesoamerican false gods and fallen spirits that had controlled its destiny since even before the arrival of Europeans (Stoll 1994: 99).

By the turn of the new century, Caballeros expanded his vision of direct engagement by neo-Pentecostals in prayer and politics toward the "redemption" of their nation. Here, he moved away from the standard Pentecostal repertoire of prayer, fasting, and deliverance toward practical interventions in the lives of church members, intended to build their social and human capital in a variety of ways, including training in extensive *capacitación* (capacity-building), self-improvement, and furthering education. All of this took place in small groups connected to the church and was the lynchpin of the formation of what Caballeros calls "Christian citizenship." A key aspect of this citizenship is preparing ordinary people for leadership, whether that be as modest as running a small business or as lofty as being summoned to the highest level

---

5   Cf. https://qz.com/734450/almost-everyone-in-buenos-aires-is-in-therapy.

of servanthood, even to the godless world of government or business. As Kevin Lewis O'Neill has shown in his work, *City of God: Christian Citizenship in Guatemala* (2010a), while Caballeros' tipping point for national transformation has remained elusive, the principles of "Christian citizenship," largely by way of small prayer and study groups affiliated with El Shaddai, have become active in networks for capacity-building and shared *confianza* among Guatemalan Pentecostals, catapulting members into prominent leadership positions in business and education within the country.

Capacitación has benefits not least of all for Pastor Harold himself, who ran for President of Guatemala in two elections. Though unsuccessful both times, his campaign for the presidency in 2011 resulted in his being named foreign minister in the administration of President Otto Pérez Molina. After his government service, Caballeros continued to expand his influence across almost every sphere of the Seven Mountain Mandate. While his wife, Cecilia, continued as the head pastor of the 12.000 member El Shaddai church that he founded (which remains the spiritual home of many government and business leaders), Caballeros actively expanded his portfolio. He served as founder and rector of Universidad San Pablo, Guatemala's largest Evangelical university, the mission of which is to train professionals in Christian moral values and principles in order to become "agents of transformation in the society they live in;" he became president and founder of Radio Visión Corporation, a network of twenty five Evangelical radio stations; he is founder and former director of FUEDES (Fundación Educative El Shaddai), a system of Christian schools in rural areas of the country "designed to inculcate a worldview of values and principles that affect the nation," and, along with his wife, headed "Manos de Amor," a church-affiliated development program that works in rural areas (El Shaddai 2010: unpaginated).

On top of all this, Caballeros is also the founder of a political party called *Vision con Valores* (VIVA), which in 2015 ran Zury Ríos, an Evangelical Christian and daughter of the genocidal general of the early 1980s, at the head of its ticket.[6] Caballeros also served as facilitator for Guatemala's 'Vision Plan' (*Plan Visión de País*), a UNESCO-sponsored initiative which consolidated the role of political parties as interlocutors between society and state during the 2020 presidential regime (Caballeros 2001).

---

6 Cf. https://www.as-coa.org/articles/six-numbers-understand-guatemalas-surprising-2023-general-election-results.

For a long moment, Caballeros' successful summiting of all the Dominionism's Seven Mountains seemed to have made him a bellwether of Pentecostal social mobilization and political ascendency. His star continued to rise until two events – the disclosure of offshore bank accounts and commercial real estate holdings in Miami he had purchased with church monies in 2016, followed by his injury in a near-fatal traffic accident while traveling in Germany in September 2022 – tumbled him from the summits of success.[7]

And yet, the rise and fall of Harold Caballeros serves as a rich case study, perhaps even an archetype, for a new type of leader in Latin America: that of a well-connected and influential religious leader who successfully uses his networks, suasion, and connections to articulate and implement a social and political program that advances Pentecostal religious values and ambitions. We can see Caballeros' successes mirrored elsewhere across the continent in the influence of highly visible, well-connected religious actors in Brazil, Bolivia, Mexico, and elsewhere in the region. We need only look toward the strong support that Brazil's former president Jair Bolsonaro received from powerful megachurch pastors such as Edir Macedo and Silas Malafaia; or to the influence that Mexico's *evangélicos* wielded in demanding that Mexico's leftist president Andres López Obrador's administration issue a national *cartilla moral* (moral primer) in return for their support; or to the prominent role that *evangélicos* played in Bolivia in the ouster of Evo Morales during his attempt to remain in the presidency in 2019 to see that the days of quiescent Pentecostal leadership is long past (cf. Cowen 2021).

4.2 Centro Esdras

Notwithstanding decades of prayer and fasting, Guatemala remains a deeply troubled nation, as far from the tipping point of redemption as ever, and even for *evangélicos*, this is a paradox that is impossible to ignore. With this in mind, in July 2009, Centro Esdras, an *evangélico* non-profit organization founded by a pastor named Israel Ortiz, convened a meeting of Evangelical and Pentecostal pastors in Guatemala City. The conference theme, *Rostros del Protestantismo en Guatemala* (Faces of Protestantism in Guatemala) did not hint at the event's

---

[7] Cf. https://www.evangelicodigital.com/sociedad/24339/harold-caballeros-sufrio-un-accidente-en-alemania; https://cmiguate.org/iglesias-politica-y-millones-de-dolares-harold-caballeros-y-los-panamapapers/; https://www.businessobserverfl.com/news/2016/may/27/stay-classy/.

subtle but urgent agenda, which was to establish a framework for developing a theology for Evangelical social engagement *en su propia manera* (in their own way). In contrast to Caballeros' *Jesus es Señor* initiative and Christian citizenship projects, which were driven by Caballeros' charisma and his 7M aspirations, Ortiz drew his inspiration from the issue that Berberian (above) articulated: the lack of a Pentecostal theology of social consciousness.

At the time, Ortiz's was a unique vision to redirect and mobilize Pentecostal social potential by channeling *evangelicos'* value-driven rational behaviors to help address secular society's most dire problems. Ortiz's proposal hoped to build on conventional Pentecostal beliefs and priorities, but it also embraced a much more capacious view of what constituted the body and boundaries of 'the church'. Specifically, Ortiz envisaged, per Turner, the building of *communitas* by creating a more porous membrane between the church and secular world[8] (Turner 1969: 96). This task was doubly complicated not only in that it required a radical re-reading of Guatemalan *evangélico* theology, but it also demanded a high degree of coordinated organizational decision making that seems almost impossible, given the highly disaggregated nature of Guatemalan Protestantism and Pentecostalism in particular (cf. Starkloff 1997).

Despite these known challenges, Ortiz threw down the conceptual gauntlet in very specific terms: "Are we feeling we are the salt and light of the world? Are we conscious of the moral and ethical role that the Gospel demands of us in society?", he asked the group. "Why have we not had more of an impact on a country that is plagued by violence, corruption, poverty, and inequality, etc.?" Ortiz challenged his colleagues to ask themselves to entertain the question of why fervent prayer alone had not saved the nation. "We continue to grabble with theories and practices of mission," he argued, "that reduce the Gospel to a spiritual force and leave aside the challenge to affect all dimensions of life" (Ortiz 2009: unpaginated). The conference attracted a wide variety of church leaders, representing some 400 different denominations. As one rural pastor plaintively called out from the audience, succinctly summarizing up Centro Esdras' challenge, "How many churches have we built? How many Bible studies, how many small groups? And yet this country still continues to get worse and worse. Isn't it time for us to ask if God wants us to do more?"[9]

---

8   Turner uses this word to describe, "society as an unstructured or rudimentarily structured undifferentiated *comitatus* [Latin: "retinue"] or even communion of equal individuals who submit together to the authority of ritual authority."
9   Quote taken from fieldnotes at conference on July 29, 2009.

Marco Tulio Cajas, a well-known Guatemalan pastor, spoke to this question directly, explicitly critiquing the churches' "anti-society" discourse as both impeding the advance of the faith and as patently disingenuous. "We pray for the authorities in power, and yet we are contemptuous of public life and those who take part in it," he noted. "We need solid argumentation [for social engagement] and innovative ideas that will permit us to be more audacious and creative in the transformation of society." Cajas, too, called for what he termed a "theology of public life," wherein "the churches as community of faith, motivate, equip, and support their members to reinterpret public life and to act within it as agents of social and political transformation" (Cajas 2009: unpaginated).

Even as the conference generated enthusiasm among its participants, it did not transform Guatemalan Pentecostalism overnight. But it did help to coalesce social groups of like-minded pastors and other religious actors (such as faculty at the Guatemala City-based *Seminario Teológico Centroamericano*) by opening venues for communication that allowed them to safely explore new hermeneutics of social engagement and to consider new social forms that might pave the path to change. This process is of yet incomplete, but in the years since the conference took place, we can see a more expansive social hermeneutics has emerged in Guatemalan Pentecostalism in several key areas. Church efforts are most visible in those areas of need where the feeble Guatemalan state has failed to provide even basic services for its people and some, perhaps, have grown weary of waiting for the soteriological unfolding of the redemption.

4.3 Hermeneutics in action: Pentecostal social forms against violence

By way of example, Guatemalan sociologist Claudia Dary (2016) writes about the community campaigns against domestic violence conducted by the Iglesia de Dios Evangélio Completo (IDEC) (a "classical" Pentecostal denomination), demonstrating ways that the church has been particularly adept at developing new biblically based strategies by which women and men learn to cope with violence in the home. The IDEC's *Baja la Voz* (literally: "lower your voice") program both empowers women (and some men) *who belong to the church* to speak up against abuse, and for abusers to learn new ways to control their anger and increase respect for their partners, providing templates for what the church calls "biblical alternatives to *machismo*" (Dary 2016: 100).

Sociologist Robert Brenneman (2012) is among the most prominent scholars who has written about other Pentecostal social interventions that have met with success; Brenneman's research focuses on religious with programs among gang members. Although it is patently dangerous work, this type of ministry appeals to Pentecostals and *evangélicos* because they view gang violence as a "spiritual problem" best tackled by the church, rather than as a social or criminal problem that the state should address (but does not). As a social group, *evangélicos* are one of only a handful of social actors who are willing to take on the gangs, one of Central America's most urgent social problems. Church workers are usually respected mediators, to the extent that the gangs themselves take their efforts seriously.

Brenneman's work on Pentecostal ministries to gang members notes that genuine religious conversion is one of the only means by which young men are able to leave *la vida loca*; the only other exit from the gang is through death. In practical terms, this means a gang member must fully abandon his criminal past, eschew all contact with his former clique and homies, begin the process of removing tattoos, and adhere to standard *evangélico* behaviors such as not drinking alcohol and attending church services with regularity, often several times per week. As sociologist José Miguel Cruz observes: "The pious lifestyle that churches encourage lets gang members easily monitor their former members" and gangs expect former members to fully live up to the Evangelical lifestyle to which they have converted. When gangs determine that a former member is not sincerely committed to their new life, they promptly eliminate him, notifying the victim's pastor with the message: "This one didn't walk right" (quoted in Miller 2023: unpaginated).

Likewise, Pentecostal ministries have improved conditions for some in Guatemala's carceral hellscape – a dangerous and lawless system of prisons that criminologist Mark Fleischer has termed "warehouses of violence" (1989; O'Neill 2010a). By using strategies such as prayer, helping break addiction and bad habits, and teaching basic literacy and other life skills, prison ministers work to improve self-esteem and teach new technologies of self to prisoners, who become less violent while still incarcerated and are less prone to recidivism when they are released (cf. Johnson 2017). As one prison minister described his work: "My objective has always been to spread the word of God, but also to teach gang members good customs and habits, how to be good people, good sons and fathers, how to be good citizens." This approach simultaneously speaks to the Christian quest to find God through inspection of one's interior life, at the same time that it provides new and practical technologies of self – soft skills – to help prisoners cope both in and outside the walls of prison (O'Neill 2010b).

As they learn an alternative to what is called in English "the thug life," Christian prisoners become part of new social forms that cohere and support them both while still in prison and once they are released. So committed are some of these groups that they police themselves while still in confinement, providing some modicum of security and order in Central America's notorious and functionally unregulated penal system, including Guatemala's El Pavón prison, one of the most lawless and dangerous such places in the world. As such, Christian prison groups – organically united by their shared conversion and sometimes united under the authority of a self-appointed incarcerated "pastor" – provide an alternative to the hierarchies of international gang and drug cartel members, extortionists, and "prison kings" that otherwise control virtually all aspects of men's lives in confinement.[10]

In short, "empowered" neo-Pentecostals have been increasingly effective in creating functional systems for improving education, security, and problems of everyday violence in places where other types of public authority, including the state, are precarious or even entirely absent. But even these successes carry with them some serious caveats. As evinced in O'Neill's work on Evangelical-run Guatemalan addiction centers, the state's abjuration of its own responsibility to provide proper care for addicts and the mentally ill opens the door wide for intentional or unintentional mistreatment when it hands them over to untrained church people, turning rehabilitation over to unregulated, unmonitored institutions, where care can range from clinically lax (again, relying mainly on prayer and tropes of redemption) to unscrupulous and dangerous (where, for example, patients are locked up and mistreated and hunted down if they leave the premises) (2019). It would also be possible, and probably fruitful, to discuss some very negative effects of Pentecostal social mobilization, for example, cases of vigilantism in parts of the country where the rule of law is largely absent that have resulted in the deaths of purported criminals without benefit of trail, or of rumors of financial ties between prominent national televangelists and the drug cartels, but these disturbing cases do not reflect the overall larger trajectory of Pentecostal life in contemporary Guatemala.

---

10   Cf. https://insightcrime.org/news/analysis/the-prison-kings-of-guatemala/.

5. Conclusion

As we have seen, Evangelical religion, especially in its majority form of Pentecostalism in the Central American nation of Guatemala, has undergone a tectonic epistemological shift from a post-temporal, apocalyptic orientation to one that is profoundly presentist and instrumentalist in its outlook. In specific terms, Pentecostals in recent decades have transitioned from an eschatological hermeneutics of separation from the world to one that embraces full-on social and political participation, cohering, in the process, into social forms that emphasize collective mobilization. This reflects a change in religious social forms and values that correspond to a shifting corpus of religious ideals and theologies. As these social relationships evolve, they change the role of the church – which previously prioritized insularity – to one of increased, outward-facing social engagement. As this evolution progresses, pastors retain charisma and sway, but the capacity building, self-realization, and leadership training that small groups nurture in congregants has made them into a social force that, over time, is beginning to chip away at the patterns of patriarchy and even authoritarianism that characterized earlier Pentecostalism.

In this milieu, we see that at least certain sectors of Pentecostalism have sacralized social values and aspirations that they heretofore perceived as secular, but which they now map onto a religious framework of understanding. It is not the allure of secular society that encourages Pentecostals to engage with the world, but rather its absence – the failure of secular modernity's 'enchantments' in modern Guatemala to provide sustenance for body *or* soul. I refer here to such things as basic public services, the rule of law, remediation programs to address poverty, violence; Pentecostals also identify as problematic the anomie that pushes young people towards drugs or gangs, for example. And yet, Pentecostal social engagement is very much on Pentecostalism's own terms, as secular social, tropes, and formulas for advancing the public good must be re-signified within a Pentecostal idiom to be acceptable, even legible, to them.

Pentecostal social mobilization holds great promise, but also certain dangers, as evinced by the role that *evangélicos* openly played in the nation's 2023 presidential campaign. In an attempt to marshal Evangelical votes, one of the leading candidates, Sandra Torres, chose an Evangelical pastor as her vice presidential running mate and adopted a morally conservative platform that she that hoped would appeal to that constituency.[11] On the other, several Guatemalan Pentecostal televangelists produced a steady flow of negative social media against Arévalo, the progressive-moderate winning candidate, denouncing him as a "communist," and even an agent of Satan. The fact that this beleaguered candidate roundly won the election offers tells us that despite these efforts, *evangélicos*, who make up over forty percent of Guatemala's overall population, voted for him despite efforts by their institutional leadership to sway them otherwise.[12] This suggests that, while Evangelical organizations' organizational logic remains inchoate, the power of social forms – notably, the small groups that exist within the large churches and among which Arévalo enjoyed much larger support – were instrumental in determining the outcome.

Many scholars have argued that Pentecostalism's attraction to converts a generation ago was its ability to offer an "alternative imaginary" to a corrupt and violent world, a symbolic resistance that demanded to keep the world at arm's length and offer believers an orderly, meaningful life framed by a particular understanding of the nature of the Holy Spirit's presence and mandates. Yet as Pentecostalism in Central America matures, there is a small but growing number of cradle and second-generation *evangélicos* who are beginning to test the boundaries of old binaries. Even today, the social spaces that Pentecostals are willing to enter remain limited, and the new hermeneutics struggle to compete with the old: Pentecostalism remains divided into those who still wish to flee the world versus those who wish to scale the Seven Mountains. As recently as September 2022, for example, *evangélicos* gathered to pray to ask God to "fill in" a massive sinkhole that had formed in one of Guatemala's major highways, but they did not propose or support any material remedy to this basic infrastructural problem.[13] It remains to be seen just how much the human capital that Pentecostal churches cultivate in their members will translate into a more fungible social capital within society at large. If so, a new hermeneutics of social engagement will require a broad expansion on the Pentecostal prerogative to bring the world to the church, *en su manera*.

---

11   Cf. https://apnews.com/article/guatemala-election-sandra-torres-74ce43addf2ec3f36f356fd034546cc0.
12   Cf. https://www.state.gov/reports/2019-report-on-international-religious-freedom/guatemala/.
13   Cf. https://progressive.org/latest/other-americans-guatemala-religious-narco-state-abbott-091422/.

Bibliography

Alexander, Jeffrey C. (2012): "The Societalization of Social Problems: Church Pedophilia, Phone Hacking, and the Financial Crisis." In: American Sociological Review 83/6, pp. 1049–1078.

Bowler, Kate (2018): Blessed: A History of the American Prosperity Gospel, New York: Oxford University Press.

Brenneman, Robert (2012): Homies and Hermanos: God and Gangs in Central America, New York: Oxford University Press.

Brusco, Elizabeth (1995): The Reformation of Machismo: Evangelical Conversion and Gender in Colombia, Austin, TX: University of Texas Press.

Burdick, John (1993): "Struggling Against the Devil: Pentecostalism and Social Movements in Brazil." In: Virginia Garrard-Burnett/David Stoll (eds.), Rethinking Protestantism in Latin America, Pittsburgh, PA: Temple University Press, pp. 20–44.

Caballeros, Harold (2001): Victorious Warfare: Discovering Your Rightful Place in God's Kingdom, Grand Rapids, MI: Thomas Nelson Inc.

Cajas, Marco Tulio (2009): "Los cristianos y la vida pública." Consulta Rostros del Protestantismo en Guatemala, July 28–30. Unpublished paper, Ciudad de Guatemala. Cowen, Benjamin A. (2021): Moral Majorities Across the Americas: Brazil, the United States, and the Creation of the Religious Right, Chapel Hill: University of North Carolina.

Dary, Claudia. 2016. Cristianos en un país violento: repuestos de las Iglesias frente a la violencia en dos barrios del área metropolitan de Guatemala. Universidad de San Carlos, Dirección General de Investigación Instituto de Estudios Interétnicos.

Diamond, Sara (1995) Spiritual Warfare: The Politics of the Christian Right, Cheektowaga, NY: Black Rose Books.

Fleischer, Mark (1989): Warehouses of Violence, Newbury Park, CA: Sage Press.

Freston, Paul (1994): Nem Anjos Nem Demônios: Interpretações Sociológicas do Pentecostalismo, Petrópolis: Vozes.

Freston, Paul (2001): Evangelicals and Politics in Asia, Africa and Latin America. Cambridge: Cambridge University Press.

Garrard-Burnett, Virginia (1998): Protestantism in Guatemala: Living in the New Jerusalem, Austin, TX: University of Texas Press.

Garrard-Burnett, Virginia (2010): Terror in the Land of the Holy Spirit: Guatemala Under General Efraín Ríos Montt, 1982–1983, New York: Oxford University Press.

Garrard, Virginia (2020): New Faces of God in Latin America: Emerging Forms of Vernacular Hermeneutics, New York: Oxford.

Garrard-Burnett, Virginia/Stoll, David (1993): Rethinking Protestantism in Latin America, Pittsburgh, PA: Temple University Press.

Gill, Anthony (1998): Render Unto Caesar: The Catholic Church and the State in Latin America, Chicago, IL: University of Chicago.

Goldberg, Michelle (2006) Kingdom Coming: The Rise of Christian Nationalism, New York: W.W. Norton and Co.

Hedges, Chris. 2006. American Fascists: The Christian Right and the War on America. New York: Free Press.

Ingersoll, Julie J. (2015): Building God's Kingdom: Inside the World of Christian Reconstruction, New York: Oxford.

Johnson, Andrew (2017): If I Gave My Soul: Faith Behind Bars in Rio de Janeiro, York: Oxford University Press.

Lessing, Benjamin (2017): Making Peace in Drug Wars, New York: Cambridge University Press, 2017.

Levenson, Deborah T. (2013): Adios Niño: The Gangs of Guatemala and the Politics of Death, Chapel Hill: University of North Carolina Press.

Levine, Daniel/Stoll, David (1997): "Bridging the Gap between Empowerment and Power in Latin America." In: Susanne Hoeber Rudolph/James P. Pescatori (eds.), Transnational Religion and Fading States, Boulder, CO: Westview Press, pp. 63–103.

Lindhardt, Martin (2011): "Introduction." In: Martin Lindhardt (ed.), Practicing Faith: The Ritual Life in Pentecostal-Charismatic Christians, New York: Berghahn Books.

Lindhardt, Martin (2012): Power in Powerlessness: A Study of Pentecostal Life Worlds in Urban Chile, Leiden: Brill.

Mariz, Cecilia Loreta (1994): Coping with Poverty: Pentecostals and Christian Base Communities in Brazil, Philadelphia, PA: Temple University Press.

Marty, Martin/Appleby, Scott (eds.) (1994): Accounting For Fundamentalisms: The Dynamic Character of Movements, Chicago, IL: University of Chicago Press.

Míguez, Daniel (2001): "Pentecostalism and Modernization in a Latin American Key: Rethinking the Cultural Effects of Structural Change in Argentina." Unpublished paper presented at Latin American Studies Association, Washington DC.

Miller, Leila (2023): "They Left Gangs and Found God. But They Weren't Spared in El Salvador's Crackdown." Los Angeles Times April 19.

O'Neill, Kevin Lewis (2010a): City of God: Christian Citizenship in Postwar Guatemala, Los Angeles, CA: University of California Press, 2010.
O'Neill, Kevin Lewis (2015): Secure the Soul: Christian Piety and Gang Prevention in Guatemala, Oakland, CA: University of California Press.
O'Neill, Kevin Lewis (2019): Hunted: Predation and Pentecostalism in Guatemala, Chicago, IL: University of Chicago Press.
O'Neill, Kevin Lewis (2010b): "The Reckless Will: Prison Chaplaincy and the Problem of Mara Salvatrucha." In: Public Culture 22/1, pp. 67–88.
O'Neill, Kevin Lewis (2012) "Pastor Harold Caballeros Believes in Demons: Belief and Believing in the Study of Religion." In: History of Religions 51/4, pp. 299–316.
Ortiz, Israel (2009): "Agentes de cambio en el mundo." Consulta Rostros del Protestantismo en Guatemala, July 28–30. Unpublished paper, Ciudad de Guatemala.
Powe, Karla O. (ed.) (1994): Charismatic Christianity as a Global Culture, Columbia, SC: University of South Carolina Press.
Rudolph, Susanne Hoeber/Pescatori, James P. (eds.) (1997) Transnational Religion and Fading States, Boulder, CO: Westview Press.
Santos, José Leonardo (2012): Evangelicalism and Masculinity: Faith and Gender in El Salvador, Blue Ridge Summit, PA: Lexington Books.
Schmidt, Volker H. (2019): "Eight Theories of Societalization: Toward a Theoretically Sustainable Concept of Society." In: European Journal of Social Theory 23/3, pp. 411–430.
Simmel, Georg (1909): "The Problem of Sociology" In: The American Journal of Sociology 15/3, pp. 289–322.
Smilde, David (2007): Reason to Believe: Cultural Agency in Latin American Evangelicalism, Berkeley, CA: University of California Press, 2007.
Starkloff, Carl F. (1997): "Church as Structure and Communitas: Victor Turner and Ecclesiology" In: Theological Studies 58/4, pp. 643–668.
Stewart, Katherine (2020): The Power Worshippers Inside the Dangerous Rise of Religious Nationalism, London: Bloomsbury Publishing.
Stoll, David (1990): Is Latin America Turning Protestant? The Politics of Evangelical Growth, Stanford, CA: Stanford University Press.
Stoll, David (1994): "'Jesus Is Lord of Guatemala': Evangelical Reform in a Death-Squad State." In: Martin Marty/Scott Appleby (eds.), Accounting For Fundamentalisms: The Dynamic Character of Movements, Chicago, IL: University of Chicago Press, pp. 99–123.

Trejo, Guillermo (2020): Votes, Drugs, and Violence, Cambridge: Cambridge University Press.
Trejo, Guillermo/Nieto-Matiz, Camilo (2022): "Containing Large-Scale Criminal Violence Through Internationalized Prosecution: How the Collaboration Between the CICIG and Guatemala's Law Enforcement Contributed to a Sustained Reduction in the Murder Rate." In: Comparative Political Studies 56/9, pp. 1328–1364. https://doi.org/10.1177/00104140221139386.
Turner, Victor W. (1969): The Ritual Process: Structure and Anti-Structure, Chicago, IL: Aldine Publishing Co.
Wallnau, Lance/Johnson, Bill (2013): Invading Babylon: The Seven Mountain Mandate, Shippensburg, PA: Destiny Image Publisher.
Weber, Max (1905): Die protestantische Ethik und der Geist des Kapitalismus (=Archiv für Sozialwissenschaft und Sozialpolitik, vol. 20), Tübingen: J.C.B. Mohr, pp. 1–54.

Web References

Jeff Abbott. "The Other Americans: Guatemala is Constructing a Religious Narco-State." The Progressive, September 14, 2022. Accessed October 30, 2023. https://progressive.org/latest/other-americans-guatemala-religious-narco-state-abbott-091422/.
BBC World News. "Bernardo Arevalo: Anti-Corruption Leader Wins Guatemala Elections." August 21, 2023. Accessed October 30, 2023. https://www.bbc.com/news/world-latin-america-66569014.
Célulares Fráter. "Reuniones Live." Fraternidad Cristiana de Guatemala, 2023. Accessed April 4, 2024. http://celulasfrater.com/reuniones-live/.
El Shaddai Ministries. "Iglesia El Shaddai." 2010. Accessed April 4, 2024. https://iglesiaelshaddai.org/.
Evangélico Digital. "Harold Cabelleros sufró un grave accidente en Alemania." September 19, 2022. Accessed October 30, 2023. https://www.evangelicodigital.com/sociedad/24339/harold-caballeros-sufrio-un-accidente-en-alemania.
Virginia Garrard-Burnett. "Time and the Maya Apocalypse: Guatemala, 1982 and 2012." The Appendix 1/1, 2012. Accessed October 30, 2023. http://theappendix.net/issues/2012/12/time-and-the-maya-apocalypse-guatemala-1982-and-2012.

Olivia Goldhill. "Almost Everyone in Buenos Aires is in Therapy." Quartz Business Journal, July 17, 2016. Accessed October 30, 2023. https://qz.com/734450/almost-everyone-in-buenos-aires-is-in-therapy.

Mark Gordon. "Stay Classy." Business Observer, May 27, 2016. Accessed October 30, 2023. https://www.businessobserverfl.com/news/2016/may/27/stay-classy/.

Elle Hardy. "How a Conservative Christian Movement Became an Important Part of Trump's Strategy." Canadian Broadcast Company, January 15, 2021. Accessed October 30, 2023. https://www.cbc.ca/radio/day6/mrna-after-covid-19-blowing-up-trump-plaza-crokicurl-history-of-swear-words-and-more-1.5874120/how-a-conservative-christian-movement-became-an-important-part-of-trump-s-political-strategy-1.5874143.

Chase Harrison. "Six Numbers to Understand Guatemala's Surprising 2023 General Election Results." Americas Society/Council of the Americas, June 26, 2023. Accessed October 30, 2023. https://www.as-coa.org/articles/six-numbers-understand-guatemalas-surprising-2023-general-election-results.

Office of International Religious Freedom. "2019 Report on Freedom of Religion: Guatemala." United States Department of State. Accessed October 30, 2023. https://www.state.gov/reports/2019-report-on-international-religious-freedom/guatemala/.

Alex Papadovassilakis. "The Prison Kings of Guatemala." InSight Crime, April 16, 2019. Accessed October 30, 2023. https://insightcrime.org/news/analysis/the-prison-kings-of-guatemala/.

Sonia D. Pérez. "Guatemalan Presidential Candidate Sandra Torres Leans on Conservative Values, Opposing Gay Marriage." AP World News, August 12, 2023. Accessed October 30, 2023. https://apnews.com/article/guatemala-election-sandra-torres-74ce43addf2ec3f36f356fd034546cc0.

Solano. "Iglesias, política y millones de dólares: Harold Caballeros y los #Panama Papers, Centro de Medios Independiente." Centro de Medios Independiente, May 9, 2016. Accessed October 30, 2023. https://cmiguate.org/iglesias-politica-y-millones-de-dolares-harold-caballeros-y-los-panamapapers/.

Statista Research Department. "Religious Affiliation in Guatemala as of 2020, By Type." September 5, 2023. Accessed October 30, 2023. https://www.statista.com/statistics/1067082/guatemala-religion-affiliation-share-type/.

Social Forms in Orthodox Christian Convert Communities in North America

Sebastian Rimestad and Katherine Kelaidis

Abstract *The Orthodox Church is considered a rather conservative body – akin to the Roman Catholic Church. Nevertheless – or precisely for that reason – it has attracted converts from the other mainstream denominations who seek an ecclesiastical home grounded on a traditional theological basis. For many Orthodox converts in the United States, the Orthodox Church is seen as a refuge from rampant liberalism and social relativism expressed in fluid gender identities and the waning of traditional values. As such, the Orthodox Church offers them a 'counter-structure' to the secular and mainstream world 'out there'. In this contribution, we analyze the way Orthodox Christian convert communities in the US use various social forms in order to create this image of the Orthodox Church as a divinely inspired counterculture. These social forms in the convert milieus pose a challenge to existing Orthodox Christian communities, who are often more concerned with ethnic and cultural affiliation and wish to integrate into Western culture.*

Keywords *diaspora, migrant religion, migration, Orthodox Church, reactive online Orthodoxy, religious conversion*

1. Introduction

The origins of the Orthodox Church lie in the eastern basin of the Mediterranean Sea, where Christianity first grew as a movement within the Roman Empire in the first centuries CE and from the 4th century as the state religion of the empire. The separation between Eastern Orthodox and Western Catholic Christianity is conventionally dated to the year 1054, although the actual alienation between the two parts occurred much earlier in a rather subtle fashion (Chadwick 2003). Numerous theological, liturgical, and political differences between the two halves of Christendom ensured that a reconciliation had become impossible by the 16th century. One of these differences was the assertion that the church did not represent a counterpart to secular society or state politics but was an integral part of it (Höpken/Rimestad forthcoming). This emphasis might not have been unique to the Eastern Orthodox Church, but it has since the early 20th century been at the center of Orthodox theology's identity vis-à-vis Western Christianity.

As such, from the emic perspective of Orthodox theology, the Orthodox Church cannot be analyzed from the vantage point of social forms. In its self-understanding, just as that of the Roman Catholic Church, the church does not have a social form, it encompasses the social in its entirety. For most of the 2000-year history of the Orthodox Church and its antecedents, it was enough to consider every baptized individual a part of the Church, which would exist wherever there was a church and parish. Ironically, this globalized narrative could only exist because Orthodoxy functioned as a "cultural church"; that is to say, a religious community embedded in a particular homogeneous cultural (and frequently geographic and political) context in which it acted as societal glue as much as ideological community. Baptism, which normatively occurred in infancy, was the only requirement for membership, as it encompassed the vast majority of members of the community without further inquiry which might produce dissension and conflict. Even today, and even in far less homogenous contexts, Orthodox theologians still actively resist looking at the church as a separate part of society at large. There is no concept of membership beyond baptism, unlike in Western churches, where membership is often connected with following rules, participating in ceremonies, or paying membership fees. Even when one looks at the Orthodox Church from a social scientific perspective, it is difficult to frame it in terms of social forms. In the core region of the Orthodox Church, it is seldom an organization with defined membership and clear goals, but rather an all-encompassing institution with a clear hierarchy, which anybody can seek out to satisfy their religious needs.

However, in those regions where the Orthodox Church has traditionally not been dominant, such as in Western Europe and North America, the Christian Orthodox presence is relatively young and does not represent the majority faith. It is therefore subject to the three processes outlined in the introduction to this volume, both within the church and in its relations to the surrounding social world: (1) the societalization of communitization implies that hierarchical structures are less important, while community elements gain in prevalence; (2) the empowering of the individual is a process that is more obvious in this part of the world than in more traditionally Orthodox regions; and (3) the competition among religions is a core feature of the North American religious landscape.

These three processes, which are usually perceived by Orthodox Christians as external influences, alien to the Orthodox faith, do play a peculiar role in the development of Orthodox Christianity in Western Europe and, especially, North America. Unlike the Western Christian denominations, which developed somewhat organically together with modernity, the Orthodox Church has developed a narrative of being at odds with modern developments. Its encounter with such developments began with the Enlightenment and secularization from the 18th century onwards, which first introduced the idea of non-religious social coherence (Roudometof 1998). However, a real encounter with Western modernity only occurred when a significant migration of Orthodox faithful, especially in the 20th century, diversified and dispersed the global Orthodox presence (Rimestad 2021).

This contribution analyzes the particular way these two processes impacted the social forms that Christian Orthodox communities have taken in the North American diaspora. They include the individual parish as a close-knit group and the auxiliary organizations that structure parish outreach. At the same time, the Orthodox Church in North America is not a single structure but consists of several parallel, ethnically connoted jurisdictional organizations. Finally, in an era the two sociologists Lee Rainie and Barry Wellman have diagnosed as "networked individualism" with its own "operating system" (Rainie/Wellman 2012: 6–7), the social form of a network is also making inroads into the Orthodox Church.

Rainie and Wellman argued that networked individualism relies on internet communication, enabled by the "Triple Revolution" of social networks beyond the tight and homogeneous group, of communication technologies involving the internet, and of mobility induced through ever-smaller cell phones (ibid.: 11–12). The two sociologists focused on the positive aspects of networked individualism, which are undeniable. However, there is an increasing awareness of the detrimental effects of the Triple Revolution, which has become rather visible among US-American converts to the Orthodox Church.

These developments do not only appear in the Orthodox Church in North America from within but are often introduced by zealous converts from Western denominations. In some cases, one can even observe that novel social forms function in opposition to more traditional Orthodox ways of community. Also, the culture wars of the 20th and 21st centuries in the US (Hartman 2019) are heavily influencing the way Orthodox Christians in North America live their faith and coalesce into the social form of networks, often displaying the same polarization of American society as can be observed in other arenas.

The remainder of this paper is divided into three parts. The following part (2.) analyzes the historical development of the Orthodox Church outside of the areas that have traditionally been Eastern Orthodox, especially North America. This is important to understand the three levels of Orthodox Christianity in the USA and their corresponding social forms. Then we turn to the phenomenon of conversion to Orthodoxy (3.). Whereas converts have never made up the majority in the North American Orthodox Church, they are arguably its most vocal representatives, who have often introduced elements into the church that the traditional Orthodox consider alien and unsuitable, including 'Protestant' social forms. The final part (4.) elaborates on the more recent development of American internet Orthodoxy, that inscribes itself into an era which has witnessed the globalization of the culture wars (Goldberg 2014). This phenomenon introduces a new social dimension into the Orthodox Church in North America that may have detrimental effects on it in the long term.

2. The globalization of the Orthodox Church – the Orthodox diaspora

The spread of Orthodox Christianity beyond its core regions in the Middle East and Eastern Europe since the end of the 19th century is primarily the result of geopolitical upheavals and migration waves, rather than missionary endeavors. While Christianity is per se a missionary religion, the Eastern Orthodox Church has always been less aggressive in its mission and therefore also less successful in terms of expansion. Instead of pro-actively traveling to the corners of the earth in order to turn people into Christians, Orthodox missions have been less visible, even though they were also quite successful, for example in the Eastern regions of the Russian Empire, as well as in Japan and Alaska (cf. Rimestad forthcoming). In the case of Alaska, which was a Russian colony before it was sold to the US in 1867, historians agree that the Russian Orthodox mission among the indigenous population was far more effective than the subsequent US Protestant attempts to evangelize the population (Kan 1999; Kan 2001). For many inhabitants, the Orthodox were perceived as peers, whereas the Protestants were foreign intruders who did not value their original culture.

Besides this arrival of Orthodox Christianity to America from the West via formerly Russian Alaska, it also, from the end of the 19th century, arrived from the East in the form of Balkan and Eastern European immigrants fleeing economic and political hardships. While most of these migrants identified as Greeks and came from either the newly formed Greek state or the Ottoman Empire, they were joined by a substantial number of Serbs, Romanians, and arrivals of various ethnicities from the Russian Empire (Durante 2015). These migrants brought with them a profoundly different kind of faith than that which had developed among the Alaskan indigenous population. In terms of social forms, though, both communities can be characterized as groups, held together by close-knit parish and family ties and often linked to a common ancestry of origin. However, the migrants were eager to integrate into the multicultural American society. They found themselves in a novel context in which the state did not involve itself in religious affairs, neither dictating the religious observance of its citizens nor (importantly) providing state support.

Moreover, ecclesiastical authorities in the regions from which they originally came were often at best uninterested in these *émigré* communities, forcing them to organize themselves independently of ecclesiastical oversight. This was further complicated in the Greek case, where the immigrants arrived from two distinct (and at times antagonistic) church jurisdictions, the Church of independent Greece and the Patriarchate of Constantinople in the Ottoman Empire. As a result, early migrant parishes were established independently, as private associations (often connected to a school in addition to a church) along the Protestant model (Kitroeff 2020). This engendered the social form of organization, but bottom-up and on a voluntary basis. Moreover, these organizations were not the main social form of the parishes, which functioned further as groups. They were necessary for the formal and legal existence of the parishes, which were the owners of the church (and school) buildings.

Meanwhile, the 'Russian' Orthodox in Alaska tried to uphold a traditional top-down episcopal church structure (dioceses), with bishops appointed by the church administration in Saint Petersburg. The diocese of Alaska was expanded to include all of the US soon after the Alaska Purchase (1867) and the bishop resided in San Francisco from 1872. His diocese was also an organization, but not congruent with the individual parishes, which remained groups and seldom had explicit organizational structures themselves. The buildings and legal obligations all lay in the hands of the diocese, which was a wholly different level from the lay faithful. It is therefore somewhat misleading to characterize the diocese as a social form. This element of Russian Orthodoxy in the USA was greatly affected by the collapse of the Russian Empire in 1917, as it opened up the way for legal disputes regarding such ownership (Sarkisian 2019). Russian Orthodoxy in North America split into several antagonistic jurisdictions (organizations) as a result, one of which eventually became the Orthodox Church in America (OCA) in 1970.

The Russians, thus, tried to uphold a diocesan structure and administer the church top-down, while the Greeks established parishes from the bottom up, starting with an association and then contacting a bishop to appoint them a priest. These two *modi operandi* have remained prevalent in the North American Orthodox Church to this day. Whereas the bishops try to run the church as a corporation with a top-down structure, independent Orthodox communities and individuals periodically appear, looking for a bishop that may legitimize them in terms of church law. Moreover, there are auxiliary organizations in all Orthodox communities in the US that provide support for the poor, healthcare, or other issues of social welfare. While these tended to be located at the individual parish level in Greek parishes, the Russians often founded regional or diocesan organizations[1], but this difference is no longer constitutive.

The ethnically connoted jurisdictional plurality of the Orthodox Church in North America is considered an anomaly in the Orthodox world. In the traditionally Orthodox regions of the world, every bishop's jurisdiction is clearly delimited in geographical terms (Rimestad 2021: 87–91), but this is not the case outside of these regions. Because there is no universally recognized Orthodox Church responsible for North America, almost all nationally connoted church structures try to lay claims on "their" co-nationals on the continent. After the Greeks, numerous migrants from all traditionally Orthodox countries entered the US over the 20th century. Such migration happened especially following the great geopolitical catastrophes of the century, such as the Russian Revolution and the Greek-Turkish War in the wake of World War I as well as the recalibration of Europe following World War II. But the fall of the Iron Curtain 1989–1993 as well as the Yugoslav Wars and persecutions of Arab Christians have also increased the number of potential Orthodox Christian Americans, which is currently estimated between three and six million, or between 0.5 and 2 per cent of the population.

The US Religion Census 2020 found that the number of actual adherents to the Orthodox parishes had dropped from almost 800.000 in 2010 to about

---

1 Cf. https://bpb-us-e1.wpmucdn.com/sites.northwestern.edu/dist/c/1549/files/2019/08/Sarkisian-Analysis.pdf.

675.000 in 2020.[2] The vast majority of these are migrants from Orthodox cultures and their descendants. The absolutely largest Orthodox structure in the US is the Greek Orthodox Archdiocese of North America (GOA) with 375.000 adherents, followed by the Orthodox Church in America (OCA), the Antiochian Orthodox Christian Archdiocese (AOCA), and the Serbian Orthodox Church (SOC), each numbering between 60.000 and 75.000 adherents.

The OCA is a structure that was founded in 1970 as a church independent of any of the national Orthodox Churches (Tarasar 1975: 261–280). However, it was to a large extent a political project of the Russian Orthodox Church (ROC), meaning that it is still considered 'Russian' by many, even though it counts among the more 'American' jurisdictions. The traditional center of world Orthodoxy, the Patriarch of Constantinople, has not recognized it as an independent church so far, probably because it considers the GOA the most legitimate structure in North America. The AOCA was originally responsible for Arabic Orthodox Christians but has accepted a number of convert communities since the 1980s, making it too a multicultural entity.

There are eleven other church structures in the US that share the remaining 100.000 Orthodox adherents, including the Russian Orthodox Church Outside Russia (ROCOR) with 24.000 adherents. This is a structure that was established in Serbia in the 1920s as an alternative to the compromised ROC in the Soviet Union (Rimestad 2015). It comprised most of the Russian bishops who fled from the Bolshevik regime and remained a staunchly monarchist and reactionary structure throughout the Cold War, considering itself the true Russian Orthodox Church. Its administrative center was relocated to Munich in 1945 and to New York in 1948. In 2007, through the mediation of Russian President Vladimir Putin, it reunited with its archenemy, the ROC of the Moscow Patriarchate (Collins 2023, 50–57). It still exists as a separate entity with a rather conservative outlook but has acknowledged the legitimacy of the Moscow Patriarchate as the center of Russian Orthodoxy.

This is a rather confusing plethora of separate structures, each of which may be seen as an organization in its own right. However, as was the case with

---

2   Cf. https://orthodoxreality.org/wp-content/uploads/2021/03/2020CensusGeneralRep ort1.pdf. There are additionally almost 500.000 Oriental Orthodox adherents in the US. This community has, despite being frequently conflated with the Eastern Orthodox, its own unique historical and sociological realities and so is beyond the scope of this paper.

the Russian diocese in the 19th century, these organizations are not primarily social forms in the sense of being arenas for social interaction, but rather providers of identity and umbrella organizations for the individual parishes that see themselves as communities for their members. The latter still correspond largely to the social form of 'group', where membership is informal and diffuse, but often tied to ethnic affiliation. At the same time, more formalized 'organizations' do exist, especially when it comes to the relationship with secular American society. There are church-linked social and cultural organizations, where there is formal membership and a hierarchical structure with clear division of labor. These organizations in most cases do not claim to represent 'the Church', however, but are auxiliary associations.

In other words, the social forms of the Eastern Orthodox Church in the US should be viewed at three different levels: the national level of dioceses and church structures (organization) is not really concerned with membership and social interaction, but mostly with church law and upholding geopolitical boundaries. The individual parishes (group), on the other hand, generally try to be inclusive but tend to become rather closed communities for people of a specific ethnic affiliation. The third level is outside of the church as such (organization/network) and includes church-affiliated organizations that labor for inclusive parishes, inter-jurisdictional cooperation, or social welfare programs. All three levels form part of the Orthodox Church in North America and make up its outward appearance. It would be a fallacy to see only one level, which would skew the image and misrepresent the complexity of US Orthodoxy.

3. Conversion to Orthodox Christianity in the United States of America

One of the factors resulting in such a skewed perception is that of American converts to the Orthodox Church. Even though the vast majority of Orthodox Christians in the US have family ties to traditionally Orthodox countries and see themselves as Orthodox faithful "in the diaspora", the most vocal views of the Orthodox Church in the English language come from converts. While most converts have personal reasons for joining the Orthodox Church, such as Orthodox spouses or formative holiday encounters with Orthodox spirituality, there is a sizeable and very vocal type of convert who approaches the Orthodox Church from readings and profound theological or spiritual search (Rimestad forthcoming; Medvedeva, forthcoming). Interestingly, such converts become very visible in the American religious field, since they are much more inclined to missionary activity than the Orthodox Church has traditionally been and often try to convince their peers of the Orthodox "truth" they have discovered. The social form thus championed is that of a group, but not in terms of social, linguistic, or ethnic proximity. Rather, the converts seek to idealize the religious aspects of Orthodoxy, downplaying its social aspects (Gallaher 2022).

One of the earliest examples of this type of convert was Seraphim Rose (1934–1982), a Californian academic who rejected Christianity as a youth and studied East Asian languages and culture before being accepted into the Orthodox Church (ROCOR) in 1962 (Christensen 1993). Six years after joining the Orthodox Church, Seraphim founded a monastery where he became a monk. He translated Orthodox theological writings into English and wrote his own theological texts, often in a rather polemical style, besides running an Orthodox publishing house and bookstore with a bi-monthly magazine. One of his main topics was the perceived depravity of Western society that could only be overcome through a rigorous adherence to Orthodox theological doctrine (ibid.). For Seraphim, secluded monasticism was the only social form that was fully compatible with Orthodox Christianity. He took an example from the Russian monastic saints of the 16th through 19th centuries, who also chose a life at the margins of civilization.

A different conversion story that also conforms to this type is that of Peter Gillquist (1938–2012), a leading member of the Evangelical Campus Crusades for Christ in the 1960s. Together with some of his fellow 'Crusaders', Gillquist became disillusioned with what he perceived as the superficiality of Protestant worship and church life and looked for the "One, Holy, Catholic, and Apostolic Christian Church" (1992: 57). He came across Eastern Orthodoxy, which he considered to embody this ideal community. Gillquist and his associates wished to retain the social form they had grown into during their search for religious truth – that of a close-knit "community of fate" – but the wish to be accepted into the Orthodox Church as a group was initially not granted by any Orthodox bishop in the US. The bishops feared that the balance between the three levels of social forms described in the previous section would suffer from such a group conversion of theologically literate and, perhaps more importantly, culturally Protestant Americans. If these Protestant Americans entered into their jurisdictions, their cultural (and one could say, ethnic) character would suffer. Considering the churches had functioned not just as centers of worship but of community life, this was a reasonable fear.

Nevertheless, the Gillquist group was finally accepted by AOCA bishop (Metropolitan) Philip in 1987, who saw these conversions as a way to provide additional visibility to his fledgling church of Arabic migrants (Herbel 2014: 103–129). The group was known as the Evangelical Orthodox Mission, an organization modeled on Protestant missionary outreach, and it grew rapidly, from 17 to 32 parishes within six years (Gillquist 1992: 175–177). Moreover, the Mission established a publishing house (Ancient Faith Publishing), which has published numerous volumes and other texts praising the AOCA as a generous haven for American converts, even though these publications have been criticized as being a "strange hybrid of evangelical Protestantism and Orthodoxy" (Gallaher 2022: 115).

For Gillquist, as well as for innumerable others, the Orthodox Church offered a place for unadulterated spirituality, a refuge from rampant secularization and liberalism (cf. Makrides 2022). At the same time, their Western, Protestant mindset made it difficult for them to imagine a religious faith where the social form of organization does not take a prime place. Instead of blending into the existing social forms of jurisdictions (organizations) and parishes (groups), the converts tend to establish parish organizations and evade obedience to traditional authority structures (cf. Gallaher 2022). This can also be seen in the rising popularity of published conversion accounts to Orthodox Christianity on the American book market in the last years (such as Gillquist 1995; Huneycutt 2018; cf. also Medvedeva forthcoming), not to mention the establishments of other media outlets, such as the radio station "Ancient Faith Radio"[3] or interactive websites, like "journeytoorthodoxy.com" and others. Common to them all is the attempt to portray Orthodox Christianity as *original* Christianity, and thus the solution to many of the problems of the modern world.

Ksenia Medvedeva (forthcoming) argues that American converts to the Orthodox Church either convert "to the Ancient Church" or they convert "against Western values". We argue that there is no substantial difference between these two motives, but rather between what may be called *theological* and *cultural* converts. *Cultural converts* are those who convert because of personal reasons or af-

---

[3] Rebranded as "Ancient Faith Ministries" in the digital era. Ancient Faith Ministries demonstrates the particular nature of these "theological converts" and the extent to which they retain their (white) American Protestant cultural perspective, seeking to create "Orthodox" alternatives to the cultural components of American Evangelical Protestantism.

ter a profound spiritual experience involving the Orthodox Church. They are generally happy to try to integrate into existing parishes, even if these retain an ethnic character. The *theological converts*, on the other hand, who see in Orthodoxy "the true church", feel distracted by the ethnic character. These latter, like Peter Gillquist and his community, may then try to establish their own Orthodox parishes, where ethnicity is not a significant marker (Gillquist 1992: 182–184; Slagle 2011: 124–142). As mentioned above, this is most easily achieved in the OCA and the AOCA, church structures that try to leave their ethnic connotations behind. That is why these two structures are the ones that tend to be most open to receiving converts and integrating fully into American culture. In terms of social forms, this means that their parishes conceive of themselves as "movements", rather than groups, in the sense that their membership is even more diffuse and informal with a high degree of symbolic integration and a clearly stated goal: to make society more Orthodox.

However, this goal is a two-pronged sword, for it can mean either of two things. For one, some converts long for a return to the "golden age" of Orthodox Christianity, which is variably situated in the time of the Church Fathers in the first Millennium CE or in the Tsarist Russian Empire, as we elaborate in the next section. The other option is more benign, a diffusion of Orthodox spirituality and Christian love into all aspects of societal life, by leading the way as positive examples. For some proponents of the first idea, the converts arguing for the second option have already lost contact with the true Orthodox faith and have succumbed to liberalism and secularization. For those in the second group, it is the other way around: the converts that long for an 'orthodoxization' of society conflate the abstract Orthodox ethos with rigorous practices and rules (Gallaher 2022).

The proponents of an 'orthodoxization' of American society want the Orthodox Church to take on the social form of a movement, which would consciously and radically counter what they perceive as harmful secularizing and liberal developments. Analytically, it is difficult to describe them as a movement, but they are rather part of a network of political and social ideas that are shared across communities and religions. They often refer to the polemic works of Seraphim Rose, which would champion 'traditional Orthodox anti-Westernism'. However, according to Robert Saler (2024), Seraphim's actual theology was not so much anti-Western as it provided a template on which anti-Westernism can easily be crafted (cf. also Riccardi-Swartz 2022: 191). The radical anti-Westernism of Orthodox Christianity is a recent phenomenon, even if it has precursors in earlier centuries (Makrides/Uffelmann 2003).

At the same time, immigrant American Orthodoxy has not been entirely immune from the effects of this mentality, absorbing it both from the converts entering Orthodoxy and from the wider culture, a culture in which religion has increasingly become a marker of political identity (Hartman 2019). The most visible example of this phenomenon is the rise of the so-called Ephraimite monasteries in the Greek Orthodox Archdiocese of America (Kostarelos 2020; Kostarelos 2022). The charismatic Elder Ephraim (1928–2019), born in Volos, Greece, and trained as an Athonite monk under the influential Joseph the Hesychast, visited North America in the late 1970s. Here, he found a Greek community in its second and third-generation post-migration that was increasingly affluent and highly assimilated.[4] Ephraim understood this as a lack of spiritual vigor on the part of the Greeks and thus resolved to come to the United States as a missionary to this Orthodox Christian community. Thus, like many American converts to Orthodoxy, Ephraim understood Orthodoxy in a much more mission-focused way than it had previously understood itself. The difference, however, is that Ephraim understood his mission primarily to the Greek diaspora, which had fallen away from their traditional Orthodox faith, not to those from other ethnic backgrounds. Despite this original focus of his mission on the Greek American community, the monasteries founded by Ephraim and his followers have also attracted a considerable number of converts, eager for the experience of 'authentic' Athonite monasticism in America (Kelaidis forthcoming). The existence of Ephraimite monasteries demonstrates the way in which Western Christian social forms have influenced Orthodox Christian understandings in the diaspora leading to the generation of para-ecclesiastical bodies under the guise of religious organizations.

4. Orthodox catechization and the internet

Sarah Riccardi-Swartz (2022) conducted fieldwork over an extended period among Orthodox Christians in a small town in the Appalachian mountains. Her findings corroborate the change occurring since 2010 and especially since the ascent of Donald Trump to the American presidency in 2016. Whereas the Orthodox community she studied initially grew out of the vision of a disciple of Seraphim Rose in 2000, it has increasingly become a home for converts who are disillusioned with current American politics and look for alternative

---

4   Cf. https://ergon.scienzine.com/article/articles/liturgical-language-crisis-of-1970.

concepts of community. This way, the Orthodox faith becomes reimagined in a way that is deeply tied to the political. This imagined world "marshals theological and political structures far removed from ancient Christian monasticism and American religion and politics, yet continually in tension with both" (ibid.: 192).

Besides this political radicalization of Orthodox communities in rural America, there is a much more dangerous radicalization that is happening online. The proliferation of internet resources and digital communication has profoundly changed the social forms of Orthodox Christianity in America. Coupled with an increasingly polarized and dichotomized political atmosphere in the US, this gave rise to the phenomenon of reactive internet Orthodoxy. Digital Orthodox celebrities, such as Josiah Trenham, Rod Dreher, Peter Heers, and Frederica Mathewes-Green, "were all players in the social drama of Reactive Orthodoxy" (ibid.: 21). These actors not only are all converts from Evangelical Protestant Churches to Orthodox Christianity, but they use internet technologies to very vocally lay the claim of representing 'true' Orthodox spirituality. At the same time, they have retained a Protestant mindset that hinders them in fully accepting universally held Orthodox truths, such as the subordination to one's bishop or the importance of community (Gallaher 2022). Although there are various parallel Orthodox ecclesiastical structures in North America that have a partially strained relationship with each other, they all agree that it is usurpation when a priest like Peter Heers is unable to disclose which bishop is blessing his work as a priest.[5]

Nevertheless, this does not diminish Heers' appeal to disillusioned Americans who find these online offerings of Orthodox faith so appealing that they decide to convert and become avid followers. Even those who are rooted in an Orthodox parish community tend to utilize online resources. For many of these converts, according to Riccardi-Swartz, "digital networks allowed them to connect, share, and be a part of the broader Orthodox community across the globe" (Riccardi-Swartz 2022: 188; cf. also Medvedeva forthcoming). While the actual discussions in Orthodox communities and the printed literature retain some level of theological nuance and differentiation, online communications tend to be more polarized and full of inflammatory rhetoric.

In terms of social forms, the actual parishes and living Orthodox communities, be they predominantly ethnic or converts, retain the characteristics of a group, focusing on the individuals as part of the community (Bringerud 2019).

---

5 Cf. https://www.assemblyofbishops.org/news/2023/communique-04202023.

The online communities, on the other hand, perceive themselves as a movement that aims at preventing further social change in the liberal direction. However, they are more concisely conceptualized as networks, since they do not rely on locations or physical interaction but only serve as echo chambers mutually reinforcing mostly far-right political opinions through specific theological interpretations that are often not condoned by the official religious experts of the Orthodox Church.[6]

A significant number of the recent converts to online reactive Orthodoxy in North America have little contact with an actual Orthodox parish since there is none in their vicinity. Furthermore, many of these converts are already part of social groups particularly prone to engagement with online radicalism – namely young men who have at least some higher education and experience some degree of alienation from society and/or peer groups (Odag et al. 2019). In keeping with their broader alienation, their exposure to everyday parish life in the Orthodox Church is minimal, to such an extent that the social form they are living in the Orthodox Church resembles a dyad, where the individual convert interacts with the church through a few self-styled internet gurus.[7] That many of these converts embrace the label "incel" (originally denoting involuntary celibate young males) further exacerbates their radicalization, as they are "outraged by the shifting social norms in the United States, fearful of potential political and religious persecution of American conservative Christians, and concerned by threats to white hegemony" (Riccardi-Swartz 2022: 188). It becomes increasingly clear that there is a growing subculture within the Orthodox Church in North America that politically leans to the right fringes while it increasingly disconnects with traditional authorities and social forms in the Orthodox Church, the bishops and the parishes as moderating communities (Gallaher 2022). This subculture thrives in the era of "networked individualism", as identified by Rainie and Wellman (2012). The more detrimental effects of the "Triple Revolution" they hold high have arguably become plainly visible only since the mid-2010s, in the "Putin-Trump era" that saw the rise of White Nationalism in the US, the eruption of inter-racial violence and the Black Lives Matter-Movement, and also the COVID-19 pandemic and rampant Trumpism (Riccardi-Swartz 2022: 187). That there is a direct link between far-right rhetoric and conversion to Orthodox Christianity is undeniable, both in terms of white nationalism (Leonova 2019) and anti-vaccinationism (Issaris et

---

6   Cf. e.g. https://theopenark.substack.com/p/from-orthobro-to-orthodox-and-the.
7   Cf. https://theopenark.substack.com/p/from-orthobro-to-orthodox-and-the.

al. 2023). When the dispute over the presidential elections of 2020 provoked the "Storm on the Capitol" on January 6, 2021, there were numerous Orthodox converts among the rioters, including at least one priest, who was later sanctioned by his bishop for his actions.[8] This radicalization is undoubtedly a result of the triple revolution, with the additional revolution in AI and algorithms, which help solidify the feeling of being part of a moral majority, even if this feeling has little basis in reality.

The fact that physical interaction as a diverse community is not necessary to spread some of these political and social views becomes a problem for the Orthodox parishes in North America. There is a tension between the traditional emphasis among the Orthodox church structures in the USA and this new English-language Orthodox discourse on the internet. The former has focused on finding a way to make Orthodox Christianity American and universal by overcoming ethnic divisions, a topic that has remained an important part of the rhetoric of converts like Gillquist and is still held high by the Orthodox Churches in the US. The other discourse, which Riccardi-Swartz terms "Reactive Orthodoxy", is a discourse happening primarily online since the mid-2010s that is seeping into convert Orthodox communities. It is a "worldbuilding form of the faith that finds its roots in an imagined nostalgia for ancient Rus', American Christian nationalism, and an apocalyptic disenchantment with democracy" (Riccardi-Swartz 2022: 173).

Instead of readily accepting the social form of the Orthodox parishes that can be conceptualized as a local group and focuses on the individual members, reactive Orthodoxy sees itself as a movement with a clear goal – to overthrow the liberal bias of contemporary American society, be it gender ideologies, infringements upon civil liberties, or race relations. At the same time, it is analytically more correct to describe reactive Orthodoxy as a network in the sense of Rainie and Wellman, as a community held together through digital links, often centering on a few controversial but media-savvy experts. Some of these experts, moreover, are more interested in followers and internet fame than in consistent theological arguments.[9]

---

[8] Cf. https://www.splcenter.org/hatewatch/2023/08/22/orthodox-priest-jan-6-participant-supports-russian-government-scheme-enticing-conservatives.

[9] Cf. https://theopenark.substack.com/p/from-orthobro-to-orthodox-and-the; https://www.euronews.com/2023/07/31/democracy-is-a-tool-of-satan-the-murky-world-of-orthodox-influencers.

5. Conclusion

What all this means for the social forms of Orthodox Christianity in North America is that there is a rising tension between the *communitizing* elements that have dominated American Orthodox discourse until recently and the *societalizing* tendencies of reactionary online Orthodoxy. Communitization for the Orthodox communities in the US means growing together to be a harmonious community of believers, which would overcome traditional and existing ethnic and cultural divisions, including with regard to mainstream society. The societalizing tendencies, on the other hand, refer to abstract and functional links between like-minded individuals who are more interested in constructing an alternative to the mainstream than growing as a community. The Orthodox Church has never been fond of the idea of the church as an organization, even though the various jurisdictions operating in North America have organizational structures. These are much more concerned with authority structures and church law than with their actual members, though. Although Orthodox parishes in the US had to register as organizations for legal reasons, most early parishes were relatively homogeneous groups of individual faithful that recognized each other as equal without any formal membership requirements. That being said, not infrequently throughout the twentieth century, Greek Orthodox parishes, for example, developed along regional lines or split from one another as political tensions in Greece found their way to the diaspora (Diamanti-Karanou 2015).[10]

Nevertheless, the conceptualization of the Orthodox Church as a movement of like-minded people of the same faith, though dispersed among various contesting ethnic structures, was prevalent, including the attempts to establish a non-ethnic American Orthodoxy – be they through inter-jurisdictional cooperation or convert communities (Bringerud 2019). This is clearly a communitizing impetus, looking to integrate diverse individuals into a united faith community. Orthodox religious organizations below the level of the jurisdiction do exist, but they are not coterminous with the parish. They help organize specific parts of its Orthodox outreach, such as support for the needy (Riccardi-Swartz 2022: 152–153) or inter-Orthodox cooperation (Kishkovsky 2004). Moreover, this work is usually perceived as the fulfillment of Christian obligations rather than as a function within an organization. For the individual parish,

---

[10] The tensions in America's growing Ethiopian Orthodox community seem to repeat this kind of development in the 21st century (Kelaidis, forthcoming).

the social form of a group is more apt, since it has a fluid, diffuse membership, where all those present are integrated into the community as individual faithful.

Reactive online Orthodoxy, on the other hand, while also perceiving itself as a movement with a moral impetus, is best described with the social form of a network. More precisely, it is a digital network, one that in some cases borders on the dyadic, meaning the relationship between a central actor and their individual followers. As such, it does not display the same community elements, but can rather be viewed as a political entity. The community is virtual and only occasionally becomes visible, most often in the term of events. Brandon Gallaher mentions several events at various North American Orthodox clergy seminaries over the last few years that have included speakers who are celebrities within reactive online Orthodoxy (Gallaher 2022: 112–113; cf. also Riccardi-Swartz 2022: 21). He laments a general trend for all these seminaries to succumb to ultra-conservative agenda-setting and fundamentalist rhetoric in their public events.

Most Orthodox believers in the US still congregate in communities, but it is increasingly difficult to avoid the discourse of reactive online Orthodoxy because it is omnipresent on the internet. Moreover, it is a self-reinforcing spiral in that even well-meaning reposts of seemingly harmless Orthodox content very easily attract comments from the reactive Orthodox milieu. This is the result of both the veil of anonymity that is offered by the internet and the mission impetus of reactive Orthodoxy. Seeing themselves as saviors of a fallen world, these actors, who are mostly converts from Protestantism, display online communication that is lecturing and polemical. Thus, the ideas circulating among reactive online Orthodox do take hold also in the parishes, especially those that have a large percentage of converts. This implies that these parishes might become more closed and dismissive of diversity of opinion. The dream of diverse and all-encompassing Orthodoxy that is harbored among many liberal Orthodox in North America is hampered by this development.

However, this development is not specific to North America, though reactive online Orthodoxy still is a predominantly American phenomenon. Because it is conducted mainly in English, however, it has a global following. At the same time, it is fueled also by the deliberate use of Russian propaganda, especially following the attack on Ukraine in February 2022. Attempts to openly split public opinion, mainly originating from Russia, can also be seen in many European contexts, although the use of Orthodox Christianity to this end has not been as successful as in the US.

Bibliography

Bringerud, Lydia (2019): Whose Tradition? Adapting Orthodox Christianity in North America, Unpublished Dissertation, Memorial University of Newfoundland.

Chadwick, Henry (2003): East and West. The Making of a Rift in the Church. From Apostolic Times until the Council of Florence, Oxford: Oxford University Press.

Christensen, Damascene (1993): Not of This World: The Life and Teaching of Fr. Seraphim Rose, Pathfinder to the Heart of Ancient Christianity, Fortesville, CA: Seraphim Rose Foundation.

Collins, Robert (2023): Global Tensions in the Russian Orthodox Diaspora, London: Routledge.

Diamanti-Karanou, Panagoula (2015): The Relationship Between Homeland and Diaspora: The Case of Greece and the Greek-American Community, Unpublished Dissertation, Northeastern University.

Durante, Chris (2015): "Ethno-Religiosity in Orthodox Christianity: A Source of Solidarity & Multiculturalism in American Society." In: Religions 6/2, pp. 328–349. https://doi.org/10.3390/rel6020328E.

Gallaher, Brandon (2022): "Fundamentalism and Conversion to Eastern Orthodoxy in the West: Reflections on the Myth of Orthodoxy." In: Davor Džalto/George Demacopoulos (eds), Orthodoxy and Fundamentalism. Contemporary Perspectives, Lanham: Lexington Books, pp. 105–126.

Gillquist, Peter E. (1992): Becoming Orthodox. A Journey to the Ancient Christian Faith, Ben Lomond, CA: Conciliar Press.

Gillquist, Peter E. (ed.) (1995): Coming Home. Why Protestant Clergy are Becoming Orthodox, Chesterton, IN: Ancient Faith Publishing.

Goldberg, Michelle (2014): "The Globalization of the Culture Wars." In: Carole Joffe/Jennifer Reich (eds.), Reproduction and Society: Interdisciplinary Readings, London and New York: Routledge, pp. 260–264.

Hartman, Andrew (2019): A War or the Soul of America: A History of the Culture Wars, Chicago, IL: University of Chicago Press.

Herbel, D. Oliver (2013): Turning to Tradition: Converts and the Making of an American Orthodox Church, Oxford: Oxford University Press.

Höpken, Wolfgang/Rimestad, Sebastian (eds.) (forthcoming): Global Secularity. A Sourcebook, vol. 4: Eastern Europe, Berlin: De Gruyter.

Huneycutt, Joseph David (2018): One Flew over the Onion Dome. American Orthodox Converts, Reverts, & Retreads, Yonkers, NY: St. Vladimir's Seminary Press.

Issaris, Vasileios/Kalogerakos, Georgios/Milas, Gerasimos P. (2023). "Vaccination Hesitancy Among Greek Orthodox Christians: Is There a Conflict Between Religion and Science?" In: Journal of Religion and Health 62/2, pp. 1373–1378.

Kan, Sergei (1999): Memory Eternal – Tlingit Culture and Russian Orthodox Christianity Through Two Centuries, Seattle: University of Washington Press.

Kan, Sergei (2001): "Russian Orthodox Missionaries at Home and Abroad: The Case of Siberian and Alaskan Indigenous People." In: Robert Geraci/Michael Khodarkovsky (eds.), Of Religion and Empire – Mission, Conversion, and Tolerance in Tsarist Russia, Ithaca, NY: Cornell University Press, pp. 173–200.

Kelaidis, Katherine (forthcoming): "Trouble Back Home: Political Conflict and Religious Division in America's Ethnic Orthodox Communities." In: Journal of American Ethnic History.

Kitroeff, Alexander (2020): The Greek Orthodox Church in America: A Modern History (= NIU-Reihe in orthodoxen christlichen Studien), Ithaca, NY: Northern Illinois University Press.

Kishkovsky, Leonid (2004): "Orthodoxy in America: Diaspora or Church?" In: Occasional Papers on Religion in Eastern Europe 24/3, pp. 35–46. https://digitalcommons.georgefox.edu/cgi/viewcontent.cgi?article=1532&=&context=ree&=&sei-redir=1&refere.

Kostarelos, Frances (2020): "Elder Ephraim and Contested Identities in the Greek Orthodox Archdiocese of North America." In: Sebastian Rimestad/Vasilios Makrides (eds.), Coping with Change. Orthodox Christian Dynamics between Tradition, Innovation, and *Realpolitik*, Berlin: Peter Lang, pp. 17–36.

Kostarelos, Frances (2022): "Fundamentalism and Dialectical Encounters in the Greek Orthodox Church in the United States: The Case of Elder Ephraim of Arizona." In: Davor Džalto/George Demacopoulos (eds.), Orthodoxy and Fundamentalism, Contemporary Perspectives, Lanham: Lexington Books, pp. 127–144.

Leonova, Inga (2019): "Orthodox and White." In: The Wheel 17/18, pp. 27–32.

Makrides, Vasilios N./Uffelmann, Dirk (2003): "Studying Eastern Orthodox Anti-Westernism: The Need for a Comparative Research Agenda."

In: Jonathan Sutton/Wil van den Bercken (eds.), Orthodox Christianity and Contemporary Europe, Leuven, Paris, and Dudley, MA: Peeters, pp. 87–120.

Makrides, Vasilios N. (2022): "The Notion of 'Orthodoxy' as the Sole True Faith: A Specific Cause of Orthodox Christian Rigorism/Fundamentalism". In: Davor Džalto/George Demacopoulos (eds.), Orthodoxy and Fundamentalism, Contemporary Perspectives, Lanham: Lexington Books, pp. 31–50.

Medvedeva, Ksenia (forthcoming): "American Conversions to Eastern Orthodox Christianity". In: Entangled Religions 15/2.

Odağ, Özen/Leiser, Anne/Boehnke, Klaus (2019): "Reviewing the Role of the Internet in Radicalization Processes." In: Journal for Deradicalization 21, pp. 261–300.

Rainie, Lee/Wellman, Barry (2012): Networked. The New Social Operation System, Cambridge, MA: MIT Press.

Riccardi-Swartz, Sarah (2022): Between Heaven and Russia. Religious Conversion and Political Apostasy in Appalachia, New York: Fordham University Press.

Rimestad, Sebastian (2015): "The Russian Orthodox Church in Western Europe. One or Many?" In: Religion, State and Society 43/3, pp. 228–243.

Rimestad, Sebastian (2021): Orthodox Christian Identity in Western Europe: Contesting Religious Authority, London: Routledge.

Rimestad, Sebastian (forthcoming): "Orthodoxes Christentum und Konversion." In: Vasilios N. Makrides (ed.), Christentum III: Das orthodoxe Christentum – interdisziplinäre Zugänge (= Religionen der Menschheit, 30), Stuttgart: Kohlhammer.

Roudometof, Victor (1998): "From Rum Millet to Greek Nation: Enlightenment, Secularization, and National Identity in Ottoman Balkan Society, 1453–1821." In: Journal of Modern Greek Studies 16/1, pp. 11–48.

Saler, Robert (2024): What you Feel Will Find Its Own Form: Kerouac, Day, Rose, and the Possibilities of Modern Christian Subculture, Eugene, OR: Cascade Press.

Sarkisian, Aram (2022): "'We go fearlessly into the maw of death.' The Influenza Epidemic of 1918 in American Orthodox Rus'." In: Journal of Orthodox Christian Studies 4/2, pp. 211–237.

Slagle, Amy (2011): The Eastern Church in the Spiritual Marketplace: American Conversions to Orthodox Christianity, Chicago, IL: Northern Illinois University Press.

Tarasar, Constance (1975): Orthodox America 1794–1975: Developments of the Orthodox Church in America, Syosset, NY: OCA.

Web References

Joshua Askew. "'Democracy is a Tool of Satan': The Murky World of Orthodox Influencers." euronews. July 31, 2023. Accessed November 23, 2023. https://www.euronews.com/2023/07/31/democracy-is-a-tool-of-satan-the-murky-world-of-orthodox-influencers.

Assembly of Canonical Orthodox Bishops of the United States of America. "Communiqué." April 20, 2023. Accessed November 23, 2023. https://www.assemblyofbishops.org/news/2023/communique-04202023.

Hannah Gais. "Orthodox Priest, Jan 6. Participant Supports Russian Government Scheme Enticing Conservatives to Move to Russia." Southern Poverty Law Center, Hatewatch. August 22, 2023. Accessed November 23, 2023. https://www.splcenter.org/hatewatch/2023/08/22/orthodox-priest-jan-6-participant-supports-russian-government-scheme-enticing-conservatives.

Noah Jefferson. "From 'Orthobro' to Orthodox and the Danger of Jay Dyer's Church Within the Church." The Open Ark. April 22, 2023. Accessed November 23, 2023. https://theopenark.substack.com/p/from-orthobro-to-orthodox-and-the.

Alexander Kitroeff. "Greek America's Liturgical Language Crisis of 1970." Ergon Greek/American Arts and Letters. 2019. Accessed April 14, 2024. https://ergon.scienzine.com/article/articles/liturgical-language-crisis-of-1970.

Alexei Krindatch. "US Religion Census 2020: Dramatic Changes in American Orthodox Churches." Accessed November 23, 2023. Orthodox Reality. https://orthodoxreality.org/wp-content/uploads/2021/03/2020CensusGeneralReport1.pdf.

Aram Sarkisian. "From Kedrovsky to Kedroff: The St. Nicholas Cathedral Cases in Their Historical Context." Teaching Law and Religion Case Study Archive. August 2019. Accessed November 23, 2023. https://bpb-us-e1.wpmucdn.com/sites.northwestern.edu/dist/c/1549/files/2019/08/Sarkisian-Analysis.pdf.

Forever Into Eternity
Social Forms of Religion in the Temple Wedding of The Church of Jesus Christ of Latter-day Saints

Marie-Therese Mäder

Abstract *The wedding in the temple, known as the "sealing" ceremony, constitutes a pivotal moment in the life of a Latter-day Saint. Beyond the eternal nature of the marriage, the exclusive sacred space of the temple holds profound significance for the couple and their community, accessible only to members of The Church of Jesus Christ of Latter-day Saints. The temple wedding establishes clear distinctions between 'us' and 'them', delineating boundaries to the outside world and creating social units that embody the cellular principle of social forms of religions. In this particular case, these units manifest as the marital dyad of the couple, fortified during the "sealing" ceremony in the temple. Marriage between a man and a woman represents the most esteemed form of living, providing access to the highest place in heaven. During the wedding, norms and values are not only actively shared but also collectively experienced. Even years later, the event is recalled in intricate detail, with certain experiences akin to the sealing ceremony in the temple. Therefore, the wedding plays a vital role in communitization. Lastly, the wedding reception fosters emotional connections among guests who actively and enthusiastically participate in the event, thereby bringing the social form of eventization into play.*

Keywords *boundary making, communitization, eventization, Latter-day Saints, marital dyad, temple, ceremony, video conversations, wedding*

1. Introduction: Drawing boundaries within temple ceremonies

In 2008, while journeying through the Western United States, I had my inaugural visit to the Latter-day Saints Temple Square. Back then, my knowledge of Mormonism and The Church of Jesus Christ of Latter-day Saints was rather limited. My initial impression of the place was vivid: the remarkable cleanliness lingered in my memory; a feature particularly noteworthy from a Swiss perspective. Moreover, the noticeable gap, the physical separation between the tourists participating in guided tours and the members of the church, left a strong impression on me (Mäder 2020).

Most of the men were dressed in white shirts with ties and jackets. It appeared that the temple square was segregated into two distinct sections: one designated for the church members and another for the visitors. Initially, I was puzzled by this division, but I later learned that access to the temple is restricted to church members only. It was not until later that I noticed the wall at the bottom of the picture and the deliberate landscaping that created a separation between myself and the guests. This setting clearly delineated a boundary between us, the visitors, and them, the insiders. It became evident to me that within Temple Square, there existed an exclusive group: individuals who stood apart from the broader world, even though the dividing line was adorned with carefully tended plants.

Latter-day Saints, who consider themselves Christians but are not fully accepted as such by all Christian communities, visit the temple to conduct various rites of passage (Van Gennep 2019: 1–14), such as baptism for the dead or couple sealings for eternity. Another important ritual practice is the "sealing ceremony". Latter-day Saint families who join the church after their children are born will, as they call it, "seal" their family in a temple ceremony for eternity, meaning that the family will continue to be bound together in the afterworld. The same ritual is conducted by couples to be sealed for eternity, meaning that the couple will still be married even after their death.[1] Due to its eternal duration, the Latter-day Saint temple wedding is called the "celestial marriage" (Daynes 2015). The ceremonies, such as the regular temple visit where members perform the "endowment ceremony" in various temple rooms, serve not only as a way to confirm and establish identity among the members but also as a way to create a social distinction between 'us' and 'them'.

The present paper centers on one specific rite of passage within the Latter-day Saint community: the temple marriage, specifically the "sealing" ceremony. It addresses three questions: First, what does the temple wedding, the "sealing" of the couple, mean within the Latter-day Saints' worldview (Fritz et al. 2018: 56–57)? Second, how is the representation of inclusion and exclusion

---

1   For more about the Latter-day Saint practices of "sealing" and "eternal marriage" cf. Hammarberg 2013: 171–196; Daynes 2015

symbolically and practically communicated in the temple wedding and other moments, like the civil marriage ceremony and the reception? Third, which social forms of religion follow from these boundaries of inclusion and exclusion and how are social forms of religion expressed in the temple wedding and its festivities?

The second question claims that the ritual of temple weddings signifies the establishment of boundaries where participants create a distinction between 'them' and 'us'. This approach draws on the ethnographer and sociologist Andreas Wimmer's understanding of the boundary concept that consists of "everyday networks of relationships that result from individual acts of connecting and distancing" and the social classifications as 'us' and 'them' (Wimmer 2008: 113). This classification allows the experience of belonging that, according to Heinrich Popitz, is a basic form of social experience. The resulting social units represent the cellular principle of social forms of religion that define the distinctions between 'us and the others' by drawing certain boundaries to the outside world (Popitz 1992: 140–143).

In the context of Latter-day Saints, this distinction from others is practiced in the sealing ceremony in the temple.[2] The latter is specifically drastic because the couples are sealed forever beyond death. The collective representation of this shared worldview is expressed, among other ways, in the temple buildings, which are only accessible to members of the church with a temple recommendation by church authorities.[3] Moreover, the various temple rituals can be viewed as identity markers used to establish boundaries between the Latter-day Saints and those outside the faith, echoing Wimmer's analysis:

> One divides the social world into social groups – into 'us' and 'them' – and the other offers scripts of action – how to relate to individuals classified as 'us' and 'them' under given circumstances. Only when the two schemes coincide, when ways of seeing the world correspond to ways of acting in the world, shall I speak of a social boundary. (Wimmer 2008: 113)

"[S]eeing the world" and "acting in the world" are intertwined and rooted in a particular worldview and distinct practices, among which a wedding can be

---

2   The temple marriage is an important step in the "Mormon Quest for Glory," as the title of Melvyn Hammarberg's monograph reads. Cf. Hammarberg 2013, 253–267.
3   A detailed account of the religious practices in a Latter-day Saint temple can be found in Mäder 2023, 201–202.

included as a specific religious social practice on several levels. Yet, the temple wedding holds significant importance in the worldview of the Latter-day Saints. The couple forms an eternal dyad between husband and wife by making eternally valid promises to each other in the sealing ceremony in the temple to enter the highest degree of heaven (out of three) in the afterlife (Daynes 2015: 334). This eternal dyad can be seen as the smallest social form, according to Popitz (1992: 152–156), in which each individual recognizes the other individual and by doing so creates a social relationship.

Additionally, the wedding also encompasses the community and the wedding guests. They partake in the ritual, listening to the couple's vows and the "sealer's" (the master of ceremony in the temple) words. During weddings collective and often emotional experiences, a strong sense of unity, and personal inclusion are communicated. These experiences contribute to the social form of religious communitization. A wedding transforms "individual experiences into collective experiences and thus makes a constitutive contribution to social forms of religion"[4] (Heiser/Ludwig 2014: 8). In processes of communitization common norms and values are shared, and the social boundary between us and them is strengthened, and a collective identity is generated (Krech et al. 2013: 54).[5] And finally, the support by other church members before, during and after the wedding reinforces a collective practice. It highlights the experience of something extraordinary, emotional bonding and active participation, that belongs to another religious social form, namely the eventization. "Acting and feeling together connects the participants, takes them out of their everyday lives and gives rise to the assumption that they are connected to something bigger", as sociologists Patrick Heiser and Christian Ludwig describe the religious social of eventization (Heiser/Ludwig 2014:10). This collective experience is exemplified, for instance, in group photographs taken in front of the temple. Following the temple wedding, the group congregates on the temple steps for immediate photographs. This moment holds particular significance as photography and videography are prohibited within the temple.

The chapter's questions are considered on the basis of three interviews that form part of a comprehensive interdisciplinary research project. This study employs a multi-methodological approach encompassing 27 narrative-biographical interviews involving both religious and non-religious couples

---

4   Translation from German by the author.
5   A detailed account of the religious social form of communitization can be found in the introduction of this volume.

across Italy, Germany, and Switzerland. These video-recorded conversations are shaped by the methodological principles of visual anthropology (Pink 2021: 81–170). They involve couples viewing and commenting on their wedding photos to reconstruct the events of their wedding day. The current chapter centers on three video interviews featuring couples affiliated with The Church of Jesus Christ of Latter-day Saints from Germany, Italy, and Switzerland. It serves as a case study within a broader research sample, where the contextual information becomes pertinent for analyzing the three interviews (Baur/Lamnek 2017; Hering/Schmid 2014).

The contribution is structured in four parts. In this introduction, I have considered the boundary concept and how it is connected to the question of social forms of religion in the Church of Jesus Christ of Latter-day Saints (1.). The main part discusses the role of Latter-day Saint temples not only in the wedding ceremony but also as spaces of collective experiences and processes of identity building (2.). Additionally, three conversations with Latter-day Saint couples show how the wedding contributes to the social forms of religion of the marital dyad, communitization, and eventization (3.). Finally, the conclusion (4.) summarises the boundary-making processes taking place during Latter-day Saint weddings and matches them with corresponding social forms of religion.

2. Latter-day Saint wedding in the temple

2.1 The boundary of the temple area

As previously mentioned, the temple is an exclusive space reserved solely for Latter-day Saints who are baptized, have reached the age of eight, and have acquired a temple recommendation issued by the temple authority (Mäder 2023, 201). This recommendation is followed by an interview with either a bishop or a representative of the church. Within the Mormon worldview, the temple is historically linked to the Tabernacle of the Israelites (Ex 25–31) in the desert and King Solomon's temple in Jerusalem.[6]

---

[6] There are 179 dedicated temples worldwide. 51 temples are under construction, 98 temples are announced, and six temples are currently being renovated. Cf. https://churchofjesuschristtemples.org/temples/.

Fig. 1: The Google Earth screenshot of the San Diego temple shows the symmetrically arranged area. The two striking towers are recognizable as shadows.

(https://www.google.com/maps/place/San+Diego+California+Temple/@32.8662322,-117.2291438,484m/data=!3m1!1e3!4m6!3m5!1s0x80dc06d32da29aff:0x3681ef10f8a92fa4!8m2!3d32.8665341!4d-117.228771!16zL20vMGQybDNi?entry=ttu)

The exclusivity of the temple is also reflected in its architecture and the surrounding grounds, which are deliberately set apart from the adjacent areas. Often, the temple area is arranged within a block, enclosed by streets and hedges. The layout of the buildings and pathways emphasizes a preference for distinctive symmetrical and square architecture, exemplified by the aerial view of the San Diego temple (cf. fig. 1). The spatial configuration of these temple complexes becomes a distinguishing characteristic (see fig. 2) (Mäder 2023: 202–208).

Fig. 2: San Diego Latter-day Saints temple.

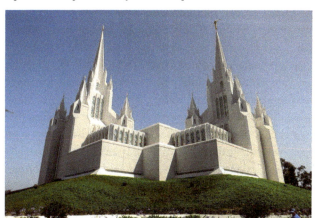

(Photo M.-T. Mäder, November 2015)

The temples' predominantly white, square-shaped exteriors establish a visual connection between the individual temple buildings and represent The Church of Jesus Christ of Latter-day Saints as a global institution. The distinctive temple architecture collectively embodies the church, in alignment with Wimmer's concept, and exudes an air of exclusivity. This architectural expression is further underscored by the surrounding garden areas, which contribute to a somewhat segregating aesthetic. When members visit the temple, they enter into an exclusive realm to which they maintain an emotional and personal relationship that is based on shared norms and values. Temple visits not only reinforce the relationships among the members but also provide a collective identity. These experiences are attributed to the religious social form of communitization. Only the visitor center serves as an inclusive space, although its pristine appearance often creates an atmosphere that seems somewhat isolated from the external world.

2.2 Communitization, societalization, and the eternal dyad in the "sealing" ceremony

In addition to the wedding for eternity, other significant rituals occur within the temple. They allow further experiences that support processes of communitization as well as societalization. The latter comes into play because the church strictly regulates these rituals, and assigned temple workers observe the procedures to be carried out correctly. These include sealings of families for eternity, particularly for those families who joined the community at a later stage. Parents and their children are eternally linked in a manner similar to the wedding ceremony. Furthermore, baptisms and confirmations for the dead are conducted within the temple, taking place in the baptismal font typically situated in the temple's basement. The baptismal font is upheld by twelve oxen, symbolizing the twelve tribes of Israel. This (presumably) imitates the architectural design of the bronze basin in the courtyard of the Temple of Solomon.[7] Members conduct rituals to baptize and confirm deceased individuals, inducting them as posthumous members of the church.

The temple itself serves as a representation of the cosmology of The Church of Jesus Christ of Latter-day Saints, featuring the so-called "telestial", "terrestrial", and "celestial" rooms.[8] These rooms symbolize the stages of existence: the telestial represents the world of creation, the terrestrial signifies Earth with the Garden of Eden, and the celestial denotes eternity. During a visit to the temple, Latter-day Saints move through these rooms consecutively. In the telestial and terrestrial rooms, visitors engage with spoken or recorded texts, with the telestial room even presenting a film depicting creation. In the celestial room, members are invited to experience the presence of God without any further instructions.

In the Rome temple, these three rooms are arranged horizontally from left to right on the middle level, with the telestial room on the left, the terrestrial in the middle, and the celestial room on the right, following the order of their cosmological significance (fig. 3).

---

[7] Cf. https://www.esv.org/resources/esv-global-study-bible/illustration-11-solomons-temple.

[8] The graphic depicting the telestial kingdom appears more akin to an infernal realm, contradicting the Latter-day Saints' belief in the absence of a traditional hell.

Fig. 3: Model of the Latter-day Saint temple in Rome.

(photo M.-T. Mäder, February 2023)

At the center of the upper level lies the sealing room, the site for weddings and family sealings. This room is distinctive due to the altar positioned in the center where the couple kneels during the ceremony. Adjacent to the wall parallel to the altar, mirrors are suspended, reflecting each other endlessly. This perpetual reflection serves as a symbol of eternity.

Members informed me in various conversations that temples are replete with symbols consistent across all temple locations worldwide. Latter-day Saints are welcome to visit any temple and will encounter a similar internal building structure and comparable interior design. Additionally, the similarity between the temples allows members to share an emotional and sensational experience that, in turn, fosters global communitization. As access to temples is restricted, non-Mormons (unable to attend a Latter-day Saint temple wedding) are guided to wait in a room adjacent to the temple reception, where on a large screen the wedding ceremony is explained by a member of the governing body of the church (Quorum of the Twelve).

It is notable that all three couples with whom I spoke about their temple wedding vividly recalled the profound significance of the endless mirroring effect during the ceremony. The social form of the dyad represents the cell of religious communitization and at the same time becomes collective on the level of experience and memory of the wedding.[9]

2.3 The temple wedding as reinforcing collective identity

The temple marriage is an integral aspect of processes of communitization within The Church of Jesus Christ of Latter-day Saints. It is exclusive not only spatially but also emotionally, as – in their self-imagination – only Mormons can comprehend the significance of being sealed for eternity. Getting married in the temple holds distinctive importance in aiming for the highest position in the celestial kingdom, as illustrated in a graphic from 1950 (see fig. 4) where the couple will live together in eternity by attaining godhood and proceeding with their procreation forever and ever (Hammarberg 2013: 267). Only these couples will be given access to the highest of the three heavens Latter-day Saints believe in.

The telestial kingdom stands as the lowest, reserved for those who have completely disregarded the moral guidelines outlined by the Mormon faith. The terrestrial kingdom is the second heaven, designated for "The good & honorable but blinded by the craftiness of men," as described in the image. Ultimately, marriage is essential for the third heaven, "the highest of which is exaltation" (Daynes 2015: 334) as highlighted by the celebratory banner displayed in front of the Salt Lake City temple in the image, but there are other paths into it as well. While several other responsibilities are essential, such as baptism, repentance, adhering to moral standards, paying tithes, and fulfilling duties, marriage holds a preeminent role in attaining the kingdom of heaven and ultimately achieving godhood as a reward. This positive appreciation of the temple wedding draws another boundary inside the Latter-day Saint community. It highlights the dyad between the couple as the smallest religious social form which is the most recognized in the afterlife.

Conversations with three Latter-day Saint couples delve deeper into social forms of religion through the sealing experience and wedding festivities. Highlighting their significance within the context of the dyad, communitization, and eventization.

---

9   Interviews with N.N., couples, September 16, 2022 near Frankfurt/M./GE (https://doi.org/10.5281/zenodo.8181413), February 1, 2023 near Zurich/CH (https://doi.org/10.5281/zenodo.8248443), and February 10, 2023 in Rome/IT (https://doi.org/10.5281/zenodo.8248549).

Fig. 4: Depiction of the Latter-day Saint worldview.

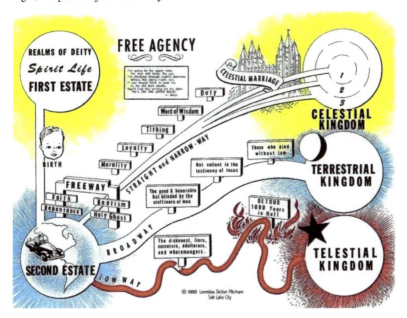

(Leonidas DeVon Mechan, Salt Lake City/US, 1950)

3. Three conversations with Latter-day Saint couples

The conversations with three Latter-day Saint couples about their wedding reveal not only the significance of the temple wedding but also express similar values connected to this experience. The couples stressed not only the social form of the dyad during the temple wedding but also reported on the personal inclusion of their guests during the sealing rite. The Latter-day Saint wedding enhances not only communitization but also provides eventization during the festivities. The conversations are recorded, and the video protocols are transcribed verbatim (Halcomb/Davidson 2006: 40) and evaluated by combining grounded theory and sociological hermeneutics of knowledge (Kurt/Herbrik 2014; Boehm 1994; Strübing 2014). The analysis focuses on the way the couples construct their wedding narrative in the temple and how they report different social forms. The video interviews are part of a larger research project with the main question of how contemporary media representations like photos and videos of religious and secular weddings in Europe communicate norms and values. In the current paper, this question is discussed in the context of social forms of religion, where the sharing of common norms and values stabilizes religious communication and plays an important role in communitization processes (Heiser/Ludwig 2014: 9). The interdisciplinary study applies a multi-methodological approach that includes, among others, the analysis of wedding shows and 27 narrative-biographical interviews (Hopf 2016) with couples from Italy, Germany, and Switzerland who married between 1968 and 2022. Within the research project's framework, the discussions with Latter-day Saint couples hold significance because these couples lack any photographs of their temple wedding.

Remembering the ceremony without visual references forges a unique connection among couples while creating a distance from others who do have photographs of the event. Despite this, their memories of the ceremony remain distinct and vivid. The subsequent analysis of these three conversations delves into how the boundary-making processes of inclusion and exclusion manifest within the memories of the temple wedding.

The three couples were married at different times: The Italian couple wed in the Bern temple in Switzerland in 1977, just two days after their civil marriage at the civil registry in Campidoglio, Rome. The wife was 25 years old, and the husband was 26. Both had converted to Mormonism at a young age after being raised Catholic. They are parents to two children and are now grandparents. The German couple married in the Frankfurt temple in 1989, holding both their temple and civil ceremonies on the same day. The wife was 20 years old, and the husband was 23 at the time of their marriage. Both were born into the church and are parents to four adult children. The Swiss couple exchanged vows in the Bern temple in 2022, following their civil wedding the day before. The wife was 24 years old, and the husband was 25. Both were born into The Church of Jesus Christ of Latter-day Saints.

3.1 The Italian couple (temple wedding in 1977)[10]

The couple – it was mainly the wife who was speaking while the husband reassured her, repeatedly distanced themselves from the civil wedding during the

---

10 The conversation took place on 10 February 2023 at The Church of Jesus Christ of Latter-day Saints visitor center in Rome/IT.

conversation. Both agreed that the civil wedding did not mean anything. It was nothing more than a tedious event, as the wife mentions:

> Nothing. Just a deadly effort. The real marriage for us would have been in the temple. We only did the civil marriage because, from a legal point of view, our marriage was valid. Otherwise, there would have been no need. It was nice because it was exciting because we shared all this with our relatives, our friends, and our parents. But while they were congratulating us, we were thinking that the best is yet to come. We are here wishing each other well, but we are married, yes, we are married by law, but our hearts are yet to be married. The chain of love, of which I spoke before, has not yet been bound. And so, the real wedding, for us, was the one up in the temple. The wedding day here in Rome was a terrible effort.[11]

The couple explicitly expressed that their civil ceremony did not feel like the "real wedding", a sentiment they reiterated multiple times during the conversation. They conveyed that they arranged it primarily for their parents and relatives. Moreover, the post-wedding lunch created an uncomfortable situation as they were expected to toast with the guests, which they refrained from doing, given the Latter-day Saint prohibition of alcohol. This act of abstaining from the toast symbolized their divergence from the group or non-members of The Church of Jesus Christ of Latter-day Saints and highlighted their sense of not fully belonging to their wedding guests. This deliberate choice served as a means to reinforce their dyad, i.e. their identity as a couple while simultaneously creating a noticeable boundary to the attendees.

Primarily, the wife portrays the civil wedding and subsequent reception as hectic and draining. In stark contrast, the temple wedding the following day is depicted as a quiet and calm occasion. However, the wife emphasizes that the spiritual experience during the temple wedding was indeed exhaustive:

> And we just went up [to Switzerland]. Nothing happened there, though, in the sense that the wedding in Zollikofen, like all weddings that take place in the temple, are extremely meaningful. In this specific case, both he and I had never done the path, so on the same day we did the spiritual path, which we talked about earlier, and immediately afterwards we went upstairs and had the wedding. So, it was a really full day for us. Also

---

11   Video conversation with NN, spouse, Rome/IT February, 10, 2023.Transcript translated from the Italian by the author.

because, besides the excitement of getting married, there was the coming to know and making covenants and commitments, which were really impactful from a spiritual point of view. And so we were exhausted.[12]

In the wife's representation, the two weddings compete against each other with regard to representation and meaning. The civil marriage proved socially exhausting due to the presence of numerous guests, family, and friends who wanted to celebrate something the couple was not entirely invested in. The great significance of the temple wedding proved to be draining also because it was additionally combined with a customary temple visit that they had not experienced before. This visit had a profound impact on them, as described by the wife: "[...] there was the coming to know and making covenants and commitments, which were really impactful from a spiritual point of view".[13] In 1977, the sealing ceremony was also logistically demanding, because there was no temple in Italy at the time. The Latter-day Saints from Italy and many other countries in mainland Europe had to travel to Switzerland to conduct the diverse temple ceremonies and make covenants with God.

The couple's firm boundary with non-Latter-day Saints, even many years after their wedding, is likely due to their conversion to the church, which sets them apart from the rest of their family and most of their friends who didn't share their worldview. On the one hand, the dyadic relationship between the couple is strengthened through this experience. On the other, they experience a strong feeling of belonging to the Latter-day Saint community even many years after the wedding. The temple wedding becomes part of their identity that they share with the other members and therefore contributes to communitization.

3.2 The German couple (temple wedding in 1989)[14]

The German couple acknowledges that the civil wedding serves as the legal prerequisite for the temple wedding, but they also do not find it particularly meaningful. They arranged the civil ceremony simultaneously with the temple wedding and the evening reception. Managing these three significant events in one

---

12 Video conversation with NN, spouse, Rome/IT, February, 10, 2023. Transcript translated from the Italian by the author.
13 Video conversation with NN, spouse, Rome/IT, February, 10, 2023. Transcript translated from the Italian by the author.
14 The conversation took place 16 September 2022 in a private home near Frankfurt/M./GE

day was stressful, as they recall, and they express a desire to do it differently if given the chance. It is not surprising that the temple ceremony held the focal point amidst this packed day. The husband even remarks that this moment is the only one he vividly recalls from the wedding:

> So, the sealing is the only thing I can still remember. [...] It was just – because it's just the ambiance, it's so beautiful. You're there in the temple. You kneel in front of an altar and there are just so many of them, there are opposing mirrors. That means you can see the others into infinity. And that's what a circle does. It's simple. It's just incredibly beautiful.[15]

It is notable that the husband becomes emotional while recalling the ceremony. Another instance of emotional depth in their conversation occurs when they discuss the certainty they had in choosing each other during their dating phase. The husband emphasizes that this decision holds a different significance within their church because it involves choosing for eternity, which, in itself, can be quite intimidating. However, surpassing this fear is rewarding and ultimately brings a sense of happiness. The husband's memories of the sealing ceremony point out again how the Latter-day Saint eternal marital dyad distinguishes itself from other weddings.

Within this conversation, the temple ceremony is revealed not only as a shared collective representation among all Latter-day Saints but also as a collective experience. Both aspects foster connections among its members while creating a sense of distance from non-Latter-day Saints and contribute to communitization. The husband classifies those who do not belong to the church when comparing the temple with the civil ceremony:

> It's just more personal than the registrar reading out his text. We thought it was unspeakable, but that's just the way it is. It is what it is. It was an official who just did his job and that was it. It wasn't very personal.[16]

Similar to the Roman couple the ceremony by the registrar is less valued by the German couple. The husband laughs when he describes the anonymous and almost mechanical civil procedure. It seems that he does not take it seriously

---

15 Video conversation with NN, husband, near Frankfurt/M./GE, September, 16, 2022. Transcript translated from the German by the author.
16 Video conversation with NN, husband, near Frankfurt/M./GE, September, 16, 2022. Transcript translated from the German by the author.

and judges the work of the official as someone who "just did his job" while the sealer in the temple who is an official chosen by the church authorities gives the ceremony meaning. In contrast, the couple positively remembers details of the sealing ceremony like when "the sun's rays shine in through the stained-glass windows",[17] as the wife describes the moment. It is also noticeable that they agree on this very detailed memory which strengthens their marital dyad. The husband says that after this moment the wedding could have been over. The reception was obligatory, but obviously not relevant to them.

It is noteworthy that although non-Latter-day Saints are usually invited to the reception, it is nonetheless exactly this part of the wedding which is less valued by the couple. It shows that the community is prioritized over the "others", the non-Latter-day Saint members, against which a boundary is drawn. Here not only communitization but also eventization take place by the inclusion of non-members. This also coincides with the experience of the German couple. The wedding reception took place in the church's community center. Many church members helped with organizing the reception, preparing food and decoration, taking photos, and tidying up again at the end. The Swiss couple, the youngest of the three, could also count on the help of the members. This also turns the wedding as an event into a shared experience during which the Latter-day Saints additionally connect.

3.3 The Swiss couple (temple wedding in 2022)[18]

In the case of the Swiss couple the shared experience of the wedding, with other members of the church, was highlighted even more during the conversation. The whole wedding was supported by church members at different moments and revealed the social forms of religious eventization and communitization. The hairdresser who also did the make-up was from the church, the wedding cake was created by the bride's father who is a professional confectioner. Church members decorated the wedding location of the reception and helped clean up afterward. The photographer was a Latter-day Saint. Additionally, the couple celebrated an extra blessing ceremony at the garden house of a member, a former bishop of the church. The husband describes their relationship as being father-son-like.

---

17   Video conversation with NN, spouse, near Frankfurt/M./GE, September, 16, 2022. Transcript translated from Swiss German by the author.
18   The conversation took place in the couple's apartment near Zurich/CH.

The wedding consisted of four different ceremonies or receptions and took place in central Switzerland in 2022. The first wedding was the civil at the registry with 50 guests. The second was the already mentioned blessing ceremony with a reception afterward in the garden of a member with 80 guests. In the evening the newlyweds celebrated with 100 guests, friends, and family members. The following day the couple was sealed in the Bern temple in Zollikofen accompanied by 25 close family members. Some of the guests, only members of the church, participated in all four weddings. The couple sent different invitations to individually assign the guests to one or more of the four celebrations. The management of the different invitations was according to the couple quite complex. Among other things, it was a way to draw boundaries between members and non-members that in turn contributes to communitization.

During the conversation, the couple shared their intricately crafted wedding album encapsulating the entire day, along with a video documenting the evening reception. They explained that the absence of photos from the temple wedding did not bother them, as it felt that they compensated for the lack of temple images with those from the blessing ceremony. Furthermore, numerous photos were taken in front of the temple, featuring the couple, family members, and friends in group shots. The wife expressed a sentiment of regret at not being able to record the words spoken by the sealer, with a slight disagreement between the couple on this matter. She believes the wording was individually tailored for them. However, the husband holds a different perspective, disagreeing with her. To his understanding, the sealer's words during the wedding are consistently the same in every temple wedding. It was noticeable that both of them made a swift attempt to resolve this disagreement during the conversation, almost as if it were inappropriate to hold differing views on the matter. Their marital dyad does not allow different memories in this issue.

When reflecting on the most significant moment of their wedding, the emotional and personal experience of the temple ceremony once again stood out as pivotal:

Husband: I had several moments like that. One of them was when I saw her for the first time. Now it's getting real. But the other one was also on Saturday itself then, inside in the temple. And in that room, it has like two mirrors, opposite each other, representing eternity. From this place, where you are, you can look into the mirror non-stop. When I was there with [my wife], I already-.

Wife: At the end when we were still two?

Husband: Yes, yes, exactly.

Wife: Everyone left the room at the end. It was really just the two of us sitting there.

mtm[19]: Is that part of the ceremony?

Husband: That you're alone? No, we just wanted it that way.

mtm: To have a moment alone.

Husband: Yes.

mtm: And did you talk to each other or just soak up the moment-?

Husband: More soak up the moment. Maybe one word.

Wife: No, not spoken much, just absorbed.

Husband: For me, I once worked in the temple for three weeks. That was before the mission. That was 2018. And I often went into that room where the sealings take place, and I used to imagine what that might be like when I was in there. That always gave me a calmness. Just such a nice feeling. You can't compare that with what happened during the day. Because it was even better then. When I think of it like that, I always looked forward to that moment. When I can be in there with my wife, and I can seal myself to her for eternity.[20]

Again, the opposing mirrors in the sealing room are mentioned as an experience of eternity by the husband. Additionally, the religious social form of the intimate dyad shared exclusively by the couple resonates with the experiences of the other couples during the temple ceremony. In this instance, the couple deliberately carved out time for themselves immediately after the ceremony. Despite having four celebrations in total, the temple ceremony stands as the

---

19 Interviewer and author of present chapter.
20 Video conversation with NN, husband, near Zurich/CH, February, 1, 2023. Transcript translated from Swiss German by the author.

pivotal event for both, holding significance beyond the other festivities. The sealing for eternity serves as a profoundly unique and deeply personal emotional experience for the couple. Simultaneously, it acts as a source of self-assurance and connection for the community, creating a distinction between them and others. These characteristics solidify as a robust boundary, delineating a clear divide between the Swiss couple and non-Latter-day Saints. The delineation aligns with the concept of boundaries in this scenario and confirms itself as the social-religious form of communitization. The couple's memory of their temple wedding represents an exclusive and highly symbolic practice that can be categorized as a collective experience that is shared with other members of the church.

4. Conclusion: Boundaries and social forms of religion in temple weddings

In the Latter-day Saints worldview, temple weddings serve as a means of establishing boundaries in the social form of an exclusive religious community, enabling members to distinguish themselves from others. These boundaries manifest in various aspects, including the architecture of the Latter-day Saints temple, its surroundings, and the couples' recollections of their weddings. The dynamics of connection and separation unfold at distinct junctures within the wedding, delineated into the civil ceremony and the temple wedding. This demarcation provides "scripts of action that aid in the identification of 'us' versus 'them' (Wimmer 2008: 113), contributing to a nuanced process of inclusion and exclusion that in turn results in social forms of religion of the bridal couple's dyad, communitization, and eventization. The concluding remarks will concentrate on three pivotal moments identified in the analysis. They answer the underlying question of how boundary-making processes and social forms of religion are expressed in Latter-day Saint weddings.

The initial moment pertains to the perception of the temple building and the collective emotions experienced by its members. The temple holds a central significance as weddings are exclusively conducted in the sealing room within its premises. The temple visit is perceived as a privilege, distinguishing Latter-day Saints from others. Members share a profound connection to this sacred space, fostering a sense of unity among them. The communal emotional attachment to the temple amplifies its impact as a collective representation and identity, which again refers to communitization reinforcing the social classification of 'them' and 'us'. This boundary contradicts their self-perception as Christians and their desire for a Christian affiliation that should include the whole of Christianity and not just The Church of Jesus Christ of Latter-day Saints. The exclusivity of the temples frequently faces criticism. A common response to this critique is the assertion that the temples are "sacred, not secret".[21]

The significance of the temple ceremony for couples is the second moment in which the social forms of the dyad on one hand and communitization on the other play a role. They are expressed in collective representations, social classifications as 'us' and 'them', and the interaction with the community. All three couples treasured their experiences in the sealing room, each in a unique way. The shared 'mirror experience' emerged as a common thread, serving as a defining aspect of the temple wedding. Emotional moments were described by all three couples, with the Italian couple expressing feeling "exhausted" due to the intense spiritual experience. Furthermore, it was the first time the Italian couple had entered the temple, experiencing the endowment ceremony for the first time. This dual encounter likely heightened the emotional intensity. Similarly, the German couple vividly recalled their temple wedding. For instance, they intricately described the sunlight streaming through the stained-glass windows of the sealing room. Both emphasized the profound shared emotional moment, noting that everything thereafter felt more like a duty toward their guests. The Swiss couple deliberately approached the temple ceremony, carving out a moment to savor the atmosphere in the sealing room. They scarcely spoke, opting to "soak up the moment", as they recollect.

Despite these three independent experiences, commonalities emerge. All three couples articulate a perception of something extraordinary during the temple ceremony, rooted in the spatial and sensory elements. This exceptional experience thus becomes an exclusive boundary between the couple and attendees of the sealing ceremony. The couple is drawing an inner boundary – now transformed into an eternal dyad by the sealing/mirroring – separated from everyone else, even other Latter-day Saints present in that room. The third moment of communitization pertains to the wedding reception held outside the temple during which the religious social form of eventization comes into play as well. Once again, the receptions varied, yet shared certain similarities as a collective endeavor. The Italian couple, compelled to celebrate for their parents,

---

21 Cf. https://www.churchofjesuschrist.org/study/eng/new-era/2006/01/how-to-talk-about-the-temple.

repeatedly underscored that the civil wedding and the ensuing reception were bothersome and held no personal significance for them. They felt estranged from the entire event and explicitly distanced themselves. Similarly, the German couple conveyed that the temple wedding was the highlight of the entire day, echoing the sentiment of the Swiss couple. Unlike the Italian couple, both the German and Swiss couples celebrated with numerous church members, creating a more comfortable atmosphere compared to the Italian couple. Additionally, the German and Swiss couples celebrated in the church meeting house with assistance from fellow members. According to the couples, the members expect and are accustomed to supporting couples in preparing and celebrating their weddings, as humorously noted by the Swiss couple. In this way, not only the temple ceremony but also the reception become a practice of inclusion and boundary-setting for the community in a collective endeavor. Therefore, the wedding reception includes both social forms, namely communitization and eventization.

To summarise, it can be stated that the multiple boundary-making processes within the context of temples and Latter-day Saint weddings unveil social forms of religion at different moments. First, the overarching boundary between outsiders and insiders (us/them) is revealed in relation to the space of the temple building which excludes outsiders. It creates a profound sense of belonging in the temple sealing ceremony and plays a constituting part in the Latter-day Saints' communitization process. From an emic perspective, it makes all the other elements, such as the civil ceremony or various receptions, pale into insignificance for the couples. Second, the ceremony also creates inner boundaries within this "sacred space" within the sealing room, formed around the couple's dyad as the smallest social form, mirrored in eternity. The couples see themselves as a unity for all eternity, distinct even from other LDS members within the sealing room. The third boundary is the common space of the wedding reception – in which LDS members and non-members share the space. In this setting, Latter-day Saints, notably the married couple, seek to express their religious identity (e.g. by not drinking alcohol) in a worldly space by applying the religious social form of eventization. The clearest example of these multiple boundary rings is indicated by the various invitations sent to different ceremonies and receptions, to members and non-members, distinguishing between the four ceremonies of the Swiss couple.[22] It shows that communitization may also include non-members for a certain time frame who participate in the event. At the same time, these guests are aware that they are only partly included, which in turn lets both sides experience the boundary during the celebration of the wedding.

Clear and robust boundaries, even multiple boundaries, impact not only insiders but also outsiders of a community. LDS weddings allow intense collective experiences that serve the social forms of religious communitization, the eternal dyad of the couple, and in some moments the eventization of religion. The boundaries established in a Latter-day Saint wedding may therefore also evoke an equal sense of exclusion for those not permitted to enter the inner boundary rings of the temple space.

Disclaimer

This project has received funding from the European Union's Horizon 2020 research and innovation programme under the Marie Sklodowska-Curie grant agreement No 101024115. The present document reflects only the author's view and the European Commission Research Executive Agency (REA) is not responsible for any use that may be made of the information it contains.

---

22   The model draws on the religious space of the Jerusalem Temple with its gradations of "holiness" increasing the closer to the center one gets of the Holy of Holies. I thank my colleague Sean Ryan for this fruitful input.

Bibliography

Baur, Nina/Blasius, Jörg (eds.) (2014): Handbuch Methoden der empirischen Sozialforschung, Wiesbaden: Springer.

Baur, Nina/Lamnek, Siegfried (2017): "Einzelfallanalyse." In: Lothar Mikos/Claudia Wegener (eds.), Qualitative Medienforschung: Ein Handbuch, 2nd ed., Stuttgart: utb, pp. 290–300.

Boehm, Andreas (1994): "Grounded Theory – wie aus Texten Modelle und Theorien gemacht werden." In: Andreas Boehm/Andreas Mengel/Thomas Muhr (eds.), Texte verstehen: Konzepte, Methoden, Werkzeuge, Konstanz: UVK, pp. 121–140.

Daynes, Kathryn M. (2015): "Celestial Marriage (Eternal and Plural)." In: Terryl L. Givens, Philip L. Barlow (eds.), The Oxford Handbook of Mormonism, New York, NY: Oxford University Press, pp. 334–349.

Fritz, Natalie/Höpflinger, Anna-Katharina/Knauß, Stefanie/Mäder, Marie-Therese/Pezzoli-Olgiati, Daria (2018): Sichtbare Religion: Eine Einführung in die Religionswissenschaft Berlin: De Gruyter.

Halcomb, Elizabeth J./Davidson, Patricia M. (2006): "Is Verbatim Transcription of Interview Data Always Necessary?" Applied Nursing Research 19/1, pp. 38–42.

Hammarberg, Melvyn (2013): The Mormon Quest for Glory: The Religious World of the Latter-Day Saints, New York: Oxford University Press.

Heiser, Patrick/Ludwig, Christian (2014): "Einleitung". In: Patrick Heiser/Christian Ludwig (eds.), Sozialformen der Religionen im Wandel, Wiesbaden: Springer, pp. 1–14.

Hering, Linda/Schmid, Robert J. (2014): "Einzelfallanalyse." In: Nina Baur/Jörg Blasius (eds.), Handbuch Methoden der empirischen Sozialforschung, Wiesbaden: Springer, 529–542.

Hopf, Christel (2016): "Qualitative Interviews – ein Überblick." In: Uwe Flick/Ernst von Kardorff/Ines Steinke (eds.), Qualitative Sozialforschung: Eine Einführung, Reinbek bei Hamburg: Rowohlt, pp. 349–360.

Krech, Volkhard/Schlamelcher, Jens/Hero, Markus (2013): "Typen religiöser Sozialformen und ihre Bedeutung für die Analyse religiösen Wandels in Deutschland." KZfSS Kölner Zeitschrift für Soziologie und Sozialpsychologie 65/1, pp. 51–71.

Kurt, Ronald/Herbrik, Regine (2014): "Sozialwissenschaftliche Hermeneutik und hermeneutische Wissenssoziologie." In: Nina Baur/Jörg Blasius (eds.), Handbuch Methoden der empirischen Sozialforschung, Wiesbaden: Springer, pp. 473–491.

Mäder, Marie-Therese (2020): Mormon Lifestyles. Religion and Ethics in Documentary Media, Baden-Baden: Nomos.

Mäder, Marie-Therese (2023): "An American Religion in Europe. How Latter-day Saints' Temples Communicate a Worldview of Sublimity and Separation." In: Daria Pezzoli-Olgiati, Stefanie Knauss (eds.), Religion in Representations of Europe. Shared and Contested Practices, Baden-Baden: Nomos, pp. 195–218.

Pink, Sarah (2021): Doing Visual Ethnography, 4th ed., London: SAGE Publications.

Popitz, Heinrich (1992): Phänomene der Macht, 2nd ed., Tübingen: Mohr Siebeck.

Strübing, Jörg (2014): "Grounded Theory und Theoretical Sampling." In: Nina Baur/Jörg Blasius (eds.), Handbuch Methoden der empirischen Sozialforschung, Wiesbaden: Springer, pp. 457–472.

Van Gennep, Arnold (2019): The Rites of Passage, 2nd ed. Chicago, IL: The University of Chicago Press.

Wimmer, Andreas (2008): "The Making and Unmaking of Ethnic Boundaries: A Multilevel Process Theory." In: American Journal of Sociology 113/4, pp. 970–1022.

Primary Sources

Video conversation, February 10, 2023, Rome/IT, https://doi.org/10.5281/zenodo.8248549.

Video conversation, February 1, 2023, near Zurich/CH, https://doi.org/10.5281/zenodo.8248443.

Video conversation, April 2022, near Frankfurt, M./GE, https://doi.org/10.5281/zenodo.8181413.

Web References

Crossway. "Solomon's Temple." ESV. Accessed November 24, 2023. https://www.esv.org/resources/esv-global-study-bible/illustration-11-solomons-temple.

Shanna Butler. "How to Talk about the Temple." The Church of Jesus Christ of Latter-day Saints. Church Magazines. January 2006. Accessed November 16, 2023. https://www.churchofjesuschrist.org/study/eng/new-era/2006/01/how-to-talk-about-the-temple.

Temples of the Church of Jesus Christ of Latter-day Saints. "Temples." Accessed January 3, 2024. https://churchofjesuschristtemples.org/temples/.

The Church of Jesus Christ of Latter-day Saints. "Style Guide: The Name of the Church." Newsroom. Accessed April 9, 2010. http://newsroom.churchofjesuschrist.org/style-guide.

The Church of Jesus Christ of Latter-day Saints. "Temple List." Accessed July 22, 2021. https://www.churchofjesuschrist.org/temples/list?lang=eng.

Organizing "Private Religion"
Types of Governance in US Protestantism

Insa Pruisken

Abstract *According to Luckmann, the new social form of religion in modern societies is the private form, which is characterized by the rise of a consumer mentality. However, religious consumers can only emerge when religious organizations provide the options for consumer choices. Consumer religion is associated with a particular pattern of church organization, which is best represented by the megachurch model and is similar to processes in the field of higher education. To identify this pattern, I introduce the "governance equalizer", an instrument that was developed for the field of higher education. The analysis of governance patterns proceeds in three steps. First, I discuss three types of elementary mechanisms of governance forms: mutual observation, influence, and negotiation. Second, I differentiate types of actors in US Protestantism: individual believers, communities, congregations, denominations, and special purpose groups. Third, building on constellations of mutual negotiation, I distinguish six types of governance forms in US Protestantism: (1) denominational regulation, (2) democratic self-governance, (3) hierarchical self-governance, (4) stakeholder guidance, (5) competition, and (6) network governance. Finally, I discuss the role of organizations in the formation of private religion.*

Keywords *governance, legitimation, megachurch model, privatized religion, social form of religion, United States*

1. Introduction

How does religion show itself in modern societies? This was the leading question for Thomas Luckmann, who considered a social form of religion broadly as a "social arrangement between collective religious representations and the social structure" (Luckmann 2003: 279). Following Émile Durkheim, Luckmann studies religious change from a functionalist perspective and states that religion is "not a passing phase in the evolution of mankind but a universal aspect of the conditio humana" (ibid.: 276). The social form of religion describes how the religious core of a worldview is related to the social and normative order of society.[1] Therefore, Luckmann's concept of the social form of religion not only refers to organizational types, such as markets, networks, and events but also considers the relationship between institutional forms and religious ideas (see the introduction to this volume). How are religious ideas and worldviews institutionalized in modern societies?

With the spread of secularization and the progressing functional differentiation of spheres – politics, economy, science, education, art, etc. – the social form of "privatized religion" emerged, which resulted from the "demonopolization" of the production and distribution of worldviews and the despecialization of religion. In this social form, the sacred cosmos depends on the private sphere and on secondary institutions[2] Knoblauch (2010) later described as "popular religion". This means that religious socialization is not necessarily a part of primary socialization, in which individuals encounter an objective social structure that is mediated by significant others (such as parents, siblings, and teachers). No general obligatory model exists anymore that relates religious values to the social and normative order of society. Instead, a plurality of worldviews and institutional forms develop that (in principle) become available to everyone. Multiple "sacred cosmoses" represent religious and nonreligious worldviews and compete with each other. Luckmann (2003) and Berger (1963) use the concept of the "market" as a metaphor to describe this new form of

---

[1] Luckmann does that by distinguishing analytically between personality, structure, and culture. Personality refers to the individual's unique pattern of thoughts, feelings, and behaviors and serves as the mediating mechanism between the individual and society. Social structure describes the organized patterns of social relationships and institutions that make up society including norms and values, roles, institutions, and patterns of social interaction. Culture provides a framework for understanding the world, shaping individual behavior, and maintaining social order (Parsons/Platt 1973).

[2] This term refers to Berger and Luckmann's distinction between "primary" and "secondary" socialization. "Secondary socialization is the internalization of institutional or institution-based 'subworlds'. (...) [It] requires the acquisition of role-specific vocabularies, which means, for one thing, the internalization of semantic fields structuring routine interpretations and conduct within an institutional area" (Berger/Luckmann 1967: 138).

religion; others talk of "event-structured", "hyper-mediatized", and "spiritual" forms of religion (Gauthier 2014).

With the rise of the private form of religion, religious communities are increasingly operating in competitive environments.[3] Unlike the fields of art, science, health, and sports, religions receive less or no financial support from the government to carry out their activities. Although many European nation-states still maintain a cooperative relationship with religion and churches enjoy special privileges, these special rights are often more historical remnants. In particular, in the United States, religious organizations must grow on their own merit. Therefore, in the discourse on the "governance of religion", the dominant question is not how to enhance the effectiveness of religion (as in the case of education and science) but rather how to manage religious diversity and restrain or contain the power of religious communities (Schuppert 2012; 2017). The state's role in this context is primarily to institutionally safeguard pluralism and nonviolence (Kern/Pruisken 2018).

In the competitive environment of private religion, religious organizations need to draw in members with their offerings. The social form of private religion necessarily builds not only on religious consumers but also on religious providers. Consequently, culturally pluralized religion also faces a pluralization of religious organizational forms. Although the rational-choice approach to religion has repeatedly emphasized the market-like nature of religion, it has neglected the pluralization of religious organizational forms. This is accompanied by the fact that established organizational sociology has only been sporadically integrated into the sociology of religion (and vice versa) (Petzke/Tyrell 2012; Tracey/Phillips/Lounsbury 2014). The development of types of social forms in religion has not been incorporated into current debates in organizational sociology.

However, despite differences from other societal fields, there is no reason to assume that established instruments of governance and organizational research should not be applicable to religious organizations as well. Religious actors in modern societies copy and enact organizational models from other

---

3   By using the concept of "competitive environments," I draw on Meyer and Rowan's (1977) distinction between competitive and institutional environments. Meyer and Rowan focus on the degree of legitimacy of organizations. While organizations in competitive environments must struggle for their survival, organizations in institutional environments can survive even if they are not successful, yet still perceived as legitimate by the environment.

societal fields, such as economy, science, and education, and from the nonprofit sector. This is particularly true for the "megachurches", which have transformed US Protestantism in the last decades. In addition, similar to religion in the United States, the state has withdrawn from direct control over many societal sectors in modern societies. Since the 1970s, management concepts have diffused to noneconomic fields and have promoted an arrangement in which the state stops regulating universities, schools, and other public organizations directly (as part of the implementation of New Public Management) (De Boer/Enders/Schimank 2007; OECD 2010). In this setting, organizations are increasingly expected to define their goals and evaluate their outcomes (Krücken/Meier 2006; Brunsson/Sahlin-Andersson 2000).

Scholars studying the governance of universities and research organizations have emphasized the need to examine the elementary mechanisms that constitute forms, such as market, state, and event. For example, markets in modern capitalism are by no means solely based on exchange under competitive conditions. Instead, markets are shaped by other elementary mechanisms, such as hierarchy and networks, as well as mutual and reciprocal adjustment (Schimank 2007b: 34). However, a systematic analysis of various governance forms, as has been conducted in higher-education research, is lacking for the field of religion so far. Although many individual studies and theoretical approaches have been conducted, they tend to lack a common analytical basis that can be built on (see for example Krech et al. 2013).

In the first part of the paper, I briefly present the state of research on the governance of religion. In the second part, I develop an analytical tool for analyzing organizational structures of religion in three steps. First, following Schimank, I discuss three types of elementary mechanisms of governance forms: mutual observation, influence, and negotiation. Second, I differentiate types of actors in religious fields. Third, building on this, I distinguish six types of governance forms in religion that build on constellations of mutual negotiation. In the third part, I discuss the role of organizations for the private form of religion.

2. The governance of religion

Research on governance originated in the economic discussion on theories of the market and the role of firms on markets (Coase 1937; Williamson 1973, 1993) and in the political science discussion on the changing role of the state and the rise of nonhierarchical forms of action coordination (Mayntz 2004). According to Mayntz, governance describes "the sum of all kinds of existing forms of the collective regulation of societal circumstances, including institutionalized forms of self-regulation of civil society, different joint activities of public and private actors as well as sovereign actions of governmental actors." (ibid.: 66, own translation). Mayntz suggests a continuum of governmental regulation on the one hand and civil self-regulation on the other. Against this background, Mayntz, Scharpf, and others define state-related sectors as those that do not fulfil core governmental functions[4] but that nevertheless bear a degree of responsibility for important social causes. Examples are science, education, and health (Mayntz/Scharpf 1995: 13–14).

Religion has not been included in these analyses of Mayntz, Scharpf, Schimank, and others. Religion can be characterized by its particular role: It is not a state-related sector that is deemed so important in a plural, secular society that it would be supported by the state. Rather, religion is considered a private matter. The public claim of religion is shifting from the state to civil society (Casanova 1994). Sociological studies on religion that use the concept of governance do so especially when examining how the state influences or regulates religious diversity. In the sociology of religion, the discussion on the governance of religion revolves around the question of how the regulatory potential of religion can be dealt with (Schuppert 2017; Burchardt 2020; Koenig 2009). From a legal perspective, many researchers have examined national differences in national constitutions, jurisprudence, and church financing (cf. Martikainen 2013). Additionally, researchers have explored how Islam is dealt with in Europe (Koenig 2007). Depending on the national context, the state can assume different roles and act as a regulator and promoter of religion, especially concerning religious peace or ecumenism (Körs/Nagel 2018).

Especially in the US sociology of religion, the rational-choice approach to religion has become established, focusing on the regulatory role of the state (Stark/Finke 2000; Finke/Stark 1992; Iannaccone et al. 1997). The more the state regulates religion and therefore favors certain religious communities, the less competition is possible, the argument goes. Consequently, this hinders religious participation. This approach has been criticized from methodological and theoretical perspectives (Kern/Pruisken 2018; Voas et al. 2002). Religious markets do not form "spontaneously", as claimed by the economics of reli-

---

4   As, for example, the police.

gion, but are the result of demanding processes of institutionalization (Kern/Pruisken 2018).

In this article, I take a different approach. I use a well-established concept in the fields of science and higher-education research and apply it to the case of US Protestantism. Initially, both fields, that of European universities and research organizations and that of US religion, differ significantly: The regulation and financing of universities and research organizations in Europe are the responsibility of the state whereas in the US, religion and the state are comparatively strictly separated. Nevertheless, the method of governance analysis can be applied to the US Protestant field because it operates at such a high level of abstraction that it can be employed across fields.

3. Governance analysis of US Protestantism

A detailed analysis of governance forms in a focal field includes three steps. First, elementary mechanisms must be distinguished. Second, the question of who the relevant actors who interact with each other are needs to be addressed. Based on these two steps, relevant governance forms in the religious field can be described.

3.1 Elementary Mechanisms

What are the elementary mechanisms that constitute joint actions and the intentional design of governance forms? Schimank distinguishes between three types of elementary mechanisms: (1) mutual observation, (2) mutual influence, and (3) mutual negotiation. These three elementary mechanisms are produced in actor constellations in which actors have to deal with the interdependencies that emerge among them. The mechanisms ensure that two or more actors can reliably coordinate their actions relative to each other, making them predictable for both parties. In this process, they establish a relatively enduring social order for this constellation (Schimank 2016: chapter 8–10; 2007b).

Constellations of mutual observation are the most elementary of the three types of constellations. In this mode, the coordination of action occurs through mutual adjustment to the perceived actions of others, including anticipated actions. In the case of one-sided adjustment, the actions of the others are considered unaffected by one's own actions. In the case of mutual adjustment, one takes into account that the other person is also adjusting to oneself – as a sequence of actions and reactions, where the initiative can come from either side at different times, or as simultaneous mutual actions that respond to each other's anticipated actions. The management of interdependencies between actors in constellations of mutual observation can occur occasionally or can solidify in recurring episodes.

For example, the worship service in any given congregation is a recurring event in which actors coordinate their behavior by observing what the other congregants are doing. A new visitor will intuitively observe how the members of the congregation dress as well as whether they stand up or sit and sing or do not sing. The new visitor can adjust her actions one-sidedly, but the members of the congregations may notice that there is a new visitor and adjust their actions to her as well, for example by way of a friendly greeting or, quite the opposite, by ignoring the newcomer. Mutual observations are the key mechanisms for the constitution of communities and markets. In constellations of mutual influence, influence potentials, such as money, knowledge, emotions, and power, are deliberately employed (Schimank 2016). Situations in which one actor possesses enough influence potential to completely impose their will on another actor are, however, relatively rare. Therefore, interdependencies between actors are managed through a balance of influence potentials. Less significant are sporadic forms of coordination; continuous influence relationships take precedence. The concept of "influence potentials" builds on Talcott Parsons's concept of "generalized media". Parsons conceptualizes power, influence, and value commitments in the spheres of community, politics, and culture as functional equivalents for money in the economic system (Parsons 1963a, 1963b, 1968). Whereas money and power directly influence an actor's situation, value commitments and influence can only be used to change actors' intentions (Habermas 1980).[5] Money and power can directly alter an actor's

---

5   Habermas employs his renowned distinction between instrumental action and communicative action to elucidate the differences in potentials for influence. Communicative action is aimed at fostering understanding or establishing social bonds. This approach relies on the mutual exchange of arguments, seeking to cultivate a consensus on specific truths, norms, or values. Conversely, instrumental action is focused on attaining particular outcomes or objectives by manipulating an actor's physical or social surroundings. In this context, power and money serve as tools, directly impacting an actor's situation. However, the influence exerted through value commitments and persuasion is more subtle, indirectly shaping actors' intentions by engaging with their convictions and beliefs.

circumstances by providing or withholding resources (in the case of money) or by exerting control or authority (in the case of power). For example, offering a financial incentive can compel someone to act in a certain way, and using authority can force compliance. Value commitments and persuasion represent a more indirect form of influence. These rely on aligning with or appealing to an actor's internal beliefs, values, or principles. Instead of compelling change through external pressure, they aim to shift an actor's intentions by convincing them to see situations differently, reevaluate their beliefs, or adopt new values. This process is more nuanced and requires a deeper engagement with the actor's perspectives and motivations.

Generalized symbolic media govern social relations. How can ego – an individual actor, an organization, or a nation-state – impel alter to do something they do not want to do? For example, a congregation can deal with new visitors attending the service in various ways. First, they can simply ignore new visitors and thereby use no influence potentials to convince them to join their church. Second, they can try influencing new visitors to get them to return the next week or to donate money. The congregation could simply force the visitor physically to return. Christian churches used this influence potential to evangelize the non-Christian population in the colonies. However, in the mode of the private form of religion, violence is not an appropriate influence potential to bind individuals to a congregation. Rather, the congregation will have to persuade the new visitor to come back by being kind and friendly, producing a welcoming atmosphere, presenting a stimulating worship service, or wielding one's moral authority. Religious promises such as the promise of eternal life in heaven are examples of influence potentials and can be used by the congregation as well.

Religious pluralism is another typical example of a constellation of influence without a dominant actor (Schimank 2016: 298). Religious groups do not solely observe each other but may use various influence potentials to win over the unaffiliated or to exert influence over the followers of other religious groups. The opposite is a constellation in which one dominant actor structures the constellation of mutual influence. An example is the "religious monopoly" (Diotallevi 2002): countries in which one religious community (e.g., Catholicism) is dominant.

Actors in constellations of mutual influence often start to negotiate "binding agreements". When formal hierarchies, legal, or other binding (especially codified) rules are present and when actors start to act on them, we refer to situations of mutual negotiation. Negotiations' outcomes are documented in laws, statutes, contracts, or organizational charts, managing interdependencies among actors without the need for influence potentials to be constantly present. In the case of the congregation mentioned above, the new visitor could formally apply for membership and fill out a membership application. Constellations of mutual negotiation can be purely episodic in nature, representing opportunities for one-time exchanges. For example, markets involve constellations of mutual observation among providers and consumers. Providers observe the offers, prices, and followers of other market actors. The cooperative interaction between the two parties typically results in prices in markets using the medium of money. In this context, providers and interested parties who wish to engage in business negotiate until they reach a binding agreement, typically in the form of a purchase contract, or they recognize the futility of further negotiations. In this sense, even one-time attendance of a church service can be considered a binding agreement: The worshipper participates in an event and contributes time and money, and in return, the congregation provides a compelling event.

Three abstract modes of negotiation are distinguished, forming the basis for the examination of concrete governance forms: networks, polyarchy, and hierarchy (Mayntz/Scharpf 1995; Lange/Schimank 2004: 22). In networks, collective agency relies on actors' voluntary agreement. Typical examples include political networks and corporate collaborations. The cooperation of major churches with the German state is also based on this mode of negotiation. Polyarchy is characterized by majority decisions. This pattern is often found in democratic governance forms, which are also partially present in churches. In hierarchies, decision-making authority lies with a superior governing body and is based on directives. I will come back to these three modes of negotiation in section 3.3.

3.2 Types of actors in religion

For the further identification of governance forms, it is now necessary to identify the actors who mutually observe, influence, or negotiate with each other. Various types of actors are considered in this context. On the one hand, these can be individual actors (e.g., individual believers, pastors, and ministers). The concept of an actor encompasses "entities that act meaningfully and intentionally, and to which action can be attributed by other actors" (Schimank 2016: 44–45). The choice of an action is always embedded in and shaped by a social context that can bring about this action. Actors can also be organizations, social groups, or social movements. These are "supra-individual actors" (Schimank 2016: 327). Each supraindividual actor is a constellation of individual actors, and their actions are therefore the collaborative actions of constellations of individual actors. What is crucial is the extent to which the actions of individual actors in the constellation form an organized whole. This means that they systematically build on each other to pursue an overarching objective (Schimank 2016: 329). In this regard, binding agreements can be used to build an organized whole oriented toward a specific goal. For example, individual believers can join forces and found a congregation together with the intention to make it a megachurch in the future.

Collective actors, however, do not only emerge based on binding agreements. Through the mechanism of mutual observation, collectively shared evaluative and cognitive interpretations can also contribute to the coordination of actions. Therefore, Schimank distinguishes between collective actors who do not require binding agreements and corporate actors who rely on binding agreements (Schimank 2016: 329). An example of collective actors that form based on mutual perception of commonalities (and not on binding agreements) is the religious community (Durkheim 1995). Membership in the community is formed through perceived commonalities (Gläser 2007: 87). In the religious community, perceived commonalities are mostly the religious creeds that members of the community share with each other. These creeds are often represented by religious symbols or codes, which help the members of a community identify each other. In this way, perceived commonalities, through mutual observation, constitute the collective self-image of a community and contribute to the shaping of an identity (Kern 2008: 119). Symbolic boundaries exist in the community and toward nonmembers of the community. In the community, common values are identified as positive whereas negative judgments are attributed to the world outside the community (Alexander 2006).

In many communities, the mechanism of mutual influence is at work, such as the emergence of charisma and power as influence potentials. The communication networks in communities often revolve around elites who have a large fanbase and many followers on social media (Gläser 2007: 87). In US Evangelicalism, these famous personalities, such as Billy Graham, Joel Osteen, and Sarah Young, are revered like celebrities and shape the community members' collective beliefs, practices, and actions.

However, communities often exhibit limited collective agency. Mutual observation of perceived commonalities and identity-driven actions alone are usually insufficient for formulating collective goals and deciding on the allocation of common resources. There is a lack of an entity capable of making decisions for the community. Even if such a decision were to be reached, it would be challenging to compel the members of a community to implement it due to membership based on perception and the autonomy of its members. This weakness in endogenous governance is characteristic of spontaneous social orders that arise without actions being deliberately coordinated (Gläser 2007: 89). Whereas informal systems of rules may indeed emerge in the community, the formulation and implementation of common political or organizational goals require networks or organizations that compensate for the community's endogenous governance deficit (Gläser 2007: 89). For example, the organization of events is not possible solely through spontaneous and identity-driven actions or on the basis of mutual observation.

The realm of religion is segmented into various faith communities – Christianity, Judaism, Islam, Hinduism, etc. – each with its own interpretative and expectation structures in the form of dogma, behavioral guidelines, and rituals. Especially in modern Christianity, formal organizations have developed in which participation is constituted by membership (Luhmann 1964: 39). US Protestantism, which is of particular interest to this article, has primarily two organizational levels: the local church and the associational organization of the denomination. There is a functional division of labor between these two organizational levels: Whereas the congregation organizes the interaction rituals of local worship, the denomination organizes the overarching community of all believers (Kern et al. 2022). Ammerman defines congregations as "locally-situated, multi-generational, voluntary organizations of people who identify themselves as a distinct religious group and engage in a broad range of religious activities together." (Ammerman 2009: 562).

In contrast, denominations are "more and less bureaucratically organized, usually at the national level, and charged with supporting (and sometimes regulating) the groups and traditions that share a religious identity" (Ammerman 2016: 143). The denominational pluralism specific to the United States is often described as "competition". Unlike the European state church model, membership in denominations is historically voluntary. However, the various denominations often do not compete with each other at the local level of the congregations because the denominations are regionally unevenly distributed. For example, whereas the Southern Baptist Convention dominates in Texas, the Evangelical Lutheran Association is strong in Minnesota.

A third type of collective organizational actors in the United States (next to congregations and denominations) is special-purpose groups (Ammerman 2016: 146). These are religious nonprofit organizations that provide social services and engage in missionary work, broadcasting, publishing, and much more (Scheitle 2010; Kern/Pruisken 2020). Unlike congregations or denominations, they are specialized in a specific goal or task.

3.3 Competing Governance Forms

In the US literature on church sociology, three fundamental "church structures" are described (Moberg 1962: 61–62): The Episcopal church structure is based on a hierarchical church order in which, for example, the bishop holds the highest authority over a local congregation. For instance, every Catholic parish worldwide is geographically defined (according to the parochial principle) and is affiliated with a diocese. The authority over the diocese rests with a local bishop, who in turn is under the authority of a higher unit, the Pope in the Catholic Church. Members are typically assigned to individual congregations near their place of residence according to the parochial principle. When moving to a new location, church members are required to register in a new parish.

In the Presbyterian church structure, an elected group of individuals known as "Presbyters" (from the Greek "presbyteros", meaning "elder") holds authority in a local congregation. The Presbyters of each congregation are, in turn, members of a broader assembly called the Synod. Because the Presbytery serves as an intermediary body between the congregation and the Synod, it can be "subject to pressure from above and below" (Moberg 1962: 94). Therefore, the Presbyterian church structure represents a hybrid form of the hierarchical Episcopal and polyarchic Congregationalist church structures.

The Congregationalist church structure advocates for the autonomy of local congregations. The responsibility for their respective ecclesiastical polity rests solely in their hands. Congregationalists may establish committees or offices for specific tasks, but the ultimate authority remains with the congregation members. The Congregationalist church structure is also referred to as "Baptist polity" because it is the prevalent church structure among Baptist churches. Membership in the congregation is based on personal choice and is exclusively related to the local congregation. The dominant mode of negotiation is "polyarchy".

The three types of church organization describe the relationship between congregations and denominations in US denominationalism. However, they are not suitable for reflecting the profound transformation that the religious field in the United States has undergone in recent decades: The denomination's relevance as the predominant form of Protestant organization has considerably declined (Roozen/Hadaway 1993; Chaves 2017; Wuthnow 1988), Evangelicalism has become a mainstream Protestant movement, and – as a central feature of this development – the megachurch, as a new type of religious organization, is always spreading (Von der Ruhr 2020; Wollschleger/Porter 2011). Consequently, the diffusion of megachurches in the United States has led to a growing concentration of more and more believers in fewer congregations: "The biggest 1 percent of Protestant churches ... contain approximately 20 percent of all the people, money, and staff" (Chaves 2017: 70). Beside their size – most studies label a congregation as a megachurch if it attracts 2000 attendees or more on Sundays – megachurches are characterized by two defining features: a relatively high degree of organizational autonomy and a strong orientation toward a religious market logic. "Organizational autonomy" means that their leadership exerts a high degree of control over the definition and attainment of the congregation's goals. The term "market logic" refers to a set of (more or less) latent background assumptions and beliefs that increasingly shape religious suppliers' and customers' behavioral expectations (Pruisken et al. 2022).

These developments are not unique to the religious field in the United States but are embedded in a global process in which patterns of marketization, economization, and commodification of noneconomic sectors are becoming prevalent worldwide (Martikainen/Gauthier 2013). Since the late 1980s, the New Public Management has become predominant in state-related sectors, such as science, education, and healthcare. With the model of the "governance equalizer", de Boer, Enders, and Schimank (2007) developed an analytical instrument with five dimensions that can be used to compare national higher education systems but has been used for the analysis of school systems as well. The instrument is designed to capture multiple governance forms at the same time: governmental regulation, democratic self-regulation, hierarchical self-regulation, stakeholder guidance and competition. All five dimensions can be more or less pronounced.

Based on the instrument of the governance equalizer, I distinguish six forms of governance that are prevalent in the field of religion in the United States: (1) denominational regulation, (2) democratic self-governance, (3) hierarchical self-governance, (4) stakeholder guidance, (5) competition, and (6) network governance. All three forms build more or less (but not solely) on binding agreements that result from mutual negotiations.

(1) The regulation of the congregation by the denomination can be compared to the regulation of universities through the state. In line with the model of the Episcopal church structure, the denomination regulates local congregations concerning finances, personnel, organization, programs, and doctrine. Regulation, as defined by Schimank (2007a: 241), means controlling behavior through conditional programs (Luhmann 1964). Therefore, the relationship between the denomination and the congregation is characterized by clear if-then rules governing various matters. Megachurches often adopt this governance form in the framework of the multisite model. The overarching main church, similar to the denomination, sets the rules, processes, and standards that the subordinate campus congregations must adhere to (Reed 2019).

(2) The democratic self-governance of congregations can be compared to the form of academic self-governance, which is characterized by professionals' involvement in decision-making processes in universities. The self-organization of Baptist congregations relies on the principle of the priesthood of all believers, which is often associated with Protestant Christianity. It emphasizes that all believers have direct access to God and are capable of interpreting and understanding the teachings of the faith. It suggests that individuals do not require an intermediary, such as a priest or clergy member, to connect with God or to mediate their relationship with him. The Congregationalist and Presbyterian church structures are marked by strong democratic self-governance. Members are involved in decision-making processes. Decisions are democratically voted on in elected committees or at a member meeting and are not decided hierarchically.

(3) Hierarchical self-governance refers to the management of single organizations (e.g., universities, schools, and congregations) that are controlled by strong leadership figures. Important decisions regarding personnel, finances, and programs as well as central religious beliefs are therefore in the hands of an individual pastor or a team of pastors. In many megachurches, democratic self-governance has been replaced by hierarchical self-governance (Pruisken/Coronel 2014; Kern/Pruisken/Schimank 2022). The relationship between be-

lievers and the senior pastor is often characterized by "charisma"[6] attributed to the senior pastor. However, hierarchical self-governance typically relies not only on charisma but also on an understanding of the pastor as a "leader" of the church similar to that position in the business world.

(4) The governance form of external control, often referred to as stakeholder guidance, is described by Schimank (2007a: 241) as a form of control through goal programs rather than conditional programs. Unlike denominational control, hierarchical instructions are not enforced from the top (the denomination) down to the local congregation but are negotiated in the form of agreements or recommendations. The interest of intermediate actors, that is, stakeholders, lies in enhancing the performance of the subordinate actor (such as the university or congregation). Here, certain special purpose organizations come into play, specifically religious counseling organizations. An example is church networks such as Acts 29[7] and Exponential.[8] These organizations advise congregations in achieving their goals. They focus on growth strategies and church planting and develop scientifically legitimated strategies for better leadership and community building. In addition, denominations increasingly use the stakeholder guidance mode. An example is the Baptist General Conference, which changed its name to "Converge" in 2015. It no longer sees itself as a denomination (as a regulating body) but as a movement that helps to start and strengthen churches.[9] Finally, megachurches that have institutionalized the multisite model can also use stakeholder guidance instead of direct forms of regulation.

(5) Competitive pressure as a form of coordination refers to the market, which consists of exchange as negotiation based on mutual observation and the use of potentials of influence, particularly time and money (Schimank 2007b: 242). Congregations (and denominations) exchange their "religious products" for resources. In this context, not only the amount of membership contributions counts as a resource; the number of worshipers can become an intrinsic value confirming the correctness of one's doctrine. Although the pressure for market formation in state-related sectors comes from the state, congregations in the United States often face real competitive pressure due to

---

6   In the sense of the concept of "charisma" in Weber's sociology of religion (Riesebrodt 1999).
7   Cf. https://www.acts29.com/about-us/.
8   Cf. https://exponential.org/.
9   Cf. https://www.converge.org/about.

actual scarcity of potential "customers" or a high density of churches (Homan 2024). A market consists of (a) a set of religious producers who observe each other mutually, (b) a set of consumers who compare these producers' offers, (c) a set of relations between these components, and (d) a comparative order that allows for categorization and evaluation of these offers (White 1981; Leifer 1985; Jansen 2013; Aspers/Beckert 2017).

(6) Unlike the higher education and science sectors, the religious sphere is additionally shaped by the mode of horizontal coordination as a sixth governance form ("network governance") (Martikainen 2013). Congregations join forces with other congregations, for example, by pooling resources to achieve collective goals. This leads to the formation of network or umbrella organizations that develop their own organizational structures. An example is the various interfaith activities that have emerged in the religious field in the past decades and that are specifically designed to build trust through networks (Körs/Nagel 2018).

With this categorization of governance forms in US Protestantism, nothing can yet be said about how common each form is and which ones might be losing influence. The question now arises of how these governance forms interact. New Public Management, and similarly the megachurch model, are characterized by a combination of hierarchical self-governance, stakeholder guidance, and competitive pressure (De Boer et al. 2007; Pruisken/Coronel 2014). The hierarchical regulation therefore shifts more strongly into the organizations. In this way, megachurches create an organizational power that enables the private social form of religion.

4. Discussion and outlook

From Thomas Luckmann's perspective, the concept of the social form encompasses the relationship among personality, social structure, and culture in a society. However, an analysis of the transformation of religion is only possible if all three levels are taken into account. In modern societies, the social form of private religion is the formative social structure of religion. Luckmann suggests that in the context of private religion, individuals in modern society experience a distinctive level of freedom in shaping their personal identity. This freedom, according to Luckmann, is akin to a consumer mindset, which extends beyond mere economic goods and encompasses the individual's engagement with the broader worldview. Luckmann's assumption was that religion loses its obligatory hierarchical character. However, this only succeeds in an organizational society where organizations or other forms exist that provide these consumer choices. In the social form of private religion, religious organizations are increasingly only considered legitimate if they provide individual believers with choices (Kern et al. 2022; Pruisken et al. 2022). However, in Luckmann's framework, the meso level of organizations and interorganizational relations (the social structure) remains underdeveloped. As Freudenberg and Reuter demonstrate in the introduction to this volume, a wide variety of forms of institutionalization of religion has developed on the meso level of religious fields.

I developed my argument that the private social form of religion must be understood in the context of the emergence of the organizational society against the background of my research on megachurches and Protestant congregations in the United States (Pruisken/Coronel 2014; Pruisken et al. 2022; Kern et al. 2022). The focus was on governance forms that are based on mutual negotiations: denominational regulation, democratic self-governance, hierarchical self-governance, stakeholder guidance, competition, and network governance. The analysis shows that hierarchical forms of governance do not disappear. Therefore, the model of the megachurch is characterized by the fact that the organization is becoming more hierarchical internally. The leadership of megachurches increasingly aligns with standards issued by external organizations and consulting firms. At the same time, there is competition at the local level, especially when multiple megachurches compete in a city. This competition allows individual believers to choose between various congregations' offers.

For future research on social forms of religion, the elementary mechanisms of mutual observation and mutual influence are equally important. In particular, the increasing digitization of religion cannot be understood without these mechanisms. On digital platforms, such as YouTube and Instagram, pastors, congregations, and other religious content providers can observe and adjust their actions to each other. The organized environment of these platforms also offers various opportunities for the emergence of influence potentials, such as the number of followers or violent outbreaks. Religious influencers can significantly increase the scope of their influence and thereby compete with established organized providers. The consequences of this development can only be understood if one understands religion, like other fields, as an "organized field" in which mechanisms of mutual observation, influence, and negotiation coexist and interact.

Bibliography

Alexander, Jeffrey C. (2006): The Civil Sphere, Oxford: Oxford University Press.

Ammerman, Nancy T. (2009): "Congregations: Local, Social, and Religious." In: Peter Clarke (ed.), Oxford Handbook of the Sociology of Religion, Oxford: Oxford University Press, pp. 562–580.

Ammerman, Nancy T. (2016): "Denominations, Congregations, and Special Purpose Groups." In: David Yamane (ed.), Handbook of Religion and Society (= Handbooks of sociology and social research), Cham: Springer International Publishing, pp. 133–154.

Aspers, Patrik/Beckert, Jens (2017): "Märkte." In: Andrea Maurer (ed.), Handbuch Der Wirtschaftssoziologie, Wiesbaden: Springer VS, pp. 215–240.

Benz, Arthur/Lütz, Susanne/Schimank, Uwe/Simonis, Georg (eds.) (2007): Handbuch Governance: Theoretische Grundlagen und Empirische Anwendungsfelder. Wiesbaden: VS Verlag.

Berger, Peter L. (1963) "A Market Model for the Analysis of Ecumenicity." In: Social Research 30/1, pp. 77–93.

Berger, Peter L./Luckmann, Thomas (1967): The Social Construction of Reality: A Treatise in the Sociology of Knowledge, Garden City and New York: Anchor Books.

Brunsson, Nils/Sahlin-Andersson, Kerstin (2000): "Constructing Organizations: The Example of Public Sector Reform." In: Organization Studies 21/4, pp. 721–746.

Burchardt, Marian (2020): Regulating Difference: Religious Diversity and Nationhood in the Secular West, New Brunswick, NJ: Rutgers University Press.

Casanova, José (1994): Public Religions in the Modern World, Chicago, IL: University of Chicago Press.

Chaves, Mark (2017): American Religion: Contemporary Trends. Princeton, NJ: Princeton University Press.

Coase, R. H. (1937): "The Nature of the Firm." In: Economica 4/16, pp. 386–405.

De Boer, Harry/Enders, Jürgen/Schimank, Uwe (2007): "On the Way Towards New Public Management? The Governance of University Systems in England, the Netherlands, Austria, and Germany." In: Dorothea Jansen (ed.), New Forms of Governance in Research Organizations, Dordrecht: Springer, pp. 137–152.

Diotallevi, Luca (2002): "Internal Competition in a National Religious Monopoly: The Catholic Effect and the Italian Case." In: Sociology of Religion 63/2, pp. 137. https://doi.org/10.2307/3712562.

Durkheim, Émile (1995): The Elementary Forms of Religious Life, New York: The Free Press.

Finke, Roger/Stark, Rodney (1992): The Churching of America, 1776–1990: Winners and Losers in Our Religious Economy, New Brunswick: Rutgers University Press.

Gauthier, François (2014): "Intimate Circles and Mass Meetings. The Social Forms of Event-Structured Religion in the Era of Globalized Markets and Hyper-Mediatization." Social Compass 61/2, pp. 261–271. https://doi.org/10.1177/0037768614524326.

Gläser, Jochen (2007): "Gemeinschaft." In: Arthur Benz/Susanne Lütz/Uwe Schimank/Georg Simonis (eds.), Handbuch Governance: Theoretische Grundlagen und Empirische Anwendungsfelder. Wiesbaden: VS, pp. 82–92.

Habermas, Jürgen (1980): "Handlung Und Sytem: Bemerkungen zu Parsons' Medientheorie." In: Wolfgang Schluchter (ed.), Verhalten, Handeln Und System: Talcott Parsons Beitrag Zur Entwicklung Der Sozialwissenschaften (= Suhrkamp Taschenbuch Wissenschaft, 310). Frankfurt am Main: Suhrkamp, pp. 68–105.

Homan, Casey P. (2024): "Understanding Competition in Social Space: Religious Congregations in Manhattan, 1949 to 1999." In: American Sociological Review 89/1, pp. 60–87. https://doi.org/10.1177/00031224231221561.

Iannaccone, Laurence/Finke, Roger/Stark, Rodney (1997): "Deregulating Religion: The Economics of Church and State." In: Economic Inquiry 35/2, pp. 350–364.

Jansen, Dorothea (2013): Einführung in die Netzwerkanalyse: Grundlagen, Methoden, Anwendungen. Wiesbaden: VS.

Kern, Thomas (2008): Soziale Bewegungen: Ursachen, Wirkungen, Mechanismen, Wiesbaden: Springer VS.

Kern, Thomas/Pruisken, Insa (2018): "Was Ist Ein Religiöser Markt? Zum Wandel der Religiösen Konkurrenz in den USA." In: Zeitschrift für Soziologie 47/1, pp. 29–45. https://doi.org/10.1515/zfsoz-2018-1002.

Kern, Thomas/Pruisken, Insa (2020): "Der Wandel religiöser Inklusion in den USA: Von Der "traditionellen" zur "vernetzten" Religiosität?" In: Hubert Knoblauch (ed.), Die Refiguration der Religion: Perspektiven der Religionssoziologie und Religionswissenschaft, Weinheim: Beltz Juventa, 147–168.

Kern, Thomas/Pruisken, Insa/Schimank, Uwe (2022): "Die Religiöse Gemeinde als Organisationaler Akteur: Das Wachstum der "Megakirchen" in den USA." In: Soziale Welt 73/3: pp. 448–476.

Knoblauch, Hubert (2010): "Popular Spirituality." In: Anthropological Journal of European Culture 19/1, pp. 24–39.

Koenig, Matthias (2007): "Europeanising the Governance of Religious Diversity: An Institutionalist Account of Muslim Struggles for Public Recognition." In: Journal of Ethnic and Migration Studies 33/6, pp. 911–932. https://doi.org/10.1080/13691830701432756.

Koenig, Matthias (2009): "How Nation-States Respond to Religious Diversity?" In: Paul Bramadat/Matthias Koenig (eds.), International Migration and the Governance of Religious Diversity, Kingston, ON, Montreal, Ithaca, NY: McGill-Queen's University Press, pp. 293–322.

Körs, Anna/Nagel, Alexander-Kenneth (2018): "Local 'Formulas of Peace': Religious Diversity and State-Interfaith Governance in Germany." In: Social Compass 65/3, pp. 346–62. https://doi.org/10.1177/0037768618787240.

Krech, Volkhard/Schlamelcher, Jens/Hero (2013): "Typen Religiöser Sozialformen Und Ihre Bedeutung Für Die Analyse Religiösen Wandels in Deutschland." In: Kölner Zeitschrift für Soziologie und Sozialpsychologie 65, Supplement 1 (Sonderheft 53: Religion und Gesellschaft).

Krücken, Georg/Meier, Frank (2006): "Turning the University into an Organizational Actor." In: Gili S. Drori/John W. Meyer/Hokyu Hwang (eds.), Globalization and Organization: World Society and Organizational Change, Oxford: Oxford University Press, pp. 241–312.

Lange, Stefan/Schimank, Uwe (2004): "Governance und Gesellschaftliche Integration." In: Stefan Lange and Uwe Schimank (eds.), Governance und gesellschaftliche Integration. 1. Auflage, Wiesbaden: VS, pp. 9–44.

Leifer, Eric M (1985): "Markets as Mechanisms: Using a Role Structure." In: Social Forces 64/2, pp. 442–472.

Luckmann, Thomas (2003): "Transformations of Religion and Morality in Modern Europe." In: Social Compass 50/3, 275–285.

Luhmann, Niklas (1964): Funktionen Und Folgen Formaler Organisation, Berlin: Duncker & Humblot.

Martikainen, Tuomas/Gauthier, François (eds.) (2013): Religion in the Neoliberal Age, Farnham and Burlington, VT: Ashgate.

Martikainen, Tuomas (2013) "Multilevel and Pluricentric Network Governance of Religion." In: Tuomas Martikainen/François Gauthier (eds.), Religion in the Neoliberal Age, Farnham and Burlington, VT: Ashgate, pp. 129–142.

Mayntz, Renate (2004): "Governance im modernen Staat." In: Arthur Benz/Nicolai Dose (eds.), Governance: Regieren in komplexen Regelsystemen, Wiesbaden: VS, 65–75.

Mayntz, Renate/Scharpf, Fritz W. (1995): "Steuerung und Selbstorganisation in staatsnahen Sektoren." In: Renate Mayntz/Fritz W. Scharpf (eds.), Gesellschaftliche Selbstregelung und politische Steuerung, Frankfurt am Main and New York: Campus, pp. 73–100.

Meyer, John W./Rowan, Brian (1977): "Institutionalized Organizations: Formal Structure as Myth and Ceremony." In: American Journal of Sociology 83/2, pp. 340–63.

Moberg, David Oscar (1962): The Church as a Social Institution: The Sociology of American Religion, Englewood Cliffs, NJ; Prentice-Hall.

OECD (2010): Public Administration after "New Public Management", Paris: OECD.

Parsons, Talcott/Platt, Gerald M. (1973): The American University, Cambridge, MA: Harvard University Press.

Parsons, Talcott (1963a): "On the Concept of Influence." In: Public Opinion Quarterly 27/1, pp. 37–62.

Parsons, Talcott (1963b): "On the Concept of Political Power." In: Proceedings of the American Philosophical Society 107/3, pp. 232–262.

Parsons, Talcott (1968): "On the Concept of Value-Commitments." In: Sociological Inquiry 38, pp. 135–160.

Petzke, Martin/Tyrell, Hartmann (2012): "Religiöse Organisationen." In: Maja Apelt/Veronika Tacke (eds.), Handbuch Organisationstypen, Wiesbaden: VS, pp. 275–306.

Pruisken, Insa/Coronel, Janina (2014): "Megakirchen: Managerialisierung im religiösen Feld?" In: Patrick Heiser/Christian Kurrat/Christian Ludwig (eds.), Sozialformen der Religionen im Wandel, Wiesbaden: Springer VS, 53–79.

Pruisken, Insa/Loebell, Josefa/Monowski, Nina/Kern, Thomas (2022): "From Denominationalism to Market Standards: How Does the Religious Market Affect Authority Relations in Protestant Congregations?" In: Research in the Social Scientific Study of Religion 32/24, pp. 508–533.

Reed, Nathan A. (2019): "A Comparative Analysis of Church Membership Practices in Large, Multi-Site Churches." Dissertation, Southern Baptist

Theological Seminary. https://www.proquest.com/openview/2c4447761f878fb066c640210b205326/1?cbl=18750&diss=y&pq-origsite=gscholar&parentSessionId=2Mrjb5vRRjD6xobdkjTxIMRJuaII282jogTL799ZkSA%3D. Accessed February 09, 2024.

Riesebrodt, Martin (1999): "Charisma in Max Weber's Sociology of Religion." Religion 29/1, pp. 1–14. https://doi.org/10.1006/reli.1999.0175.

Roozen, David A./Hadaway, Christopher Kirk (eds.) (1993): Church and Denominational Growth, Nashville: Abingdon Press.

Scheitle, Christopher P. (2010): Beyond the Congregation: The World of Christian Nonprofits, New York: Oxford University Press.

Schimank, Uwe (2016): Handeln Und Strukturen, Weinheim: Juventa.

Schimank, Uwe (2007a).): "Die Governance-Perspektive: Analytisches Potenzial und anstehende konzeptionelle Fragen." In: Herbert Altrichter/Thomas Brüsemeister/Jochen Wissinger (eds.), Educational Governance, Wiesbaden: VS, pp. 231–260.

Schimank, Uwe (2007b): "Elementare Mechanismen." In: Arthur Benz/Susanne Lütz/Uwe Schimank/Georg Simonis (eds.), Handbuch Governance: Theoretische Grundlagen und empirische Anwendungsfelder. Wiesbaden: VS, pp. 29–45.

Schuppert, Gunnar Folke (2012): When Governance Meets Religion: Governancestrukturen und Governanceakteure im Bereich des Religiösen (= Schriften des Münchner Centrums für Governance-Forschung, 6), Baden-Baden: Nomos.

Schuppert, Gunnar Folke (2017): Governance of Diversity: Zum Umgang mit kultureller und religiöses Pluralität in säkularen Gesellschaften, Frankfurt am Main: Campus.

Stark, Rodney/Finke, Roger (2000): Acts of Faith: Explaining the Human Side of Religion, Berkeley and Los Angeles: University of California Press.

Tracey, Paul/Phillips, Nelson/Lounsbury, Michael (eds.) (2014): Religion and Organization Theory (= Research in the Sociology of Organizations, 41), Leeds: Emerald.

Voas, David/Crockett, Alasdair/Olson, Daniel V. (2002): "Religious Pluralism and Participation: Why Previous Research Is Wrong." In: American Sociological Review 67/2, pp. 212–230.

Von der Ruhr, Marc (2020): "Megachurches in the Religious Marketplace." In: Stephen Hunt (ed.), Handbook of Megachurches, Leiden and Boston: Brill, pp. 131–151.

White, Harrison C. (1981): "Where Do Markets Come from?" In: American Journal of Sociology 87/3, pp. 517–547.
Williamson, Oliver E. (1973): "Markets and Hierarchies: Some Elementary Considerations." In: The American Economic Review 63/2, pp. 316–325.
Williamson, Oliver E. (1993): "Transaction Cost Economics and Organization Theory." In: Industrial and Corporate Change 2/1, pp. 107–156.
Wollschleger, Jason/Porter, Jeremy (2011): "A 'WalMartization' of Religion? The Ecological Impact of Megachurches on the Local and Extra-Local Religious Economy." In: Review of Religious Research 53/3, pp. 279–299. https://doi.org/10.1007/s13644-011-0009-2.
Wuthnow, Robert (1988): The Restructuring of American Religion: Society and Faith Since World War II, Princeton: Princeton University Press.

Web References

Acts 29. "About Acts 29." Accessed February 9, 2024. https://www.acts29.com/about-us/.
Converge. "Starting and Strengthening Churches Together Worldwide." Accessed February 9, 2024. https://www.converge.org/about.
Exponential. "You're a Multiplier. We're Here to Help You Multiply." Accessed February 9, 2024. https://exponential.org.

Authors

Valérie Aubourg is Professor of Anthropology and Ethnology at Lyon Catholic University, where she heads the 'Confluence: Sciences et Humanités' research unit. From 2005 to 2011, she conducted research on Charismatic-Pentecostal movements in Réunion Island, published under the title *Christianismes charismatiques à La Réunion* (Karthala 2014). Her work then focused on the evangelical influence within French Catholicism. This resulted in her study *Réveil catholique* (Labor et Fides 2020).

Samuel Dolbeau holds a Ph.D. in Religious Studies from the UCLouvain (Belgium) and in Sociology from the EHESS (France). His doctoral research investigated the process of institutionalization of the Emmanuel Community in French-speaking Europe. In a broader sense, his work examines New Ecclesial Movements and the transformations of contemporary Catholicism from a socio-historical perspective.

Maren Freudenberg is Senior Lecturer of the Sociology of Religion and the Comparative Study of Religion at Ruhr University Bochum, Germany. Her research interests include the intersections of religion and the economy, theories of charisma and authority, global Pentecostal-Charismatic Christianity, as well as conservative Evangelicalism in the United States and Germany/Switzerland.

Virginia Garrard is Professor Emerita of History at the University of Texas at Austin and past Director of LLILAS Benson Latin American Studies and Collections. She is currently the Greenleaf Distinguished Scholar in Latin American Studies at Tulane University and is currently researching a new book on revolutionary Catholic priests in Central America during the 1970s and 1980s.

Hannah Grünenthal studied Religious Studies, Modern Indology, and Psychology at the University of Heidelberg. In 2021, she completed her doctorate in Bremen on the construction of authority and positioning processes of the Catholic Charismatic Renewal in Germany. Her areas of specialization are Catholicism in Germany, religion during the Covid-19 pandemic, and qualitative research methods.

Hillary Kaell is Associate Professor of Anthropology and Religion at McGill University, where she holds a William Dawson Chair. Her most recent book is Christian Globalism at Home: Child Sponsorship in the United States (Princeton, 2020), winner of the 2021 Schaff Prize from the American Society of Church History. Currently, she is co-researcher on MuREL, a long-term study of municipalities, religion, and secularism in Quebec, from which the research in this article derives.

Katherine Kelaidis is Director of Research and Content at the National Hellenic Museum in Chicago and a Research Associate of the Centre for Orthodox Christian Studies, Cambridge. She studied Classical Languages at the University of California, Berkeley and the University of London.

Ariane Kovac is a Ph.D. candidate in religious studies at Leipzig University and a research associate at the Center for Religious Studies at Ruhr University Bochum. Her research interests include contemporary Christianity in the US and Germany, emotions and therapeutization, and digital religion.

Marie-Therese Mäder is a scholar of religion, media, and philosophy with particular expertise in the field of media and religion. Since 2020 she is a Senior Lecturer at the Ludwig-Maximilians-Universität in Munich (DE) and teaches Media Ethics at the Universities of Applied Sciences of the Grisons (FHGR) and Bern (HKB) in Switzerland. In 2021 she won a two-year Marie Sklodowska Curie Fellowship for her research about the mediatization of weddings (www.promising-images.eu) at the university in Macerata/IT.

Insa Pruisken is an Assistant Professor in Sociological Theory at the University of Bremen, Germany. Her research interests are the sociology of religion, the sociology of organization, social network analysis, and sociological theory.

Astrid Reuter is Professor of Religious Studies at the University of Münster. Her main research areas are the history and theory of the study of religion, Charismatic Catholicism, and religions in Brazil.

Sebastian Rimestad studied Political Science and Religious Studies in Aberdeen, Tartu, and Erfurt, with a focus on Orthodox Christianity. He holds a research position at Leipzig University, working on religious conversion and current developments in the Orthodox Church.

Sebastian Schüler is Professor of Religious Studies at the University of Leipzig. His research interests include Evangelical Christianity and New Age movements in Europe and the United States. He has done extensive fieldwork on the Emerging Church Movement and has recently begun research on the Human Potential Movement in California from 1960 to the present.